# VICTIMS AND VIRAGOS:

## Metropolitan Women, Crime and the Eighteenth-Century Justice System.

**Gregory Durston**

I.A., Dip.L., LL.M., Ph.D., of the Middle Temple and Lincoln's Inn, Barrister

Published 2007 by arima publishing

www.arimapublishing.com

ISBN 978-1-84549-221-2

Printed and bound in the United Kingdom

Typeset in Garamond 11/16

Abramis is an imprint of arima publishing

arima publishing
ASK House, Northgate Avenue
Bury St Edmunds, Suffolk IP32 6BB
t: (+44) 01284 700321

www.arimapublishing.com

# Contents

## Acknowledgements

I would like to acknowledge the invaluable assistance provided by the staff of Kingston University Library, the British Library, the British Newspaper Library at Colindale, Lambeth Palace Library, the Institute of Advanced Legal Studies, the libraries of the Middle Temple and Lincoln's Inn, the National Archives (formerly the Public Record Office) in Kew, the City of London Record Office, the Westminster City Archives and the London Metropolitan Archives. The completion of the book was assisted by a small grant from Kingston University's HEFC allocation. I am extremely grateful for assistance and advice from a wide variety of people, on many different aspects of the book. Amongst them are Professors Rab Houston and Nicole Rafter, Dean Joanna Innes, and Dr. Stephanie Hayman. On a personal basis, I owe a debt of gratitude to the late Barry Rose. Additionally, I would like to thank Philippa Russell for assistance with the preparation of the manuscript. Parts of chapters four and six first appeared in articles published in the *Griffith Law Review* and the *British Journal of Eighteenth-Century Studies*.

Gregory Durston.

London, Whitsun, 2007.

# Chapter 1. Introduction:
# Women and the Eighteenth-Century Metropolis.

## Introduction

This book will consider the experiences of eighteenth-century women, in the Metropolitan area, as both the victims and perpetrators of crime, and as participants, in various forms, in the era's criminal justice system. However, although, in recent decades, gender has become as much a category for historical examination as class and race, this still does not preclude asking *why* women should be deserving of a specifically gendered account, rather than being examined together with men. In part, the answer to this question lies in the tendency for existing studies to universalise men's experiences, to view crime and 'male crime' as synonymous, an attitude that was largely unchallenged until the 1970s. The experiences of women were sometimes markedly different to those of their male counterparts and are consequently deserving of special consideration.

However, for much of the past, the explanation for this focus on males and crime, and the relative neglect of females, is also readily apparent, and does not rest purely on prejudice or a male-centric view of the world. Historically, women have constituted a relatively small minority of offenders, defendants and, except as sexual and domestic violence complainants, even victims, of crime. Of course, this does not mean that their experiences of crime and the criminal justice system are insignificant; they can tell modern observers a great deal about wider attitudes towards women in earlier societies, and this is as true for the eighteenth century as for any other period. This alone might make them worth special study. Nevertheless, the lack of distinction between the genders is especially unsatisfactory for the Metropolitan area during the 1700s because, as will be seen, the proportion of women committing, and prosecuted for, crime appears to have been extremely (and abnormally) high by historical standards. Although most offenders, in most eras, are male, the level of female engendered crime is not fixed, nor does it remain constant across the centuries or between different societies. Unusually, men's experiences in the London area during much of the 1700s, and particularly the early years of that century, do not, necessarily, encompass the 'vast majority' of offenders, especially when property crimes are considered.

Despite this, eighteenth-century female criminality has been somewhat ignored academically, at least when compared to its male counterpart.[1] Nevertheless, examinations of women, crime and the legal process, within geographically confined areas, during designated historical periods, are certainly not new. Thus, there has been an excellent study of female criminality in Cheshire during the seventeenth century, and an important analysis of women and crime in Victorian England.[2] This book deals with the transitional century between these two periods, and focuses on a predominantly urban and suburban, rather than rural, area. However, it should also be stressed that, in this context, any historical 'period' that is defined by a century is highly artificial. As will be shown, many of the attitudes towards female criminality and the ideals of femininity that have been ascribed to Victorian England can be seen emerging or developing (from more distant roots) during the 1700s, even if they only reached their peak in the later decades of the following century. There were also major changes in levels of offending and attitudes towards both women and crime during the century. Even more intriguingly, there are some remarkable parallels between patterns of female offending and punishment in this place and period and that of the modern era, as well as important differences.

The book's different chapters explore women's experiences as the perpetrators of crimes such as murder, infanticide and various instrumental offences (like theft and burglary); as principals in the 'victimless' crime of prostitution; as victims of rape; and as both perpetrators and victims in domestic violence cases. The crimes covered are sufficiently wide-ranging to provide valuable insights into gender relations and female offending/victimisation while remaining focussed enough to keep the task within manageable bounds. Additionally, the text considers the experiences of women as actors within the era's criminal justice system, whether as defendants, convicts, prosecutors or witnesses, and, in particular, how their roles differed from those of their male counterparts. The chapters are written to be largely 'self-standing', so that they can be read individually. As a result, some themes are touched on briefly at some places in the text that are also dealt with more fully elsewhere. Footnotes provide assistance in locating such connections.

## Sources of Information

As with all studies of this type, this book is based on a mixture of primary and secondary sources. A major source of primary information has been the contemporary reports of the Metropolitan area's serious trials that are contained in the Old Bailey Sessions Papers. These were published (initially erratically)

---

[1] Gwenda Morgan and Peter Rushton, *Rogues, Thieves and the Rule of Law: The Problem of Law Enforcement in Northeast England,* London, University College London Press, 1998, p.98.

[2] See generally, Lucia Zedner, *Women, Crime and Custody in Victorian England,* Oxford, OUP, 1991, and Garthine Walker, *Crime, Gender and Social Order in Early Modern England,* Cambridge, CUP, 2003. For the period around the turn of the century, these have recently been joined by Deidre Palk's *Gender, Crime and Judicial Discretion: 1780-1830,* Woodbridge, Boydell Press, 2006.

between 1674 and 1914, at first being similar to the populist chapbooks of the era (cheap tracts about crime focussing on gruesome offences) but gradually developing into proper law reports covering most offences tried at each sessions. The Sessions Papers provide information about all offences that were indicted at the Old Bailey, i.e. that were not thrown out by the Grand Jury finding that a tendered Bill of indictment was unsupported by sufficient evidence to justify it going before a trial jury, and so returning a verdict of 'ignoramus' (literally 'I do not know').

Important pioneering work on the uses and limitations of these reports was conducted by John Langbein during the 1970s. Overall, he concluded that the reports were accurate in what they reported, but that what they recounted was not necessarily the whole story; much of significance might be omitted from them. As a result, if something was mentioned in the papers, it probably occurred; however, that it was not reported did not necessarily mean that it did not happen. This also means that offences that were of lesser interest at the time, such as 'run of the mill' thefts, and technical aspects of the trial process that were of limited appeal to a general audience, such as arguments on points of pure law, were not always covered very fully. Nevertheless, the frequent involvement of literate Londoners in the era's criminal justice process, as jurors or constables, mean that many legal issues were viewed as being of general interest, while the reports themselves became increasingly 'legal' (and so technical) as the century progressed. Although not ideal, they are probably the best source of information available on the eighteenth-century criminal trial, in a system that, unlike its inquisitorial continental counterparts, generated few records.[3]

As the eighteenth century advanced, the level of detail increased in those cases that were properly covered, though this was compensated for by a growth in the number of what Langbein termed 'squibs'; these are truncated reports that specify little more than the defendant's name, the indictment and the verdict. They were commonly employed to cover trials that were felt to be of less interest to readers, perhaps because the matter charged was not serious, was a routine example of its type, had already been heavily covered in other reports or had occurred during a particularly busy sessions. Obviously, the problems occasioned by such squibs are much less of an issue for offences such as murder than they are for 'typical' examples of crimes like shoplifting, which were much more likely to receive this type of coverage. When making quantitative analysis, using the Sessions Papers as a source, a potentially serious problem would arise if the use of squibs were to affect one gender more than the other, as it could then have a distorting effect on any conclusions drawn. However, work on the

---

[3]John Langbein, "The Criminal Trial Before the Lawyers", *The University of Chicago Law Review*, 1978, vol. 45, pp.263-316, at pp.267-272.

1780s suggests that male and female thieves were, proportionately, almost equally the subjects of such abbreviated reports during that decade.[4]

The most complete collection of the Old Bailey Sessions Papers available has been digitalised and is now available online at www.oldbaileyonline.org (all citations identified as OBSP will refer to this source unless otherwise indicated). This is a major project, funded by a variety of sources and under close academic supervision. It contains the reports of over 100,000 trials. Although enormously convenient to access, some caution must be exercised in using the site's search engine as, unsurprisingly in such a massive project, a few mistakes have crept in, leading to occasional 'double counting' and misclassification of offences (amongst other problems). It should also be noted that the reports for the initial 14 years of the century are not complete, almost half of the sessions being missing. This means that any quantitative assessment of the first half of the eighteenth century is actually for the equivalent of about 43 years. Additionally, acquittals were not reported for two years between 1790 and 1792, for fear of encouraging criminals, also leading to some statistical distortion. Furthermore, after c.1790, the court responded to increasingly delicate public sensibilities by expressly forbidding the publication of all but the most basic facts about rape hearings and some other potentially salacious cases.

Another fruit of popular literacy during the era were the Newgate Ordinary's short biographies of the criminals, both male and female, awaiting execution after capital conviction at the Old Bailey. One of the perquisites of this prison chaplain's office, they were commercially sold accounts based on extensive interviews conducted by the cleric with the condemned convicts and his attempts to render spiritual assistance to them, while also extracting confessions, criminal intelligence and expressions of repentance. Although, in theory, taken from the convict's own words, in reality they reflected the chaplain's personal agenda to a considerable degree. Only rarely, for example, were the prisoners allowed to attribute their offending to their immediate social environment and life chances, rather than personal, and progressively worse, moral failings, and, in particular, their neglect and ignorance of the precepts of religion.[5] Nevertheless, there were limits as to how far even a prison chaplain could depart from his subject's own account, especially if he wished them to be marketable (they were a useful addition to a relatively modest salary) and much valuable information can be gleaned from them. Additionally, of course, enormous numbers of books and tracts, on a huge range of topics, were published during the 1700s, many of which provide valuable insights into both women and crime during the period and will be regularly cited.

---

[4] Lynn Mackay, "Why they stole: women in the Old Bailey, 1779-1789", *Journal of Social History*, 1999, vol. 32, p.636.

[5] See for example, the account of Jane Bowman, in Rev. Paul Lorrain, *The Ordinary of Newgate his Account of the Behaviour, Confessions, and Dying words…21th of July 1703*, London, 1703, p.2.

A major source of information can be found in the crime reports published in contemporary newspapers, journals and periodicals. The eighteenth century was an era of near mass literacy. After the mid-century, about 40 per cent of labourers and women could read, a figure that continued to expand gradually.[6] In London, literacy amongst females was especially high, reflecting the capital's ability to 'cream off' better educated women from provincial society. By the 1720s, fully 56 per cent of females there could sign their names.[7] As a result, the eighteenth century was also the first great newspaper age, and this was an industry that was centred on London. To the occasional news-sheets of the seventeenth century were added regular newspapers in a modern sense; the *Daily Courant* appeared in 1702 and was swiftly followed by numerous others. By the end of the century, there were about twenty London papers. Unsurprisingly, given their location, these were disproportionately interested in what went on in and about the Metropolis. Their circulation was greatly increased by the large number of coffee and teahouses to be found in the capital; each newspaper available in such establishments, whether placed there by their proprietors or left by customers, had multiple readerships.

Then as now, crime made good copy, and from the reign of Queen Anne newspapers carried a steadily increasing number of reports detailing Metropolitan felonies. Of course, like the Sessions Papers, and as today, the medium was often more interested in lurid offences than the more mundane (and typical) crimes to be found in the capital. Some journals were quite loose about checking reported 'facts'. Nevertheless, they provide a valuable source of information about, and (perhaps much more reliably) contemporary attitudes towards, both crime and women.

Finally, it should be remembered that examining crime in a historical context presents special difficulties when it comes to the interpretation of the available evidence. This is especially the case when less 'vocal' social elements, such as women, are involved. Most published writers, whether newspaper journalists or authors, were male, as were those who kept legal or other records.[8] They also tended to be drawn from the middle and upper social orders.

## The Role of Women in Eighteenth-Century Society

For eighteenth-century women, the historical legacy of previous eras was, in theory, clear. Female autonomy and power had little place in a well-ordered society. Women were seen as physically, psychologically, emotionally, intellectually and, by a few commentators (especially early in the century), morally weaker than men. Even sympathetic male observers could freely assert

---

[6]Douglas Hay and Nicholas Rogers, *Eighteenth-century English Society*, Oxford, OUP, 1987, p.9.

[7]Peter Earle, "The female labour market in London in the late seventeenth and early eighteenth centuries", *Economic History Review*, 1989, 2nd series, XLII, 3, pp.328-353, at p.334.

[8]See generally, Mary Bosworth, "The Past as a Foreign Country? Some Methodological Implications of doing Historical Criminology", *British Journal of Criminology*, 2001, vol. 41, no.3, pp.431-442.

that men had "superior" intelligence and critical faculties, something that was further enhanced by their greater access to all the advantages bestowed by education and fortune.[9] This analysis appeared to be supported by passages drawn from the Bible and authors from the ancient world, age-old and inscrutable custom, and even aspects of contemporary medical science. As a result, it was, ostensibly, quite natural to believe that females should live obediently under the control (or at least supervision) of the nearest appropriate male, whether such men were their husbands, fathers, brothers or masters.

However, it was also accepted that this did not give men carte blanche in their treatment of women. As clerics sometimes pointed out, although a woman should submit to her husband, as she would to the Lord: "This subjection is not a slavish servile one."[10] There were reciprocal duties imposed on men to treat their spouses with understanding and respect. More importantly, English society had never fully matched the 'ideal typical' model. Theory and reality often parted company. For example, ostensibly, the doctrine of coverture, by which husband and wife were deemed to be one, imposed harsh legal and economic limitations on married women. Certainly, it was resented bitterly by some females. Nevertheless, in *practice*, it was often circumvented by a variety of legal devices and jurisdictions that gave women individual property rights and the chance to seek legal redress in a personal capacity; amongst these were customary and ecclesiastical law. Additionally, the doctrine was sometimes tacitly disregarded, even at common law.[11] Nor, on close examination, was it entirely beneficial for males. Many men complained that they got a harsh deal from coverture; not only were they liable for their wives' debts, but they could be imprisoned for them if they failed to pay up (unlike the wife herself).[12]

In reality, gender relations frequently departed from the fundamental tenets of a patriarchal society, even in rural areas. Many women were not docile, as the contemporary emphasis on 'hen pecked' husbands makes clear. Additionally, they quite often lived independently of men, as widows, spinsters or abandoned spouses, and frequently exerted a measure of real power via a variety of forums, stratagems and accommodations with the male dominated world.[13] As a result, men often alleged that women could impose their wills on males, so that they were: "…wheedled or huffed, and sometimes tired, if not beaten, into measures

---

[9]Jonas Hanway, *A Plan for establishing a Charity-House of Charity Houses for the reception of repenting prostitutes*, London, 1758, at p.xiii

[10]William Giles, *A Treatise on Marriage*, London, 1771, p.16.

[11]Joanne Bailey, "Favoured or oppressed? Married women, property and 'coverture' in England, 1660-1800", *Continuity and Change*, 2002, vol. 17 (3), pp.351-372, at pp. 351-353. See also chapter two.

[12]*Gentleman's Magazine*, vol. 6, 1736, p.649.

[13]Bernard Capp, "Separate Domains? Women and Authority in Early Modern England", *The Experience of Authority in Early Modern England*, P. Griffiths et al (Eds.), Basingstoke, MacMillan, 1996, pp.117-145.

very disadvantageous to themselves."[14] By contrast, some men were considered 'effeminate' and made little effort to live up to the duties of their sex. This was particularly evident in the Metropolitan area, where, even at the start of the century, some people were ignoring their appointed gender roles. Thus, there were complaints about foppish men who behaved like women, discussing at length the price of muslin or recipes for sweetmeats. Against this, it was noted that there were masculine women who instead of soothing men into "tenderness and compassion" (as they should), liked nothing better than to talk about horses and hounds, aggressively discuss politics or jest boisterously with males.[15]

Furthermore, society itself changed significantly during the course of the 1700s, especially in the Metropolis. Indeed, the later decades of the eighteenth century may have witnessed the beginning of a major shift in attitudes towards femininity and the social role of women generally. Arguably, England started to become truly 'modern' in the eighteenth century, and this was a view that some contemporary observers subscribed to even at the time. Certainly, the era was strongly influenced by, *inter alia*, the growth of individualism, use of the scientific method, rationalism, industrialism, commercialism, the political and philosophical ideas of the enlightenment and, towards its close, those emanating from the French Revolution. It also witnessed an ongoing rise in the social and political importance of what might loosely be termed the 'middling' orders.

The position of women was also being questioned to a hitherto unprecedented degree. Of course, as in previous centuries, most women appear to have accepted the gender division in eighteenth-century society, and the distinct social roles accorded to males and females that came with it, whether willingly or with resignation. There was no formally organised feminist movement, campaigning for a measure of equality between the sexes in public life. Instead, there were relatively disconnected, if courageous, individuals, such as Mary Astell, a classical scholar who dreamed of organising college retreats for academic spinsters, and a variety of other assorted misfits and rebels.[16] However, despite this limitation, a perhaps surprising range of proto-feminist writing was produced by women (and some men) during the century, in essays, novels, poems and polemical works, of which Mary Wollstonecraft's *Vindication of the Rights of Women* (1792) is merely the best known.

Contemporary debates about philosophical rationalism and political authority gave such early feminists a conceptual framework with which to challenge the power of age-old custom. Thus, in 1735, one female author could claim that the position of wives was "more disadvantageous than slavery itself." She pointed out that Thomas Hobbes had been unable to find any foundation in nature for the enormous superiority ascribed to men and asserted that, taken

---

[14]*Gentleman's Magazine*, vol. 6, 1736, at p.649

[15]*The Spectator*, No.57 (5th May 1711) reproduced in D.F. Bond (Ed.), *The Spectator*, vol. 1, Oxford, Oxford Clarendon Press, 1965, p.241.

[16]Roy Porter, *English Society in the 18th Century*, London, Penguin, 1991, at p.23

individually, many women were physically stronger than men.[17] Another polemical feminist tract complained of the "tyrannical usurpating authority" that men exerted over women, alleged that the "haughty sex" were largely a prey to their own brute passions and animal appetites, and stressed that inscrutable custom on gender relations was not necessarily correct; it noted that a belief that the sun circled the earth had been centuries old before it was clearly repudiated by modern science.[18] Yet another female author declared that if women were not denied access to education, they would swiftly excel men in the study of letters. She went on to claim that, in so far as they existed, many base and lewd females were actually the work of the men who had first led them astray.[19]

The greater London area, in particular, was the epicentre for many of these trends, some of which manifested themselves in bizarre ways. Thus, on occasion during the 1720s, women boxed each other in public prize-fights held at Hockley in the Hole.[20] Amongst well-to-do females, as well, there were growing displays of independence. In the late 1700s, John Collet's popular illustrations frequently portrayed affluent women engaging in a number of 'unladylike' pastimes, such as shooting and gaming, in the process demonstrating a marked degree of personal freedom.

## The Eighteenth-Century Metropolis

The conurbation that comprised the two adjoining cities of London and Westminster, along with the built up and adjacent parts of the county of Middlesex, was termed the 'Metropolis' during the eighteenth century. However, government remained in the hands of its three main component parts (four if the urbanised parts of Surrey south of the Thames are included). Thus, in the City of London, the Mayor, Sheriff, Aldermen and Common Councilmen ruled, acutely jealous of their ancient privileges. The neighbouring City of Westminster was, at least nominally, governed by its court of twelve Burgesses. Other parts of the Metropolis were still controlled by the Middlesex Justices of the Peace (JPs) in, theoretically, the same way as other parishes in the country (Middlesex being the county immediately surrounding the two cities north of the river). These JPs also had an important function in the government of Westminster (but not the City), while in the built up areas south of the river, the Surrey JPs held sway (except in the City dominated and controlled Borough). The main unifying characteristic of the entire area north of the river, including the rural parts of Middlesex, was their shared use of the Old Bailey Court to determine serious crimes.

---

[17]Anon (female author), "The Hardships of the English Laws in Relation to Wives", (1735) in *Women in the Eighteenth Century*, Vivien Jones (Ed.), London, Routledge, pp.217-225, at p. 223.
[18]Anon ('By Sophie, a person of quality'), *Women not Inferior to Men*, London, printed for John Hawkins, 1739, at pp.2-4.
[19]Anon ('By a Lady of Quality'), *Women Triumphant or the Excellency of the Female Sex*, London, 1721, pp.vi and 16.
[20]*The London Journal*, June 23rd 1722, p.3.

During the eighteenth century, the whole area experienced massive population growth as a result of inward migration and a huge expansion in its built up parts. In 1695, one informed estimate had placed the population of the parishes within the bills of mortality area alone at 530,000. By 1716, this had reached 630,856.[21] At the end of the century, the Metropolitan area encompassed at least a million people. However, population growth in the City, the 'square mile', both within and without its historic walls, though significant, was relatively modest compared to the expansion west of Temple Bar, where many richer people started to settle, soon being followed by less prosperous elements. Although much smaller than the City, Westminster's population had reached about 130,000 by 1700; growth slowed thereafter, so that it had expanded to 165,000 by the time of the first census in 1801.[22] Additionally, there was enormous growth in the poorer Middlesex parishes that lay to the east of the City or beyond its northern borders; these were often heavily engaged in brewing, distilling and other forms of commercial activity.

This expansion also meant that, by the early 1700s, although still administratively totally distinct, the two cities at the core of the Metropolis were completely joined together, meeting along the Strand in one continuous built up area.[23] Throughout the eighteenth century, the conurbation continued to gobble up what had previously been rural and suburban villages such as Chelsea and Marylebone. In London, urbanisation, a phenomenon that is often associated with the industrial revolution had, in reality, long preceded it. Of course, this process should not be exaggerated; at the end of the period, much of Middlesex still remained rural. However, even here, proximity to the Metropolis meant that undeveloped parts of the county were dominated by the requirements of the capital. Its agriculture was shaped by the need to supply the city with fruit, milk and vegetables while it was littered with the brickworks and gravel pits that supplied much of the raw material for urban building.

As the death rate in London during this period exceeded its birth rate by a considerable degree (especially before the 1750s), the increase in population was necessarily the result of a large-scale immigration of people from all parts of the British Isles as well as some areas of continental Europe. Influxes of poor Irishmen were a particularly regular feature, with many complaining that too many Metropolitan beggars came from the neighbouring island.[24] Over half (56 per cent) of women indicted at the Old Bailey between 1791 and 1793 came

---

[21] *The Gentleman's Magazine*, 1735, vol. 5, p.355.

[22] Elaine Reynolds, "Sir John Fielding, Sir Charles Whitworth, and the Westminster Night Watch Act, 1770-1775", *Criminal Justice History*, 2002, vol.16, pp.1-29, at p.3.

[23] E.A. Wrigley, "A simple model of London's Importance in Changing English Society and Economy 1650-1750", *Past and Present*, 1967, no.37, p.44.

[24] Anon (a 'Citizen in London'), *The Vices of the cities of London and Westminster trac'd from their original …*, Dublin, G. Faulkner, 1751, p.20.

from other parts of Great Britain and Ireland.[25] However, this was not much greater than their proportion in the adult female population as a whole. Although a high proportion of male Londoners were also migrants, proportionately more women appear to have travelled long distances to the capital, from Scotland, Ireland or the Continent, fewer to have moved there from the Home Counties.[26] Taken together, these changes also meant that the area was markedly different to the rest of the country in several key respects; for example, in degree of urbanisation, population density, level of commercial activity, forms of recreation and even social control mechanisms.[27] Additionally, the rapid expansion brought with it numerous problems associated with overcrowding, poor sanitation, vagrancy, increased social segregation and disorder.

## Metropolitan Courts and Policing

Criminal courts in the Metropolis sometimes differed markedly from those in the rest of England. In the eighteenth century, most offences were tried on indictment. Less serious crimes, termed misdemeanours, including most frauds, cases of riot and assault, were normally heard by juries at the Metropolitan equivalent of provincial Quarter Sessions. These were usually held at the Guildhall for the City and at Hick's Hall in Clerkenwell for Middlesex. Westminster also had its own Quarter Sessions, separate from those for the rest of Middlesex, and conducted in a tavern, near Westminster Hall, until the eighteenth century, when a purpose built court was constructed. Although held more frequently (usually eight times a year) than their provincial equivalents these were, in reality, broadly similar to other Quarter Sessions found elsewhere in England.[28] More serious crimes, such as murder, robbery and rape, were classified as felonies, and normally heard (before juries) at the Old Bailey Sessions. These were usually held immediately after the Quarter Sessions, and the inferior courts' clerks drew up the indictments that would be determined at the higher forum. Hearings at the Old Bailey were rather different to their provincial counterparts, the Assizes.[29]

Although the Old Bailey was a joint court, serving both the City of London and the county of Middlesex, its two jurisdictions were kept quite distinct, each having its own clerical staff, records and returning two separate juries to conduct trials from each location. Inevitably, this meant that as the population of the City declined relative to that of the rest of the Metropolis, so did its share of the trials

---

[25]Peter King, "Female offenders, work and life-cycle change in late-eighteenth-century London", *Continuity and Change*, 1996, vol. 11, pp.61-90, at pp. 72-74.

[26]Earle, "The female labour market in London", at p.333.

[27]Peter King, *Crime, Justice and Discretion in England: 1740-1820*, Oxford, OUP, 2000, p.111, and, generally, Dorothy George, *London Life in the Eighteenth Century*, London, Penguin Books, 1965.

[28]E.D. Mercer and K. Goodacre, *Guide to the Middlesex Sessions Records, 1549-1884*, London, Greater London Record Office, 1965, p.14.

[29]Anthony Babbington, *A House in Bow Street*, 2nd edn, Chichester, Barry Rose, 1999, p.51.

(an extra jury had to be added for Middlesex as the century progressed because of its increased numbers). However, although a joint court, the Old Bailey was dominated by officials from the City, which paid for its upkeep and provided the court's Recorder (its most important judicial figure). Additionally, the City's Common Sergeant, the legal adviser to the Court of Common Council was, *ex officio*, one of its judges. In strict order of precedence, the Lord Mayor was the Chief Judge of the Old Bailey Court.[30] In practice, his lack of legal training meant that he was not ideally equipped to conduct trials of any complexity, which were usually left to the Recorder or one of the Westminster judges (taking a turn to sit temporarily at the court). As a result, the Lord Mayor would normally sit next to the judges, as the Old Bailey, unlike provincial assizes, saw the frequent use of collegiate benches. Occasionally, however, he might conduct some of the more straightforward hearings on his own account. The legal representatives of the adjacent county had very much a secondary role. Indeed, the City officials long refused to allow Middlesex magistrates even to sit on the bench, although permitting them to attend court as part of the gaol delivery commission, considering them (often correctly) as socially inferior to its own Aldermen.[31] The only other Metropolitan forum with the power to determine serious crimes was the Crown Side of the Court of King's Bench, whose three separate criminal jurisdictions included a local power to hear offences committed in Middlesex and Westminster. However, it was very rarely used for 'normal' criminal trials, being largely confined to matters with a political or aristocratic connection, and was, usually, statistically insignificant.

At the other end of the spectrum to serious felonies were minor offences that did not require a jury trial, but could be determined by JPs, either when sitting alone or, more commonly, with colleagues. Nationally, magisterial powers were much greater when JPs sat in pairs or larger groups, though, in the City of London, the Aldermen (the square mile's equivalent of JPs) had unusually extensive powers when sitting by themselves. Although summary offences were rare in 1700, their numbers expanded gradually throughout the century, occasioning concern amongst jurists such as William Blackstone (who preferred to see the use of juries). The Metropolitan area was at the forefront of this expansion, and most committals to the City's Bridewells were made by summary courts, whether by the Aldermen sitting at the Guildhall Justice Room and Mansion House, or the institution's own court (presided over by its governors, amongst who was to be found the Lord Mayor).[32]

At petty sessions magistrates would deal with as much of the business that came before them as possible, even if, sometimes, they might not have a sound legal basis for their actions. As well as discharging matters that appeared to be

---

[30] James Howel, *Londinopolis*, London, 1657, p.392.
[31] John Beattie, *Policing and Punishment in London, 1660-1750*, Oxford, OUP, 2001, pp.13-14.
[32] Faramerz Dabhoiwala, "Summary Justice in Early Modern London", *English Historical Review*, 2006, vol.cxxi no. 492, at pp.799-800.

without foundation, and committing other cases for trial on indictment (whether at Quarter Sessions or the Old Bailey), they would deal summarily with many allegations. Thus, when Margaret Jones was brought before the Alderman sitting at the Guildhall Justice Room, accused of "quarrelling" in the street and insulting a male passer by (the complainant), she was discharged "after promising not to offend again." Similarly, in 1780, Ann Cummings and Ann Stockwell, two local prostitutes, were produced at the Guildhall Justice Room for: "…making a disturbance in the street, & collecting a mob." Nevertheless, they, too, were discharged by the magistrate after "promising better behaviour in future."[33] This approach was particularly manifest in the City of London, where Aldermen would record their decisions in Minute Books, many of which still survive. A cursory examination of these (often hard to decipher) documents suggest that a large number (perhaps over half) of the complainants and defendants that came before the magistrates were women.[34]

Policing was largely parish based and organised, with a major input coming from amateurs rather than professional officers. The constables were unpaid men (or their paid substitutes) fulfilling a part-time, year-long parish office for healthy, moderately well to do, male ratepayers; they were normally selected by rota. By contrast, members of the watch were the poorly paid and sometimes elderly or physically infirm guardians of the night streets. They were placed at stands and in strategically situated watch-houses or, occasionally, patrolled fixed beats. Normally, they would be under the immediate supervision of the allotted 'constable of the night', a parish constable taking his turn by rota at what was an unpopular nocturnal task. This individual would check up on the watchmen while they were on duty and also investigate suspicious activity.

## Females and Crime

Historically, crime has been viewed as an essentially masculine activity, a few notably "feminine" offences, such as malefic witchcraft and infanticide, apart. The latter continued to be an overwhelmingly female crime during the eighteenth century, while allegations of the former swiftly dwindled to near non-existence prior to complete abolition of the offence in 1736. Although two women were prosecuted and acquitted for witchcraft at the Old Bailey in 1682 and 1683, these were amongst the last such cases to be tried at this forum. However, occasional claims of witchcraft were still being made against women in the early 1700s, even in and about the Metropolitan area, though hardly any survived magisterial examination. By then, a much more common accusation was that females were claiming to be 'cunning women' as a way of fraudulently

---

[33]Minute Book of the Guildhall Justice Room 28th June to 28th July, 1780, LMA CLA 00501, entry for 3rd July.

[34]Minute Book of the Guildhall Justice Room 25th May to 19th June, 1752, LMA CLA 00501, entry for 11th June. A forthcoming Ph.D dissertation by Drew Gray should clarify many issues pertaining to these records.

earning money. In 1731, a woman was tried at Hick's Hall (the forum for the Middlesex Sessions) for defrauding one Mrs. Newton of more than twelve pounds by claiming to be able: "…to bring home her son from the East-Indies in a whirlwind; and also of procuring 3 men to fall in love with the said Mrs. Newton." Despite the large sums of money involved, and a long hearing, the defendant was acquitted.[35] Such cases continued throughout the 1700s and into the following century, so that in 1822 Elizabeth Cousens was sentenced at the Guildhall to a month in the Bridewell, after promising to tell fortunes and identify and cure hidden diseases.[36]

At a less serious level, minor gender specific offences, such as 'scolding', which, whatever its medieval origins, had become a purely female offence, committed by an obstreperous woman who had become a "public nuisance to her neighbourhood", during the early modern period, was also very rarely prosecuted by 1700 (though discussed by Blackstone as late as 1769),[37] even in the provinces, and died out completely in the Metropolitan area shortly afterwards.[38] Nevertheless, such 'female' offences, even taken together (and ignoring prostitution) made up only a tiny minority of crimes perpetrated by women, the vast majority of which were for 'conventional' offences such as theft.

Women's involvement in crime had a long history in the London area. In the previous century, the transvestite Mary Frith, popularly known as 'Moll Cutpurse', had become one of London's first master criminals, finishing as a large-scale commercial fence. Operating out of domestic premises she had acted as an intermediary between crime victims and felons, negotiating the return (at a price) of stolen items. This was fully 50 years before the notorious Jonathan Wild adopted the same technique in the early 1700s. Frith was so influential that, when criminals had a dispute between themselves, she was often asked to be an "umpire in their quarrels."[39] A few women involved in crime emulated Moll Cutpurse's 'masculine' behaviour, but even more thoroughly, and simply joined the ranks of those eighteenth-century females who dressed, lived as, and were thought to be, men, a number of whom also served as pirates, sailors, marines and soldiers during the era. Thus, 'George' Kelf, sentenced to transportation for stealing from his lodgings, was only suspected of being a woman after being incarcerated in Newgate prison. 'He' was then "search'd, and found to be so." Kelf explained that she had gone as a man for the previous 16 years.[40] Seventy years later, Sarah Stanley, a "masculine looking" woman who had served as a

---

[35]*Grub-street Journal,* 22 July 1731.
[36]*The Times,* Aug. 9th, 1822, p.3.
[37]William Blackstone, *Commentaries on the Laws of England,* 1769, vol. 4, at p. 169.
[38]Walker, *Crime, Gender and Social Order in Early Modern England,* p.104.
[39]Anon, *The Life and Death of Mrs Mary Frith, Commonly Called Mal Cutpurse,* London, Printed for W. Gilbertson, 1662, pp.2-6.
[40]*Weekly Journal or British Gazetteer,* 26 July 1726.

corporal in a cavalry regiment, was convicted at the Old Bailey of petty larceny, after being driven by "mere necessity" to steal a cloak.[41]

Despite the presence of such individuals, most women offended as women, and did not commit specifically 'female' offences. There were few crimes, however outlandish, in which Metropolitan women were totally unrepresented. Thus, some were charged as accessories to rape, others accused of sodomy with animals. In a bizarre case from 1677, a married woman of 'lewd conversation', who regularly took men back to a rented room, where she was spied on by her neighbours through peepholes, was seen to bring a dog home and have sexual relations with it. The dog was brought to court, put in front of the defendant and: "…owned her by wagging his tail, and making motions as it were to kiss her, which 'twas sworn she did do when she made that horrid use of him." She was convicted of sodomy and sentenced to death.[42] By contrast, Jane Martin perpetrated an early and extremely sophisticated example of what has since become known as 'long firm' fraud. She established a bogus business (a shop), ordered about 700 pounds worth of goods on credit from various merchants, and then suddenly decamped and disappeared with the proceeds of her venture which she hid in the Mint and, presumably, swiftly sold on in that nefarious area.[43] As late as 1819, it was noted that many women were adept at taking elegant lodgings, dressing fashionably as members of the upper social orders, assuming false names, and then ordering large quantities of goods on credit, before disappearing with the valuables they had acquired. Some of these well attired women would also infiltrate society functions and steal whatever came to hand.[44]

Women were also heavily involved in coining offences, at a time when the national currency was under almost constant attack. Of the c.750 people accused of the crime during the eighteenth century, just over a third (c.270) were female. Although some were married women working with their husbands, many acted on their own or with other females. Sometimes, their techniques were extremely sophisticated. Thus, in 1710, Jane Housden, Mary Pitman and Elizabeth Roach were caught with a melting ladle, metal and a flask, amongst "other things fit for counterfeit coining." After her arrest, Housden threw five pounds of forged shillings in the Thames, from where they were retrieved by a diving boy.[45] Women were also frequently involved in uttering forged bank notes and wills.

---

[41]J L Rayner and G T Crook (Eds.), *The Complete Newgate Calendar*, London, Privately printed for the Navarre Society, vol. 4, 1926, at pp.221-222.

[42]OBSP, Trial of unnamed woman, 11th July 1677.

[43]Arthur Hayward (Ed.), *Lives of the Most Remarkable Criminals: Who have been Condemned and Executed for Murder, the Highway, Housebreaking, Street Robberies, Coining or other offences. Collected from Original Papers and Authentic Memoirs, 1735*. London, Routledge & Sons, 1927, pp.381-383.

[44]Samuel Leigh, *Leigh's New Picture of London*, London, Printed by W. Clowes, Northumberland, 1819, pp.106-107.

[45]OBSP, Trial of Jane Housden, Mary Pitman and Elizabeth Roach, 6th September 1710.

In the popular mind there were many similarities between the way in which both men and women entered criminal life. A progressive moral deterioration after the commission of minor sins, such as Sabbath breaking, that ultimately culminated in the commission of capital felonies, like murder, was one of the most common. In his various *Accounts*, the Newgate Ordinary would regularly stress how irreligion and libertinism had led many females to disaster. Thus, Jane Dyer, a Scottish woman who had moved to London and was executed there for theft in 1705 admitted to the cleric, prior to being hanged, that she had been guilty to the highest degree of "Lewdness and Debauchery, of swearing, lying, cursing, [and] Sabbath breaking" before resorting to out and out crime.[46] Similarly, shortly before her execution, the murderer Elizabeth Brownrigg attributed her own fall from an earlier life of moral rectitude to neglecting her prayers and failing to observe the Sabbath, which was the "first inlet to the wickedness she had unhappily fallen into."[47] Women were thought to be especially susceptible to the effects of vanity, being inherently prone to extravagance, frivolous, generally incapable of "sober application" and often possessed of an innate craving for baubles and fine clothes, factors which could make them vulnerable to temptation.[48]

To modern observers, of course, such explanations do not satisfactorily explain the comparatively high incidence of female crime found in the Metropolis at this period. Other attempts to account for it in the intervening 200 years have been more plausible. In 1876, the Victorian criminal historian Luke Owen Pike suggested (erroneously) that female crime was increasing in his own era because women were becoming more independent of men in gaining their livelihoods. He went on to argue that they had: "...thrown off the protection against competition and temptation which dependence on men implies. [and] It follows that, so far as crime is determined by external circumstances, every step made by woman towards her independence is a step towards that precipice at the bottom of which lies a prison."[49] Although wrong with regard to his own age, and despite not considering exactly what male 'protection' may have entailed for the women concerned, and whether it was always welcome on their part, his analysis is not devoid of merit. In the modern era, it has been at the root of what has been termed the 'gender equality hypothesis', a belief that the gender gap in crime is smaller in social environments in which female roles differ less from those of men, whether in urban settings or (in the twentieth century) during wartime.[50]

---

[46]Paul Lorrain, *The Ordinary of Newgate …4th May 1705*, at p.1.
[47]Anon, *God's Revenge Against Murder!*, London, 1810, at p.23
[48]Rev. Wettenhall Wilkes, *A Letter of Genteel and Moral Advice to a Young Lady*, London, 1751, p.194 and Thomas Gisborne, *An Enquiry into the Duties of the Female Sex*, 1797, London, p.34.
[49]Luke Owen Pike, *A History of Crime in England*, vol. 2, London, Smith Elder & Co, 1876, at p.527.
[50]Darrel Steffensmeier and Emilie Allan, "Gender and Crime: Toward a Gendered Theory of Female Offending", *Annual Review of Sociology*, 1996, vol.22, pp.459-487, at pp.467-468.

Eighteenth-century London was a novel society; unprecedented in English history and not replicated in Western Europe since the fall of the Roman Empire. It was an environment characterised by anonynimity, social mobility and transient, increasingly contractual (rather than affective) relationships. As a result, social cohesion sometimes became attenuated, whether manifest in family or friendship ties, an ability to rely on others, participation in communal activities or personal attachment to a specific neighbourhood. In this environment, social boundaries also became more flexible and individuals were free to re-invent themselves, no longer invariably being bound by 'reputation' or their status at birth. Perhaps indicative of this change, by the early eighteenth century, impostors were regularly pretending to be parish officers in Westminster, well aware that in a society of strangers, people no longer took it for granted that they could recognise local constables and watchmen.[51] In some (but not all) respects, the novel society that emerged in the Metropolitan area was profoundly unsettling to many longstanding social mores. Thus, it has been observed that the luxury economy found in parts of Westminster generated social expectations and a sexual license that had the potential to undermine traditional courtship practices.[52]

The process of urbanisation inevitably also had a major impact on both crime and gender relations. It is now generally accepted that women's offending must be seen in its socio-economic context, rather than as being purely a product of innate physical or psychological characteristics. Although women in rural areas had relatively free lives by much European comparison, they still lived under considerable constraint. However, these social controls and socialised habits of obedience must frequently have become attenuated in the Metropolis, where there were more single, working, females, many of whom had migrated from the country to what was a huge and frenetic city. In this environment, they were often dependant on their own resources to survive. As a result, some of the 'traditional' distinctions between the sexes appear to have been loosened.

This phenomenon, widely remarked upon by modern urban historians, had been observed by visiting foreigners to London, such as Allessandro Magno, as early as the 1500s. It had, if anything, become more pronounced over the ensuing 150 years, so that, in the wider nation, Metropolitan women became the epitome of pride and independence, often ignoring the demands of tradition and exercising "very great…liberties" in the process.[53] Frequently divorced from

---

[51]Jennine Hurl-Eamon, "The Westminster Impostors: Impersonating Law Enforcement in Early Eighteenth-Century London", *Eighteenth-Century Studies*, 2005, vol.38, no.3, pp.461-483, at p.462.

[52]Nicholas Rogers, "Carnal Knowledge: Illegitimacy in Eighteenth-Century Westminster", *Journal of Social History*, 1989, vol. xxiii, part 2, 1989, pp. 355-375, at p.369.

[53]See Lucia Zedner, "Women, Crime, and Penal Responses: A Historical Account", Michael Tonry (Ed.), *Crime and Justice; A Review of Research*, Chicago, University of Chicago Press, 1991, p.247 and Laura Gowing, "The Freedom of the Streets: Women and Social Space, 1560-1640", *Londinopolis*,

family assistance (and control) by migration, many women, like other Londoners, had to become personally assertive, if they were to survive in what was often an unforgiving environment. Some were single, whether spinsters or widows, others in unstable relationships (even if 'married' or cohabiting), in which they could be abandoned at any time. Many more were married to men, such as sailors, who might be away for long periods of time. The effect that this independence had on Metropolitan women, their life strategies and daily conduct, will be a recurring theme in this book.

As a result of these factors, women experienced an unprecedented degree of personal autonomy, but it was a freedom that was combined with a need to show a novel degree of self-reliance. The effects of this combination produced a widespread feeling that some Metropolitan women were 'out of control'. In 1678, a judge (the infamous Jeffreys) at the Old Bailey, sentencing a group of female pickpockets and shoplifters, had referred to them as a "parcel of Sluts" bent on stealing to maintain a luxurious lifestyle and drawn from: "...those Women, that have the impudence to smoke tobacco, and gussle in Ale houses."[54] The notorious judge was certainly not unique. Many visitors to the Metropolis were shocked by the aggressive behaviour, apparent 'vanity' and impudence of local females.[55]

One specific example of this process at work was female participation in the 'gin craze' that swept the Metropolitan area in the early decades of the eighteenth century. This produced the first occasion in which men and women (especially single working women) had access to alcohol and the social world with which it was associated on even vaguely equal terms. Female consumption of the spirit, often ingested side by side with men, was high, and many others were involved in 'hawking' it for a living.[56] Indeed, it has been argued that, historically, the eighteenth-century Metropolis saw women emerge as serious drinkers in their own right for the first time, something that was to be recorded by William Hogarth in graphic detail in his print 'Gin Lane' (1751). In this, London differed from the rest of the nation. Alcohol was far more readily available to urban females than it was to women in rural areas. Metropolitan women, especially those from the lower social orders, often visited gin and brandy shops and taverns, buying and imbibing 'quarterns' of spirits. These establishments provided them with an escape from cramped, damp and cold domestic environments. By the end of the century, the magistrate Patrick Colquhoun was alarmed to note that women were even frequenting tavern taprooms, though he seems to have been guilty of rose tinted thinking in

---

P. Griffiths et al (eds.), Manchester, Manchester University Press, 2001, p.130 and Henri Misson, Memoirs *and Observations in his Travels over England* (J. Ozell, Trans.), London, 1719, p.364.
[54] OBSP, Punishment Summary, 12th Dec., 1678.
[55] Anon *A View of London and Westminster: or, the Town Spy, etc. By a German Gentleman*, 1725, pp.54-58.
[56] Jessica Warner and Frank Ivis, "Gin and Gender in Early Eighteenth-century London", *Eighteenth-Century Life*, vol.24, 2000, pp.85-105, at p.86.

believing that, only a few years earlier, this would have been considered a disgrace.[57]

Compounding the problem, numerous Metropolitan chandlers' shops sold gin, and many of them appear to have catered primarily to a female clientele, whether wives or servant-maids. Thus, the pickpocket Sarah Nut stole from the proprietor of such an establishment after she "came into the house [shop] to drink."[58] If Henry Fielding is to be believed, many women used the pretext of buying household goods to tipple, sometimes visiting such establishments up to ten times a day. As a result, some observers even demanded that the sale of spirits to women be made illegal.[59] As attitudes towards the effects of drunkenness to criminal responsibility became more varied during the 1700s, some women (like men) sought to place the blame for their misconduct on alcohol, or, as with Sarah Hatchet in 1726, attribute an allegedly false confession (to murder), to the effects of gin.[60]

However, and crucially, this freedom of action occurred in a society where the traditional limitations on female employment, and so remuneration, even if slightly relaxed, were still a potent force, greatly limiting legitimate opportunities and recourse to legal survival mechanisms.[61] This situation was made worse by the willingness of Metropolitan males to impinge on the relatively limited number of traditionally female occupations. As a female journal correspondent complained in 1739, it was "absurd and ridiculous" to see young men, dressed up in wigs and ruffles, selling needles, lace and small quantities of silk; such occupations were, in theory, "much below the honour and dignity of their sex."[62] (As will be seen, some observers even blamed this phenomenon for forcing women into prostitution). Perhaps as a result, women, especially those with children, appear to have outnumbered male beggars in the London area throughout the eighteenth century. However, their mendicancy had a lower public profile than that of their male counterparts, usually being conducted more discreetly, as many went about it by knocking on kitchen doors, ostensibly to ask if there was work available, but usually accepting alms instead.[63]

Taken together, these factors (personal independence in difficult economic circumstances), may have had a major impact on female behaviour in general, and offending in particular, explaining why patterns in the Metropolis differed

---

[57]Patrick Colquhoun, *A Treatise on the Police of the Metropolis*, 1796, Printed by H. Fry, London, at p.41.

[58] OBSP, 5th Dec. 1722, Trial of Sarah Nut.

[59]Jessica Warner, *Craze: Gin and Debauchery in an Age of Reason*, London, Profile Books, 2003, pp.61-62 and p.66.

[60]Dana Rabin, "Drunkenness and Responsibility for Crime in the Eighteenth Century", *Journal of British Studies*, 2005, vol.44.3, pp.457-477, at p.474,

[61]Earle, "The female labour market in London", p.339.

[62]*Gentleman's Magazine*, vol. 9, 1739, p.525.

[63]Tim Hitchcock, "Begging on the Streets of Eighteenth-Century London", *Journal of British Studies*, 2005, vol.44.3, pp.478-498, at pp.489-490.

from those found elsewhere in the country. In turn, the fact that females often had to act in what might have been considered a 'masculine' manner by their rural counterparts, might also explain why, as defendants, although still advantaged in comparison to men, they were less favoured than women being tried in the provinces. Generally, as will be seen throughout the book, the capital appears to have had something of an 'equalising' effect on the genders. Women were more likely to behave, and be treated, like men than were their rural sisters, especially when it came to crime, though this was, of course, always a matter of degree, and more indulgence was shown towards urban women in the final decades of the century than had previously been the case.

Any discussion of women and crime in a historical context cannot divorce itself from what are still sensitive issues over gender relations. Questions about personal empathy and sympathy (or a lack of it) cannot be ignored.[64] However, any examination of the eighteenth-century Metropolis also quickly makes clear that partisan generalisations about the sexes can be extremely dangerous. Unsurprisingly, straightforward misogyny in some male perpetrated crimes (and some male officials) is well evidenced. As in all ages, women could be the victims of brutal sexual violence at the hands of men. For example, in 1718, John Price, a Metropolitan executioner, was himself hanged, and his body suspended from chains in Bunhill Fields, for savagely murdering an elderly woman who had resisted his drunken advances. In the process, he almost knocked one of her eyes "out of her head."[65] At the other end of the social spectrum, and at about the same time, the 'Mohocks', a group of Aristocratic rakes, would viciously attack women in the streets, solely for their own amusement, even if their activities (and numbers) were greatly exaggerated by contemporary observers. Several females were scarred for life in such incidents. Typically, Jonathan Swift could note that two members of the gang had attacked a lady's maid outside her mistress's house, during which assault: "They cut all her face, and beat her without any provocation."[66]

However, there was also a marked absence of 'sisterhood' amongst many eighteenth-century females. Thus, women could manifest extreme violence towards each other (as well as men), over comparatively minor matters. When Mary Dodson visited a woman named Greensword to ask for payment of a (disputed) debt for the supply of liquor, Greensword did not respect her heavily pregnant condition. Although eight months gone, she was beaten "black and blue," with blows being rained on her arms, stomach and breasts.[67] Greensword, who was fined £20, was not an aberration. Despite their gender, females were disproportionately represented amongst defendants in assault cases in which

---

[64] See generally Mary Bosworth, "The Past as a Foreign Country?", pp.431-442.
[65] Alexander Smith, *A Compleat history of the lives and robberies of the most notorious highwaymen ... for above an hundred years past,* London, Briscoe, vol. 2, 1719, pp.329-330.
[66] Jonathan Swift, *Journal to Stella,* entry for March 9, 1711, London, Methuen & Co., 1901.
[67] *The Times,* 10th Jan. 1792, p.3

pregnant women were attacked. Of 87 such cases recorded in the Westminster area between 1685 and 1720, almost a third (27) were perpetrated by other women.[68] Women also seem to have been more likely to 'sexually' humiliate other females when engaged in fights with members of their own sex, than were men who assaulted women. This might be done by exposing their breasts or private parts in public. Whatever may have been the female ideal amongst educated commentators of the time, with its emphasis on mutual support, nurturing and gentleness, many women did not remotely conform to the approved stereotype. Despite this, in a society that was dominated by men, there was also a sometimes surprising degree of official sympathy for women forced into difficult situations, such as those who killed their partners after they had themselves been assaulted.

---

[68]Jennine Hurl-Eamon, *Gender and Petty Violence in London, 1680-1720*, Columbus, Ohio State University Press, 2005, p.50.

# Chapter 2: Women, Criminal Litigation and Punishment

## Introduction

This chapter will consider Metropolitan women's experiences within the eighteenth-century criminal justice system, whether as defendants, convicts, complainants/prosecutors, witnesses or members of the 'jury of matrons'. As this rather limited list suggests, the era's courts and prisons were dominated by men. Nearly all of the personnel found in them, whether judges, attending dignitaries, magistrates, jurors, clerks, lawyers, ushers, gaolers or executioners were male. Other than as the accused, women were largely confined to giving evidence or, occasionally, being spectators in the public gallery.

In all ages, society's approach towards the prosecution and punishment of women has been shaped by contemporary attitudes towards femininity and its conventions for dealing with women. (Of course, this also applies to its treatment of 'masculinity'). At every stage in the eighteenth-century criminal litigation process, cultural understandings as to what women were like, and how they ought to behave, determined forensic and penal responses. In general terms, this manifest itself in a widespread, though not universal, lenience towards females accused of crime, coupled with some gender specific, and occasionally rather theatrical, forms of penal sanction.[69]

It is extremely difficult to factor in the many variables *other* than their sex that might have contributed to this phenomenon. It is possible that the apparent lenience shown towards women could be explained without requiring recourse to a specifically gendered account at all. For example, they may have received milder treatment because they were not as 'hardened' as male criminals, perhaps committing less serious examples of the crimes with which they were charged, or having fewer previous convictions. Nevertheless, such explanations do not appear to be supported by most of the available evidence. Thus, it seems that women at the Old Bailey were no more likely than men to be neophytes to crime, nor was there an enormous difference in the value of goods stolen. As a result, other explanations must be sought for their milder treatment.[70] The most obvious is that male 'sympathy' towards accused women favoured beneficial

---

[69]David Garland, *Punishment and Modern Society: A Study in Social Theory,* Oxford, Clarendon, 1990, p.202.

[70]Peter King, "Gender, crime and justice in late eighteenth-and early nineteenth-century England", *Gender and Crime in Modern Europe,* M. Arnot et al (eds.), London, University College London Press, 1999, pp.44-74, at p.46 and pp.62-64.

outcomes for them in the criminal litigation process, at a time when there was enormous scope for this to have tangible results.

Although discretion is found in all legal systems, throughout all eras, the eighteenth century was a golden age for discretionary justice. The decision to prosecute (and for what) was largely in the hands of the victim; examining magistrates and Grand Juries had considerable power as to whether to allow matters to proceed for trial; most importantly, perhaps, jury nullification and mitigation was at its peak and there was huge discretion vested in the judiciary and the executive to award post-conviction reprieves from execution.[71] This discretion could be disproportionately exercised on behalf of women, if there was the will to do so, as frequently appears to have been the case. Feminist historians have long argued that the rhetoric of criminal justice systems can mask a bias in favour of patriarchy, the sociological process by which men come to dominate positions of power. Nevertheless, this does not necessarily result in negative outcomes for female defendants; indeed, quite the reverse can occur. Indulgent paternalism can be a part of patriarchy. This could manifest itself in the most surprising situations. Thus, in the early decades of the nineteenth century, women who had been convicted of possessing forged bank notes, and were awaiting transportation to Australia, wrote regularly to the Bank of England (their prosecutor) asking for financial relief and other assistance. This was usually in the form of cash payments while they were held in Newgate and an embarkation bounty on their departure. Remarkably, these were frequently granted, and not insignificant sums provided to them by the Bank. By contrast, the relatively small number of men who petitioned in similar terms were nearly always unsuccessful.[72] The Bank's attitude was not an institutional eccentricity; to a large extent, it encapsulated prevailing 'establishment' attitudes towards female offenders within the criminal justice system of the period.

However, it should also be noted that such sympathetic judicial and prosecutorial treatment of females is not without parallel in other periods. It has been identified in the modern era and was even more marked in the Victorian period than in the 1700s.[73] Indeed, it is arguable that, in this respect, the eighteenth century laid the foundations for attitudes that became prevalent during the 1800s. Nevertheless, these had certainly not been universal prior to 1700. In Cheshire, at least, during the previous century, the picture was more mixed. In that county it appears that there was little judicial leniency (comparative to men) shown towards women accused of larceny *apart* (albeit significantly) from the down-valuing of stolen goods, where they were at a marked advantage. Against this, they were more likely to be indicted by a Grand

---

[71] Peter King, *Crime, Justice and Discretion in England 1740-1820*, Oxford, OUP, 2000, at p.355.

[72] Deirdre Palk, "'Fit Objects for Mercy': gender, the Bank of England and currency criminals", *Women's Writing*, 2004, vol. 11, no. 2, pp.237-258, at pp.252-254. William Blackstone, *Commentaries on the Laws of England*, 1769, vol. 4, at p.320.

[73] Lucia Zedner *Women, Crime and Custody in Victorian England*, Oxford, Clarendon Press, 1991, p.26.

Jury and to be convicted at trial.[74] Neither of these phenomena were true of their Metropolitan counterparts of the 1700s.

Why should eighteenth-century justices, judges, jurors and even prosecutors be more sympathetic towards female offenders than to those of their own gender? A number of potential explanations can be considered, several of them are examined in the context of specific crimes in other chapters but can be outlined here. During the eighteenth century, and especially after about 1750, women came to be seen as less 'culpable' when offending than men. This appears to have rested on a number of physical and psychological assumptions about their sex. Thus, it seems that the Bank of England's indulgence was based on a ready acceptance that women were poor, likely to have been led astray by others (usually men), in distress, raising children or otherwise 'deserving' in a way that men were not.[75] As this suggests, females were also increasingly seen as weak, easily led, emotional and essentially passive in their behaviour. This meant, according to *The Times*, that females were more deserving of charity than men; as women were "the weaker body, [they] are more liable to error, and less entitled to severity."[76] William Hogarth's print, 'Cruelty in Perfection' (1751), provides a neat contemporary illustration of such attitudes. In it, Ann Gill, a servant maid, has had her throat and wrists cut by Tom Nero, a career criminal, who has seduced Gill into stealing her kindly mistress's valuables. Unfortunately, at their nocturnal rendezvous, he murders her for the stolen items, rather than eloping with her, as Gill had expected. Nevertheless, the dead woman has brought along her Prayer Book, a letter to Nero explaining her reluctance to rob her employer and a treatise condemning murder, indicating that she is, fundamentally, not a bad person, albeit one who has been corrupted by an evil man.

Offending women were also increasingly likely to be seen as 'troubled' individuals, rather than 'troublesome' deviants, suffering from psychological and emotional disturbances, instead of being possessed by evil. Such attitudes were to be long lasting. Although Edwardian psychiatrists, such as Henry Maudsley, popularised the notion that women were innately more disposed to hysteria and nervous disorders than men, these ideas had been in circulation, in proto-form, well over a century earlier.[77] As one observer noted, towards the end of the eighteenth century, it was widely believed that women suffered from an inherent "unsteadiness of mind."[78] Indeed, this analysis was longstanding even then. In a letter written to his daughter, in 1688, the first Marquis of Halifax had noted that

---

[74]Garthine Walker, *Crime, Gender and Social Order in Early Modern England*, Cambridge, CUP, 2003, p.178.

[75]Palk, "'Fit Objects for Mercy', pp.252-254.

[76] *The Times*, June 27th 1788, p.3.

[77]Ginger Frost, "'She is but a Woman': Kitty Byron and the English Edwardian Criminal Justice System", *Gender & History*, 2004, vol. 16, no. 3, pp.538-560, at p.547

[78]Thomas Gisborne, *An Enquiry into the Duties of the Female Sex*, 2nd edn., London, 1797, p.34.

one aspect of the inequality of the sexes, along with men's superior physical strength, was that: "Your sex wanteth our reason for your conduct."[79]

The origins of a more general belief that women were inherently less criminal than men, being intrinsically more chaste, honest, less likely to cheat or steal, and naturally more sociable, far from being a creation of the nineteenth century, was also rooted in the later 1700s.[80] Such attitudes are most clearly manifest in judicial pronouncements from the bench and in comments made by practising lawyers. Thus, when sentencing Mary Blandy at the Oxford Assizes, for poisoning her father, Baron Legge observed that it would have been hoped that the "natural softness of your sex, might have saved you from an attempt so barbarous and so wicked."[81] Similarly, it appeared particularly shocking and astonishing to many observers that Elizabeth Brownrigg: "...a midwife by profession, and herself a mother of many children [at least 15] should murder, by slow cruelties, the children of other unfortunate women."[82] In 1775, when twin brothers, Robert and Daniel Perreau, were accused of attempting to negotiate a forged bond, such attitudes were also clearly evident. When they claimed that Daniel's mistress, Margaret Rudd, was behind the crime, her supporters, including a barrister, stressed that, as a woman, Rudd was "subject to all the little weaknesses of her sex." It was also argued that it was inherently unlikely that she could have imposed her will on two men and that she was not worldly enough to understand complicated financial matters: "It required more intelligence than she possessed."[83]

The trial of Anne Broadric provides a classic example of how such attitudes could produce beneficial outcomes for women in even the gravest of cases. She was accused of the murder of a wealthy man named Errington, whose live-in lover she had been for several years, but who had jilted her to marry another woman. Although the dead man had made financial provision for her future needs, this did not satisfy Broadric, who sent him a threatening letter declaring that nothing was "more terrible than the rage and vengeance of a disappointed woman." Subsequently, she shot him dead at his home. At her trial, at the Essex Assizes, her lawyer called non-medical witnesses to say that they suspected her to be insane. Their testimony, despite not being given in a professional capacity, went unchallenged by prosecuting counsel, although, during the eighteenth century (and as today), the legal burden of proving insanity was, in theory, on the defendant. The jury swiftly returned a verdict of not guilty by reason of insanity and the presiding judge directed that Broadric be returned home, with a

[79] Elizabeth Foyster, "Male Honour, Social Control and Wife Beating in Late Stuart England" *Transactions of the Royal Historical Society*, 6th Series, vol. 6, 1996, pp.215-224, at p.215.

[80] Zedner, *Women, Crime and Custody in Victorian England*, p.39.

[81] R William (Ed.), *The Trial of Mary Blandy*, Edinburgh and London, William Hodge & Coy, 1914, p.134.

[82] Anon, *God's Revenge Against Murder!*, London, 1810, at p.29

[83] Donna Andrew and Randall McGowen, *The Perreaus & Mrs. Rudd: Forgery and Betrayal in Eighteenth-Century London*, London, University of California Press, 2001, pp.181-4.

special recommendation that she "be taken all possible care of." Her case apparently excited "universal pity", despite being the long premeditated killing of a man in front of his wife.[84] These attitudes were to have numerous unfortunate social ramifications for women, being used, *inter alia*, to deny them access to education and the professions. However, they could, and did, bring about beneficial outcomes for many female defendants.

Of course, not all women could be pigeon-holed in this way. Those female offenders who, with the best will in the world, could not be contained within such gendered stereotypes were likely to be viewed as beyond the pale and capable of the most extreme immorality, as: "When a woman has once broken thro' that modest decency which confines the sex, she is not to be restrained within any boundaries."[85] Thus, it was not possible to keep the former prostitute and kept mistress, Elizabeth Richardson, within the realm of 'respectable' women when, in a case that was not wildly dissimilar to that of Broadric, she stabbed an attorney named William Pimlot in a fit of sexual jealousy. Unlike Broadric, she was swiftly convicted of murder and executed.[86] As a result, a general lenience towards women was qualified by the selective stigmatization of certain females.

Additionally, and very importantly, it seems that claims of need were much more readily accepted if made by women than when advanced by their male counterparts, especially (and with justification) if they had infants to care for. Thus, when Ann Flynn was indicted for stealing a shoulder of mutton from a butcher's shop, she admitted the theft but told the court that she had been driven to it by "the most afflicting distress." Her husband had been ill and unable to earn anything for 12 weeks, and she had two small children to support. In the light of this pitiful story, and mindful that she had already spent five weeks in custody awaiting trial, the jurors "found her guilty, with a faltering accent." The judge, noticing and sharing their compassion, sentenced her to a shilling fine, which the jury paid themselves.[87] Given the difficulties that such women faced, this reaction is, perhaps, understandable.[88]

A number of other factors probably contributed to women's advantageous situation. On a practical basis, in many cases, if females with small children were executed, transported, or imprisoned for long periods on hulks or in jails, family breakdown would ensue and their infants would be forced onto the parish. This would occasion expense for local ratepayers and, if the children were lucky enough to survive to adolescence, might contribute to the large and criminogenic 'blackguard' of Metropolitan street youths. In such circumstances,

---

[84]JL Rayner and GT Crook (Eds.), *The Complete Newgate Calendar*, London, Privately printed for the Navarre Society, vol. iv, 1926, pp.199-202.

[85]George Parker, *A View of Society and Manners in High and Low Life*, London, 1781, p.90.

[86]OBSP, Trial of Elizabeth Richardson, 7th Dec. 1768.

[87]Rayner and Crook, *The Complete Newgate Calendar*, vol. iii, p.177.

[88]For further discussion of this phenomenon see chapter five.

acquittals or less drastic punishments could become highly attractive.[89] Additionally, and very importantly, it is likely that, because men were expected to be aggressive, male crime was perceived as inherently more threatening than that committed by women, and so was more likely to be prosecuted to conviction, even if it had not actually involved violence. Male housebreakers, if cornered or surprised, might kill out of a desperation to escape; women were less likely to do so. Finally, it should be noted that, to a considerable extent, the era's criminal trials were moral theatre. Gestures of deference and submission towards the court, and public penitence for offending behaviour, could have decisive effects on the outcome of a hearing.[90] It is possible, though difficult to prove, that women were better at adopting such postures than were men.

## Arrest and Prosecution

Women in the eighteenth-century Metropolis entered the criminal process in much the same way as men. They were arrested and produced before a sitting justice in Middlesex and Westminster, or an Alderman (an ex officio magistrate) in the City of London. The arrest was often made by the victim himself at the crime scene (and detaining women was usually easier than holding men), though they might be assisted by passing watchmen or a nearby constable. If the woman was detained but not caught red handed, some extempore (and not always fair) questioning might be used by members of the public to confirm initial suspicions. Thus, in 1677, it was recorded that a 16-year-old girl, suspected of attempting to poison her mistress, was "strictly questioned" by bystanders. Initially, she denied the crime, but eventually: "...after much importunity and some suggestions of pardon, she declared that she did do it."[91] Other women would be caught as they fled from a crime scene by members of the public or patrolling parish officers (especially watchmen), arrested later by thief-takers seeking the bounty on their heads, or detained after being incriminated by a criminal associate seeking to turn Crown evidence. Both of the latter two possibilities explain the behaviour of Mary Burton, a notorious shoplifter. Fearing capture, because of the substantial reward on her head, she: "...surrender'd herself in order to be made an evidence against her Confederates." When examined by a magistrate, she admitted to dozens of crimes and incriminated many of her colleagues.[92]

Unusually, it was fairly common for prostitutes who stole from their clients to be detained a few days after the offence was committed. Such women were often geographically constrained in their movements, working the same streets on a regular basis. If a man became aware that he had become their victim it was

---

[89]King, "Gender, crime and justice...," at p.46 and pp.62-64.

[90]King, *Crime, Justice and Discretion*, p.372.

[91]Anon, *Horrid News From St. Martin's, or, Unheard-of Murder and Poison: Being a true relation how a girl not full sixteen years of age, murdered her own mother at one time and a servant-maid at another with Ratsbane,* London: printed for D.M., 1677, pp.1-3.

[92]*Weekly Journal, or The British Gazetteer,* 9th July 1726.

often not too difficult to track them down. Thus, in 1730, Peter Watkins noted that it had taken him "8 or 9 days before he could take" Jane Tyrrel, after she picked his pocket. Doubtless, most men were too embarrassed to do anything in such situations and merely wrote their losses off to experience.[93] If detained at night, women would normally be held in custody at a watch-house or a local prison (such as one of the compters) until the following morning, when they would be produced before a JP. If arrested during the day, they might be taken straight before a magistrate. This individual would conduct a formal examination of the suspect, decide whether to commit for trial and, if so, to what forum (Quarter Sessions or the Old Bailey) and for what crime. He would also make a decision about bail in lesser matters.

Given the considerable discretion that was, in practice, vested in Metropolitan magistrates, a degree of prudence was advisable in women when being examined. Sometimes, an awareness of this was misused by those in authority. Even laudatory obituaries of Thomas de Veil, one of the most influential and significant Metropolitan Justices prior to the advent of the Fielding brothers, made no secret of the fact that he was a philanderer who had grossly abused his position. To facilitate this, he apparently constructed a "private closet for the examination of the fair sex."[94]

However, not all women were so accommodating, or even respectful, towards their magistrates. In 1745, Mary 'Cut and Come-again' was arrested for a low value robbery in which she had slapped a woman and taken her apron. Lactating at the time, when parish officers arrived to detain her, she: "…pulled her breasts out, and spurted the milk in the fellows faces." Once produced in front of the examining Justice she refused to provide her name (hence the use of a pseudonym) and announced that "she would spit upon the Justice's seat, and she did so." The magistrate had her fettered and handcuffed for her journey to Newgate prison, where she was held pending trial. In due course, she was convicted at the Old Bailey and, unusually, given the circumstances, not subsequently reprieved from execution.[95] As Mary's experience also suggests, those in custody pending trial at the Old Bailey would normally be committed to Newgate to await the next sessions, though a variety of other Metropolitan prisons were also used.

## The Trial Process

### The Indictment

Metropolitan females accused of theft in the 1700s were twice as likely as men to avoid trial altogether, either because prosecutors failed to attend to testify at their hearings or because Grand Juries returned indictments marked

---

[93]OBSP, Trial of Jane Tyrrel, 13th May 1730.
[94]*The Gentleman's Magazine*, 1747, vol. 17, p.563.
[95]OBSP, Trial of Mary Cut and Come-again, 24th April 1745.

'ignoramus'.[96] There was an especially well marked reluctance to pursue actions against the more pathetic type of female criminal, such as former prostitutes reduced by illness to picking pockets. Such a woman would often spend a period in Newgate: "…'till she is discharged because the plaintiff will not appear to prosecute her."[97] Some notorious female criminals experienced this phenomenon on several occasions during their careers.

However, although women benefited from the Grand Jury process when accused of crimes, females who attempted to prosecute serious matters in the criminal courts appear to have been at a slight disadvantage, tending to attract a greater degree of scepticism from this body than did men. Thus, the Middlesex Grand Jury was much more likely to dismiss misdemeanour indictments prosecuted by women than those brought by men (females made up less than a third of prosecutors at the Middlesex Sessions). At the Old Bailey, the situation was even more extreme.[98] By contrast, women appear to have had more success, and felt more comfortable, with less elevated, more 'user friendly', forums. For example, early in the eighteenth century, they made up a majority of those who brought actions in the ecclesiastical courts for, *inter alia*, defamation. Additionally, more women than men in the Metropolitan area instigated recognisances (unlike the pattern found in rural locations). These were the simplest, cheapest and, in their consequences, least draconian method of bringing a criminal prosecution, especially for offences against the peace and minor assaults.[99]

*The Plea*
The number of defendants of both sexes who formally admitted their crimes in court was tiny by modern comparison; the guilty plea was not favoured by the judges, lawyers or court officials of the time. Nevertheless, at provincial assizes it seems that women were slightly more likely than men to plead guilty, perhaps because they hoped (with justification) that their gender would attract more lenient treatment. However, in the Metropolitan area, and taking the full range of offences tried at the Old Bailey during the 1700s together, women appear to have been somewhat less likely than men to plead guilty, despite enjoying the same beneficial outcomes in the litigation process (albeit to a much smaller extent than their rural counterparts). Thus, approximately one man in 80 who was indicted at the Old Bailey admitted his guilt without going to trial, while for women it appears to have been about one in 140, though some specific offences, such as murder, attracted a higher rate of female guilty pleas. Of course, these numbers remain, statistically, very small.

---

[96] King, "Gender, crime and justice…", pp.44-74, at p.46 and p.62-64.
[97] *The Gentleman's Magazine*, 1749, vol. 19, p.126.
[98] Robert Shoemaker, *The London Mob*, London, Hambledon & London, 2004, pp.229-230.
[99] Shoemaker, *The London Mob*, pp.229-230.

Women might come under acute pressure from the judiciary not to enter such a plea, especially if the outcome would be capital. When Mary Price, accused of murdering a child in 1718, insisted on admitting her guilt, the presiding judge was astonished, and would have permitted her to withdraw her original plea, pointing out that the case: "…might not be proved upon her, but if she confessed it she must be hanged."[100] It is possible that this pressure was more acute on female, rather than male, defendants, though this would be difficult to establish. Nevertheless, the situation during the 1700s, when execution was less likely to result from such a plea, was still an advance on the previous century, when almost no women had pleaded guilty prior to the extension of benefit of clergy to their sex in 1692.[101] Standing 'mute of malice', that is refusing to enter any plea at all (whether guilty or not guilty), would have had disastrous consequences for the woman involved, just as it did for men, and very rarely occurred.

*Women and the Peine*

A deliberate refusal to plead would (theoretically) result in the imposition of the *peine forte et dure* prior to 1772, when remaining mute of malice was made tantamount to a guilty plea (though the *peine* does not appear to have been applied for 30 years prior to this date). This was amongst the worst brutalities of the era, albeit only very rarely administered in the eighteenth century. It entailed being gradually pressed to death under a board holding progressively increasing weights, unless a plea was forthcoming (which could then be accepted with permission from the court). It could be applied to women as well as to men, being administered "without any distinction of sex or degree."[102] Occasional instances of this occurred throughout the seventeenth century. Thus, in 1676, two women who adamantly refused to enter a plea were both ordered to be pressed, and then returned to Newgate to have the procedure carried out.[103] Even worse, and unlike women facing execution, a woman who faced death by pressing would not be allowed to plead pregnancy to avoid such a disposal, because her conduct manifest a "wilfull contempt of her tryall."[104]

By the early 1700s, however, although still legally available, its use against women seems to have fallen drastically, and there are very few, if any, instances recorded of it actually being applied in the Metropolitan area. In 1721, Mary Andrews initially refused to plead to her felony indictment at the Old Bailey, despite warnings from the court about the consequences of her "obstinancy." However, as was common in such cases at the Bailey during the eighteenth century, the public executioner was then called in to bind her thumbs tightly

---

[100]OBSP, Trial of Mary Price, 9th July 1718.
[101]John Beattie, *Policing and Punishment in London, 1660-1750*, Oxford, OUP, 2001, p.338.
[102]William Blackstone, *Commentaries on the Laws of England*, 1769, vol. 4, at p.320. See also John H. Baker, "Criminal Justice at Newgate 1616-1627", *The Irish Jurist*, 1973, vol. 8, p.316.
[103]OBSP, Trial of two anonymous women, 28th June and 23rd Aug 1676.
[104]Baker, "Criminal Justice at Newgate 1616-1627", vol. 8, p.316.

with whipcord to see if it would force her into entering a plea, without the full peine having to be applied. This proved effective as, after he began to: "…draw her thumbs very hard, as usual on such occasions, she finding her self unable to bear the little pain of the whipcord, was persuaded not to try whether she could suffer the superior torment of the pressing, and so yielded to plead." This also turned out to be in her interests as, at trial, she was acquitted.[105]

Of course, there was much less incentive for married women to refuse to enter a plea, as most of 'their' property was legally vested in their husbands, and so not forfeit to the Crown if they were convicted. Traditionally, this was the main reason for refusing to plead, as it meant that the defendant was not formally convicted of a felony, a prerequisite for confiscation. Furthermore, many unmarried women would have had little to their name worth seizing. However, it is also likely that contemporary notions of 'manliness' encouraged a greater male willingness to undergo such an ordeal, some men accepting it in preference to the social stigma of conviction, even if their estates were very modest.[106]

*Evidence*

When it came to testifying at trial, females were less important than males. In early modern England generally, they appeared much less frequently to give evidence than men, a few exceptions to the general pattern (crimes like witchcraft and infanticide) apart. For example, in felony cases heard at the Hertfordshire Assizes between 1610 and 1619, only one in 12 of those called to give evidence were women.[107] The position at the Old Bailey in the eighteenth century was less extreme, but followed the same general pattern. Thus, of 150 non-defendant witnesses, whose gender can be identified, and who gave evidence at the Sessions that commenced on the 14th September 1752, 34 (about 22 per cent) were women and 116 men. (This is a fairly crude figure, as there were a considerable number of 'squibs' in this Sessions' reports, which do not make clear what the gender was of those who testified at trial). There are some obvious explanations for this phenomenon; for example, only about an eighth of the legal 'victims' of crime at the Old Bailey were women. One reason for this was that victims were also usually prosecutors, theft was the most common offence indicted, and most marital property was deemed to be in the possession of the husband. Thus, if a married woman's clothes were stolen from her home, her husband would often be identified as the loser. (Spinsters and widows would

---

[105] *Applebee's Original Weekly Journal*, 3 June 1721.

[106] See on this generally Andrea McKenzie "This Death Some Strong and Stout Hearted Man Doth Choose": The Practice of Peine Forte et Dure in Seventeenth- and Eighteenth-Century England", *Law and History Review*, 2005, vol.23, no.2, pp.279-314.

[107] James Sharpe, "Women Witchcraft and the Legal Process" in Jenny Kermode and Garthine Walker, *Women, crime and the courts in early modern England*. London, UCL Press, 1994, at p.112.

be prosecutors in their own right). However, and less obviously, only 10 per cent of those who prosecuted offences against the peace at the Bailey were female.[108]

It seems that some women were reluctant to prosecute cases in the Old Bailey courtroom, especially if they were single, when the potential court costs entailed may have been alarming (unlike less formal legal procedures). This also applied to the prosecution of misdemeanours by indictment at the Middlesex Sessions, though, during the early decades of the eighteenth-century, the proportion of female prosecutors increased steadily. This expansion was the continuation of a trend that had been evident from as far back as the Restoration period. As a result, female prosecutors doubled to just over a quarter of the Middlesex total in the 60 years prior to the early 1720s. A number of reasons have been mooted for this change, amongst them being the increased level of female literacy, which may have made women more self-confident in using the indictment process.[109]

The lack of female witnesses is also partly explained by the fact that some common 'male' crimes, such as assaults arising out of tavern or street game brawls, were likely to be committed in circumstances in which there were few women present. Furthermore, the male total is greatly increased because any constables and watchmen called to give evidence would necessarily have been men, as would magistrates (or their clerks) called to testify on disputed confessions and physicians giving medical evidence (though most midwives were female). However, the number of female witnesses is also considerably bolstered by the fact that female defendants (of whom there were a considerable number) often called women, rather than men, as their character witnesses; calling such evidence was an important part of eighteenth-century criminal trials. As a result, the proportion of women who 'spoke to an issue' would probably be considerably smaller than 22 per cent (though equally, the evidence of male parish officers was often not in dispute).

There is limited evidence that juries treated women more sceptically than men when they appeared as witnesses. Contemporary attitudes suggested that females were more likely to be dominated by their emotions and thus, perhaps, less reliable than men. Richard Bernard in his *A Guide to Grand-Jurymen* (1629) was probably verbalising a widespread seventeenth century belief when he suggested that women were "more credulous, and apt to be misled." Such attitudes persisted into the following century. Given the dominance of males, and the absence of females, in Metropolitan courts, the process of testifying may also have been inherently more intimidating for women, perhaps making them less persuasive. Nevertheless, the cases also make it clear that men could be capitally convicted on purely female evidence without too much difficulty. Indeed, at the Middlesex Sessions, in the early 1700s, trial juries were more likely

---

[108]Shoemaker, *The London Mob*, pp.229-230.
[109]Robert Shoemaker, *Prosecution and Punishment: Petty Crime and the Law in London and Rural Middlesex*, c. 1660-1725, Cambridge, CUP, 1991, pp.211-212.

to find defendants prosecuted by women to be guilty than they were those indicted by men.[110] For jurors, it seems that the social background and 'respectability' of the witness, rather than their gender, was often the most significant factor when it came to assessing the weight of their testimony.

## Verdicts

Generally speaking, women secured higher outright acquittal rates than men and were more likely than males to be convicted of a lesser offence than that initially charged. There was nothing unique to the Metropolis in this; indeed, this trend was less pronounced there than in the provinces or some earlier periods. At the Hertfordshire assizes, in the late sixteenth and early seventeenth centuries, only 30 per cent of the women arraigned for felony were convicted, compared to 52 per cent of men.[111] As will be seen when property offences are considered in detail (in chapter five) and homicides discussed (in chapter three), the beneficial outcomes enjoyed by Metropolitan females during the 1700s were more modest, though still tangible. More specifically, an analysis of the c.750 people accused of coining offences during the eighteenth century indicates that the c.270 women accused of the crime fared somewhat better at trial than their c.480 male counterparts. Over 60 per cent (302) of the men were convicted, while fewer than half of the women (119) were found guilty. One explanation for this phenomenon is probably to be found in the number of wives prosecuted with their husbands, but who were seen as sufficiently peripheral to what was occurring to secure an acquittal. However, a more generally sympathetic attitude towards women also appears significant.

Additionally, women were more likely to benefit from jury nullification in other forms. During the eighteenth century, trial juries frequently convicted for less serious offences than those originally charged on the indictment. In many cases, this was not the result of real doubt about the commission of the graver matter, but an attempt to mitigate the consequences for the defendant of being found guilty. This was termed 'pious perjury' (on the part of the jury). In many cases, it seems to have been almost institutionalised, and either tacitly accepted or even actively encouraged by the judiciary, with verdicts to lesser offences being routinely returned in certain well-established situations. Thus, juries might methodically downgrade small sums of a few shillings that, nevertheless, were above the 12d. (non-capital petty theft) threshold to an almost customary amount of 10d. This could produce bizarre results; for example, thefts in which cash had been taken being reduced in value to an amount that was well below the face value of the coins and notes stolen. It also seems that jurors, some of whom had extensive experience of sitting at sessions, were well aware as to where other clergyable amounts ended. Thus, in the right circumstances, trials

---

[110]Shoemaker, *The London Mob*, p.211
[111]John Bellamy, *The Criminal Trial in Later Medieval England: Felony Before the Courts From Edward I to the Sixteenth Century*, Toronto, University of Toronto Press, 1998, p.124.

for house-breaking, might be "found by the jury to be thirty-nine shillings worth", i.e. below the non-clergyable 40s 'cut-off' for this crime, even where valuables worth well over a hundred pounds had been taken.[112] A similar approach might be taken to the five shilling limit for capital forms of pick-pocketing.

Although such 'pious perjury' was sometimes almost ritualised, in other situations, its presence would depend on the individual characteristics of the defendant or the case for which they were being tried; overt repentance and co-operation with the authorities could be vital. Thus, Sarah Trevalion was convicted of theft to the value of 10d., despite being indicted for stealing sheets and a riding hood worth a total of 15s. Although the theft appears to have involved a breach of trust, the victim having taken Trevalion into her house out of pity for her impoverished state, the defendant swiftly confessed to the offence when examined and identified where she had pawned the proceeds of her crime.[113] This seems to have been enough to attract mercy.

Overall, women were significantly more likely than men to benefit from pious perjury. In the late seventeenth century, it was far more common for Metropolitan juries to reduce a charge for female defendants than for men, even where the woman faced no legal disadvantage when compared to a male accused. Thus, it might be explicable that charges of larceny (where women were at a disadvantage vis a vis claiming clergy until 1692) were reduced in 15 per cent of male cases but fully 64 per cent of female ones. However, in burglary cases, where clergy could not be claimed by either sex, the rate was only 33 per cent for men but still 64 per cent for women.[114] This continued to be the case during the following century.

*Feme Covert*

In the criminal law, what has been termed the 'relentless logic of patriarchy' sometimes worked to women's advantage. There were some legal doctrines that expressly favoured their trial prospects, coverture being foremost amongst them. Once married, an eighteenth-century woman had the status of *feme covert*, unlike spinsters and widows (who were *feme sole*). Her legal existence largely became merged with that of her husband. Although she lost most of her rights to personal property, her husband frequently became liable for her torts and debts.[115] Despite being primarily a civil law concept affecting property rights and responsibilities, the doctrine, and women's legal passivity, had significant consequences for criminal matters as well. Thus, the law was reluctant to find

---

[112]John Beattie, *Crime and the Courts in England 1660-1800*, Oxford, OUP, 1986, p.424.

[113]OBSP, Trial of Sarah Travalion, 6th Sept., 1710.

[114]Val Edwards, "German Princesses and Common Prostitutes: Women and Crime in Restoration London", *Holdsworth Law Review*, 1981, vol.6, pp.2-16, pp.9-13.

[115]Anon, *Baron and Feme: A treatise of Law and Equity Concerning Husbands and Wives*, 3rd edn., London, R. Nott, 1738, p.29. There was an extensive list of other legal consequences in civil matters.

that a married woman who stole with, and in the presence of, her husband - unless it was in an overtly active role - was implicated in the crime, even as an accessory. Instead, it was assumed that "she did it by the coercion of her husband." As a result, the: "… wife is no felon, but it shall be wholly judged the husband's fact."[116]

William Blackstone traced this doctrine back to the Anglo-Saxons. It was unique to wives; "constraint of a superior" did not extend to children, servants or any of a man's other dependants who committed crimes at his behest.[117] Naturally, the converse did not apply. Indeed, if a man became aware that his wife was involved in theft or receiving stolen goods he could only absolve himself from personal complicity by drastic steps; her "husband so soone as he perceive it [must] waive and forsake their company." By contrast, assuming she did not get excessively involved in her spouse's crimes, his wife, even though: "…not ignorant of it may keepe his Company still notwithstanding, and not be deemed accessory."[118] The doctrine did not apply if a woman stole at her husband's command, but in his absence: "…much less is she excused if she commit a theft of her own voluntary act."[119] Presumably, the former factor was what prompted the Newgate Ordinary to stress that Margaret Green, who was hanged for burglary in 1705, although pressured into offending by her male partner: "…always did [so] by herself, as she did (that is, she was alone) when she attempted to rob [steal from] Mr. May."[120] Additionally, it did not extend to a few serious instrumental felonies, such as robbery. Unsurprisingly, it did not apply to homicide, though women who concealed or assisted their husbands *after* the latter had committed murder escaped being accessories to their spouse's crime.[121] A variety of other, fairly arcane, offences were also specifically exempt from the doctrine. For example, a woman could be indicted for the misdemeanour of managing a brothel with her husband, and in his presence. It seems that the justification for this was that the offence involved the government of a domestic house, in which it was assumed the "wife has a principal share."

An important rationale for the doctrine was manifest in one of the justifications advanced for denying it to women accused of treason, even where they had worked at their spouse's behest. Along with the crime's inherent gravity, this was because a man who was a traitor had: "…no right to that obedience from a wife, which he himself as a subject has forgotten to pay."[122] More practically, as late as 1785, the Recorder of London noted that women

---

[116]Anon, *The Laws Resolutions of Womens Rights,* London, John More, 1632, p.6 and p.206.

[117]Blackstone, *Commentaries on the Laws of England,* Book iv, p.28.

[118]Anon, *The Laws Resolutions of Womens Rights,* p.6 and p.206.

[119]Anon, *The Laws Respecting Women,* London, Printed for J. Johnson, 1777, pp.70-71.

[120]Rev. Paul Lorrain, *The Ordinary of Newgate his Account of the Behaviour, Confessions, and Dying words…4th May 1705,* p.2.

[121]Anon, *The Laws Respecting Women,* pp.70-71.

[122]Blackstone, *Commentaries on the Laws of England,* Book iv, p.29.

were often legally exempt from punishment: "…because they were supposed to be acting under the influence of their husbands, whose orders the law did not suppose them daring enough to resist."[123]

Despite Blackstone's endorsement, the criminal implications of *feme covert* were increasingly questioned during the 1700s, and its application gradually restricted.[124] This could be done without rejecting the doctrine altogether because it created a presumption that a wife was being compelled to offend by her husband, not a rule of law, so that "like other presumptions it may be repelled."[125] The courts could reduce its scope simply by being more willing to conclude that it had been successfully rebutted in any instant case. Although coverture was being claimed at the Old Bailey as late as 1816, when, for some reason, two women, Jane Drummond and Mary Lynch, successfully advanced the defence at separate trials, its use was fairly rare after 1700. There were only five successful cases recorded in the Old Bailey Sessions Papers during the entire eighteenth century. Thus, in 1702 Martha Rogers, tried on a writ of restitution, was acquitted of receiving stolen goods because: "It appeared that she was a Feme Covert, thereupon the matter was quasht."[126] In like manner, in 1792, Ann Cropper was acquitted of burglary, despite being found with stolen goods on her person, although her husband was convicted and sentenced to death. Similarly, when Richard Field was convicted of murder and theft, his wife, although charged with receiving part of the stolen cash, was acquitted "by reason of her coverture."[127]

Nevertheless, the Sessions Papers do not mention the doctrine when recording that Margaret Sloper was acquitted after being tried with her husband in 1785, although other reports make it clear that *feme covert* was the reason. Presumably, a significant number of other female acquittals at the Old Bailey during the century were for similar reasons, though not expressly recorded as such in the Sessions Papers. Additionally, on a practical basis, the doctrine often seems to have influenced the initial decision to prosecute and indict, so that women received a considerable measure of protection if involved in criminal ventures with their husbands.

On many occasions, the protection of *feme covert* appears to have extended to 'common law' wives and co-habitants, even if not legally married. As the Recorder of London expressly recognised in 1785, the criminal courts did not usually "act so rigorously" as to require the production of a marriage certificate and would normally assume marital status from a relationship in which a couple

---

[123]*The Times,* January 15th 1785, p.3.
[124]Even the civil ramifications came under growing scrutiny as the century advanced. In a controversial decision, aimed at reflecting 'modern' developments, Lord Mansfield concluded in *Corbett v. Poelnitz* (1785) that a *feme covert* who lived apart from her husband, with her own maintenance, could be personally sued on a contract made by her.
[125]Peregrine Bingham, *The Law of Infancy and Coverture,* London, 1816, Butterworth & Son, p.228
[126]OBSP, Trial of Martha Rogers, 14th Jan. 1702.
[127]OBSP, Trial of Richard and Mary Field, 9th Dec 1714.

lived openly as 'man and wife' (as had the Slopers), though, by then, some legal observers could deplore such laxity and apparent support for "prostitution" as bad law.[128] In any event, prior to Hardwicke's Marriage Act of 1753, which was aimed at controlling clandestine and irregular marriages, challenging marital status was often very difficult.

Even late in the period, and in situations where coverture might not apply in theory, the attitudes reflected in the doctrine could produce benign outcomes for female defendants. Thus, in 1805, Susan Cowdell from Shoredith was acquitted at the Middlesex Quarter Sessions of viciously assaulting her own sister. Her husband, having had an angry domestic argument with the victim, struck her and then ordered his wife to beat her sister, on pain of being thrown out of the matrimonial home. Although the two women had been chatting amicably up to this point, Susan, being a "dutiful wife", immediately obeyed and gave her sibling a severe thrashing, which occasioned extensive bruising. At trial, the jury convicted the husband, but "acquitted the wife, as acting under his influence."[129] The doctrine was also particularly important because 'habitual' female criminals tended to have spouses or partners who were themselves felons. Thus, to take an extreme example, Sarah Oakly, a Newgate escapee, was simultaneously the widow of an executed felon hanging in chains and the wife of another being held in the Surrey county jail.[130] As a result, the number of 'married' women who assisted their partners in criminal ventures is probably significantly greater than the records suggest.

## Women and Benefit of Clergy

Throughout the eighteenth century women could claim 'benefit of clergy' on equal terms to men. This ancient privilege was a relic of the Church-State struggles of the medieval era. It had allowed clerics who committed secular offences to escape temporal punishment (including execution) in favour of being disciplined by the (very lenient) ecclesiastical courts. However, during the early modern period, it was extended by a series of legal fictions to include most men, and, by two seventeenth century Acts, women (technically, they claimed 'benefit of statute', the notion of female clerics being unthinkable), though the number of offences for which it could be claimed was simultaneously greatly reduced. Women were allowed clergy for minor thefts by an Act of 1623. In 1692, another statute (3 and 4 Will. and M. c. 9), granted them clergy on the same basis as men. During the seventeenth century, clergy would be allowed to all men who were literate, the convict proving this by reading a verse of the Bible in court. This might have favoured males (though by the early 1690s, the magistrate

---

[128]Peter King "Female offenders, work and life-cycle change in late-eighteenth-century London", *Continuity and Change*, 1996, vol. 11, pp. 61-90, at p.68. See also letters from an "English Crown Lawyer" *The Times*, January 27th 1785, p.2 and February 9th 1785 p.4.

[129]*The Times* Sept. 18, 1805, at p.3

[130]*Mist's Weekly Journal*, 10th Dec. 1726.

Edmund Bohun could note that literacy had increased so much that it extended to many women).[131] However, under the two statutes that granted clergy to women, females were, in any event, not required to prove literacy, and so were, theoretically, in a favoured position when compared to their male counterparts.[132] Nevertheless, by 1700, any pretence to it being a real test, rather than a legal fiction, had been largely abandoned, as male convicts would usually be quietly told what to say by the Ordinary (court and prison chaplain).[133] The almost pointless 'test' was finally abolished in 1706, when everyone became entitled to its benefit (where it still existed), whether literate or not, male or female. Thus, men and women were entirely equal in respect of clergy throughout most of the century.

Laymen, and all women, who were clergied would be branded until 1779 (when the procedure was replaced with a whipping), to prevent them receiving it on a second occasion, and would then be released, rather than being executed for what would otherwise be a capital felony. Branding was normally on the braun of the thumb, the years from 1699 to 1706 apart, when it was on the cheek (possibly to make it more visible and thus harder to claim more than once). Thus, after the Sessions held at the Old Bailey in May 1701 it was noted that: "A great many were burnt in the cheek, and one woman in the hand, her crime she was tried for having been committed, before the law for burning in the cheek was in force."[134]

However, by the 1700s, branding was usually a perfunctory and often ineffectual process. A German visitor to London in 1710 was amused to note that women who were clergied were prone to scream in court when the iron was picked up to mark a T on their thumbs, even though, in the case of minor thefts, this was usually done with a purely symbolic 'cold' iron, rather than one that had been rendered red-hot.[135] As a result, many women, just like men, appear to have received clergy more than once. For example, both of the two women, Jane Bowman and Elizabeth Smith, executed at Tyburn on the 21st July 1703, admitted to the Newgate Ordinary that they had been 'branded' on numerous previous occasions.[136] Similarly, it was noted that shoplifters who were convicted of a clergyable felony (i.e. not under the 1699 Shoplifting Act), having previously been burnt in the hand for a like offence, could be found guilty a "second, third, or fourth time, [and] escape with the same punishment, by reason of the difficulty in proving the record." The women concerned would use multiple

[131]Edmund Bohun, *The Justice of Peace: His Calling and Qualifications,* London, 1693, p.23.
[132]Blackstone, *Commentaries on the Laws of England,* vol. IV, pp.362-363.
[133]Henri Misson, *Memoirs and Observations in his Travels over England,* J. Ozell (Trans.), London, 1719, pp.17-18.
[134]*London Post,* 2nd–5th May, 1701.
[135]W. H. Quarrell and Margaret More (Trans. and Eds.), *London in 1710 From the Travels of Zacharias Conrad Von Uffenbach,* London, Faber & Faber Ltd. 1934, p.124.
[136]Lorrain, *The Ordinary of Newgate …21th of July 1703,* p.2.

aliases to make identification harder, and sometimes survived as many as seven such convictions.[137]

## Pleading the Belly

A female convicted of felony and sentenced to death could 'postpone' her execution if found to be pregnant. Like benefit of clergy, this practice was rooted in the medieval era. Its rationale was founded on the need to protect an innocent (if unborn) life, though this reasoning was somewhat attenuated because, in theory, the privilege could not be used more than once for the same offence.[138] Nevertheless, despite these limitations, the career criminal John Hall felt that women who were tried at the Old Bailey in the early 1700s had a "great advantage over the men, by pleading their bellies."[139] He may have been thinking of women like Sarah Faircloth, who, in 1708, was convicted of shoplifting gold lace worth 44s. and sentenced to death but successfully claimed pregnancy and had her sentence respited.[140]

Once a female convict made such a claim the sheriff would have to return a jury of "matrons or discreet women" to try the issue.[141] This was the only time, other than when testifying as witnesses, that women were given significant importance in the criminal litigation process. The judge would direct the matrons to determine whether the convict was "quick with child." Carrying a dead or newly conceived child was not sufficient.[142] Quickening was normally thought to occur at some point after the third month of pregnancy, the operation of the female ovum not being fully understood until the start of the nineteenth century. Courts used the all-female jury for reasons of delicacy and because they viewed the women concerned as experts in identifying the physical signs of pregnancy.[143] The matrons were usually midwives or, at the least, married or widowed women with extensive personal experience of pregnancy. Not infrequently, they might include the wives of court personnel, such as the jailer. Unlike the trial jury, the matrons received their evidence in private, normally conducting an intimate physical inspection of the convicted woman after being led by the court bailiff to a closed room. A range of tests were employed, though most were not conclusive of the issue. Amongst the most important was squeezing the convict's breasts for signs of lactation.[144] The

---

[137] Anon, *The Great Grievance of Traders and Shopkeepers, by the Notorious Practise of Stealing their Goods out of their Shops and warehouses by persons commonly called shop-lifters* ND but c.1720, London, at p.1
[138] Anon, *The Laws Resolutions of Womens Rights*, 1632, p.207.
[139] John Hall, *Memoirs of the Right Villainous John Hall*, London, 1708, p.33.
[140] OBSP, Trial of Mary Ingram and Sarah Faircloth, 8 Dec 1708.
[141] Blackstone, *Commentaries on the Laws of England*, vol. 4, p.388.
[142] Blackstone, *Commentaries on the Laws of England*, vol. 4, p.388.
[143] Judy M. Cornett, "Hoodwink'd by custom: The exclusion of women from juries in Eighteenth-Century English Law and Literature", *William and Mary Journal of Women and the Law*, 1997, vol. 4, pp.18-28.
[144] Laura Gowing, "Secret Birth and Infanticide in Seventeenth-Century England", *Past and Present*, vol.156, 1997, at pp.157-187.

matrons would act publicly only when they were sworn (according to a special oath) and when announcing their verdict. Although the jury of matrons could be the same size as a trial jury (twelve people), it was usually much smaller, often containing as few as three women.

In theory, if the jury gave an affirmative answer, execution would be delayed until after the baby's delivery, or until it became apparent that the woman was not pregnant. Pregnancy did not put off the initial trial or the formal passing of sentence after conviction, merely the hanging that followed them.[145] Thus, in December 1703, Moll Hawkins, a thief who had been sentenced to death in March that year, was executed, having been reprieved for nine months after being found (mistakenly) to be quick with child.[146] Similarly, in 1708, although Deborah Churchill was condemned to death for murder on the 26th of February, she was temporarily reprieved for pregnancy; however, when it transpired that she was not with child, her sentence was reinstated and she was executed at Tyburn on the 17th of December.

Nevertheless, after a female felon had been temporarily reprieved for pregnancy a warrant for her execution had to be issued by the Sheriff before she could be hanged. In practice, such an execution would often not be authorised, especially for less serious capital offences, though there were periods, such as the reign of Queen Anne, when a more robust approach was followed, particularly in London. However, in many cases, after the child was born or (more commonly) the woman proved not to be pregnant, she would spend a few months in jail and then be permanently reprieved and released, though, after 1718, this might be on condition of transportation to America. As a result, some women escaped death several times via this mechanism. For example, in December 1738, when Constantia James finally failed in her attempt to claim pregnancy after conviction at the Old Bailey for theft, it was claimed that she had previously "got off 9 times by pleading her belly." (On this occasion, however, she was executed at Tyburn).[147] Indeed, such a reprieve was sufficiently predictable that in 1692, when Susan Lucas was respited from execution (for clipping coins) by dint of her pregnancy, the Newgate Ordinary: "...charged her not to grow secure upon this, as if her sentence would be forgotten." His warning prompted Lucas to promise to attend chapel regularly and repent of her former life. Presumably, the chaplain might have influence on the eventual decision to grant a permanent reprieve.[148] Quite often, this decision would be made by the King's cabinet when it was considering other post-sessions reprieves. Thus, after two women successfully pleaded their bellies at the December 1704 sessions, the council decided that one, the robber Patience

---

[145]Anon, *The Laws Resolutions of Womens Rights: or, the Lawes Provision for Women*, London, John More, 1632, p.207.

[146]Rayner and Crook, *The Complete Newgate Calendar*, vol. II, p.172.

[147]*The Gentleman's Magazine*, 1738, vol. 8, p.659.

[148]The Rev. Samuel Smith, *The Ordinary of Newgate his Account of the Behaviour Confessions, and Dying Speeches of the Condemned Criminals that were Executed at Tyburn on 2nd. March 1692*, pp.1-2.

Cooper, was to be executed after giving birth, while the case of the other, a shoplifter, was to be reviewed again at a later date.[149]

Given its obvious benefits, it is unsurprising that many women who were capitally convicted should have had recourse to pleading their bellies. Of course, in the largely unregulated, and often (effectively) unsegregated, prisons of the eighteenth century it was not too difficult for women of child-bearing age to become pregnant, and anecdotal evidence suggests that some female prisoners actively sought impregnation while in custody. Many, however, would make such a claim as a matter of course, even if well aware that it was unfounded. As Henri Misson observed, females in early eighteenth-century London who were condemned to death "never fail to plead that they are with child."[150] It is apparent that most who claimed the privilege were not pregnant.

In practice, the privilege mitigated some of the harshness of the criminal law, and particularly the death for felony rule. Until 1692, it had also given many women the same leeway that was available to men via benefit of clergy. As a result, the willingness of matrons and the courts to grant it during the seventeenth century had often depended on forum. At quarter sessions, which, even in the early 1600s, were usually very reluctant to inflict a death sentence, it seems that the matrons were often tacitly encouraged to return a positive finding when a woman was capitally convicted. In forums where a death sentence was more willingly passed and expected, such as the Crown side of Assizes and the Old Bailey, the matrons were usually stricter and more likely to produce a negative verdict. Nevertheless, the eminent judge Mathew Hale felt that even in the higher criminal courts during the latter 1600s any doubt would normally be decided in favour of the examined woman, as the: "…compassion of their sex is gentle to them in their verdict, if there be any colour to support a sparing verdict." More cynically, early in the following century, John Hall thought that some women convicted at the Old Bailey were undeservingly being "brought in quick with child" because the matrons at that court had been bribed.[151]

However, in reality, and probably, in part, because women had the same right to clergy as men throughout the 1700s, the matrons employed at the Old Bailey during the eighteenth century do not seem to have been at all reluctant to find that a woman was not pregnant, and normally appear to have been highly discriminating about such claims. (By this time the quarter sessions for Westminster, Middlesex and the City almost never passed death sentences, making the doctrine largely irrelevant in those courts). This became even more marked after 1718, when capitally convicted women could be reprieved on condition of transportation, further reducing any need to use the fiction of pregnancy to circumvent draconian laws, and encouraging the court and matrons to be even stricter in their application of the test. As a result, there was

[149]Beattie, *Policing and Punishment*, p.354.
[150]Misson, *Memoirs and Observations in his Travels*, p.329.
[151]Hall, *Memoirs of the Right Villainous John Hall*, p.33.

a steady reduction during the century in the number of women who successfully pleaded their bellies.

Although, as late as 1830, Rachael Oddy, accused of stealing a large amount of cash from a dwelling house, had her sentence of death respited for pregnancy (by then she would almost certainly have been reprieved had it not been), the Sessions Papers record that only 12 women were reprieved for pregnancy in the second half of the eighteenth century, and eight of these cases occurred in the 1750s. By contrast, in the first half of the century there were at least 94 successful claims, 75 of them between 1700 and 1724 (despite many Sessions Papers prior to 1714 being lost). Even this was a decline on the previous century, when there had been at least 69 cases in the final decade of the 1600s alone. Most Old Bailey claimants during the eighteenth century were unsuccessful, even in the early 1700s. Typically, at the Sessions held in January 1719, all six women who received sentence of death pleaded their bellies, but only one of them, Mary Jones, gained a positive result from the Matrons.[152] Indeed, some women who received negative findings during the century may have been pregnant, or at least truly believed themselves to be so. In 1726, it was noted that the shoplifters Jane Holmes and Katherine Fitzpatrick, having unsuccessfully pleaded their bellies: "…seemed exceedingly uneasy that their children should die violent deaths within them."[153] It should be noted that this phenomenon was not special to the London area; pleading the belly was a declining practice in the second half of the century in the provinces as well.[154]

## Reprieves

Even if not clergied or pregnant, capitally convicted women (like men) could be reprieved and so avoid execution. Women who were sentenced to death at the Old Bailey were usually executed several weeks after their sentence had been passed (unless convicted of murder in the years after 1752). In the meantime, the Recorder of London's report on the Sessions' capital convictions, prepared after the trials had been heard, would be submitted to the King, his Secretary of State and the Privy Council. It would recommend whether the convicts under sentence of death should be reprieved or "left for execution." Although the final decision was for the Crown, the judge's advice was normally followed. In making his recommendation, he would be influenced by the nature of the offence and the age, previous history, degree of involvement, motivation and (it seems) gender of the convict.

The delay between conviction and execution also gave individual women with friends and contacts, especially influential ones, the opportunity to petition

---

[152] OBSP, Punishment Summary, 15th January 1719.
[153] Arthur Hayward (Ed.), *Lives of the Most Remarkable Criminals: Who have been Condemned and Executed for Murder, the Highway, Housebreaking, Street Robberies, Coining or other offences. Collected from Original Papers and Authentic Memoirs, published in 1735*, London, Routledge and Sons, 1927, at p.379.
[154] King, *Crime, Justice and Discretion in England 1740-1820*, p.28.

for a reprieve, even if one had not been suggested by the Recorder. Thus, a very young female murderer, who had also tried to kill her employer, unavailingly spent her time while awaiting execution: "… begging of those that come to visit her, that they would mediate for her to her lady, to use her interest to get her a pardon."[155] Most reprieves were granted for offences against property, though there were occasional instances of women being pardoned for more serious crimes.

Generally, women did well out of the reprieve system, at least when compared to men, although, after 1718, it was often on condition of transportation for 14 or more years. Even in the late seventeenth century, 68 per cent of London women under capital sentence had received a reprieve, compared to just 37 per cent of men.[156] It seems that over the course of the following century, over three quarters of women sentenced to death had their sentences commuted, the proportion increasing gradually over time. Thus, in the years from 1690 to 1714, only 21.3 per cent of women who were capitally convicted for property offences in the City of London were definitely hanged, most of the rest being pardoned (the figure for executions may have been slightly higher due to gaps in the record); by contrast, the execution figure was at least 46.6 per cent for men.[157] By the late eighteenth and early nineteenth centuries, when capital sentences were being passed more sparingly (and reprieves granted more willingly) only eight per cent of Metropolitan female property offenders were even being sentenced to death, compared to 13 per cent of men. More significantly, in *practice*, hardly any women (one individual or 0.15 per cent) were actually executed, rather than being reprieved, for such crimes during this period, whereas 89 men (2.85 per cent) were hanged.

It has long been apparent that the proliferation of theoretically capital offences that constituted the eighteenth-century 'Bloody Code' was more 'bark than bite,' such crimes only rarely resulting in execution. This was especially true for women. Indeed, of the confirmed female executions during this period, over half were for various forms of homicide, whether murder, infanticide or petty treason.[158] The remaining women were hanged for a variety of offences including coining, forgery, housebreaking, burglary, shoplifting and pick-pocketing (though the last two crimes only rarely resulted in death, especially after the mid-century). This bias in favour of women was not unique to London, and was often very much more marked in the provinces. In Essex, between 1740 and 1804, 271 men went to the gallows for property offences. Only one woman experienced a similar fate, and this case had involved a particularly heinous breach of trust at a time when there was acute local concern about

---

[155] Anon, *Horrid News From St. Martin's*, pp.1-3.
[156] Edwards, "German Princesses and Common Prostitutes", vol.6, pp.2-16, pp.9-13.
[157] Beattie, *Policing and Punishment*, p.357. Some cases cannot be determined.
[158] King, "Gender, crime and justice…", pp.44-74, at p.46 and pp.62-64.

burglary.[159] In the North East, too, they were much less likely than men to be hanged if convicted (though more likely to be found guilty, unlike the Metropolitan position).[160]

## Execution

Predictably, given its population and crime problems, London and Middlesex witnessed the highest incidence of female executions in England and Wales. It seems that almost 200 women were executed in the Metropolitan area during the eighteenth century. This is from a total of 1,644 people put to death there between 1701 and 1800.[161] This makes female executions more than 12 per cent of the whole, far below the proportion of female convicts and a cumulative reflection of the effects of pleading the belly and reprieve.

An examination of the 92 women executed at Tyburn between 1703 and 1772 reveals that 32 of them (about 35 per cent) were born outside the capital. Among them were 17 women (19 per cent) from Ireland.[162] Thus, non-native Londoners were certainly not over-represented amongst women who were executed, though it seems that those from across the Irish Sea were. It may be that the latter found it especially difficult to find reputable people to intervene on their behalf and were more strongly associated with crime and social problems in the capital, at least in the minds of the authorities. As with males, youth was not a bar to execution (though it might encourage clemency), and several teenage girls were hanged for property offences during the century. Among them was Mary Pyner, a maid who was hanged in 1766 for stealing almost 20 guineas from her master, despite being only 15 or 16 years old. However, by then, such a disposal was relatively rare for young females and usually the result of aggravating features in the crime; Pyner appears to have started a dangerous fire in the stable of her employer to create a diversion.[163] After the Gordon Riots of 1780, women made up six of the 25 people hanged for offences committed during the disturbances.

Executions were normally carried out at the ancient fixed gallows (the 'Triple Tree') at Tyburn, until 1783, when the place of execution was moved to a space immediately in front of Newgate prison. Additionally, a few women (like men) were hanged close to the scene of their crimes, on ad hoc gallows, for exemplary effect. The process of awaiting execution was, inevitably, traumatic. In 1741, when Mary Diver, held in Newgate pending her trip to Tyburn, said goodbye to her small child it even "drew tears into the eyes of the turnkey."[164]

---

[159]King, *Crime, Justice and Discretion in England 1740-1820*, p.282
[160]Gwenda Morgan and Peter Rushton, *Rogues, Thieves and the Rule of Law: The Problem of Law Enforcement in Northeast England*, London, University College London Press, 1998, p.118.
[161]V.A.C. Gatrell, *The Hanging Tree: Execution and the English People 1770-1868*, Oxford, OUP, 1996, p.616.
[162]Peter Linebaugh, *The London Hanged*, Harmondsworth, Penguin, 1991, pp.142-143.
[163]OBSP, Trial of Mary Pyner, 11th December 1765.
[164] *The Gentleman's Magazine*, vol. xi, 1741, at p.162.

The Newgate Ordinary - the prison chaplain - and visiting outside clerics (especially those attending non-conformists) would minister to them both in the prison and on their way to the gallows.

At the scaffold, some women, like some men, would die very 'penitent', while others would maintain their innocence to the end. However, a few would be openly defiant, aided on occasion by a liberal consumption of alcohol, though the pressure to put up a show of bravado seems to have been less acute than it was amongst men. Nevertheless, in 1699, it was recorded that a woman awaiting execution at Tyburn: "...behaved her self very impudently, and seemed no way sensible of her condition."[165] Similarly, in 1763, Hannah Dagoe, a convicted thief, who had appeared to James Boswell to be a "big unconcerned being" when he visited the condemned prisoners in Newgate, resolutely ignored the ministrations of the Roman Catholic priest who accompanied her to the gallows (she was an Irishwoman). Once there, she struggled to get her arms free and then attacked the public executioner, Thomas Turlis, punching him in the chest. Dagoe also threw her hat and cloak into the crowd so as to deny Turlis his customary right to the possessions of those executed. Eventually, however, she was overpowered and a rope placed around her neck. Undaunted, and before the execution carts could move off so that the convicts were 'launched into eternity', Dagoe threw herself from the cart so forcefully that she broke her neck and died instantly.[166]

Dagoe's sang froid saved her from the slow throttling that often accompanied a hanging using the thick hemp ropes of the era at gallows without a 'drop' (as was normal until the end of the century). It also meant that it was almost impossible for a hanged woman to die with 'dignity', most struggling for several minutes and often spontaneously emptying their bladder and bowels in the process. The potential for indecency that this created occasioned concern amongst both female convicts and a wider society that was increasingly squeamish about the public exposure of women's bodies. Thus, as she was led up the ladder at the Oxford gallows, Mary Blandy was moved to implore her executioners: "Gentlemen, do not hang me high for the sake of decency." Unfortunately for her, after she had been cut down, she was slung over one of the sheriff's men's shoulders and carried through the crowd: "...in the most beastly manner, with her legs exposed very indecently."[167]

*Female Execution for Treason/Petty Treason*
Historically, women who were guilty of high treason would normally be burnt 'alive' rather than being hung, drawn and quartered, unlike men convicted of the same crime. This was for reasons of decency, as the: "...natural modesty of the

---

[165] *The Flying Post*, 24-26 January 1699.
[166]Rayner and Crook, *The Complete Newgate Calendar*, vol. 4, pp16-17.
[167]William (Ed.), *The Trial of Mary Blandy*, p.189.

sex forbids the exposing and publicly mangling their bodies."[168] Exceptional cases, such as that of Alice Lisle in 1685 apart (and her sentence was eventually commuted to beheading), the punishment would have been of little more than academic interest but for the fact that high treason encompassed coining (or otherwise counterfeiting money), as well as plotting against the Crown. Coining was, traditionally, a crime with a strong female involvement and numerous women were burnt for the offence prior to 1790. Even during the following century, women continued to be heavily associated with an offence that required skill but little strength, and which was best conducted in the secrecy of private homes.[169] As a result, in May 1699, a newspaper noted that a woman who had been convicted of coining with two male colleagues, and who had witnessed their hanging at Tyburn only moments earlier, was fastened to a post, after which: "... she was immediately choak'd [throttled], and faggets and brushes, being placed around her, she was burnt to ashes."[170] Similarly, almost a century later, in 1786, Phoebe Harris was convicted of coining fake shillings in Drury Lane, sentenced to burn, and executed accordingly.[171] Margaret Sullivan suffered the same fate when found guilty of an identical offence two years later. She had been colouring circles of base metal silver so that they resembled sixpences and shillings.[172] Because coining was socially injurious, it was acutely unpopular with ordinary people. As a result, Barbara Spencer, a 24 year old woman from St. Giles, Cripplegate, had to face her death by burning against the: "... clamour of the mob, who also threw stones and dirt, which beat her down and wounded her."[173]

However, this special punishment regime evinced a progressively greater degree of distaste amongst educated observers as the century progressed, in part because of an increased sensitivity towards the public exposure of female bodies and what has been termed a growing reverence for domesticated womanhood.[174] Thus, after Phoebe Harris's execution, the *Universal Daily Register* declared that her death was "shamefully indelicate and shocking." It was also appalled at the way women received what was, ostensibly, a severer punishment than men convicted for the same offence (who would normally, by this time, merely be hanged rather than being drawn and quartered as well). Its criticism became even more virulent when Margaret Sullivan was burnt.[175] In light of this, by the 1780s, the strangled woman's body was normally completely covered in faggots

---

[168]Blackstone, *Commentaries on the Laws of England,* vol. 4, p.93.
[169]Zedner, *Women, Crime and Custody,* p.39.
[170]*The Flying Post,* 1-3rd June 1699.
[171]*The Times,* May 1, 1786, p.3.
[172]*The Times,* June 23, 1788, p.3.
[173]Hayward (Ed.), *Lives of the Most Remarkable Criminals,* pp.31-34.
[174]Simon Devereaux, "The Abolition of the Burning of Women in England Reconsidered", *Crime, History & Societies,* 2005, vol. 9, no. 2, pp.73-98, at p.78.
[175]Gatrell, *The Hanging Tree,* pp.337-338.

prior to burning, to preserve public decency.[176] Even so, in 1788, *The Times* referred to the punishment as a "barbarity" that evoked horror throughout London.[177] The punishment was finally brought to an end after Sir Benjamin Hammett raised the issue in parliament. He had been acutely distressed at witnessing Sophia Girton's immolation, in April 1790, in his capacity as Sheriff of London. During the ensuing debate, Hammett also pointed out that the normal indulgence of first strangling a condemned woman prior to burning her was, in fact, technically illegal. A statute of 1790 (30 George III c.48) substituted conventional hanging for such offences.[178]

Nevertheless, and arguably even more unfairly, burning was not confined to women accused of high treason, it was also the punishment imposed on those who were convicted of 'petty treason'. Sir Francis Bacon defined this crime as occurring in three situations: "Where a servant killeth his Master, the wife, the Husband, the Spirituall man his prelate." In domestic situations, the protection afforded to employers was also extended to their spouses, so that if a servant killed the wife of his master it was petty treason.[179] The vast majority of cases tried during the eighteenth century involved women who had murdered their husbands, though a few servants were prosecuted for killing their employers.

In practice, despite its specific form of indictment, the only significant difference between petty treason and any other type of murder was that those convicted of the crime were subject to a special execution regime. This was intended to preserve, in a very visible form, deference to social superiors. For the handful of men convicted, the punishment was much less draconian than that imposed for high treason, and almost the same as for a normal felony execution, merely involving the symbolic modicum of extra shame and discomfort involved in being taken to the gallows on a flimsy wattle sledge, drawn behind a horse, rather than in the customary cart. Once there, execution was by conventional hanging and there was no drawing and quartering.

For women, however, there was no difference between the punishment for the two forms of treason: "In petie Treason, the corporall punishment [for men] is by drawing on an hurdle, and hanging, and in a woman burning."[180] (Women, too, would be drawn to the gallows on a wattle hurdle). Even to some contemporary observers, the special punishment for female spouse killers seemed unfair, given that it was not reciprocated. One German visitor complained that husband murders: "...are put to death in what I consider to be an unjust way: they are condemned to be burnt alive. Men who murder their

---

[176]Shoemaker, *The London Mob*, p.94.

[177]*The Times*, June 27th 1788, p.3.

[178]Ruth Campbell, "Sentence of Death by Burning for Women", *Journal of Legal History*, 1984, vol. 5, pp.44-48.

[179]Sir Edward Coke, *Institutes of the Lawes of England, Part Three, Concerning High Treason, and other Pleas of the Crown and Criminal causes*, London, W. Lee, 1644, p.20.

[180]Sir Francis Bacon, *Cases of Treason*, London, printed by the Assignes of John More, 1641, pp.7-8.

wives are only hanged."[181] As late as 1773, Elizabeth Herring was sentenced to burn after murdering her husband with a knife during a tavern dispute. She had unavailingly argued that they were not legally married, despite cohabiting for 11 years. This appears to have been the last burning in the Metropolitan area for petty treason.[182] The final such sentence to be imposed for the crime in England as a whole took place at Winchester, in 1784. When Henrietta Radbourne was found guilty of killing her mistress in 1787, the conviction was revised to allow her to be hanged outside Newgate, and normal hanging was used for all husband killers after that date, though petty treason, as a category of offence, was only abolished in 1828.

*Execution by Burning*

In London, during the seventeenth century, burnings had often been conducted at Smithfield. However, by the 1700s, they were usually carried out near the gallows at Tyburn, until, like other executions, they were moved to a space outside Newgate prison in the 1780s (though abolition followed soon after). When women were burned, their executions would usually take place a few minutes after the other condemned prisoners had been hanged, and they would be led past their suspended bodies to the stake. The women involved would often be draped in cloth, or dressed in clothes, impregnated with tar, to facilitate easy combustion. Traditionally, their bodies were fastened to the stake by irons. However, and as some of the reports already discussed suggest, after 1660 it became increasingly common for the executioner to strangle women so that they were dead, or at least unconscious, before the flames reached them. By the start of the 1700s, nearly all women burnt at the stake were granted the "indulgence of being first strangled" using a pulley system.[183] This practice had long been universal by the time of abolition in 1790.[184]

Even so, this mitigating process was not always successful, and signally failed in the case of the husband-killer Catherine Hayes in 1726. Some observers thought that this was done deliberately, to: "…strike a proper terror in the spectators of so horrid a crime."[185] However, the reality seems to have been much more mundane. After two cartloads of faggots had been piled around Hayes and lit, the executioner took the end of a cord attached via a pulley to her neck and began to tug on it; unfortunately, a change in wind direction meant the flames blew towards him, burning his hands, and forcing him to let go. Hayes reportedly gave three dreadful shrieks before she was engulfed by the fire and

---

[181]Madame Van Muyden (Trans and Ed), *A foreign View of England in the reigns of George 1 and George II*, p.127.

[182]OBSP, Trial of Elizabeth Herring, 8th Sept. 1773.

[183]*London Journal*, 14 May 1726.

[184]Frederick Augustus Wenderborn, *A View of England Towards the Close of the 18th Century*, Dublin, printed for P. Wogan, vol.1, 1791, p.80. See also Blackstone, *Commentaries on the Laws of England*, vol. 4, at p.370.

[185]*London Journal*, 14 May 1726.

fell silent, though she was also seen trying to push away the burning faggots with her hands. Some contemporary reports claimed that the executioner, seeing her plight, mercifully threw a large piece of wood at her head, which broke her skull and brought her suffering to an end. It took an hour for the fire to reduce her body completely to ashes.

To prevent such problems, after the first decades of the century, the process of strangulation was increasingly conducted before the fire was lit and, in the years immediately prior to abolition, women were, in effect, 'hanged' at the stake before being burnt, as happened in 1789 with the last woman to suffer this fate, Catherine Murphy. Indeed, Murphy's dead body was left dangling for half an hour before the faggots were lit. Despite such mitigation, in a pre-cremation age, being burnt seems to have elicited special alarm, as it deprived the woman of a proper burial. Thus, prior to her death in 1726, Catherine Hayes fainted several times in the Newgate Chapel, horrified at the fate that awaited her. She declared that although quite prepared to die, a: "...hat-full of guineas, if she had them, she would bestow to save her from being burnt."[186] Much of the attendant ceremony was the same as for a hanging, though the wording of the death sentence was suitably altered in such cases, the judge informing the convicted woman that: "...you are to be drawn on a hurdle to the place of execution; where you are to be burnt with fire until you are dead." As with any other execution, there would be a clergyman present and the condemned woman would be encouraged to confess and repent. Typically, Hayes admitted her guilt prior to her immolation and, though "somewhat confused in her thoughts", begged God and the world for forgiveness.

## Transportation

After execution, transportation was the most severe punishment in the penal repertoire, becoming especially common after the Transportation Act came into force in 1718. Nationally, women were much less likely to be sentenced to this punishment than men, only about 20 per cent of transports being female.[187] However, in London, the discrepancy was much smaller, if only because Metropolitan women appear to have been more prone to offending than their provincial counterparts. Between 1718 and 1776, of the almost 14,000 such sentences handed down at the Old Bailey, nearly 5,000 were given to women. For much of the century, women appear to have been proportionately almost as likely to be transported as were men convicted of the same crimes, unless, perhaps, they had small children who would then be left on the parish.[188] Some clearly found the prospect appalling. Mary Standford, a prostitute who was (unusually) capitally convicted of theft from a client, was unwilling to petition

---

[186]*Weekly Journal or The British Gazetteer,* 30 April 1726.
[187]Eric Monkkonen (Ed.), "Bound for America: A Profile of British Convicts Transported to the Colonies, 1718-1775", *Crime and Justice in American History,* 1991, vol.1, p.99.
[188]Beattie, *Policing and Punishment,* p.444.

for a pardon on condition of transportation, being terrified of conditions in the New World.[189] In April 1789, seven women, under the leadership of Sarah Cowden, initially refused to accept transportation to Australia as a condition of their reprieves.

## Corporal Punishments

A few physical punishments that had been specifically associated with women lingered into the eighteenth century. By the early modern era, the cucking-stool, which allowed an offender to be dunked in a pond or river, was used almost exclusively for females, often in cases where they had been convicted of 'scolding' (a gender specific offence). As late as 1688, the inhabitants of Deptford were ordered to provide a cucking-stool to punish the area's "idle, lewd and disorderly scolding women."[190] This would be used to 'duck' such females into a pond or river, this being part of the punishment.[191] Henri Misson, who visited England in the late 1690s, described its operation: "They fasten an arm chair to the end of two beams, twelve or fifteen feet long … They place the woman in this chair, and so plunge her into the water, as often as the sentence directs, in order to cool her immoderate heat."[192] However, prosecution for scolding, and use of the cucking-stool to deal with scolds, seems to have died out very early in the eighteenth century, at least in the Metropolitan area.

The pillory and stocks were used for both sexes, punishing, *inter alia*, impostors, those who libelled the Crown, gave false testimony, blasphemed in the streets or, in some cases, could not pay minor fines. They both involved detention in a public place, the first by the wrists and neck and the second by the ankles; however, far more men than women received such disposals.[193] Shame and popular hostility were an implicit, and often essential, part of the punishment. In 1777, Ann Marrow, who had dressed as a man to marry three other women before defrauding them of their money, was sentenced by the Westminster Quarter Sessions to three months imprisonment and to stand in the pillory once at Charing Cross. Unfortunately for her, so great was the resentment of the spectators: "…particularly the female part, that they pelted her to such a degree that she lost the sight of both her eyes."[194] Crimes that attracted less social opprobrium would usually result in more benign treatment from onlookers.

Public flogging was the traditional punishment imposed for offences against morality, some other misdemeanours, and for petty theft (the only felony

---

[189]Hayward, *Lives of the Most Remarkable Criminals,* pp.368-371.
[190]Elizabeth Melling (Ed.), *Crime and Punishment, Kentish Sources VI,* Maidstone, Kent County Council, 1969, p.193.
[191]Blackstone, *Commentaries on the Laws of England,* 1769, vol. 4, at p. 169.
[192]Misson, *Memoirs and Observations of his Travels,* p.65
[193]Misson, *Memoirs and Observations of his Travels,* p.218.
[194]Rayner and Crook, *The Complete Newgate Calendar,* vol. IV, pp.113-114.

not to carry a theoretical death sentence). Historically, the whipping was carried out either with the convict tied to a cart's 'tail' and paraded through the streets while being beaten or, alternatively, attached to a stationery post. Thus, in 1725, after Sarah Kettleby was convicted of various offences of immorality, her poverty meant that she was unable to pay a fine; in lieu of a fiscal penalty, she was sentenced to be whipped from the cart's tail while being led in a circle around the Spittle Fields area (as well as to 14 days hard labour in a house of correction).[195] In the same year, Elizabeth Carter was whipped from Ludgate to Temple-Bar for running a brothel. It was later reported that several prosperous mercers who had frequented her establishment contributed towards keeping the mob that attended the procession from insulting or abusing her "as has been usual on such occasions."[196]

However, as the eighteenth century advanced, both judges and magistrates became increasingly reluctant to sentence females to corporal punishment, especially if it was to be carried out in public. The Sessions Papers record only 12 women being sentenced to a public whipping during the eighteenth century, albeit that all of these cases occurred in the years after 1742. This contrasts to over 40 in the last quarter of the previous century alone (and probably many more), though, of course, the paucity of cases reflects the fact that this forum only rarely tried the minor crimes that attracted such punishment. When floggings were imposed on women, they were much more likely to be carried out in private. Sometimes, as with Mary Sidon in 1783, it was even expressly stipulated that they be conducted "in the presence of females only."

This change in judicial attitudes reflected a wider change in popular mores towards women and their bodies. Typical of this transformation, the poet Samuel Coleridge was outraged when he read of the public flogging of a woman in 1811; this, he felt, was at odds with the era's "progressive refinement and increased tenderness." He also thought that beating females was not something that was worthy of men.[197] As a result of such sentiments, the public whipping of women declined markedly after the 1770s. Thus, in the 1760s, 77 women were whipped at the cart's tail, compared to 106 men, with slightly more females being whipped privately than males (46 compared to 39). In the following decade, however, only 19 women were whipped at the cart's tail compared to 178 men. During the 1790s, only 5 women were whipped publicly, while 47 were flogged privately (compared to 393 men).[198] The whipping of female vagrants was formally ended in 1792, and all flogging of women abolished in 1817 (a couple of decades before it was ended for men, except for those being disciplined in prison). No woman was sentenced to be publicly whipped or

---

[195]*Weekly Journal or The British Gazetteer*, 23rd January 1725.
[196]*Mist's Weekly Journal*, 30th October 1725.
[197]Gatrell, *The Hanging Tree*, p.338.
[198]Devereaux, "The Abolition of the Burning of Women", pp.83-84.

pilloried in London after 1798.[199] As this also suggests, the pillorying of women followed a similar pattern of decline to that of flogging. By the 1760s, three times as many men as women were being pilloried, with the proportion of women falling to only 20 per cent in ensuing decades, until abolition brought the practice to an end.[200] Fiscal penalties or short periods of imprisonment were used instead.

## Women and Custody

Although the Metropolis had numerous jails, confinement in mainstream eighteenth-century prisons was primarily a means of securing those awaiting trial, or, after conviction, holding those awaiting execution or transportation. It was only rarely used as a punishment in its own right, and long sentences of imprisonment were rare. In the largely unsegregated prisons and unsupervised penal regimes of the era it is, perhaps, not surprising that many women's experiences of custody were similar to those of men. Women had separate accommodation to men throughout the 1700s; however, they were only properly separated from male prisoners in the nineteenth century. In 1700, a Bridewell Keeper, William Robison, was even found to be charging men 6d. for admission to the women's quarters. Understandably, in these circumstances, women appear to have been just as vulnerable to the corrupting environment of the era's jails as were men. As a result, in 1708, the female felons detained in the women's part of the commonside of Newgate, where those unable to afford the high fees of the exclusive masterside were accommodated, could be described as a "troop of hell-cats lying head and tail together in a dismal, nasty, dark room." There was a grate in their cell, connecting it to a passage that ran past the outside of the prison, allowing them to beg alms from the public, something that was often necessary given the meagre bread allowance provided by the authorities; unfortunately they also used it to subject passers by to volleys of obscenities. One observer felt that it would be an "unpardonable crime to describe their lewdness."[201]

Little had changed a century later. Elizabeth Fry, who was to be instrumental in reforming the conditions in which female prisoners were held in Newgate, was shocked, when visiting the prison at Christmas 1816, to see the "dreadful proceedings that went forward on the female side." The women were swearing, fighting, begging, gambling, dancing and spending their cash on drink in the prison 'tap'.[202] Nevertheless, although the changes associated with Fry and what 'Whig' historians might term the triumph of humanitarian idealism, were significant, it is also possible to exaggerate the horrors that faced prisoners in

---

[199]Shoemaker, *The London Mob*, p.93.
[200]Devereaux, "The Abolition of the Burning of Women", pp.73-98, at p.85.
[201]Hall, *Memoirs of the Right Villainous John Hall*, p.30
[202]Stephen Halliday, *Newgate: London's Prototype of Hell*, Stroud, Sutton Publishing, 2006, p.32 and p.173.

eighteenth-century jails. Additionally, not all of the reforms of the early nineteenth-century, such as the abolition of alcohol and playing cards, were popular with inmates, including female ones.

Many of the customs found amongst imprisoned women were the same as those adopted by men. Thus, women followed the long established tradition in Metropolitan prisons whereby new prisoners would 'tip' older established inmates and turnkeys, on their arrival, so that they could purchase alcohol. Such enforced donations were termed 'garnish'. Failure, or an inability, to pay might result in the new prisoner being stripped of her clothes. In 1711, when Mary Hall, detained in the Gatehouse prison, was unable to pay her garnish money, she recorded that the turnkeys and other prisoners "took off her gown and threatened her." Similarly, in 1733, Sarah Malcolm, accused of a notorious set of murders, was forced to hand over all 18d. that she was carrying on her person as garnish after her arrival in Newgate. Fortunately for her, and apparently anticipating this, she had concealed other money in her hair.[203] However, the custom worked to Elizabeth Turner's advantage in 1734. Unable to pay money for her garnish, she was stripped of her coat by the other inmates, who also discovered a set of baby clothes sewn up inside it, something that subsequently afforded her a defence to a charge of infanticide.[204]

Like men, women might seek to escape from custody. In March 1738, women lodged on the common side at Newgate attempted to break out of the prison by cutting the iron bars of their window with a saw, with a view to climbing down a lead water pipe. Unfortunately, they were overheard by one of the turnkeys, who foiled their plans. The ringleaders were then separated from the rest and held in the condemned cells.[205] More successfully, Sarah Oakly and another female felon named Honeyman escaped from the Surrey County Goal by scaling a 15 foot high wall, using nails "fasten'd in the wall on the inside", though Honeyman broke her leg when jumping down. Oakly immediately returned to her normal Metropolitan haunts and was swiftly arrested in Whitechapel, being found in bed with a male companion.[206]

Unlike the Metropolis' other prisons, however, the Bridewell and the capital's Houses of Correction had been specifically designed as short-term carceral institutions for minor offenders. Many of their inmates were female, if only because of the large number of prostitutes who were committed to them. As a result, the Committee of Governors that was established in 1798 to investigate the Bridewell Hospital noted that, over the previous four years, it had held an average of 40 occupants, either serving seven day sentences for vagrancy

---

[203]OBSP, Trial of Sarah Malcolm, 21st Feb. 1733. Although taking such items could found indictments for robbery, and the courts were willing to "reprove" the perpetrators for committing an "unlawful act," such cases often resulted in acquittals where prosecutions were brought; see for example, OBSP, 16th Jan., 1752, Trial of Simon Jones et al.
[204]OBSP, Trial of Elizabeth Turner, 30th June 1734.
[205]*Daily Gazetteer,* 23 March 1738.
[206]*Mist's Weekly Journal,* 10 December 1726.

or a month for being disorderly. Of these, typically 25 were women and only 15 men. At the Bridewell they would be put to work, either at oakum picking or beating hemp (as they had been for decades) though the Committee thought that it would be better, and more constructive, if the women worked as seamstresses, under their designated Task mistresses, the women who supervised the female inmates' work (earlier in the century the supervisors had normally been men, even for female prisoners).[207] Although they had reformist origins, by the eighteenth century they were as corrupt (and corrupting) as any other Metropolitan prison.[208] In 1786, Mary Dixon claimed that she had been raped in the shop "where the bad people pick hemp," by an official from the Tothill Fields Bridewell. She had been committed to the Apprentices' wing of that institution by her master, for running away and tearing a hole in a piece of muslin (it was her third time there).[209]

## Conclusion

During the eighteenth century, Metropolitan women were normally favoured as defendants at trial, and as convicts when it came to punishment. At most stages of the proceedings they appear to have received better outcomes than their male counterparts. However, this was not special to London. Indeed, it seems to have been much less manifest in the Metropolis, especially in the early and middle decades of the century, than it was in most provincial courts; this is, perhaps, yet another indication of the 'equalising' effect of the capital.

Although women benefited from the formal legal advantage of *feme covert*, this was of relatively minor significance. Much more important were the attitudes that underpinned it. Women received favourable outcomes because male judges and jurors looked indulgently upon them. This was for a number of reasons, some of which were undoubtedly justified; for example, single and impoverished women with dependant children were in a quite invidious position and often treated with corresponding sympathy. Others were based on the era's much more dubious take on female psychology and physiology. Nevertheless, although such attitudes may have been highly patronising, female defendants benefited from them.

Additionally, and despite the grim theatricality of the periodic burnings of women for petty treason, females did relatively well out of the era's penal system, being much less likely to be executed (if capitally convicted) or whipped, than their male counterparts. Indeed, it seems that a popular reluctance to see women hanged, at a time when there was a heavy female involvement in Metropolitan crime, contributed to the emergence of a more general view that

---

[207] Anon, *Reports from Select Committees, Respecting The Arts-Masters and Apprentices of Bridewell Hospital,* London, 1799, p.8.
[208] N Morris and D J Rothman (Eds.), *The Oxford History of the Prison*, Oxford, OUP, 1995, p.329.
[209] OBSP, Trial of William Flint, 25th October 1786.

capital punishment needed to be supplemented by more moderate sanctions.[210] By contrast, non-defendant female participants in the criminal trial were not so favoured. Thus, it seems that as witnesses women were often not viewed in quite the same light as men, although, in international terms (for example, by comparison with contemporary Mediterranean and Middle Eastern societies) their disadvantage was relatively minor.

---

[210]Beattie, *Policing and Punishment*, pp. 474-5.

# Chapter 3: Murder

## Introduction

This chapter will consider the nature and incidence of female perpetrated homicide in and about eighteenth-century London, with a particular focus on those cases in which a verdict of guilty to murder (rather than manslaughter) was returned. Violence, though universal amongst human beings, is also very specific to time, place and cultural context. Despite this, it is frequently argued by criminologists that female violence, of all forms, is relatively unusual, and that its gravest manifestations, such as homicide, are "definitively masculine." As a result, it is claimed that violence is "recognized as a problem and consequence of masculinity." By contrast, it is suggested that women "rarely participate" in its extreme manifestations.[211] A recent history of violence in England since 1750 was even titled *Hard Men*.[212]

Nevertheless, it has also been argued that violence committed by women is neglected in academic studies because it is mistakenly assumed to be absent. Certainly, the anthropological and historical literature reveals that there are, or have been, societies where women are (or were) almost as violent as men, such as the female inhabitants of Margarita Island off the coast of Venezuela and some Australian aboriginal communities.[213] However, these have been relatively peripheral areas, especially to the developed world, and thus might be viewed as rather singular aberrations. This is something that could not be said of the London area, which was already Europe's largest conurbation by the early 1700s. In examining female homicide a number of other themes can also be explored. Amongst them is the impact of a predominantly urban environment on violence, along with change in murder rates over time and in contemporary legal attitudes towards women accused of murder.

The incidence and gender distribution of murder is a particularly valuable statistic when analysing violence as, unlike some lesser forms of physical aggression, it is an offence to which a 'blind eye' has rarely been shown. Even in eighteenth-century England, it had an apparently high level of both reporting and prosecution. Obviously, disposing of bodies in built up areas (such as the Cities of London and Westminster) without detection was particularly difficult,

---

[211]Michele Burman et al, "Researching girls and violence: facing the dilemmas of fieldwork", *British Journal of Criminology*, 2001, vol. 41, pp.443-459, at p. 443.

[212]Clive Emsley, *Hard Men: The English and Violence Since 1750*, London, Hambledon and London, 2007.

[213]Patricia Pearson, *When She Was Bad: How Women Get Away with Murder*, London, Virago Press, 1998, pp.13-14.

explaining the complicated dismemberment and scattering of their spouses' corpses employed by both Mary Hobry and Catherine Hayes. The prosecution process was also greatly assisted by the coroner's active involvement in homicide cases, something that was absent for other crimes, and which usually ensured a relatively thorough investigation of obviously suspicious deaths. Additionally, the coroner had the power to indict for trial on his own initiative. Furthermore, by the 1700s, government (whether national or local) was normally prepared to fund prosecution by counsel in murder cases, at least in the capital. Thus, in 1726, the Treasury Solicitor managed the trial of the notorious husband-killer Catherine Hayes. After the rape and murder of Anne Bristol, by four watermen in 1723, the King personally intervened to ensure that "so barbarous" a matter should not escape unpunished through lack of counsel for the Crown. He directed the Attorney General to "take this prosecution under your care and appear at their trials at the Old Bailey." Similarly, in 1790, when William Cooper was indicted for murdering his wife, when she died some days after he had beaten her, it was the defendant's local parish, Enfield in Middlesex, which paid for the prosecution.[214] This introduced a degree of professionalism to the Crown's preparation of such cases.[215]

The Old Bailey Sessions Papers are especially valuable for homicide offences, as the court dealt with nearly all prosecuted murders from the Metropolitan area. The only other forum that conducted such trials, the Crown Side of the Court of King's Bench, confined itself to exceptional cases; for example, those with a political or aristocratic connection. These were statistically insignificant. Although the inferior sessions for the City, Westminster and Middlesex theoretically had jurisdiction to conduct such trials (as they would until the nineteenth century), by 1700 they had long abandoned hearing murder (or other potentially capital) cases.[216] Of course, the Sessions reports do not mention murder bills that were thrown out by the Grand Jury prior to trial. However, the coroner's power to indict for murder on his own account meant that, even if this happened, it was still theoretically possible for a matter to proceed to trial, something that probably encouraged some consistency of approach.

It is quickly apparent that Metropolitan homicide, *apart* from infanticide of the newborn, was a predominantly male activity during the eighteenth century. This chapter will not consider the killing of recently delivered babies, although this was the most common single form of homicide amongst women. (The phenomenon is specifically dealt with in chapter four). The crime was particular in its circumstances, being substantially confined to single women (at least in

---

[214]*The Times*, Oct 30, 1790, p.4

[215]For the growth of prosecuting counsel generally see John Langbein, *The Origins of Adversary Criminal Trial*, Oxford, OUP, 2003, pp.146-147.

[216]Elizabeth Melling (Ed.), *Crime and Punishment, Kentish Sources VI*, Maidstone, Kent County Council, 1969, p.2. I am grateful to Dr. Ruth Paley for information on the work of the Court of King's Bench in the eighteenth century.

incidence of prosecution), tried pursuant to special (Jacobean) laws and procedures until 1803, attracted different judicial and jury attitudes and can, as a result, largely be considered *sui generis*. Such killings apart, some estimates have suggested that men were responsible for as much as 93 per cent of Metropolitan homicides between 1690 and 1791.[217] This appears to be an overestimate; the same author has suggested that female homicide may have been as high as 13 per cent.[218] For those convicted of murder (rather than manslaughter), and taking the whole of the eighteenth century as the unit of measurement, and the Sessions Papers as the source of information, the percentage of women increases, but is still only about 15 per cent of the male total.

Nearly all homicides that came for trial were indicted as murder. Although manslaughter was a regularly returned lesser verdict, it was very rarely prosecuted in its own right. It appears that only three women were actually indicted for manslaughter during the century at the Old Bailey, two of whom were acquitted while one received a 'special' verdict allowing further legal consideration (it was, proportionately, almost as rare amongst men). It was not until the first half of the following century that indictments for manslaughter *per se* started to increase substantially, as magistrates and grand jurors gradually assumed the task of discriminating between homicides prior to trial.[219]

## Statistical Summary and Comparison

In summary, from the trials of 134 women for murder (or an equivalent crime, such as petty treason) 34 (about 25 per cent) were capitally convicted of the full offence; 25 (about 19 per cent) were acquitted of murder but convicted of the much less serious (in its legal consequences) offence of manslaughter, and 75 women (about 56 per cent) received an outright acquittal. By contrast, about 241 men were convicted of the full offence from more than 900 male murder trials between the start of 1700 and the end of 1799, making the female conviction level (i.e. the proportion of all murder convictions) for the full offence 15 per cent of the male one. However, the male conviction rate for murder (the proportion of male murder defendants found guilty) was only a little higher than that for women. Against this, almost 300 men were convicted of manslaughter (or, much more rarely, 'chance medley') on murder indictments (about 30 per cent of those prosecuted), a much higher disposal than for women, while well over 400 men (about 45 per cent) were acquitted outright.

Consequently, men were seven times more likely to be indicted for murder than women, slightly more likely to be convicted of the full offence when

---

[217]Robert Shoemaker, "Male Honour and the decline of public violence in eighteenth-century London", *Social History*, 2001, vol.26, no.2, pp.190-208, at pp.190-193.
[218]Robert Shoemaker, *The London Mob: Violence and Disorder in Eighteenth-Century England*, London, Hambledon and London, 2004, p.168.
[219]Martin J. Wiener, "Judges v Jurors: Courtroom Tensions in Murder Trials and the Law of Criminal Responsibility in Nineteenth-Century England", *Law and History Review*, vol. 17, no.3, 1999, pp.467-506, at p.470.

prosecuted than were females, significantly more likely to be convicted of the lesser offence of manslaughter (possibly a reflection of the greater incidence of brawling amongst males) and markedly less likely to secure an outright acquittal. Of the Metropolitan men convicted of murder, 74 had female victims and 167 male ones. Thus, less than a third of male murderers crossed the gender line. However, of the 34 women convicted of the full offence, 20, about 58 per cent, had male victims. This higher proportion is partly explained by the significant number of husband/partner killers in the female total. By contrast, for lesser assaults, at least in the early 1700s, it *seems* that men were 75 per cent more likely to have female victims than women were to attack men.[220]

Some of the patterns disclosed in the Metropolitan area correspond with other locations and eras, while several differ to a significant degree. For example, the number of females convicted for an offence of homicide in modern England (as a whole), about 10 per cent of all killings, makes up a broadly similar (albeit slightly lower) proportion of the total to that found in London in the 1700s.[221] However, the proportion of female perpetrated killings in the Metropolis was higher than that found in most of rural England or continental Europe at this time.[222] In early modern rural Germany, between the sixteenth and eighteenth centuries, women committed only 2.2 per cent of homicides.[223] Even in the nineteenth century, although Irishwomen appear to have been more willing to use violence than their English counterparts, only 71 of the 1,926 Irish killings between 1866 and 1892 (under four per cent) were carried out by females.[224]

Additionally, and as with many other types of case, Metropolitan females were much less favoured in litigation outcomes than those prosecuted at provincial Assizes. Women accused of murder in Lancashire during the late eighteenth century were six times less likely to be convicted and executed than were men. Even in Surrey, during the same period, they were 50 per cent more likely to be acquitted than their male counterparts.[225] The willingness of female killers to cross the 'gender line' is also in marked contrast to the situation that prevailed in some other major European cities in this period. Thus, in Amsterdam, of 14 female perpetrated murders, only one (a spouse killing), had a

---

[220]Jennine Hurl-Eamon, *Gender and Petty Violence in London, 1680-1720*, Columbus, Ohio State University Press, 2005, p.71.

[221]J. Cotton "Homicide" in *Crime in England and Wales 2001/2002: Supplementary Volume*, C. Flood-Page and J. Taylor (eds.), London, Home Office, 2003, pp.1-23.

[222]Julius Ruff, *Violence in Early Modern Europe 1500-1800*, Cambridge, CUP, 2001, p.125.

[223]Eva Lacour, "Faces of violence Revisited. A Typology of Violence in Early Modern Germany", *Journal of Social History*, vol.34, no. 3, pp.649-667.

[224]Carolyn Conley, "No pedestals: women and violence in late nineteenth-century Ireland", *Journal of Social History*, vol. 28, no. 4, pp.801-818, 1995, p.802.

[225]Peter King, "Gender, crime and justice in late eighteenth-and early nineteenth-century England", M. Arnot et al (Eds.), *Gender and Crime in Modern Europe*, London, University College London Press, 1999, pp.44-74, at p.55.

male victim.[226] However, it was less unusual by wider English comparison; during the sixteenth and seventeenth centuries, between a quarter and a third of spouse killings had been perpetrated by women.[227]

## Female Homicide and General Violence

The predominance of male murderers during the 1700s would have caused little surprise to contemporary observers. Women were not expected to be violent; it was considered unfeminine, a masculine trait that was, or should be, alien to the 'passive' and submissive sex. Female violence was more likely to be seen as deviant and against 'nature', while much male aggression accorded with approved contemporary notions of masculinity. As a result, females who indulged in violence were likely to be termed 'masculine women'.[228] Cases that conformed to such stereotypes were emphasized in popular reports, such as that of a "gigantic" woman who was brought into court for assaulting another female, and who, it was claimed, was possessed of the bruised face of a prize-fighter and was generally of "terrific appearance." When told by the Mayor that she would have to find bail, she obligingly assaulted the complainant in open court.[229]

However, there is, as always, a question as to the extent to which such attitudes were descriptive or normative. Some women in the 1700s overtly defied the dominant cultural constructions of femininity, even if they occasionally had to resort to cross-dressing to do so. Much more significantly, and whatever may have been the social ideal, and even, amongst the middling social orders, the usual practice, of gender relations and behaviour, the realities, stresses and strains of proletarian life frequently dictated different outcomes. Both sexes might have to adopt opposite gender roles. Just as men sometimes nurtured children, for poor women, at least, survival in the harsh Metropolitan environment often did not permit excessive fastidiousness about the use of violence. Several Metropolitan women in the eighteenth century were publicly identified as 'viragos'; among them was Mary Barber, a Drury-Lane innkeeper, who was committed to prison for "beating" the local constables.[230] When women did fight, it was often 'tooth and nail', and not confined to minor scratching, hair-pulling and slapping. Kicking, biting and punching were all frequently employed.[231] Indeed, it has been (speculatively) argued that the comparative rarity of female violence also meant that there were fewer 'rules' to

---

[226]Peter Spierenburg, "How Violent were women? Court Cases in Amsterdam, 1650-1810", *Crime, History & Societies*, vol.1, no.1, 1997, pp.9-28, at p.25.

[227]Frances Dolan, *Dangerous Familiars: Representations of Domestic Crime in England, 1550-1700*, Ithaca and London, Cornell University Press, 1994, p.25.

[228]Shoemaker, *The London Mob*, pp.168-169.

[229]*The Times*, August 12 1819, p.3.

[230]*Grub-street Journal*, 26th November 1730.

[231]Garthine Walker, *Crime, Gender and Social Order in Early Modern England*, Cambridge, CUP, 2003, p.77.

regulate it when it did occur, so that it was more likely to get 'out of hand'.[232] The degree to which this reflects specifically Metropolitan factors, as opposed to urban ones, is difficult to assess. For example, and in contrast, very few women appear to have been prosecuted for offences of violence in eighteenth-century Buenos Aires, and when they were, it was usually as accomplices.[233]

Comparing murder rates across time is fraught with difficulties, as legal definitions of the offence can change and the medical survival rates of victims improve. However, with this caveat, it can be noted that the eighteenth century is firmly situated within a long period of dramatically declining homicide rates, one that began as early as the late medieval period in some parts of Western Europe (especially England), and which continued into the early twentieth century. Thus, in England as a whole, there was an average of 2.3 homicides per 100,000 head of population during the first half of the eighteenth century. In the second half, it was only 1.4. Much recent work explaining this phenomenon has supported Norbert Elias's emphasis on the process of modernisation, whereby the state gains a monopoly of power (and legitimate violence), while also emphasising the significance of social disciplinary institutions such as the growing number of schools, and the impact of religious reform movements. As a result, there is also stronger self-control on the part of individuals. This also explains why the process appears to have started first in socially 'advanced' countries such as England and the Netherlands.[234]

A major decline in homicide rates was found throughout England, albeit that the speed at which it occurred varied with location.[235] It may have been more marked in the Metropolitan area than elsewhere. On one (albeit fairly extreme) calculation, between 1690 and 1791, the per capita homicide rate amongst Londoners fell from 3.9 to 0.6 per 100,000 inhabitants, the first two decades being especially decisive in the process of decline. Most of this fall is explained by a decline in male killings, and it has been claimed that this was, in large part, a result of changing male attitudes towards notions of masculinity and honour in an urban society.[236] Although the figure cited is rather high, at least 118 males were convicted of the full offence of murder in the first half of the century (and probably about 125 given statistical gaps in the Sessions Papers), and 123 in the second 50 years. Allowing for the substantial increase in Metropolitan population over the same time (well over a 50 per cent increase), this amounts to not far short of a halving on a per capita basis. It has been suggested that, although women's homicides (of all types) also declined

---

[232]Shoemaker, "Male Honour", p.202.

[233]Susan Socolow, "Women and Crime: Buenos Aires, 1757-1797", *Journal of Latin American Studies*, 1980, vol.12, no.1, pp.39-54, at p.43.

[234]Manuel Eisner, "Modernization, Self-control and Lethal violence", *British Journal of Criminology*, vol. 41, 2001, pp.618-638, at p. 629.

[235]Lawrence Stone, "Debate: The History of Violence in England, A Rejoinder", *Past & Present*, vol. 108, 1985, pp.214-216.

[236]Shoemaker, "Male Honour", pp.190-193.

significantly over the same period, the fall was slightly less dramatic. According to the 1690-1791 estimate, there was, broadly, a reduction from one to 0.5 people per sample year compared with a general decline of 16.75 to six amongst men. *However*, taking the number of female perpetrators recorded in the Sessions Papers as a measure, it seems that about 60 per cent of killings carried out by women occurred in the first half of the century (despite the later increase in population), making their per capita decline during the course of the century at least as marked as that found amongst men, and suggesting that they were equally affected by whatever was encouraging a 'gentler' society.

Of course, murder constitutes the tip of a pyramid of illegal violence, and the breadth of that pyramid's base, in relation to its peak, varies from era to era, and between societies and genders. The incidence of killing does not necessarily provide a reliable indicator for that of minor assaults.[237] Even so, statistics for lesser offences of violence indicate that they, too, were predominantly a male phenomenon (albeit to a significantly smaller extent than their lethal counterparts), something that becomes progressively more manifest as the degree of gravity in the violence declines. Throughout the early modern period, women made up between 10 and 20 per cent of those prosecuted for crimes of violence generally, with the higher figure being more 'typical' than the lower.[238] This broadly remained the case during the eighteenth century in the Metropolis, where, even at the lower end of the spectrum, women were the recipients of about 20 per cent of recognisances issued for assaults in which a weapon was used.[239] In Westminster, during the early years of the century, the proportion was somewhat higher. In 1792, it was noted that the whole day's business at the Middlesex Quarter Sessions had involved "women of spirit who had torn each others caps to pieces."[240]

Additionally, the figures for non-lethal violence amongst women may be an underestimate, as many male victims of minor female aggression might have been reluctant to risk public humiliation by prosecuting such attacks. Furthermore, the authorities throughout eighteenth-century Europe appear to have been less concerned about low-level female violence generally, especially when it was intra-gender (such as fights between market women), again leading to under-reporting.[241] Such violence could often be dismissed as a manifestation of sexual pathology that might more properly be addressed by agencies other than the criminal law. Perhaps typical of such attitudes, in a 'female on female' assault brought to the Guildhall Justice Room in 1752, the sitting Alderman

---

[237] For example, in the 1990s, Scottish men were much more likely to be the victims of homicide than those in England and Wales, but less likely to be the victims of non-lethal violence, K. Soothill et al, *Homicide in Britain: A Comparative Study of Rates in Scotland and England and Wales*, Edinburgh, Scottish Executive Central Research Unit, "Main Findings", 1999, p.1.

[238] Walker, *Crime, Gender and Social Order in Early Modern England*, at pp.25 and 75.

[239] Shoemaker, "Male Honour", pp.190-193.

[240] *The Times*, 10th Jan. 1792, p.3

[241] Ruff, *Violence in Early Modern Europe 1500-1800*, p.125.

noted that: "It appears to be a family dispute & frivolous- & doubtful who was the aggressor." He discharged the accused woman. [242]

## Female Perpetrated Murders

Between 1700 and 1799, the Sessions Papers record that there were 122 murder trials involving female defendants (two women being prosecuted for the crime twice). Additionally, 12 women were prosecuted for petty treason. This was the crime committed when: "...one out of malice takes away the life of a subject to whom he oweth special obedience."[243] In practice, this meant a husband, employer or clerical superior. All but one of these dozen cases involved the murder of husbands, the exception being the killing of her mistress by a maid. Despite the special indictment and unusual method of executing such women (by burning up to 1784), they were essentially what, today, would be classified as domestic murders, and can be added to the total. Thus, 134 women were prosecuted for murder or an equivalent offence. In 27 of the murder trials women were convicted of the full offence charged. To these can be added the five women convicted of 'petty treason' for killing their husbands. Additionally, two women prosecuted for petty treason were convicted of simple murder for technical reasons (doubts about the validity of their marriages or over other legal requirements for the crime), and can also be included in the murder total. For example, Henrietta Radbourne (the only employer killer) appears to have been convicted of murdering her mistress, rather than the petty treason with which she was charged, because, by the 1780s, it was felt that the latter crime required the evidence of two witnesses.[244] This produces a final tally of 34 women convicted of murder or an equivalent offence (two of whom pleaded guilty), these having killed a total of 37 people (Sarah Malcolm accounting for three victims in 1733). These 34 women will be considered in further detail.

Of course, some cases of female murder would have gone entirely undetected. In others, a woman died before trial. Thus, one night in 1701, a prostitute from Marsom Street, convinced that her 'gallant' was involved with another woman, cut his throat with a razor in a fit of jealousy. She did not show up in the statistics as, shortly afterwards, she was committed to the Gate-House prison where she hanged herself.[245] One of the successful prosecutions is also quite difficult to classify. Mary Jones was part of the MacDaniel gang that entrapped Metropolitan vagrants into committing felonies with a view to securing their convictions and the attendant rewards. At trial in 1756, she was found guilty of the 'murder by perjury' of one of their victims, who had been

---

[242] Minute Book of the Guildhall Justice Room 25th May to 19th June, 1752, LMA CLA 00501, entry for 8th June.

[243] Letter from "Philalethes" in *Mist's Weekly Journal*, 21st May 1726.

[244] OBSP, Trial of Henrietta Radbourne, 11th July 1787.

[245] *Post Boy*, 26-29 July 1701.

hanged on the gang's evidence; the legality of this finding was later referred to the 12 Westminster judges, sitting together, for consideration.

Of the 34 women, about 28 were prosecuted as principals, rather than accessories. This figure could, at first sight, appear surprising, as it might be expected that a higher number of females would be convicted of aiding or abetting male killers, as Jane Housden was in 1712 (she handed a pistol to her lover so that he could shoot another man), rather than playing a more active role. Additionally, of the 34 women, 21 (about 60 per cent) acted alone when carrying out their killings, without support from members of either sex. Taken together, these facts could, perhaps, be viewed as indicating that women were less 'passive' when it came to homicidal violence than is sometimes assumed. However, considerable caution is necessary when extrapolating such conclusions, as it also seems that the courts were often reluctant to prosecute women who, technically, could have been considered to be accessories, if they worked with men, unless it was in an overtly active role. Theoretically, women were subject to the same rules on aiding, abetting, counselling or procuring murder as their male counterparts; the doctrine of 'feme covert' did not apply to homicide, though women who concealed or assisted their husbands after the latter had committed murder escaped being accessories to their spouse's crime.[246] In practice, however, the attitudes that underpinned the doctrine, especially a feeling that women were easily led and controlled by men, meant that some indulgence was often shown to females who had a minor or peripheral role in killings. Thus, Mary Price was acquitted as an accessory to murder, despite shouting "kill him, kill him" to the principal in the killing.[247]

Nevertheless, occasionally, and sometimes to the astonishment of the women concerned, practice did follow theory, as can be seen in the case of Deborah Churchill, in 1707. Churchill, a domestic servant, was "Debauch'd" by her master. Subsequently, she took a succession of prosperous lovers who provided for her, as well as a man of her own, a soldier named Lewis. One night, however, while in Drury Lane, she was accosted by a man named Ware, who made the mistake of thinking that she was a common prostitute; an argument ensued in which Ware insulted Churchill by calling her a "bitch". Infuriated, she ran to a nearby tavern where her soldier lover and another man were drinking, and demanded redress. Lewis immediately ran after Ware, with the other man and Churchill alongside. He challenged, then stabbed and mortally wounded him. The two men swiftly appreciated the gravity of what they had done, and fled. However, instead of following them, and presumably assuming normal gender roles would leave her safe, Churchill: "…who rather glory'd in the Thing, staid, and was apprehended for the same." She was then committed to Newgate, accused of murder. Churchill was apparently confident of an acquittal and was

---

[246]Anon, *The Laws Respecting Women*, London, Printed for J. Johnson, 1777, pp.70-71. This important legal doctrine is discussed in detail in chapter two.
[247]OBSP, Trial of Elizabeth Armstrong and Mary Price, 15th October 1735.

confounded when, at trial, and "contrary to her expectations," she was convicted. This appears to have been because a number of eye-witnesses testified that she had publicly incited Lewis to "crucifie" Ware and "egg'd him onto revenge." To her great surprise, she was also refused a reprieve and executed.[248]

## Acquittal and Conviction for Manslaughter

A total of 82 women were tried for murder and acquitted outright between 1700 and 1799. Similarly, four of the 13 women accused of petty treason for husband murder were acquitted outright, perhaps because the evidence suggested that the injury inflicted did not occasion death, making 86 women altogether. Four of these 86 women were acquitted because they were "lunatick", although there was no dispute as to their commission of the killing for which they were indicted. This compares to only nine men who received the same verdict. Given the disparity between the number of male and female prosecutions, it appears that women were about three times as likely as men to receive this disposal. This may have reflected a popular reluctance to find 'normal' women capable of such extreme violence and preference for an analysis of 'mad not bad' as its explanation. One murder prosecution, that of Mary Adey in 1779, produced a 'special' verdict, the trial jury being unable to apply the law to the facts of the case and, having made a finding as to what had occurred, leaving the 12 Westminster judges to determine, in a reserved judgment, whether the case was one of murder or manslaughter. Another 23 women were prosecuted for murder and convicted of the lesser crime of manslaughter during the 1700s (including the bellicose Frances Coats from Holborn, who received the same favourable verdict, on two separate occasions, in 1720 and 1723). Additionally, two women were found guilty of manslaughter after being prosecuted for petty treason. Thus, in 1744, Lydia Adler, who seems to have been both short tempered and annoyed with her husband's philandering, gave him a vicious kick in the groin. He suffered severe bruising and, when combined with an existing internal problem, complications ensued so that 12 days later he died from his injuries. Had he not declared on his death bed that the "wicked woman had killed him" and asked his relatives to prosecute her, it is likely that no further action would have been taken over the matter.[249] This produces a total of 25 women convicted of manslaughter after being indicted for murder (or its equivalent).

Manslaughter covered a class of homicides that were seen as being much less culpable than murder, usually because they involved killings committed without 'malice aforethought' (the mental state necessary for the more serious conviction), perhaps because the lethal incident developed out of a spontaneous quarrel and was committed in 'hot blood', or was one in which the victim had

[248]Rev. Paul Lorrain, *The whole life and conversation, Birth, Education and Parentage of Deborah Churchill…*, London, Printed for J. Dutton, 1708, pp.1-8.
[249]OBSP, Trial of Lydia Adler, 28th July 1744.

contributed to the fracas.[250] Eighteenth-century England had a high tolerance for lethal violence that was not premeditated or a facet of instrumental crime. Manslaughter was a 'clergyable' offence for which the normal punishment, early in the century, was branding with the letter M on the brawn of the thumb followed by discharge. Unlike property crimes, transportation was not usually used (after 1718) to supplement this minor penalty in manslaughter cases. Perhaps significantly, at least three of the 25 women had been indicted for murder by the Old Bailey Grand Jury, not by the investigating coroner, who had merely committed them to stand trial for the lesser form of killing. (There were good reasons for the Grand Jury indicting for the more serious offence, given the trivial consequences of clergied manslaughter and the need for 'open' justice).[251]

The significant number of women convicted of the lesser crime is in contrast to the situation that prevailed in much of provincial England during the early modern period, where its rarity as a verdict for females has led to it being called a "distinctly *masculine* form of homicide." These findings appear to have been linked to a male 'brawling' culture that was not perceived as extending to women.[252] Such a culture also explains the high incidence of homicides between relative strangers during the early modern period. For example, little more than a fifth of killings in early seventeenth-century Essex were domestic, compared to over half in early twenty-first century England generally (this figure is itself a reduction from its twentieth century peak). Many fatal assaults in the early modern era were the consequence of (often drunken) quarrels in alehouses and other public spaces, and resulted in manslaughter (rather than murder) convictions, because of the attendant lack of malice aforethought. Women were only rarely involved in such incidents.[253] The significant rate of female manslaughter verdicts in the Metropolitan area raises the possibility that urban women in the 1700s were more likely to act, or at least to be perceived as acting, 'like men' than had previously been the case (again, perhaps, indicative of the 'equalising' effect of the area on behaviour).

However, and as with their male counterparts, the dividing line between female murder indictments that produced convictions for manslaughter, and those that resulted in convictions for the full offence, could be very thin. It is not always easy to identify the factors that led juries to distinguish between such cases, in a system that was heavily premised on the exercise of discretion. Generally, it seems that the presence or absence of provocation, initial aggression or willing participation in a 'fight' by the victim, the use of a weapon, the degree of injury, the social background of victim and perpetrator, the import

---

[250]John Baker "The Three Languages of the Common Law", *McGill Law Journal*, 1998, vol. 43, p.9.

[251]Babington, *Advice to Grand Jurors in Cases of Blood*, p.73.

[252]Walker, *Crime, Gender and Social Order in Early Modern England*, pp.124-125

[253]Steve Hindle, "Crime and Popular Protest", in B Coward (Ed.) *A Companion to Stuart Britain*, Blackwells, Oxford, 2003, pp.130-147, at p.133

of any words used during or before the incident (such as a threat to kill), a substantial delay between wound and death and 'moral' disapproval of the defendant and/or approval of her victim all had a role to play. Thus, Elizabeth Hely appears to have been acquitted of murder during a fracas, in which she and an inebriated male associate fought with several men late at night, because the dead man had initiated the incident by complaining about the bad language that they were using in their (private) conversation.[254] The lack of intent could also be extrapolated from the surrounding circumstances, and especially the nature of any weapon employed. Frances Coats, annoyed by a group of small children who were playing in her courtyard, threw a half-brick at them from an upstairs window when they failed to heed her warning to leave. A six-year old boy was struck on the head and mortally wounded. Nevertheless, Coats was merely convicted of manslaughter.[255] Similarly, in 1710, Elizabeth Gratrix struck Sarah Surupsal on the head with a pewter pot during a heated argument, occasioning a wound from which she died a month later. She, too, was convicted of the lesser offence.[256]

The use of a blade (rather than a blunt instrument like a tankard) seems to have made it harder (though not impossible) to deny intent. Any prior threats of lethal violence towards the victim were highly influential, even if uttered without deliberation. For example, in 1719, Jane Griffin murdered her maid, Elizabeth Osborn, in what seems to have been a fit of temper. Unfortunately, during some heated arguments on earlier occasions, Griffin had uttered threats which: "...though she might mean nothing by them when she spoke them, yet proved of the utmost ill consequence." One night, while making her children's supper, she quarrelled bitterly with her maid about the whereabouts of a missing key. Griffin then snatched up the knife with which she had been cutting poultry, and stabbed Osborn in the breast. Initially, she was hopeful of securing a manslaughter verdict, but the jury, hearing of her earlier threats, convicted of murder.[257] Similarly, Mary Hanson was convicted of murder (again a fatal stabbing), partly because: "The warm expressions she had been guilty of before the blow, prevailed with the jury to think she had a premeditated malice."

Nevertheless, in the absence of such expressions, jurors were often indulgent to female defendants who killed during heated quarrels (as they were to men). Thus, Frances Coats and Elizabeth Richardson were tried for beating to death the impoverished Dorothy Fennel. Their victim was Richardson's lodger, whose accommodation was being funded by the overseers of the poor of St. Andrew's Holborn. A stormy relationship apparently culminated in an argument in which Fennel was pulled by the hair and repeatedly hit on the head

---

[254] OBSP, Trial William Smith and Elisabeth Hely, 16th Jan. 1723.

[255] OBSP, Trial of Frances Coats, 12th July 1720.

[256] OBSP, Trial of Elizabeth Gratrix, 6th Sept. 1710.

[257] Arthur Hayward (Ed.), *Lives of the Most Remarkable Criminals: Who have been Condemned and Executed for Murder, the Highway, Housebreaking, Street Robberies, Coining or other offences. Collected from Original Papers and Authentic Memoirs, and Published in 1735*, London, Routledge and Sons, 1927, pp.11-15.

and stomach, suffering internal injuries from which she died a few hours later. However, in her defence, Coats claimed that the dead woman had: "....call'd them Bitches and Whores, and pull'd her down before she struck." This seems to have persuaded the jury to convict her merely of manslaughter, and to acquit Richardson altogether.[258]

## Social Background to Murders

Much of the immediate background to female perpetrated homicide was determined by women's lifestyles. Men were more geographically mobile than women, and spent a higher proportion of their waking hours in 'public' spaces. Unsurprisingly, a higher proportion of male killings -almost half- took place outdoors, especially early in the century; others occurred in or about taverns. This was comparatively rare amongst women, the great majority of whose homicides either took place inside buildings (commonly domestic ones) or on or around their doorsteps.[259] In the North East of England, female perpetrated homicides occurred almost entirely within the context of family or close social relationships, rather than between strangers. In this, they differed markedly from those committed by males in the same area, where there were a significant number of stranger killings.[260] This is not surprising; men were much more likely, for example, to have arguments in taverns with people with whom they were not familiar. Although the great majority of female killings in the Metropolitan area also occurred in a social or familial context, the number of stranger homicides committed by women appears to have been somewhat greater than in the provinces, making up about 15 per cent of female murder convictions (ignoring those for petty treason), perhaps another indicator of the 'equalising' effect of the capital.

Nevertheless, for both sexes in the Metropolis, homicides were frequently the result of domestic and social stresses that engendered sudden and violent conflicts. These often differed from many other fights only in that a fatality ensued.[261] Thus, Elizabeth Bostock had a long history of mutually violent quarrelling with her 'spouse' (there were serious doubts about their marital status), long before she mortally wounded him with a case-knife. These disturbances had led to the periodic involvement of the local constable and watchmen, on earlier occasions.[262] Similarly, Elizabeth Pew killed Richard Ward, a fellow servant, after a bitter quarrel over some bread and butter, during which he told her "she was a Bitch and a Whore." However, and crucially, he did not

---

[258]OBSP, Trial of Frances Coats and Elizabeth Richardson, 10th July 1723.
[259]Shoemaker, "Male Honour", p.200.
[260]Gwenda Morgan and Peter Rushton, *Rogues, Thieves and the Rule of Law: The Problem of Law Enforcement in Northeast England*, London, University College London Press, 1998, p.112.
[261]James Sharpe, "Domestic Homicide in Early Modern England", *Historical Journal*, vol.24, 1981, pp.29-48, at p.34.
[262]OBSP, Trial of Elizabeth Roberts, 30th June 1725.

physically threaten her. Unfortunately, Pew was holding a knife at the time, which she threw at Ward, mortally wounding him. At trial, Pew was not helped by other witnesses giving evidence that she was aggressive and quarrelsome. The presiding judge probably sealed her fate when he directed the jury that: "If one Person kills another without a just provocation, it is Murder: And words alone are not a just provocation." A conviction for the full offence resulted, even though the defendant had immediately asked a watchman to summon a surgeon.[263]

Amongst men (i.e. most homicide perpetrators), this process was greatly compounded by a widespread and acute sensitivity to perceived slights to male honour, something that often meant that even the smallest 'insults' could not pass unmarked, whether it was jostling in the street, verbal abuse or even a dispute over who was to have the wall (rather than gutter) side of the pavement. Recourse to violence restored a man's status. Such notions of 'honour', especially strong early in the century, were much less common amongst women, so that the spontaneous tavern or street quarrels, over apparently trivial causes, that lay behind many male homicides were rarer in females. They were certainly not totally absent, especially where sexual slights, such as 'whore', were involved, as the case of Deborah Churchill makes clear. (Insults to their sexual chastity seem to have been far and away the most common form of slight to females in early modern Europe generally.)[264] Nevertheless, their comparative rarity is significant, as the eighteenth-century decline in male homicide rates is sometimes attributed to a simultaneous decline in their 'prickliness' over affairs of honour and personal affronts, yet is matched in women.

## Methods of Killing

Many of the 34 women who were found guilty of murder would have committed nothing more serious than an assault if a weapon had not come readily to hand. Stabbing was by far the most frequent method of killing employed by female murderers, and a kitchen knife or some other form of domestic blade the most common weapon, being used by 15 women in the sample (with one other female aiding and abetting a man to stab someone to death). In a majority of cases, the instrument used was the ubiquitous case-knife, found in most domestic environments. However, several other sharp or pointed tools were also pressed into service. Thus, one evening, the rowdy Esther Levingston and her male partner became involved in a particularly severe disturbance, as a result of which a constable attended her apartment in the Minories. The two occupants barricaded the premises, and, when a parish officer attempted to force entry with some local men, Levingston stabbed one of them with a shoemaker's awl, inflicting a mortal wound.[265] Elizabeth Richardson used

---

[263]OBSP, Trial of Elizabeth Pew, 16th Oct. 1734.
[264]Lacour, "Faces of violence Revisited", pp.649-667.
[265]OBSP, Trial of Esther Levingston, 14th Sept. 1763.

a pen-knife to stab her lover to death. By their nature, it was much easier to inflict a lethal wound with such weapons than with a blunt instrument, especially when they were used by a person of limited strength. In eighteenth-century Portsmouth, less than 10 per cent of non-lethal assaults involved the use of a knife, while a quarter involved a stick.[266]

However, the use of purposely manufactured, bladed, weapons was absent amongst women. No females used swords, daggers or hangers to kill their victims, although they were a significant component amongst the weapons used in male homicides, and especially common in killings carried out by members of the upper social orders (who, for much of the early century, publicly wore such weapons). Thus, in a survey of 315 homicide inquests conducted by coroners in London and Middlesex between 1673 and 1782 (in about 300 of which some form of foul play was suspected), 30 cases (about 10 per cent) involved killings by such weapons (only three of which could be considered as 'duels'). This contrasts to 45 killings (about 15 per cent) that were the result of a stabbing occasioned by other types of bladed instrument, such as a knife.[267] As a result, female perpetrators made up a substantial component of those who committed fatal knifings using blades manufactured for domestic use.

A variety of other methods were employed by female murderers. Four women personally strangled their victims (most of whom were children), usually with a ligature made of rope, string or a strip of leather. Several others had recourse to battering, punching and kicking. Drowning was used by two females (to kill children). However, no woman was convicted as a principal in a murder in which a firearm was used (and only one as an accessory to a fatal shooting), although one female was found not guilty of murder by reason of insanity after shooting a former suitor who had jilted her. In the popular mind, women were particularly associated with the use of poison, killing by stealth and strength rather than direct physical aggression and confrontation. There had been several notorious incidents in the capital, which formed part of Metropolitan myth. In a case from 1677, a Westminster maid of less than 16 years of age was suspected of attempting to murder her mistress and another woman by mixing ratsbane into their meals after being chided by them. While being questioned she also admitted to having murdered her mother who was, apparently, "very sickly and troublesome," and another maid, who was ill with small pox, in a similar fashion, over the previous two years. Had a physician not induced vomiting on the part of the girl's employer and her friend, so that the poisons were expelled, she would have been guilty of four murders. Despite her youth, the maid apparently

---

[266]Jessica Warner "'My Pappa is out, and my Mamma is asleep': Minors, their routine activities, and interpersonal violence in an early modern town, 1653-1781" *Journal of Social History*, 2003, vol. 36, issue 3, pp.561-584. at p.578.
[267]T. R. Forbes, "Inquests into London and Middlesex Homicides, 1673-1782", *Yale Journal of Biology and Medicine*, 1977, vol.50, pp. 207-220, at p.217.

demonstrated considerable knowledge of the poison's working.[268] In the early years of the eighteenth century, the case of Mary Channing (1687–1706), from Dorset, who had poisoned her husband's morning milk to allow her to live with a lover had also become notorious.[269]

However, the statistics would suggest that female poisoners loomed much larger in popular myth and debate than in reality. Nevertheless, there were occasional instances throughout the eighteenth century, particularly amongst intimates. As women normally had responsibility for preparing food and drink, it is, perhaps, not surprising that they should have greater recourse to it than men, especially in domestic killings. Even so, during the 1700s, only one Old Bailey murder case that resulted in the conviction of a woman involved the use of poison, though four other females were acquitted of the crime and, in the case of Alice Hall, accused of using ratsbane to poison the broth of two women in 1709, this was by dint of insanity. Doubtless, some other cases went entirely undetected as, by its nature, poisoning was not always easy to identify.

When brought to court, such cases were also hard to prove and (unusually) could result in large amounts of expert medical evidence being called. Thus, the trial of Dorothy Longley, for poisoning her husband, lasted the (then) highly unusual time of 13 hours when held at the Surrey assizes in 1732. This was partly occasioned by the enormous amount of medical evidence called on behalf of both the Crown and defendant. The trial resulted in an acquittal.[270] Perhaps significantly, the only conviction of a woman for poisoning in the Metropolitan area was supported by concrete evidence *other* than that provided by motive and physicians. Elizabeth Cranbery of Twickenham was found guilty in 1720 of murdering Thomas Biggs, her father-in-law, by putting white arsenic in his breakfast porridge. She had earlier had a fierce domestic argument with the dead man, with whom she lived, and who had threatened to "turn her out of Doors." After Biggs fell sick, the porridge was tested on a domestic dog, and the defendant was immediately suspected. Her possessions were searched and a suspicious powder discovered and examined by a doctor, who confirmed it to be poison.

## Alcohol

In the modern era the heavy consumption of alcohol has frequently been linked to violence, whether via a psychopharmacological disinhibition process, physical

---

[268] Anon, *Horrid News From St. Martin's, or, Unheard-of Murder and Poison: Being a true relation how a girl not full sixteen years of age, murdered her own mother at one time and a servant-maid at another with Ratsbane*, London: printed for D.M.,1677, pp.1-3.

[269] Anon, *Serious admonitions to youth, in a short account of the life, trial, condemnation and execution of Mrs Mary Channing who, for poisoning her husband, was burnt at Dorchester in the county of Dorset on Thursday, March the 21st 1706*, London, 1706, printed for Ben Bragg, pp.1-52.

[270] *The Gentleman's Magazine*, 1731, vol. 1, pp.454 and 492, and 1732, vol. 2, p.676.

handicap, isolation in vulnerable settings or some other mechanism. Alcohol was also thought to be a major contributory factor in eighteenth-century violence. Even in 1678, the 'fall' of Sarah Elestone, a 46-year-old woman from Southwark, who was burnt at the stake for stabbing her husband to death, was attributed to her becoming hardened to the "filthy sin of drunkenness." She had, allegedly, been introduced to this vice by her acquaintanceship with several 'lewd' women, and eventually sold most of the household furniture to fund her habit. She committed the lethal act itself after consuming "a cup too much."[271] However, in the years after 1688, the problem became more severe, as the Dutch practice of distilling and consuming gin became increasingly widespread, supplementing traditional consumption patterns of beer and wine. The drinking of cheap brandy also became widespread. In 1782, the young Prussian clergyman, Karl Moritz, though impressed by much of London life, was surprised by the prevalence of 'Dealer[s] in foreign spirituous liquors' and observed that the: "...propensity of the common people to the drinking of brandy or gin is carried to a great excess."[272] Cheap spirits were thought to be particularly likely to engender violence. After the short-lived Gin Act of 1736 was introduced, some optimistic observers even claimed that an attendant reduction in consumption meant that Westminster JPs were less troubled by poor people prosecuting assaults.[273]

It appears that at least three (and possibly several more) of the women convicted of murder during the century had acted while heavily under the influence of drink (as had others who were found guilty of manslaughter). As with men, when intoxication was combined with the ready availability of a weapon, sudden and spontaneous quarrels over essentially petty matters could produce fatalities. Thus, Mary Hanson stabbed her sister-in-law's brother to death in 1725. She had been in a house where he was tending his sick sister (married to Mary's brother) while "very drunk", wandering around with a knife in her hands looking for 'victuals'. Although warned not to make a disturbance that could upset the sick woman, she persisted in making a noise so that the dead man tried to: "...put her out and she immediately stab'd him with the knife." This occurred despite there having been "no former quarrel betwixt them."[274] Prior to her execution, she left a paper at Newgate blaming her action on drink and warning: "...all women to take heed how they give way to drunkenness."[275]

Similarly, in 1735, Patrick Darling, an Irishman drinking in a brandy shop, made a personal joke at the expense of another customer, Mary Price. Incensed,

---

[271]Anon, *The Last Speech and Confession of Sarah Elestone at the place of execution who was burned for killing her husband April 24 1678 with her deportment in prison since her condemnation*, 1678, London, printed for T.D. pp.1-2.
[272]Karl Moritz, *Travels in England in 1782*, London, Cassell and Company, 1886, p.24.
[273]*Daily Gazetteer*, 13th October 1736.
[274]OBSP, Trial of Mary Hanson, OBSP, 7th April 1725.
[275]Hayward, *Lives of the Most Remarkable Criminals*, pp.219-221.

she kicked him in the groin, prompting him to box her ears in response. Price then summoned her cousin, Elizabeth Armstrong, who was drinking in a neighbouring gin shop. Armstrong arrived with an oyster knife she had been using to eat shellfish, and a further disturbance ensued, during which she stabbed Darling in the chest and leg.[276] Mary Eager was more fortunate. Although a JP informed the court that she was an 'infamous' woman, she was merely convicted of manslaughter after stabbing John Essex to death with a fruit knife (she sold pears for a living) in a gin shop. Eager had earlier accepted a dram from him and seems to have been offended when he demanded a kiss.[277] Additionally, of course, alcohol could make the victims of female instigated homicide aggressive or obstreperous, either provoking their attackers, or, like Elizabeth Rock in 1778 (knocked down some stairs by a minor blow), so unsteady that they sustained mortal injury where they would otherwise have not. These cases normally resulted in manslaughter verdicts.

## 'Disciplinary' Procedures resulting in Murder

In the eighteenth century, the use of 'correctional' violence and physical mistreatment of inferiors was widespread and often considered quite legitimate, whether directed against young employees, such as apprentices and servants, or children. However, the extent to which the courts condoned such violence should not be exaggerated. The power to chastise had to be exercised in a proportionate manner, and a failure to do so could result in court action.[278] Throughout the era, the deliberate use of potentially lethal force was viewed as quite unacceptable, in any context. Additionally, during the course of the 1700s, the courts appear to have shown a progressively lower level of tolerance towards such behaviour.[279]

Women could be the perpetrators of such violence, as well as its victims, and about 10 per cent of women convicted of murder were found guilty after occasioning deaths by administering excessively harsh discipline. In the process, they sometimes exercised a power and authority that was normally foreign to them. However, their victims were usually children or adolescents. Thus, in 1755, Mabell Hughes was convicted of the murder of Alexander Knipe, the eleven-year old inmate of the Aldgate work-house, where Hughes also lived and had achieved the position of overseer of the resident children's silk-winding. She seems to have taken a particular dislike towards Knipe, for reasons that are not obvious. Finding fault with his behaviour one Sunday (he was one of a group of children allegedly making a noise) she beat him with a thick oak stick and then

---

[276]OBSP, Trial of Elizabeth Armstrong and Mary Price, 15th October 1735.

[277]OBSP, Trial of Mary Eager, 11th Sept. 1734.

[278]Jennine Hurl-Eamon, "Domestic Violence Prosecuted: Women Binding Over Their Husbands for Assault at Westminster Quarter Sessions, 1685-1720", *Journal of Family History*, vol. 26, no. 4, 2001, pp.435-454, at p.417. See also chapter two.

[279]John Beattie, "Violence and Society in Early-Modern England", *Perspectives in Criminal law. Essays in Honour of John Edwards*, A. Doob et al (Eds.), Ontario, Aurora, 1985, pp.50-51.

kicked and stamped on the boy when he was on the ground. This seems to have ruptured him (he had a congenital weakness) and caused particular injuries to his genitals, from which he died during the night, having gone to bed groaning that: "Mrs Hughes had killed him." Although Hughes had a reputation for being very bad tempered towards the children, she had been expressly authorised to beat them. Her fault seems to have lain in going 'too far', especially as the court received evidence that the dead boy was of a mild disposition and not "hard to be governed", which would have justified more robust treatment. The use of her feet, in particular, appears to have prejudiced the tribunal. Hughes was sentenced to death and hanged and dissected at Surgeon's Hall.[280]

Similarly, in 1762, Sarah Metyard, a widow, and her identically named unmarried daughter, were convicted of murdering Ann Nailor, their 13 year-old servant girl, by shutting her up in a room and starving her to death. Nailor had been bound out to their service by the parish, and immediately subjected to a brutal regime, being beaten by the mother and denied food. Her various attempts to escape were unavailing, and severely punished, and she was frequently tied up with string. After her death, the two women dismembered her body and dumped it in the street.[281]

Perhaps the most notorious case, that of Elizabeth Brownrigg, occurred in 1767. Brownrigg, who came from relatively modest origins, reached a stage in life with her upwardly mobile husband where she could take as bound servants impoverished girls from her local parish or from the Foundling Hospital. Despite being thought of as a midwife of "great skill and humanity" she appears to have discovered a sadistic pleasure in beating and abusing them, flogging the girls with horsewhips, brooms, staves and anything else that came to hand. Eventually, she mortally wounded a fifteen year-old, during a savage thrashing.[282] Brownrigg went to her execution as a figure of popular hate, a crowd assembled in the yard of the Sessions House cheering her conviction. Her husband and son escaped this fate, being seen to have taken a merely 'supportive' role in the assaults, and so only being guilty of misdemeanours. Although this is a decision that is of some interest in itself, Elizabeth was thought to have dominated her weak spouse, who had clearly taken a lesser role in the events.[283]

However, some women in this situation were more fortunate, and merely convicted of manslaughter. Amongst them was Mary Smith, who, in 1755, struck and mortally wounded her carpenter husband's assistant, Joseph Oliphant, with one of his own tools, after words passed between them. The court enquired closely of all the witnesses to the incident as to whether the defendant's disposition was "humane or cruel." The universal acknowledgment

---

[280]OBSP, Trial of Mabel Hughes, 10th September 1755.
[281]OBSP, Trial of Sarah Metyard and daughter, 14th July 1762.
[282]OBSP, Trial of Elizabeth Brownrigg et al, 9th September 1767.
[283]*The Gentleman's Magazine*, vol. 37, 1767, at pp.419 and 433.

that she was a charitable and gentle woman seems to have told in her favour, although wives, unlike their husbands, were not allowed to physically chastise apprentices.[284]

## Domestic Killings by Women

About a third of the 34 murders carried out by women were committed in an obviously domestic environment (not including quasi-domestic incidents against or between servants). Parents, in-laws, children and infants (ignoring new-born babies) were amongst their victims. This is similar to the proportion of domestic killings in modern England as whole (about 35 per cent, itself a decline from the 1950s) and slightly higher than that for modern Greater London (about 25 per cent). Thus, Ann Walsham, a single mother, was widowed early, and left with a child of only a few months of age. She found the infant thoroughly inconvenient for her future prospects, and attempted to put her upon the parish, but was refused by the local church-wardens because she only had one child to support and was able bodied. Walsham resolved to kill her offspring, and unavailingly tried first to poison her, and then to bring about her death by leaving her exposed to the elements; eventually, she strangled the infant. She was able to pass this off as a natural death. However, within a couple of weeks, Walsham was overcome with remorse, attempted suicide and eventually confessed and pleaded guilty to murder. At times she seemed unhinged, and at her execution "appeared like one perfectly distracted."[285] Similarly, in 1743, Sarah Wilmshurst drowned her three-month old child in a privy.

For the lower classes, at least, the strain of living in a crowded domestic environment, with an uncertain income, could easily lead to violence against minors. This might affect women as well as men and also occasionally resulted in domestic murder. Thus, tragedy ensued when Mary Anderson decided to follow her mother into nursing newborn babies for money. She took in three week old Hannah Clark, the offspring of a Westminster joiner and his wife, for 4s a week. At first, the arrangement seemed to work reasonably well. The infant's parents visited periodically for a month, until they received the news that their child had died as a result of a "violent fit." Although they were suspicious, wondering if Anderson might have negligently killed Hannah by, for example, 'overlaying' the infant while she was sleeping, they did not pursue the matter or suspect the reality. What had actually happened was that the baby had been prone to violent crying. At 4 am one morning she had started bawling and Mary Anderson, becoming "wickedly incensed" at this disturbance of her sleep (and that of her natural daughter, all of whom were in the same room), drowned Hannah in a pan of water. Her mother, fearful that Mary would be executed for the crime, told her how to dry out the infant's body and advised her to claim

---

[284]OBSP, Trial of Mary Smith, 22nd October 1755.
[285]Rev. John Taylor, *The Ordinary of Newgate's Account...of the Sixteen Malefactors who were executed at Tyburn on Monday the 23rd of March, 1752.*

that its death was due to a fit. However, when the mother died three years later, her 'ghost' or, as contemporary observers realistically noted, Mary's own conscience, plagued her, and she eventually owned up to the murder. She had, apparently, been "very melancholy and dejected" ever since the killing.[286]

As these two cases suggest, the domestic murder of a significant number of small children (other than that of the new born) *may* have gone undetected. London appears to have witnessed a markedly higher proportion of certain forms of infant deaths, such as drowning, than was the case in the provinces, without an obvious explanation. It is possible, indeed likely, that within the total of suffocated and drowned children under the age of five, were a number who were killed by their parents (including, as in these cases, their mothers).[287] The two cases are also indicative of the emotional price paid by such women, even if typical familial relationships were not quite the same as today.

However, the majority of domestic killings by women involved spouses or partners. A tiny number were premeditated and calculating, as can be seen from the notorious case of Catherine Hayes in 1726. Hayes had worked informally as a prostitute before marrying John, the son of a Warwickshire farmer, and moving with him to London. Once there, her husband purchased a house, took in lodgers and became a pawn-broker. She seems to have been a promiscuous and quarrelsome woman who found her husband and his thriftiness tiresome, telling a friend that she would think it "no more sin to murder him than to kill a dog." She started an affair with two of her lodgers and persuaded them to assist her in killing her spouse in return for payment. Having got John drunk, they hacked him to death. Afterwards, the ruthless Catherine proposed that the body be decapitated before disposal to make subsequent identification harder.[288]

Nevertheless, most spouse killings occurred more spontaneously. Thus, Anne Boswell stabbed and mortally wounded her husband at the public house they ran together in Whitechapel, after hearing from a local gossip that he had been with "some fresh women." (As with many such killings, the wound would probably not have been lethal in the modern era).[289] Elizabeth Herring, the last Metropolitan husband killer to be sentenced to burn, seems to have harboured a longstanding resentment towards her spouse (she disputed that he was even legally married to her). She claimed that he had regularly abused her in the past, and a neighbour confirmed that she had been beaten by him with a poker and stabbed with a fork. The Watch had also been called to break up domestic disturbances between the couple on previous occasions. Unfortunately for Herring, she had been heard to make threats to her husband's life and,

---

[286]Anon, *Concealed Murther Revealed*, 1699, London, Printed for William Aldredge, at pp.1-2.
[287]Thomas R. Forbes "Deadly Parents: Child Homicide in Eighteenth-and Nineteenth-Century England", *Journal of the History of Medicine and Allied Sciences*, 1982/3, vol. 41, at pp.175-199.
[288]*Weekly Journal or The British Gazetteer*, 5th March 1726.
[289]OBSP, Trial of Anne Boswell, 16th January 1747.

eventually, publicly stabbed him in the throat with a case-knife, after the mildest of disagreements over a piece of bread.[290]

Even so, by the eighteenth century, the notion that men could legally and 'acceptably' beat their partners had been in retreat for decades, amongst both lawyers and educated men. It was increasingly seen as 'dishonourable' and unmanly.[291] Although it was still tacitly accepted by some commentators that husbands could use 'moderate correction' against their spouses, this was often mentioned with embarrassment, and any suggestion that men could inflict serious violence on their partners was deprecated.[292] Such changes were reflected in the attitudes of judges and juries towards women who killed their partners. If men were killed after resorting to significant violence against 'their' women, even if it was not potentially lethal and did not involve the use of weapons, it was normally viewed as sufficient 'provocation' to prevent a murder (rather than manslaughter) conviction from being returned. Thus, Catherine Lewis was acquitted of murder and simply branded and discharged after stabbing her husband Richard during a quarrel over whether he had "been with his whore." Richard had kicked her during the altercation and neighbours gave evidence that they fought several times a day and that he had frequently beaten her in the past.[293] In 1743, Elizabeth Freeman was also acquitted of the more serious charge after killing her violent husband with a shoe-maker's knife during a similar quarrel. This was despite her telling a churchwarden, called to the scene, that she "had done murder, and deserved to be hanged for it."

If anything, this process seems to have become even more pronounced as the century advanced. In 1796, Jane Churn stabbed James Scofield to death after he asked her for some thread. When she failed to reply, he called her a "bloody bitch" and struck her about the head. They started fighting, the dead man eventually pinning Churn to the floor with his knees. At this, an eye-witness, fearing that "there would be murder" asked both parties to desist. This produced a temporary respite, which Churn used to go to a table, pick up a fork, and stab Scofield in the side, subsequently also hitting him with a poker. He died shortly afterwards. Even so, Churn, too, was merely convicted of manslaughter and sentenced to a 1s. fine (branding having been abolished). In 1798, Mary-Ann Stone received the same favourable verdict when she stabbed and mortally wounded her 'common law' husband of two years, Abraham Winter, after he abused, struck and beat her during a quarrel.[294]

---

[290]OBSP, Trial of Elizabeth Herring, 8th September 1773.

[291]Elizabeth Foyster, *Manhood in Early Modern England: Honour, Sex and Marriage*, London and New York, Longman, 1999, pp.189-191.

[292]See on this, Anon, *Baron and Feme: A treatise of Law and Equity Concerning Husbands and Wives*, 3rd edn., London, R. Nott, 1738, p.9 and Anon, *A Treatise of Feme Coverts or the Lady's Law*, London, Printed for R. Nott, 1732, p.48. For a more detailed discussion of this phenomenon, go to chapter two.

[293]OBSP, Trial of Catherine Lewis, 4th July 1727.

[294]OBSP, Trial of Mary-Ann Stone, 4th July 1798.

'Active' conflict prior to the lethal incident was vital for such a verdict; there was no notion of 'slow burn' provocation that would reduce murder to manslaughter, even under the most pressing circumstances (a situation that has only been softened in recent years, even in the modern era). It was widely accepted that Mary Hobry, a French midwife who killed and dismembered her husband (a fellow countryman), had been the subject of considerable abuse. Her spouse had beaten her regularly, frittered their household money on alcohol and other pleasures and even subjected her to perverse sexual practices, or "villainies contrary to nature." However, she pleaded guilty to murder without hesitation (quite unusually) after she strangled her drunken husband with his garters, when he fell asleep after assaulting her for the final time.[295] Nevertheless, the cases make it apparent that, although flexible, eighteenth-century criminal law was also a system of rules. There were firm limits as to how far these could be avoided or ignored. Such rules shaped the analysis and constrained the deliberations of tribunals. Juries at the Old Bailey applied roughly the same, well-established, criteria when returning verdicts in murder cases, whether the defendants were male or female, married or single.

## Murder in the Course of Instrumental Crime

Only four or five murders were committed by women engaged in carrying out instrumental crimes. However, several of them became eighteenth-century *causes celebres*. Most famous amongst them was that of Sarah Malcolm, accused of murdering three women in the course of a robbery in 1733. (Hogarth even produced an engraving of the defendant). Malcolm, who was only 22 at the time of her death and originally from county Durham, had worked for her elderly (primary) victim some time earlier, and still did the old lady's laundry on a piecework basis. She subsequently claimed to have had two accomplices in the ensuing robbery (one of them female) who actually committed the multiple killing (though these were never caught).[296] Some observers attributed her fall to a period of employment at the Black Horse, a 'low' public-house near Temple Bar, where she allegedly made bad connections. It was even rumoured that she had been involved in the earlier (1729) murder in Drury Lane of a Mr. Nisbet, for which a man had already been hanged.[297]

Another, equally notorious, case was that of Susan Perry, in 1713. Perry, also a woman of 22, lured away John Pace, a child of four who was walking home from school, by pretending to be familiar with his parents. Having got the infant into a secluded place she strangled him with a piece of wool, stripped him of his clothes and abandoned the body in a ditch. His hat, coat and frock were

---

[295]Anon, *A hellish Murder Committed by a French Midwife, on the Body of her husband*, London, 1688, at pp.30-34.

[296]Sarah Malcolm, *A True Copy of the Paper Delivered the Night before her Execution by Sarah Malcolm*, London, 1732, p.8.

[297]*Gentleman's Magazine*, vol. 3, Feb. 1733, p.100.

swiftly sold onto a woman who dealt in second-hand clothes for 9d (their identification was to be the cause of her discovery). Women were well noted for robbing children, and such a scenario formed a cameo in Daniel Defoe's *Moll Flanders* (he may have been influenced by the case), presumably because it was easier for them to gain the trust of infants and they were guaranteed to be physically stronger than their victims. Nevertheless, most such cases did not end in murder, and why Perry should have been willing to kill for such a trifle is hard to say, unless it was to avoid subsequent identification.

## Brutality

Many female homicides (like male ones) were the result of a momentary loss of control, sometimes instantly regretted. However, Perry was certainly not unique in the considered and extreme brutality manifest in her killing. Thus, in 1734, Judith Dufour, an illiterate gin soaked member of the Metropolitan underclass, got leave to remove her illegitimate two-year-old daughter for a few hours from a Bethnal Green workhouse (where the infant was an inmate). She then strangled the child and discarded her body in a ditch after stripping it of its clothes, which she promptly sold for 16d. before immediately spending the proceeds on drink. At trial, Dufour claimed to have been encouraged into committing the crime by a female associate that she could not identify.[298] Similarly, in 1718, Mary Price strangled a three-year-old girl to exact revenge on the child's father for taking her tobacco box. In 1751, Rachel Beacham, a married woman, cut the throat of the five year old daughter of a work colleague, for reasons that she could not explain, other than by saying that "she was tempted to do it." The court enquired about her mental state and whether she was prone to drinking but without gaining any explanation for her action.[299] After she was sentenced to death, the Ordinary probed a little deeper, and seems to have concluded that some kind of mental disturbance lay behind what was a relatively impulsive decision to murder a young girl who had never given her offence, and whose mother was, apparently, on friendly terms with Beacham.[300] As with men, some of this brutality was, perhaps, also a symptom of an environment in which life was often lived close to the margins of survival and in which levels of public exposure to violence and attendant squeamishness were necessarily lower than today. (A theme that was to be graphically explored by William Hogarth in his 'Four stages of cruelty').

## Conclusion

Although it appears that Metropolitan women were, proportionately, much more involved in instrumental crime during the eighteenth century than their

---

298OBSP, Trial of Judith Dufour, 27th February 1734.
299OBSP, Trial of Rachel Beacham, 4th December 1751.
300Taylor, *The Ordinary of Newgate's Account...* pp.1-4.

modern counterparts, this did not extend to homicide.[301] The statistics lend credence to what has been termed a 'constant phenomenon' and probably reflect a combination of physical, cultural and situational factors, many of which remain unchanged. Women are still much less likely to resort to lethal violence than men, though their advantage over males in the outcome of such cases at trial appears to have largely disappeared. Despite this, however, there are sufficient examples of extreme female brutality during the 1700s to make any observer cautious over coining generalisations about the 'gentler' sex. A number of striking continuities between the eighteenth century and the modern era are also apparent: the most common method of killing is still stabbing, followed by hitting or kicking and then strangling or asphyxiation. The most frequent background to homicide is still a quarrel, act of revenge or loss of temper.[302]

However, the fact that the proportion of Metropolitan killings carried out by women during the eighteenth century matches that for modern England is suggestive. Although women were, on average, not as strong as men, their smaller representation in offences of violence can also be explained by contrasts in socially expected behaviour.[303] As previously noted, women in rural and more traditional kin-based societies, lived under considerable (often male) constraint. This might be imposed by fathers, husbands, brothers, neighbours, magistrates or clerics. However, these social controls and socialised habits of obedience frequently appear to have become attenuated in the Metropolis, where there were more single, working, females, many of whom had migrated from the country to what was a huge, frenetic, socially mobile and sometimes anonymous city. In this environment, they were often dependant on their own resources to survive. In consequence, some of the 'traditional' distinctions between the sexes appear to have been loosened. Perhaps as a result, where they did occur, many female perpetrated killings in the Metropolis during the 1700s were notably similar in background and *modus operandi* to those of their male counterparts. Women could not only drink alcohol freely but also might have to be self-assertive, even if this risked them getting drawn into lethal quarrels. This also means that many of the era's female perpetrated homicides appear remarkably 'contemporary' to modern observers.

It can also be noted that the per capita incidence of homicide amongst women appears to have declined significantly during the course of the century, just as it did for men (of all classes), suggesting that they, too, were not immune to a general change in attitudes towards the use of potentially lethal violence. This softening of manners, increased intolerance for social violence generally and growth in personal restraint can be traced to at least the previous century.

---

[301]Malcolm Feeley and Deborah Little, "The Vanishing Female: The Decline of Women in the Criminal Process, 1687-1912", *Law and Society Review*, 1991, vol. 25, no. 4, pp.719-757, at p.721 and p.736. See also chapter five.
[302]Cotton "Homicide", pp.1-23.
[303] John Beattie, "The Criminality of Women in Eighteenth Century England", *Journal of Social History*, 1974, vol.8/4, pp.80-116, at p.96.

Although first identified by Norbert Elias over 70 years ago, the explanation for such a "civilizing process" is still a matter of fierce debate.[304] Nevertheless, in the Metropolis, at least, it seems that it cannot be explained purely by changing social constructions of masculinity. An increased aversion to violence appears to have been one facet of a general rise in a culture of self-control, rather than something that was specifically linked to men. It was probably as much associated with the influence of a growing middle-class as with gender.

An ongoing question for criminologists is the extent to which women being 'processed' in the criminal justice system are treated differently to men; whether better, as members of the 'weaker' sex (the 'chivalrous' approach), or worse, because of their degraded status as females who would resort to crime. As with many of the other crimes discussed in this book, it seems that, when it came to prosecutions for murder, women were generally favoured during the 1700s, rather than being at a disadvantage. Those on the 'fringes' of killings were less likely to be indicted than men. Those who came for trial were more likely to be acquitted or found insane, albeit that the degree of 'chivalry' seems to have been small compared to that shown in the provinces (again, perhaps, a reflection of the 'equalising' effect of the capital). Furthermore, and despite contemporary notions of patriarchy and the generally subordinate role of women to men, it seems that females within heterosexual relationships who killed their partners were subject to largely the same criteria for determining culpability as men. Finally, a scrutiny of female perpetrated killings in the eighteenth-century Metropolis reveals just how fine, even arbitrary, the distinction between life and death in the crimes themselves, and guilt and innocence in the ensuing trials, often was; frequently, it turned on chance or random factors.

---

[304]See generally, Norbert Elias, *The Civilising Process*, vols. 1 and 2, Oxford, Blackwells, 1982.

# Chapter 4: Infanticide

## Introduction

This chapter will consider Metropolitan infanticide during the 1700s. In modern England, 'infanticide' is used, legally, to refer to the killing of those under a year in age, and colloquially for the murder of small children generally. However, this chapter will deal with neo-naticide, the killing of newborn babies. (The murder of older infants is considered in chapter three). Additionally, the chapter will focus on the killing of illegitimate babies rather than the era's *apparently* much rarer killing of babies born within marriage, though it seems that the benefit of any doubt was usually given to suspicious deaths amongst the newborn offspring of married couples, which very rarely resulted in court proceedings.[305] Doubtless, in an era of high infant mortality, many went entirely undetected. There is an excellent general study of eighteenth-century infanticide using evidence drawn from the court records for northern England as its primary source.[306] Some of its conclusions apply with equal force to the metropolitan area; nevertheless, as will be seen, there are also some significant differences.

Historically, infanticide has been found in most societies, being motivated by a huge array of factors ranging from eugenics, gender selection and economic/subsistence issues to post-natal depression. Although the Church vigorously condemned the practice, it continued an illicit existence in pre-modern England. How frequently it occurred is hard to establish. By its nature, infanticide is committed in secret and a lack of prosecutions does not necessarily establish its absence. Some observers, such as Daniel Defoe, feared that exposed cases were merely the tip of an early eighteenth century infanticide 'iceberg': "But alas! What are the exploded Murders to those which escape the Eye of the Magistrate, and dye in Silence?"[307] Nevertheless, there is no tradition in English folklore even tacitly justifying it. In this, the country contrasts with, for example, eighteenth-century Japan, where it seems that infanticide was quite frequently practiced, by all social groups, as a method of planning the gender balance and ultimate size of families.[308] Although, in England, many cases undoubtedly went entirely undiscovered, an analysis of those in which there was exposure would

---

[305]For an example of this see, OBSP, Trial of Elizabeth and John Tyrant, 5th July, 1727.
[306]See generally Mark Jackson, *New-born child murder: women, illegitimacy and the courts in eighteenth-century England*, Manchester, Manchester University Press, 1996.
[307]Daniel Defoe, *The Generous Projector*, London, Printed for A. Dodd, 1731, p.9.
[308] Thomas Smith, *Nakahara: Family Farming and Population in a Japanese Village, 1717-1830*, California, Stanford University Press, 1977, at pp.11-14.

suggest that a relatively small minority of unmarried pregnant women had recourse to such a drastic solution.

## Social Background to the Crime

Unsurprisingly, cases of infanticide almost invariably involved female suspects, if only because, in the case of illegitimate births at least, the putative fathers had usually disappeared. As a 'typical' example might be considered the case of Ann Mabe, a servant who was impregnated by her employer's coachman in 1718; unfortunately, he vanished shortly afterwards, despite Mabe sending him several imploring letters asking for assistance.[309] Many women were abandoned without any means of contacting (or sometimes even identifying) their former partners. As a result, of the cases heard at the Old Bailey Sessions between December 1714 and December 1799, only four involved male defendants as principals, and all of these were married men who had assisted their wives in killing their babies or, in one case, committed the crime after his wife died in childbirth. All led to acquittal. This meant that infanticide was unusual in being a very serious offence in which the defendants were normally women. With the *de facto* abandonment of witchcraft prosecutions, in the latter part of the seventeenth century, it was almost unique in this.

Royalty apart, most people in the early modern era were well into adulthood before they wed. In late eighteenth-century England, the average groom was about 26½ years of age when contracting a first marriage and his bride was almost 25, although the figures were slightly lower for the London area.[310] As a result, and even allowing for a somewhat later onset of puberty, many people had to wait years between sexual maturity and the arrival of socially sanctioned sexual intercourse within marriage. Indeed, some individuals, such as servants and, for as long as they were indentured, apprentices, may never have been able to experience such approved coitus.[311] This inevitably produced 'fornication', the existence of socially (if ineffectively) sanctioned sexual intercourse outside marriage. As one observer realistically noted in 1799, in nearly all countries there were: "...vast numbers of young men and young women, who, from the narrowness of their circumstances, dare not entertain a hope of marriage, whose passions, inflamed by continual recurrence of stimulating occasion, overwhelm all powers of reasoning." In such a situation, it was inevitable that the most virtuous resolutions and even religious piety would: "...give[s] way to the ardour of a susceptible constitution, and the temptations of intoxicating opportunity."[312]

---

[309] OBSP, Trial of Ann Mabe, 27th Feb 1718.
[310] Douglas Hay and N. Rogers, *Eighteenth-Century English Society*, Oxford, OUP, 1987, pp.44-46.
[311] Alan Macfarlane, "Illegitimacy and illegitimates in English history", in *Bastardy and its Comparative History*, P Laslett, K Oosterveen and R Smith (Eds.), London, Arnold & Co, 1980, p.71.
[312] Anon, *Thoughts on Means of Alleviating the Miseries attendant upon Common Prostitution*, London, 1799, p.12.

Additionally, the incidence of fornication appears to have expanded considerably during the eighteenth century, as attitudes towards penetrative intercourse changed and people became more sexually active generally.[313] In particular, mutual masturbation and various forms of 'heavy petting' seem to have been replaced by a new emphasis on full intercourse.[314] Certainly, the level of illegitimacy increased during the century, especially in urban areas, rising from 1.5 percent of recorded baptisms in 1660 to over 5 per cent in 1815.[315] As a result, some demographers have even referred to the 1700s as the 'century of illegitimacy.'[316] The transformation in sexual mores seems to have been particularly strong in and about the London area, where adultery had also become more common, some even claiming that it "rage[d] in our voluptuous Metropolis."[317] Instances of extra-marital pregnancy almost inevitably resulted when such behaviour was combined with bad luck, poor contraception and dishonoured promises of betrothal should such an eventuality occur. The latter was a very common feature of sexual dalliances outside marriage during the period.[318] It was a special criticism of Alice Meadows, a servant convicted of infanticide after being impregnated by a lodger in the house where she worked, that she admitted to having: "...easily consented, when solicited to the act of whoredom, without any hope of gain or promise of marriage."[319]

However, and even allowing for the apparently liberalising effect of the Metropolitan area on sexual attitudes, it should also be noted that many mothers of illegitimate babies, in agreeing to full intercourse, were simply practising the pre-marital sexual customs that were common in the rural areas they had grown up in. Unfortunately for them, in an urban context, it was often very much harder to produce the social pressure that might prod a reluctant father into honouring promises of marriage (when pregnancy ensued) than was the case in a rural environment.[320] Many bastards were the result of serious courtships that had turned sour.

Despite the propagation of 'official' morality, via pulpits and chapbooks, the absence of virginity in unmarried females, even if discovered, seems to have been viewed as a *relatively* minor sin at a popular level in eighteenth-century England. (In part, this was, perhaps, influenced by the lack of significant

---

[313]Timothy Hitchcock "Unlawfully begotten on her body': Illegitimacy and the Parish Poor in St Luke's Chelsea", *Chronicling Poverty*, P King et al (eds.), 1997, pp.70-87.

[314]Tanya Evans "'Unfortunate Objects': London's Unmarried Mothers in the Eighteenth Century", *Gender & History*, 2005, vol.17, no.1, pp.127-153, at p.128.

[315]Hay and Rogers, *Eighteenth-Century English Society*, pp.47-48.

[316]Lisa Zunshine, *Illegitimacy in Eighteenth-Century England*, Columbus, Ohio State University Press, 2005, p.1.

[317]Anon, *Thoughts on the Frequency of Divorce in Modern Times*, London, 1800, p.4.

[318]Jonas Hanway, *A Candid historical Account of the Hospital for the Reception of exposed and Deserted Young Children*, London, 1759, p.43.

[319]Rev. Samuel Smith, *The Ordinary of Newgate his Account of the Behaviour Confessions, and Dying Speeches of the Condemned Criminals that were Executed at Tyburn on 2nd. March 1692*, p.2.

[320]Evans, "Unfortunate Objects", p.136.

amounts of heritable property, something that made the risk of bastardy of some concern to the 'political' nation). It did not usually bring intolerable shame on the individual concerned. As Francis Place noted in later life, when looking back to the Metropolis of the 1780s, "want of chastity" in a girl did not necessarily indicate that she was an abandoned person.[321] Unlike some Mediterranean societies, there is little evidence that such women found it difficult to marry once suspected of unwedded sexual intercourse, and there was no physical inspection of prospective brides to ensure virginity, though, it seems, some men may have tried to check for 'intactness' on their wedding nights.[322] Indeed, one contemporary observer claimed that of: "Twenty reputed virgins, scarce seven carry their maiden-heads to the marriage-sheets."[323] In any event, given the size of the capital and the frequent transience of its social relationships, especially those involving servants, it would often have been easy for women to put their 'pasts' behind them, *provided* there was an absence of children.

By contrast, the consequences of giving birth to bastards could be *fairly* drastic for poor women. The simple begetting of illegitimate children was not a crime during the eighteenth century. If an illegitimate baby could be supported by its mother no civil offence was committed, if only because the "very maintenance of the child is considered as a degree of punishment."[324] However, producing bastards that might become a burden to the community was still, theoretically, punishable in the mainstream criminal courts. A Jacobean statute of 1610 (7 James, cap. 4) had provided that: "Every lewd woman which shall have any bastard which may be chargeable to the parish, the justices of the peace shall commit such woman to the house of correction, to be punished and set on work, during the term of one whole year." Public whipping and pillorying were also potentially available. Such punishments had frequently been administered in the seventeenth century. Nevertheless, although much of this legislation remained on the statute book during the 1700s, by then, the courts were much less assiduous about imposing physical punishment for the offence, and it was probably not this that acted as a primary deterrent. Although summary courts were heavily involved in dealing with bastardy examinations, most were primarily concerned with ensuring that the cost of raising an infant was borne by the man responsible for bringing about the pregnancy, rather than punishing the woman concerned, unless she was a repeat 'offender'. Indeed, in many parts of the country, imprisonment was more likely to be used against putative fathers who failed to pay maintenance than against bastard bearing women.[325]

---

[321]Hay and Rogers, *Eighteenth-Century English Society*, p.50.

[322]Anon, *A Dialogue Between A Married Lady and a Maid*, London, 1740, p.B3

[323]Father Poussin, *Pretty Doings in a Protestant Nation*, London, 1734, at p.8.

[324]William Blackstone, *Commentaries on the Laws of England*, Oxford, Clarendon Press, 1765-1769, vol. 4, p.65.

[325]Peter King, "The Summary Courts and Social Relations in Eighteenth-Century England", *Past & Present*, no. 183, 2004, pp.125-173, p.152.

However, illegitimate children still had to be supported at the expense of the parish, and it was this, as much as any inherent immorality, that alarmed local authorities. It also explains the concern shown by contemporary parish officers about apparently pregnant single women who moved into their communities. Thus, in 1739, Elizabeth Harrard claimed to have been forcibly moved on by the Richmond beadle when she went into labour in his suburb and then to have experienced exactly the same treatment when she arrived in Twickenham on the same day, being escorted out of the town by its beadle and left in adjoining fields.[326] If the parish were landed with a bastard, it would have to be put out to nurse and, when old enough, apprenticed. In practice, little care and less expense would be taken over this, so that eighteenth century survival rates for bastards thrown on the parish were quite appalling, as cheap but neglectful nurses, institutions and dubious apprentice masters were selected by church wardens. For example, the notorious and homicidal Elizabeth Brownrigg's maids were 'apprenticed' to her by her local parish, along with a donation of five pounds to the Brownriggs' own coffers and clothing for the girls for two years. Given that the husband was a house painter, and Elizabeth a midwife, her neighbours: "…could not conceive what occasion she had for any apprentices at all, or what trade she could learn them."[327] Many illegitimate children survived only a few months, relatively few (under a quarter) to adulthood.

Despite this, there was still considerable expense involved for even the most economical vestry. As a result, the parish would either try to obtain a lump sum, perhaps ten pounds, if it was to take immediate responsibility for a bastard or, alternatively, support and an undertaking from the genitor to meet any future expenses, if he could not be coerced into marriage.[328] Typically, in 1683, a man who had been established as the father of an illegitimate baby might be required to pay 12d. a week until the child was 12 years old, and a five pound lump sum at that age to pay for an apprenticeship.[329]

If paternity was acknowledged, and the father could provide maintenance, the offence would not usually come before the civil courts. Consequently, poor unmarried women who were pregnant or had produced bastards were pressured to reveal the identities of those who had impregnated them. Thus, in March 1726, it could be laconically noted in a London journal that a pregnant woman had: "…hang'd herself with her handkerchief in Covent Garden Round House, where she had been committed for being with child, and not discovering the

---

[326] OBSP, Trial of Elizabeth Harrard, 6th Sept 1739.

[327] Anon, *God's Revenge Against Murder*, London, 1810, at p.5

[328] Dorothy George, *London Life in the Eighteenth Century*, Harmondsworth, Penguin, 1965, pp.214-215.

[329] Anon, *An Assistance to Justices of the Peace, for the Easier Performance of their Duty*, Joseph Keble, London, 1683, p.200.

father."[330] For the same reason, it was ordered that midwives at childbirth should try to extort a genitor's name out of an unmarried woman.[331]

On their own, the hostility of local taxpayers, coupled with the moral shame of bearing a bastard, gave considerable incentives for pregnancies to be concealed and the resultant children disposed of. However, there were other, practical, consequences that were equally severe. These would normally include loss of position for female servants and employees and, without a reference and with a small child in tow, little prospect of securing another one. This might necessitate falling back on one of the rapidly increasing number of workhouses in and around the capital. As Sarah Hayes explained, when accused of concealing her delivery in 1746: "I was a servant, and would not disgrace myself." Hopes of making a future marriage would also be severely damaged if the child survived. Given these consequences, many felt that it was not surprising if a woman in such a position did not try to: "…screen herself from censure, by the commission of a more dreadful sin in the murder of a spurious infant."[332]

Of course, some desperate women managed to pre-empt such a situation. Although the law was, theoretically, strict on infanticide there were: "…so many ways of evading it, either by destroying the infants before their birth, or suffering them to die afterwards by wilful neglect, that there appears but little hope of putting a stop to this practise."[333] The latter option, though useful to married women (and again helping to explain their low incidence of prosecution) was of less use to single females seeking to avoid the stigma of bastardy. Nevertheless, women who were able to pay a token fee could turn to wet nurses, popularly nicknamed "killer-nurses," who would discreetly starve and neglect illegitimate babies left in their care until they died. (The cost of a genuine nurse, willing to take proper care of a child, was often equivalent to the woman's annual wage).[334] Metropolitan 'baby farming', although it only became a focus of acute public and political concern in the 1870s (after the trial and execution of Mary Waters) had its roots in the eighteenth century and appears to have been tacitly accepted until well into the Victorian period.[335]

Attempting to secure an abortion was a stratagem that was open to all women. Defoe was convinced that induced miscarriages to avoid embarrassing or inconvenient pregnancies were widespread in the early 1700s, and deplored the: "… Abortions, which wicked Wretches make use off to screen themselves from the Censure of the World."[336] Bernard Mandeville shared his view and, in

---

[330] *Weekly Journal, or The British Gazetteer,* 19 March 1726.
[331] Macfarlane, "Illegitimacy and illegitimates in English history", p.71.
[332] *The Gentleman's Magazine,* 1749, vol. 19, p.126.
[333] Poussin, *Pretty Doings in a Protestant Nation,* pp.42-43.
[334] Zunshine, *Illegitimacy in Eighteenth-Century England,* p.4.
[335] Barry Godfrey and Paul Lawrence, *Crime and Justice: 1750-1950,* Collompton, Willan Publishing, 2005, p.132.
[336] Defoe, *The Generous Projector,* p.10.

1736, Ronald Brome claimed (untruthfully) to have dismissed his servant because he caught her boiling up an abortificent in his kitchen.[337] Many contemporary books on household management contained herbal recipes that were designed to bring on the 'courses', the primary purpose of which was, in reality, to produce miscarriage. More typically, and probably more effectively, when, in 1732, Eleanor Beare was tried for acting as an abortionist in Derby, her preferred method was not ingested 'physic' but, instead, to get her patients suitably anaesthetised with alcohol and then to insert a long metal needle into them.[338] Legally, abortion was not viewed nearly as seriously as infanticide, especially in the early stages of pregnancy (prior to the foetus 'quickening'), although, if a woman who was quick with child took a potion or used some other method to kill the child she was carrying and, as a result, although "born alive, [it] dieth of the potion, battery, or other cause, this is murther."[339] However, abortion was, medically, a very risky and highly uncertain path.

If the foetus did survive to term, many other women took the less drastic step (to killing) of simply abandoning the infant in an environment in which it was likely to be found and, perhaps, succoured, or at least handed over to the parish authorities. Thus, in 1701, a woman left her baby in an attractive bandbox in Fleet Street, where it was picked up by a man who had no sooner "opened his prize, e're a child within it fell a crying."[340] How frequently the streets of London served as a dumping ground for illegitimate children, both from the city and its environs, is not clear, but there are many descriptions of bastards being abandoned by both residents and visitors.[341] The parish would then be forced to take on the financial burden involved, unless a kindly (and perhaps childless) stranger intervened. For example, in the first six months of 1743, 12 babies were abandoned in the parish of St. George, Hanover Square, alone.[342] The prosperous nature of this locality may have encouraged its selection for 'dropping'. With Thomas Coram's establishment, in 1739, of the London Foundling Hospital for "exposed and deserted children", near Brunswick Square, such mothers were presented with a practical alternative, and numerous babies were abandoned there. In its first day of operation (2nd June) 117 babies were admitted; in the first month, 425, all under two months in age, arrived.[343] At one time, they could simply be put into a basket placed outside the hospital's door. (It was even occasionally argued that the presence of the Foundling

---

[337]OBSP, Trial of Elizabeth Skinner, 15th Jan 1736.

[338]*The Gentleman's Magazine*, vol. 2, August 1732, pp.931-932.

[339]Zachary Babington, *Advise to Grand Jurors in Cases of Blood*, London, Printed for John Amery, 1677, p.141.

[340]*English Post*, 12-14 November 1701.

[341]Macfarlane, "Illegitimacy and illegitimates in English history", p.71.

[342]R W Malcomson, "Infanticide in the eighteenth century" in *Crime in England 1550-1800*, J.S. Cockburn (Ed.), London, Methuen, 1977, p.188.

[343]Hanway, *A Candid historical Account*, p.25.

Hospital actually encouraged 'whoring').[344] By the end of the century, almost 19,000 children had been admitted, though indiscriminate admissions had been ended in 1760 due to lack of funds (it should also be noted that mortality rates reached 60 per cent of all admissions).[345] Some English observers blamed an apparent increase in infanticide north of the border, at the end of the century, on the absence of a Scottish equivalent to the Hospital.[346]

Nevertheless, and for a variety of reasons, many probably based on physical practicalities, such as an inability immediately after birth to move any great distance and the frequent lack of privacy in an urban environment, a few women resorted to killing their babies. Despite being detested as an 'unnatural' crime, the immediate background to many cases of neo-natal infanticide were depressingly similar. Although the modern crime is often the result of extraordinary psychological pressures, that found in the eighteenth century was usually the consequence of much more mundane social and environmental circumstances. A general (i.e. nationwide) survey for the era suggests that many, if not the majority, of suspected perpetrators were servant girls, most killings were committed almost immediately after birth, and that the sex of the infant was largely irrelevant to the mother's decision; it was fear of the shame and practical consequences of giving birth that was the motivation.[347] A recent and localised survey of Cheshire has produced much the same pattern.[348] It also seems to have been fairly common in northern Europe generally. Thus, in eighteenth-century Stockholm, the typical infanticide defendant was also an unmarried female servant who had become pregnant by a fellow servant, the employee of a neighbouring household or, more rarely, by her master.[349] Similarly, the overwhelming majority of prosecuted offenders in the eighteenth century German cities of Hamburg and Nuremburg were maidservants.[350]

Unsurprisingly, then, these patterns and findings seem to have been substantially replicated in a specifically Metropolitan context. Thus, in eighteenth-century Westminster, the majority of bastard-bearers were either servants or ex-servants.[351] Their motivation in committing infanticide was

---

[344]M Ludovicus, *A Particular but Melancholy Account of the Great Hardship, Difficulties, and miseries that Those Unhappy and much to be pitied Creatures, the Common Women of the Town, Are plung'd into at this Juncture*, London, 1752, p.22.

[345]Evans, "'Unfortunate Objects', p.129.

[346] *The Times,* May 16th 1799, at p.3.

[347]Malcomson, "Infanticide in the eighteenth century" (1977) p.192.

[348]J P Dickinson and James A Sharpe, "Infanticide in early modern England: the Court of great Sessions at Chester, 1650-1800", *Infanticide: Historical Perspectives on Child Murder and Concealment, 1550-2000,* M Jackson (Ed.), Aldershot, Ashgate, 2000, p.49.

[349]Maria Kasperson, *Infanticide in Eighteenth Century Stockholm,* Paper delivered to The British Criminology Conference 2000.

[350]Otto Ulbricht, "Infanticide in eighteenth-century Germany" in *The German Underworld,* Routledge, Evans R.J. (Ed.), 1988, p.111.

[351]Nicholas Rogers, "Carnal Knowledge: Illegitimacy in Eighteenth-Century Westminster", *Journal of Social History* vol.xxiii, part 2, pp. 355-375, 1989, p.365.

usually practical. As Bernard Mandeville suggested in 1724, many young women, especially domestic employees, were "chiefly mov'd to this Action by the fear of losing their services, and wanting bread."[352] (Some also argued that shame was likely to be felt most acutely by women who were naturally most 'modest').[353] Usually, the woman involved had concealed her pregnancy as best she could during gestation, given birth in secret and then swiftly disposed of the baby's body.

The situation was probably even worse than in the provinces, because London was seen as sexually highly corrupting for female servants, especially those who came from the country, and women poured into the Metropolis as prospective servants "from all corners of the universe."[354] Jonas Hanay warned that they could not: "...suspect half the wicked arts which are played off to seduce young females."[355] The threat came from numerous quarters: masters, their sons, apprentices and male fellow servants. Although employers could, and often did, abuse their very considerable power, the social status of the putative fathers of illegitimate children in Westminster examinations was only significantly superior to that of the mothers (i.e. gentlemen, officers or masters etc.) in 33 per cent of cases, even at the start of the century. This figure fell steadily to 14.1 per cent by the 1780s, though the extent to which this reflected incidence or, instead, a change in upper class attitudes towards their responsibilities to illegitimate offspring is debateable.[356] Most genitors came from similar social backgrounds to their partners. Male servants, in particular, were frequently considered to be "very pert and saucy where they dare, and apt to take liberties" with their female colleagues. Apprentices were equally bad, and could not (legally) marry during their indentures, whatever they might promise. Women who thought that they might lure a man into marriage were vulnerable to men who were equally determined to entice them into sexual relationships, using the promise of wedlock as "bait."[357]

Of course, most domestic service was 'live in' and so provided accommodation, something that could be invaluable to desperate women who were already pregnant, further increasing the number of servant perpetrated infanticides. For example, in 1701, Christian Russell was impregnated by a man in Teddington who: "...having made a whore of her, would not afterwards make her his wife." She moved the short distance to London when a swelling belly

---

[352]Bernard De Mandeville, *A Modest Defence of Publick Stews*, London, printed for A. Moore, 1724, p.27.
[353]William Hunter, *On the Uncertainty of the Signs of Murder in the Case of Bastard Children*, London, printed for J Callow, London (first published 1783), 1812, p.9.
[354]Poussin, *Pretty Doings in a Protestant Nation*, p.4.
[355]Jonas Hanay, *Advice from Farmer Trueman to his Daughter Mary, upon her going to Service*, Edinburgh, 1789, p.209.
[356]Nicholas Rogers, "Carnal Knowledge: Illegitimacy in Eighteenth-Century Westminster", *Journal of Social History*, 1989, vol. xxiii, part 2, pp. 355-375, at pp.359-361
[357]Eliza Heywood, *A Present for a Servant-Maid*, London, 1743, pp.35-48.

threatened to reveal her true situation. Once there, she took employment as a servant and, 10 weeks later, gave birth to a baby that she immediately killed in her master's privy.[358] Interestingly, few of the women accused of infanticide appear to have been prostitutes, despite their heavy presence in the Metropolitan area. Many observers thought that street-walkers were able to control their fertility, notwithstanding the general lack of effective contraceptive techniques at this time. Others speculated that prostitutes did not conceive readily because of the physical effects of having sex with numerous different men, something that, it was thought, "imbecilitates the feminary parts."[359] No doubt, many more had recourse to abortion. Nevertheless, Bernard De Mandeville freely conceded that among the problems occasioned by prostitution was bastardy and its attendant risk of infanticide.[360] It would appear that streetwalkers who had recourse to such desperate measures were more successful in concealing their crimes than were domestic servants, possibly because they enjoyed more privacy.

## The Statistics for London

Between December 1714 and December 1799, 125 women (and four men) stood trial accused of infanticide. Of these, 20 were convicted and sentenced to death.[361] Thus, the conviction rate for women was about 16 per cent. Of the women who were convicted, nearly all had killed their babies within an hour of birth (usually almost immediately). Of the 20 dead babies, 19 infants (95 per cent) were described as illegitimate. There was a very roughly equal division between the sexes, with 11 female babies being killed, eight male ones, and one in which the sex of the infant was not identified in the reports. The case of the single married woman to be found guilty, Mary Morgan in 1724, appears to have occasioned surprise. Half (10) of those convicted were clearly domestic servants, though their job descriptions varied: cook, housemaid etc. The number may have been greater as the reports are not always clear; some others appear to have been the employees of small businesses. The great majority of women committed their crimes alone, though a handful were assisted by family members or friends who were sometimes charged as accessories; such cases, like that of Grace Gates, her mother and a male friend in 1752, often resulted in acquittals.

An examination of the Old Bailey Sessions Papers also reveals an unequal distribution amongst the 129 cases (including the four with male defendants) between 1714 and 1799. There are localised peaks in prosecutions for the crime. Thus, in 1716 there were two cases. In 1718 nine women were indicted (albeit that four came from one incident, with three being accessories), falling to four in

---

[358] Rev. Paul Lorrain, *The Ordinary of Newgate his Account of the Behaviour Confessions, and Dying Speeches of the Condemned Criminals that were Executed at Tyburn on Wednesday Jan. 28ᵗʰ 1701*, pp.1-2.

[359] Ludovicus, *A Particular but Melancholy Account*, at p. 5.

[360] De Mandeville, *A Modest Defence of Public Stews*, p.23.

[361] Francis Whalley is inaccurately listed as having been convicted on the search engine.

1719. As a general rule, however, prosecutions declined as the century advanced, despite a major increase in the Metropolitan population at the same time, from c.600, 000 to about a million. (On one analysis, London and Middlesex witnessed a halving in the number of indictments per capita between 1670 and 1770).[362] Thus, taking June 1757 as the mid-point between December 1714 and December 1799, only 36 of the 129 accused were indicted in the second half. Additionally, only five of the convictions occurred in this period, and none between the end of 1775 and 1799. The last 15 trials all produced acquittals. Not all women condemned to death were actually executed, some sentences being commuted, or at least not carried out, for a variety of reasons. Thus, according to the Ordinary's *Account*, during the eighteenth century only ten women were hanged for the crime at Tyburn, the normal place of execution. Significantly, these occurred prior to 1752, though several, such as Ann Hullock in 1760, have been missed by this source. Even so, they still constitute 12 per cent of all female executions at this place.[363] This pattern seems to have been broadly replicated nationwide and in the English colonies in America. However, and also perhaps significantly, the decline in convictions at the Old Bailey, prior to 1775, seems to have been less marked than elsewhere in the country. Thus, on the Northern Circuit Assizes, only six women were found guilty out of almost 200 indicted between 1720 and 1800, producing a conviction rate of about three per cent, less than a fifth of that found at the Old Bailey. Additionally, the last conviction at the Northern Assizes occurred in 1757, 18 years earlier than in London. [364]

## Infanticide and the Law.

Infanticide had not been viewed as seriously as other homicides in medieval England. Although deprecated, its prosecution was frequently left to the Church courts, which could not shed blood (though they might impose penance). Thus, in the early sixteenth-century, the unmarried Alice Ridyng was dealt with by such a forum after she gave birth at her father's home in Eton and, within hours of the birth, suffocated the child and then buried it in a dung heap.[365] However, during the second half of the sixteenth century, there was a significant increase in concern about the crime and it became a regular topic for discussion amongst Elizabethan legal writers such as Richard Crompton. The extent to which this was part of the era's general quest for order, a response to new social and

---

[362]Peter C Hoffer & N E H Hull *Murdering Mothers: Infanticide in England and New England 1558-1803*, New York, New York University Press, 1981, pp.66 and 80.

[363]Peter Linebough, *The London Hanged: Crime and Civil Society in the Eighteenth Century*, Harmondsworth, Penguin, 1991, pp.148-149.

[364]Mark Jackson, *New-born child murder*, p.3 and p.134, and Mark Jackson "Suspicious infant deaths: the statute of 1624 and medical evidence at coroners' inquests", *Legal Medicine in History*, M Clark and C Crawford (Eds.), Cambridge, CUP, 1994, p.70.

[365]Jeremy Goldberg,"Girls growing up in later medieval England", *History Today*, June 1995, vol.45, pp.25-32.

religious mores or the result of increasing early modern sentimentality towards children (itself perhaps the consequence of a reduction of the risks attendant on investing in such relationships) is difficult to assess. Whatever the reasons, the crime fell into the province of the secular courts, with prosecutions on indictment multiplying from the 1580s.[366] Again, this pattern was widely replicated elsewhere in Europe. Thus, in Sweden, the offence had also been dealt with by the Church courts in the medieval era, and did not have its own secular legal regulation until after the Reformation. It was only in the latter part of the sixteenth century that Swedish courts began to develop special procedures to deal with cases of infanticide.[367]

### The 1624 Statute

In England, the Crown faced inherent difficulties in prosecuting the offence. It was necessary to prove that the dead baby had been born alive and had then been deliberately killed to obtain a conviction. Given the surreptitious nature of the act, witnesses were rare, so the prosecution was usually forced to rely on circumstantial evidence, something that early modern juries were notably reluctant to convict on. This led to the passing of a special statute in 1624, after which most unmarried women accused of murdering their newborn children were tried under an 'Act to prevent the Destroying and Murthering of Bastard Children' (21 James I, cap. 27). In theory, the new Act apart, the only difference to ordinary murder cases involved in the killing of a baby was that the latter did not permit of a number of defences, such as self-defence, that were otherwise potentially open to those accused of killing adults: "…there can be no provocation, it cannot be manslaughter; that is the only difference: the single question is, whether the child was wilfully and intentionally killed or not?"[368] By contrast, the wording of the 1624 statute effectively reversed the burden of proof: "Whereas many lewd women that have been delivered of bastard children, to avoid their shame, and to escape punishment, do secretly bury or conceal the death of their children, and often, if the child is found dead, the said women do allege, that the said child was born dead … Be it enacted … in every such case the mother so offending, shall suffer death as in the case of murther, except such mother can make proof by one witness at the last that the child…was born dead." Strictly speaking, if narrowly construed, the statute was potentially less far-reaching than at first might have seemed the case. Arguably, it was concealing the baby's death, not its body post-mortem, that brought the presumption into play, and the intention of the mother was crucial in determining guilt.[369]

---

[366]Hoffer and Hull, *Murdering Mothers*, p.7.
[367]Kasperson, *Infanticide in Eighteenth Century Stockholm*.
[368]OBSP, Trial of Elizabeth Curtis, 15th Sept. 1784.
[369]Jackson, "Suspicious infant deaths", p.67.

In practice, the court records suggest that such subtleties were usually ignored in the early decades of the statute's existence, and that a woman who hid the death of an illegitimate newborn baby was presumed to have murdered it, unless she could prove it had been stillborn by calling a plausible witness. The statute is also indicative of a fairly advanced understanding of concepts of burden and standard of proof, despite occasional claims that these were largely a product of the following century.[370] The Act's effects were initially dramatic; in the decades immediately after 1624, up to 40 per cent of unmarried women accused of the crime were convicted and hanged. The number of prosecutions also rose significantly. These reached a peak during the Puritan attempt to put offences of immorality at the core of the criminal canon during the Interregnum. In Essex, for example, there were 14 in the years between 1656 and 1660, compared to only three between 1661 and 1665.[371] Similar provisions were also introduced into the criminal codes of many European countries, including Scotland, Denmark, Sweden and France.[372] Indeed, it has been argued that there was an early modern European 'infanticide craze', costlier in lives than that over witches.[373] Thus, faced by the same evidential problems as were found in England, the Swedish legislature developed similar solutions. The most important of these meant that an accused unmarried woman was considered to have murdered her child if she had concealed her pregnancy, deliberately given birth in solitude and then hidden the body of the dead baby. As in England, this meant the tacit abandoning of accepted notions of due process.[374] In Scotland, an infanticide statute passed (rather late in the era) by the Scottish Parliament in 1690 was based, to a significant degree, on the English Act of 1624, and had much the same evidential effect.[375] France had introduced legislation as early as 1556, requiring "declarations de grossesse" by pregnant but unmarried women, so that an 'unregistered' dead baby was presumed to have been murdered.

In theory, given that it remained in force until 1803, unmarried English women accused of infanticide during the eighteenth century had to avoid its draconian provisions, if at all possible. The legal operation of the statute, and one way of circumventing it, can be seen in a case from 1717. This involved a servant named Ann Hasle, from St. Giles without Cripplegate, who was accused of drowning her newborn baby in a large copper. On the discovery of its body, Hasle claimed that the infant had been stillborn. Although a midwife and surgeon who examined its body gave evidence that there were no marks on the baby indicative of injury or drowning, the accused woman still faced the reverse

---

[370]Barbara Shapiro, "To A Moral Certainty: Theories of Knowledge and Anglo-American Juries 1600-1850", *Hastings Law Journal*, 1986, vol. 38, p.156.

[371]Keith Wrightson, "Infanticide in earlier Seventeenth-Century England", *The German Underworld*, Evans R J (Ed.), London, Routledge, 1975, p.12.

[372]Blackstone, *Commentaries on the Laws of England*, vol. 4, p. 198.

[373]Dickinson and Sharpe, "Infanticide in early modern England, pp.35-36.

[374]Kasperson, *Infanticide in Eighteenth Century Stockholm*.

[375]Its use north of the Border declined rapidly after 1750, the statute being repealed in 1809.

onus clause contained in the 1624 Act. Indeed, the wording of the Act was read to the jury so that they appreciated that: "…concealing the Birth and Death of Bastard-Children should make the Mothers deem'd the Murtherers of them." The prisoner, too, realized that she had to "put her self out of the Reach of this Act." To do this, she alleged that she had been a married woman at the time of conception, and claimed that her husband had since died. Prior to Hardwicke's Marriage Act of 1753 the documentation of such events was often poor, and she called her sister to prove her nuptials. Her evidence on this issue being accepted, Hasle was "deemed not to be affected by that [1624] Statute." This transformed the situation, as it then became a normal murder case and thus the: "Prosecutor's Business to prove the Child was born alive and that she murthered it." The lack of conclusive evidence on this issue was enough to create a doubt in the jurors' minds, and she was acquitted.[376]

The working of the 1624 Act can also be seen in a case from 1784 in which it was, again, not operative, because there had been no Grand Jury indictment under the Jacobean law, so that the barrister prosecuting the case had to inform the petty jury that because it was a trial: "…upon the Coroner's Inquisition at common law, not under any indictment on the [1624] statute, it is necessary that there should be some evidence to satisfy you, that the mother by violence and wilfully was the cause of the child's death."[377] In 1745, an interesting legal point was raised by the Old Bailey trial of James Leger, who was accused of being an accessory to an infanticide allegedly committed by Grace Usop, in his house. Unusually for the era, Leger was legally represented (something that had only been possible for a decade). His counsel argued that, as a married man, unlike the accused woman, he, too, was not affected by the statute, and thus it "must first [be] proved that the child was born alive" before he could be convicted. He, too, was acquitted.

### The Act in Practice

However, in many eighteenth century trials it *should* have been almost impossible to avoid the theoretical reach of the 1624 Act. Despite this, it seems that the statute was being regularly ignored by judges and juries by the late 1600s, and almost entirely disregarded after the middle of the following century, as the reverse onus clause was increasingly seen as draconian and smacking: "…pretty strongly of severity, in making the concealment of the death almost conclusive evidence of the child's being murdered by the mother."[378] This was quite overtly recognised at the time, although one sessions report from 1743 suggested, wholly implausibly, that ignorance of the statute was widespread, and that such killings would "not so frequently occur" if it was better known.[379]

---

[376] OBSP, Trial of Ann Hasle, 17th July 1717.
[377] OBSP, Trial of Elizabeth Curtis, 15th Sept. 1784.
[378] Blackstone, *Commentaries on the Laws of England*, p. 198.
[379] OBSP, Trial of Elizabeth Shuddrick, 12th Oct 1743.

Apparently more sympathetic judges and juries began to accept a range of special defences, such as 'benefit of linen', in which the defendant demonstrated that she had made bed clothes and similar items in preparation for the birth of her baby, and 'want of help', in which the defendant argued that the infant died despite her manifest efforts to secure assistance. Indeed, whatever the original intention of the Jacobean legislators, the precise, and rather technical, wording of the 1624 Act did provide *some* legal justification for such defences. Thus, as early as 1664, Sir John Kelyng had concluded that a woman who knocked for help, *during* her labour, was not caught by the statute.[380] Both of these defences are well evidenced in the Old Bailey Sessions Papers. Typically, in 1718, Francis Bolanson was acquitted at trial, largely because she had "made provision" for her child.[381] By the late eighteenth century, this defence was being applied in an almost mechanistic fashion, so that in 1784, a prosecuting barrister observed in court that he could not blame the Grand Jury for earlier returning an infanticide bill *ignoramus* in his case, as the woman concerned had "provided some things for the child."[382] Strictly speaking, the significance of such evidence should have been a matter for the trial jury.

Some, like Daniel Defoe, complained bitterly about the willingness of seemingly intelligent men to accept such flimsy defences and their gullibility in believing that the presence of a 'scrap' of linen disproved a deliberate killing. He feared that women contemplating infanticide were well aware of this and planned for it, either before or after committing their killings.[383] Although this may seem far-fetched, in fairness to Defoe it should be noted that there were occasional cases that supported his claim. Thus, in 1734, when Mercy Hornby asked one of the prosecution witnesses if she had not discovered children's bed linen in her trunk, the witness acknowledged finding an infant's shirt, blanket, night cap and other items there, but damningly added that these had not been discovered until a day after the crime came to light, and suggested it was: "…much to be fear'd, that you did not put them there; for indeed I was inform'd they were borrow'd of a Neighbour."

However, and even more significantly, acquittals were frequently being secured even in the complete absence of these special defences. Indeed, during the 1700s, it seems that the 1624 statute was only expressly mentioned to Old Bailey jurors on rare occasions and that numerous judges were ignoring it without having a fig-leaf of legitimacy for doing so. By the 1760s, William Blackstone could frankly note that the statute's implementation had been severely watered down: "I apprehend it has of late years been usual with us in England, upon trials for this offence to require some sort of presumptive evidence that the child was born alive, before the other constrained presumption

---

[380]Jackson, "Suspicious infant deaths", p.67.
[381]OBSP, Trial of Francis Bolanson, 15th Oct 1718.
[382]OBSP, Trial of Elizabeth Curtis, 15th Sept 1784.
[383]Defoe, *The Generous Projector*, p.10.

(that the child, whose death is concealed, was therefore killed by it's parent) is admitted to convict the prisoner."[384] The Act was certainly not unique in experiencing this fate. The early modern era was much more willing than the present age to allow statutes to fall into desuetude. This was widely recognised, and even approved, by eminent judges, who sometimes urged that if penal laws had been: "…sleepers of long, or if they be grown unfit for the present time, [they should] be by wise judges confined in the execution."[385] Indeed, in the eighteenth century, the jurist William Eden cited the court's practice of dispensing with the 1624 Act as a classic illustration of the way in which: "…cruel laws have a natural tendency to their own dissolution in the abhorrence of mankind."[386] However, as Eden's remark also suggests, such a process did not occur at random. Statutes were abandoned when they were considered anachronistic. Like witchcraft prosecutions, the decline in convictions under the Act reflects a transformation in judicial and, via the jury, social, attitudes. Judges were no longer striving after guilty verdicts and juries were happy to follow their lead. The 1624 statute was belatedly repealed in 1803, when all infanticides became subject to the same evidential rules as other types of murder. Indeed, the part of the 1624 Act that "subjects the offendor to death" had been expressly recommended for repeal by a parliamentary committee in 1772, though nothing came of this proposal.[387] There were also several calls for abolition from individual M.P.s.

Further complicating the issue, on rare occasions the 1624 Act *was* actively invoked in the capital during the first half of the century. Thus, in January 1723, Mary Radford was convicted and sentenced to death for the murder of her newborn infant, although it was frail and very small and the prisoner's mistress testified that she was an apparent simpleton. Despite this: "The prisoner's Case being evidently within the Statute for Bastard Children, the Jury found her guilty." Similarly, at the trial of Mercy Hornby in 1734, the statute was read in full to the jury before they considered their verdict. As with several other cases in which this happened, a guilty verdict was returned. Why such cases should occur is hard to explain. It might have been a reflection of personal idiosyncrasy or 'old fashioned' attitudes on the part of the presiding judge (though the collegiate nature of Old Bailey benches would argue against this); it could have been a response to a sudden 'panic' about infanticide in the wider community, or even personal antipathy towards the individual accused on the part of judge or jurors. Whatever the motivation, it does seem that some judges would stress the provision to secure convictions in cases where they thought a guilty verdict was

---

[384] Blackstone, *Commentaries on the Laws of England*, p. 198.
[385] Francis Bacon, "On Judicature", *The Essays*, London, Everyman edn. J M Dent, 1906, pp.162-165.
[386] Jackson, "Suspicious infant deaths", p.74.
[387] Anon, "The Criminal laws as they relate to capital offences", *Journals of the House of Commons* vol.33, 1772/03/04, reprinted 1803, p.612.

deserved. Where they were not so persuaded, they would tacitly downplay or ignore it.

*Securing an Infanticide Conviction*

Despite such cases, to secure an infanticide conviction in the eighteenth century it was normally: "…necessary that there should be clear proof of the child's being born alive, and having appearances of violence, and that the Jury should be clearly satisfied that the mother intentionally killed the child."[388] Essentially, this was the traditional common law legal onus for all murder prosecutions. As a result, it was unusual to see a conviction in the London area unless the method used to kill the infant was unequivocally murder or, if the physical evidence of deliberate murder was absent, the suspect made explicit admissions to the crime, whether to an examining JP, coroner or third party. One way of proving deliberate killing was to find wounds that were clearly of human origin, unlike the majority of cases in which smothering, strangling or drowning appear to have been the likely cause of death. Thus, Mary Morgan's conviction in February 1724 was the result of her baby having two stab wounds to its belly, one of which was so deep that its "Bowels came out."[389] In 1737, Mary Shrewsbury was convicted and sentenced to execution after cutting the throat of her illegitimate baby so deeply that: "It could not be cut worse, unless it's Head had been cut quite off."

The importance of such incontrovertible injury to sustaining a prosecution was widely appreciated, as can be seen from the reaction of Ann Palmer, a midwife instructed by a Parish Officer to examine Shrewsbury. After she adduced an admission from the suspect that she had thrown her baby's body into a vault, accompanied by a claim that it was dead when she did so, Palmer immediately responded by saying: "I hope you have not havock'd it."[390] This was in marked contrast to the situation that had prevailed in the seventeenth century. During that era, in Essex, for example, although prosecutions in which blows were the alleged cause of death were the least likely to result in acquittals, well over half of those accused of killing their babies by strangulation, suffocation or drowning were also convicted and sentenced to hang.[391] However, where such methods of killing were employed in the eighteenth century they usually required specially incriminating circumstantial factors to produce a conviction. This was partly because eighteenth-century juries were willing to accept faintly plausible, if far fetched, explanations for otherwise suspicious facts in a way that their predecessors had not. For example, breeches deliveries apart, in the usual course of birth the neck and head of a baby appears first and is consequently the most obvious place for an unaided mother to "lay hold of to assist herself." In doing

[388]OBSP, Trial of Elizabeth Curtis, 15th Sept 1784.
[389]OBSP, Trial of Mary Morgan, 26th Feb 1724.
[390]OBSP, Trial of Mary Shrewsbury, 16th Feb. 1737.
[391]Wrightson, "Infanticide in earlier seventeenth-century England", vol. 15, p.15.

this, it was sometimes argued, she might inadvertently put pressure on the child's throat, strangling it. Similarly, in 1778, although the baby of a servant, Anne Taylor, was recovered from the privy of her master's house, and a surgeon gave evidence that its head was almost severed from its body, the court 'accepted' her argument that this was the result of her self-delivering it or, alternatively, of it slipping into a deep and sharp edged privy while she was relieving herself.[392] As this case suggests, the requirement that evidence of an injury's provenance be unequivocal grew progressively stronger as the century advanced.

Making admissions to the crime, even if the injuries were not clear-cut, could also produce a guilty verdict. Thus, in 1744, Ann Terry was convicted of throwing her baby to its death because she openly admitted doing it "to hide her shame."[393] In like manner, in 1761, Esther Rowden was found guilty after making admissions to a woman from St. Martin's-workhouse, whose lying-in room she had used after giving birth. This woman had pressed Rowden about widespread suspicion that she had recently given birth and eventually extracted a confession as to where the infant's body was to be found and, far more seriously, that her baby had been born alive and then been strangled with a string.[394]

## Special Features of Metropolitan Infanticide

### Disposal of the Body

After a baby had been killed, its mother would have to dispose of its body. A failure to hide the corpse or gore effectively was likely to lead to exposure. Thus, in 1736, Jane Cooper left her baby's corpse sewn up in a bundle, with a friend, for 'safe-keeping', with strict orders that no one be allowed to open it. However, her friend ignored this command when, after a few days, the package began to smell like rotting meat and exude maggots. This led to Cooper's arrest. Similarly, in 1775, a maid employed at the Roe-Buck tavern in Lewisham, south of the Thames, apparently got up suddenly from her dinner, went into an adjoining stable, and gave birth to a baby boy: "...which she immediately killed on the spot, by beating out its brains, either with a stick or the heel of her shoe." She then returned to her meal. However, one of the other diners, appreciating what had happened, went to "proper persons" and informed on her, so that she was arrested and the evidence discovered.[395]

Concealment posed far greater problems in an urban environment than in the countryside. In rural areas, bodies could be buried in fields and woods, submerged in ponds, lakes and rivers or even burnt. This was not usually

---

[392]OBSP, Trial of Anne Taylor, 9th Dec 1778.
[393]OBSP, Trial of Ann Terry, 10th May 1744.
[394]OBSP, Trial of Esther Rowden, 21st Oct 1761.
[395]*Middlesex Journal,* May 30-June 1, 1775.

possible in London and explains the astonishingly high number of cases in which the infant's body was discovered in a 'house of office', 'little room' or 'vault' (i.e., a public or domestic privy), producing routine newspaper observations such as: "Yesterday, a Servant was committed to Newgate for murdering her Bastard-Child, by throwing it into a House of Office."[396] Thus, taking the 15 prosecutions for infanticide from January 1760 to the end of 1770, over half (eight) involved the use of a privy. Sometimes, it had not been employed merely to dispose of the baby's corpse, but was actually the method by which it was killed, usually by smothering as a result of immersion. So common was this, that when the mistress of Ann Bartleet, a nursery maid, suspected that her employee was pregnant, she ordered another servant to sleep with her and to ensure that their room was kept locked so that Ann could not creep downstairs to the privy to deliver and kill her offspring.[397] Occasionally, the condition of the deposits of excrement in such places could itself become a vital issue at trial, especially when, as periodically occurred, the accused woman claimed that she had suddenly given birth as she defecated and then been unable to retain hold of her (slippery) baby. As a result, those responsible for emptying privies might be called to give evidence on how deep and liquid the 'night-soil' in them was. If it was soft and could readily cover a newborn baby it was more likely to have been deliberately chosen. If firm and shallow, the woman's account became more plausible.

*Coming to Notice*

The discovery of infanticide usually came from a failure to conceal the telltale signs of pregnancy, birth or the infant's body from neighbours. The Metropolitan area differed little from the provinces in how this occurred. However, the relative lack of privacy made concealment much harder. One other factor that made London unusual was the social isolation of many female employees. In Cheshire, for example, it seems that a high proportion of cases in which exposure for the crime was avoided involved close family members rallying round the pregnant woman to assist in hiding the birth.[398] The city attracted huge numbers of immigrants from all over the country and beyond. Of the women hanged (for all crimes) at Tyburn between 1703 and 1772, only 35 per cent had been born in London, and 19 per cent came from as far away as Ireland.[399] Many Metropolitan women, miles from their places of origin, had no prospect of any form of help in concealing a killing. Of course, it also meant an absence of social support to encourage them to keep a baby and intimate family pressure against killing it.

---

[396]*The Post-Boy,* 22-24 November 1711.
[397]Randolph Trumbach, *Sex and the Gender Revolution: Heterosexuality and the Third Gender in Enlightenment London,* vol.1, Chicago: University of Chicago Press, 1998, at p.294.
[398]Dickinson and Sharpe, "Infanticide in Early Modern England", p.36.
[399]Linebough, *The London Hanged,* p.143.

Frequently, births came to light after someone was prompted to make enquiries about a sudden loss of weight in the suspected woman, the discovery of blood and afterbirth on the floor, soiled linen or the medical problems often attendant on an unassisted delivery. Of course, not everyone who found out about such an event would inform on the mother. In 1737, Elizabeth Bell appears to have been sympathetic to the plight of her lodger. After seeing blood, being told by the young woman that she had miscarried, and despite the circumstances being extremely suspicious, she merely fetched her lodger some hot ale, and then went to bed, after being sworn to secrecy. The court was unimpressed by her conduct, telling her: "You have behav'd very ill in this Affair, and you deserve to be severely reprimanded. You saw all the Symptoms of the Woman's being deliver'd, and instead of making a Discovery, you ran out of the Way."[400] How common such a reaction was is hard to establish. However, it does not appear to have been typical. In the North of England, it has been noted that there was considerable popular hostility towards those who committed infanticide, and this seems to have been matched in London. Thus, in 1747, it was observed that a misguided and mistaken allegation of baby killing in a poor area meant that the accused woman was "like to fall a sacrifice to the Mob."[401]

Many people, especially women, seem to have gone out of their way to expose such cases. Typically, one landlady whose newly arrived lodger appeared to have given birth, locked her into the house and went for the authorities. Similarly, Rebecca Prince, from St. Brides parish, was accused of murdering her baby after she gave soiled linen to another woman to wash. This woman: "...perceiv'd some Tokens on them, that made her suspect the Prisoner had had a Child, whereupon she went and acquainted her [Prince's] Mistress." In turn, her employer immediately sent for a midwife who examined Prince and extracted a confession.[402] It has been noted that in the North East of England during this period, women were instrumental in detecting most cases of newborn child killing.[403] This seems to accord with the situation in the Metropolitan area. (It was also noted in contemporary France, that it was popular opinion, particularly the "clamor" of women, that was often the driving force behind infanticide prosecutions).[404]

It was not simply the birth that presented problems. Unlike the supportive female groups that assembled for legitimate childbirth, for those who became pregnant out of wedlock, other women, even if neighbours, companions or

---

[400]OBSP, Trial of Mary Shrewsbury, 16th Feb.1737.
[401]OBSP, Trial of Elizabeth Fletcher, 9th Sept 1747.
[402]OBSP, Trial of Rebecca Prince, 27th Feb 1723.
[403]Gwenda Morgan and Peter Rushton, *Rogues, Thieves and the Rule of Law: The Problem of Law Enforcement in Northeast England*, London, University College London Press, 1998, p.117.
[404]Tracey Rizzo: "Between Dishonor and Death: infanticides in the *Causes celebres* of eighteenth-century France" *Women's History Review*, vol.13, no.1, 2004, at p.11

friends, were potential dangers, threatening to expose their condition.[405] Most servant girls would have to hide their pregnancy and its tell tale signs in an environment that afforded little privacy, domestic staff usually sharing rooms and frequently sharing beds. Morning sickness could be explained away as a stomach upset, unless very severe. However, rapid and localised weight gain was much harder to account for. Although the loose and voluminous shifts of the era gave some scope for concealment, it was often not enough. As a result, when challenged, some women, such as Mary Mussen in 1757, claimed to be suffering from a medical condition, such as the dropsy.[406] Others would allege that they had a familial history of putting on weight in a distinctive fashion, one suspect averring that her prominent pot-belly was shared by all her relatives. Ann Haywood attributed her portliness to the bunching of her stays and petticoats.[407] Nevertheless, in many cases it was widely suspected that individuals were pregnant long before they actually gave birth, especially if they continued with the same employer throughout the pregnancy (London was noted for its very high turnover of domestic staff, something which afforded an opportunity to avoid continuous surveillance). Thus, Martha Shackleton's master had "long suspected" she was pregnant in 1743. Similarly, Mussen's employer had been suspicious for at least two months. Fellow servants, who lived more intimately with the women, would often notice the symptoms earlier and frequently seem to have ignored them, in what may almost have amounted to a 'code of silence'.

## Involving the Authorities

Infanticide was a serious felony. However, it differed from other grave crimes in the diverse manner in which the authorities became involved, especially in the Metropolis. Although a midwife would usually investigate at an early stage of proceedings, it was often the suspected woman's neighbours who called her in. Nevertheless, a variety of local and public officials might also become involved. Obviously, if an infant's body was discovered in a public place, a constable might initiate an enquiry, as Peter Debrather did in 1735.[408] Church-wardens, overseers of the poor and parish beadles might also become involved. Thus, in 1737, a Mr. Bay noted that he was called to the scene of an alleged infanticide in Moorfields, by virtue of his position as an overseer. Once there, he put a guard on the house and made other arrangements for the investigation. In theory, most women accused of the crime should have been examined by a magistrate. However, this does not always appear to have been a very important part of the process. This may have been because it was appreciated that the coroner would also question them. Nevertheless, the magisterial questioning could result in

---

[405]Laura Gowing, "Secret Birth and Infanticide in Seventeenth-Century England", *Past and Present*, vol.156, 1997, at pp.157-187.
[406]OBSP, Trial of Mary Mussen, 26th May 1757.
[407]OBSP, Trial of Ann Haywood, 8th Dec. 1762.
[408]OBSP, Trial of Elizabeth Ambrook, 16th Jan 1735.

admissions that were hard to deny later at trial. Thus, in June 1727, after Elizabeth Archer fled to London, having killed her baby in Staffordshire, she "sign'd her Confession of the Fact" in front of Sir Thomas Clarges JP Although she was returned for trial to her native county's Assizes, her confession would go with her.[409]

## The Coroner's Role

A coroner and his jury would investigate cases of infanticide, like any other form of homicide. They might view a surgeon's autopsy, and would receive other evidence at their hearing. This investigation was significant, because coroners had the power to commit cases for trial direct to the Old Bailey without the matter having to be indicted by the Grand Jury. Normally, of course, that body would consider the case as well, and, in most cases where the coroner had decided there should be a hearing, the Grand Jury would also find a *billa vera* ('true bill'), so that the defendant would stand trial on both the coroner's Inquisition (a standard parchment document) and the Grand Jury indictment. However, this was not *invariably* the case. Coroners seem to have been rather more willing to commit for trial than Grand Juries, apparently not requiring so clear-cut a prima facie case. (Indeed, some observers complained that eighteenth century coroners' jurors were too willing to attribute suspicious deaths to murder).[410] As a result, the Grand Jury would sometimes return a finding of *ignoramus* on the bill of indictment and trial would take place solely on the coroner's inquisition. This occurred, for example, at the trial of Elizabeth Fletcher in 1741, and of Elizabeth Curtis in 1784. Curtis was prosecuted by the celebrated barrister William Garrow, who felt that it was necessary to open the trial by informing the jury about the unusual nature of the committal, as normally: "...after the inquisition is found, and the woman committed, the next step in point of law is to prefer an indictment before the grand Jury for the same offence, that was preferred [in this case], and has been thrown out."[411] Almost invariably, in trials held solely on a coroner's inquisition, an acquittal followed.

Occasionally, however, the converse could happen; for example, where a coroner negligently failed to submit an inquisition to the Old Bailey. Thus, at the trial of Frances Whalley in October 1761, the hearing took place solely on the Grand Jury indictment, and the coroner for Middlesex, George Grew, was fined £50 for failing to return an inquisition and not appearing in person at the Old Bailey. The coroner's investigation and the information it threw up could also be alluded to in evidence given at the subsequent trial on indictment. Thus, at Whalley's hearing, a constable involved in the case was asked if an autopsy had been performed on the baby's body in open court, to which he replied "No it

---

[409] *The British Journal*, 17 June 1727.
[410] R Baldwin, *Considerations on some laws relating to the office of Coroner*, Newcastle, printed for T. Saint, 1776, p.63.
[411] OBSP, Trial of Elizabeth Curtis, 15th Sept. 1784.

was not; it lay in the room all the time the jury sat." The coroner's oral examination of the accused woman would also be produced for the court, sometimes in person by the coroner.

## Expert Evidence

The use of 'expert' witnesses in criminal trials, though sanctioned in England for over 150 years before 1700, was still rare in the eighteenth century. However, cases of infanticide were an important exception to this general situation, especially in and about the London area. There were good reasons for this. Giving birth was an extremely dangerous business throughout the era and many children were stillborn for entirely natural reasons. For example, in one week in 1680, returns from the bills of mortality for 131 Metropolitan parishes show that there were 236 Christenings and 12 children who were still born.[412] This was typical for the whole of the following century. In the year 1707, the same area produced 547 still born infants; in 1727, the figure was 590; in 1764, it was 729, and in 1784 it was 528.[413] This meant that claims that a baby had been 'dead on arrival' were often very plausible. As a result, infanticide frequently attracted medical opinion evidence to rebut such a defence. At least ten per cent of all eighteenth and early nineteenth century prosecutions in which expert medical evidence was called at the Old Bailey involved such cases.

This type of evidence was also readily available in London, the centre of England's medical profession. It was usually given in the form of testimony from midwives and surgeons or (very much less frequently) physicians and apothecaries, who had examined the infant's body and who could give evidence about what was 'normal'.[414] Of the 20 cases alone in which convictions were secured, at least 18 involved the calling of a midwife *or* a doctor (usually a surgeon), and at least six cases involved both (including William Complin, in September 1765, who described himself as both "surgeon and man-midwife").[415] In the others, at least one professional was called (midwives being more common than surgeons as sole expert witness). This is a minimum figure; the existence of some experts may not have been mentioned in the sketchier trial reports. Even in the 18 cases between the start of 1740 and the end of 1750, which resulted in acquittals, the great majority involved the calling of a medical expert.

The use of different types of professional at the same trial was partly because many infanticide cases raised two distinct medical questions: firstly, whether an infant had been born (rather than miscarried); and secondly, whether it had survived birth and then been deliberately killed. The era's usual obstetrical

---

[412]British Library tract L.23.C.7.(62)
[413]Hoffer and Hull, *Murdering Mothers*, pp.186-187.
[414]Stephen Landsman, "One hundred years of rectitude: medical witnesses at the Old Bailey 1717-1817", *Law and History Review*, vol.16, 1998, p.451.
[415]OBSP, Trial of Maria Jenkins, 18th Sept.1765.

practice meant that the first issue was often addressed by a midwife, while the second, if contested, was more likely to come within the remit of a surgeon (though the division was not rigid). Thus, in 1750, when a surgeon giving evidence strayed outside his area of primary expertise, the Court asked: "Are you [also] a man midwife?"[416] On gynaecological issues, if nothing else, a "skillful woman" might be accorded primacy. Indeed, occasionally, especially early in the period, an ordinary female witness who had given birth could be treated as a *de facto* expert and asked to give an opinion to (male) judges and juries on a natal issue, as occurred when Mary Soy's servant of six weeks was taken ill with stomach pains in 1784; her mistress was asked if she had had children, and when she responded in the affirmative ("Four dead ones"), was questioned about whether her servant's symptoms were reminiscent of labour pains. However, as the century advanced, the courts became increasingly reluctant to allow lay people to venture such opinions.

A large majority of those who gave expert testimony did so on behalf of the Crown, rather than the defendant, this being an extreme version of the general pattern in the period, and unsurprising, given the differences in resources and education between those representing the authorities and suspects. Only a handful of eighteenth-century Old Bailey infanticide cases produced a 'battle of experts' between prosecution and defence witnesses. However, this did not mean that unchallenged medical experts were necessarily partisan or actively sought a conviction, especially early in the century, when notions of adversariality were weaker. Thus, in the unusual case of Mary Mullen, in 1757, in which two medical witnesses appeared for the Crown and another for the defendant, each expert readily conceded the limits of his or her knowledge and that they might be mistaken in their conclusions. All were restrained in giving their testimony, and none appear to have seen their role as that of advocate.[417]

There seems to have been a greater general willingness to consider experts, especially those instructed by public authorities such as a JP or coroner, as being 'neutral', and many experts seem to have shared such a view. Nevertheless, Defoe was convinced that numerous acquittals were being secured by bogus defence experts, paid for the purpose, and that for infanticide defendants it was common practice: "...to hire a set of old–bedlams, or pretended midwives, who make it their trade to bring them off for three or four guineas, having got the ready rote of swearing the child was not at its full growth."[418] However, this was certainly not invariably the case. Mercy Hornby was damned by the testimony of a mid-wife she herself had sent for, after exposure, to ensure the removal of the afterbirth. How helpful such evidence was is a matter of debate. In 1783, Dr. William Hunter was very sceptical about the value of medical testimony in infanticide cases. He felt that many who gave it did not have sufficient specialist

---

[416]OBSP, Trial of Jane Trigg, 12th Sept.1750.
[417]Landsman, "One Hundred years of Rectitude", p.451 and p.476.
[418]Defoe, *The Generous Projector*, p.9.

experience in the subject, were "not so conversant with science as the world may think", sometimes mistook natural marks for violence and were inclined to express their views to coroners and courts too quickly and too firmly.[419]

Bodies might be examined for signs of violence and autopsies performed, often under a coroner's supervision, to establish whether the child was born alive or dead. Given that the 1624 Act was widely ignored, establishing a live birth was usually vital to a successful prosecution, as a claim to have suffered the miscarriage of a premature baby was an obvious defence. To establish that an infant had gone to term, evidence might be given on the presence of nails, hair and its general size. Even if gestation was complete, it did not prove that the baby was alive at birth. To do this, a number of tests, of varying degrees of scientific value, were developed and other indicators of a live birth identified. One regular test conducted at infant autopsies was to remove and then float the baby's lungs in a bowl of water, on the basis that their floating would be indicative of the presence of air. This was deemed to be a sign that the infant had breathed after (a live) birth. This test was often accorded considerable significance by surgeons such as Richard Stevens (1750) in the early and middle decades of the 1700s. It was also widely use din parts of continental Europe, including eighteenth-century France.[420]

Nevertheless, as the eighteenth century advanced, many Metropolitan doctors appear to have become more sceptical about its value. Thus, at a trial in 1762, both surgeon and man-midwife were cautious about its worth, both rejecting the suggestion from the court that it 'proved' the issue, and one noting that he had very recently seen a 'false positive' returned from the test in controlled conditions.[421] For some, such doubts matured into near contempt for the test by the later decades of the century, so that the surgeon at Elizabeth Parkins' trial in 1771 observed that although its validity was "formerly thought decisive; but now that opinion is exploded."[422] At Anne Taylor's trial, in 1778, a witness, mentioning that the coroner had ordered the "usual experiment" to be made on the baby's lungs, was firmly told by the court: "That is nothing. We never suffer that to be given in evidence."[423] Other judges, however, even at the Old Bailey, continued to accord it value, while accepting, as the court observed at the trial of Ann Spinton in 1771, that it was not conclusive of the issue. Indeed, many surgeons were still according some significance to what they called the 'hydrostatic test' in the early 1830s, albeit qualifying it so heavily as to render it as little more than indicative of post-natal survival.[424] Whatever its value, there

---

[419]Hunter, *On the Uncertainty of the Signs of Murder*, p.18.

[420]Tracey Rizzo, "Between Dishonor and Death: infanticides in the *Causes celebres* of eighteenth-century France", *Women's History Review*, vol.13, no.1, 2004, at p.14.

[421]OBSP, Trial of Mary Samuel, 8th Dec. 1762.

[422]OBSP, Trial of Elizabeth Parkins,10th April 1771.

[423]OBSP, Trial of Anne Taylor, 9th Dec 1778.

[424]Charles Severn, *First Lines of the Practice of midwifery: to which are added remarks on the forensic evidence requisite in cases of foeticide and infanticide*, London, published by S Highly, 1831, pp.140-141.

were also instances of highly sophisticated forensic analysis, based on the close observation of a dead baby's body. Thus, in 1757, a testifying surgeon noted the presence of dried blood in the nostrils of an infant whose throat had been cut. He explained its presence as being the result of this injury having been inflicted while the baby was still breathing (and thus alive) and its breath having then forced the blood upward. The jury convicted.[425]

Another well-recognised test was to examine the baby's body to see if it had its fists clenched, something popularly thought to be a sign that it was dead at birth. One of the main reasons for Mabe's acquittal in 1718 was: "...the opinion of the Midwife and Court, that a child that is new born, if alive, [is born] with its hands expanded."[426] The discovery of faeces, passed by a newly delivered infant, was also viewed as indicative of a live birth. Indeed, in 1757, Ann Farrer, a midwife, was adamant that it was impossible for a dead baby to pass a stool.[427] Obviously, a baby's crying after delivery was also conclusive if established. By contrast, there were also signs that were viewed as indicative of a still-birth. The position of the afterbirth might be one of these. Thus, the midwife who examined Rebecca Prince's baby, after it was retrieved from a vault in 1723, believed the child was still born because "what should have come away with it, came not away till the Night after."[428] If it was necessary to prove that a woman had recently given birth, perhaps because a baby's body had been found outside the suspected mother's personal quarters and she resolutely denied that it was hers, evidence could be given that she had been searched by a midwife, either at home or when being questioned by a JP, and found, *inter alia*, to be lactating, as occurred with Francis Whalley. However, gynaecological knowledge was uncertain and the accepted signs of recent pregnancy could often be the subject of alternative explanations. Some of these tests (always carried out by women) seem to have come close to being physical assaults, but were already centuries old by the eighteenth century, as evidenced by Alice Ridyng's experiences in the early 1500s.

Nevertheless, as some of these case studies indicate, despite the importance given to medical testimony it was widely recognised, even at the time, that it was still a rather inexact science and thus frequently inconclusive. As a result, it was probably more likely to help a defendant, by raising a doubt, than to advance a prosecution by eliminating one. This was expressly recognised in 1782, when a presiding judge observed that floating a dead baby's lungs was only conclusive if the test favoured the accused. It was merely indicative if the converse occurred: "... it has been held to be conclusive, if the lungs sink; but not to be conclusive, if they float: it is a common experiment, and, in that case, gives a degree of

---

[425]Landsman, "One Hundred Years of Rectitude", p.451.
[426]OBSP, Trial of Ann Mabe, 27th Feb 1718.
[427]OBSP, Trial of Mary Mussen, 26th May 1757.
[428]OBSP, Trial of Rebecca Prince, 27th Feb 1723.

probability." The surgeon being questioned agreed with the court's general assessment of current medical opinion.[429]

Interestingly, the psychiatric condition of the mother appears to have provided few avenues of defence for an accused woman in England (unlike France), unless, like Mary Tate in 1714, she had a longstanding previous history of mental illness. Tate "talk'd very ramblingly" at her hearing and was able to call witnesses to say that she had been considered ill for several years. She was acquitted as 'non compos mentis'.[430]

## The Eighteenth-Century Legacy

The attitudes towards infanticide established during the eighteenth century were to lay the foundations for those that were prevalent in the following one. Many observers thought the crime remained widespread in the 1800s. Indeed, there were claims in the mid-nineteenth century, by men such as Dr. Lankester (an M.P. and Middlesex coroner), that in London the police thought no more of finding a dead newborn's body than they did that of a cat or dog. Lankester estimated that there could be thousands of women living in London alone who had secretly disposed of a baby without being discovered. Benjamin Disraeli even suggested that it might be as common in England as it was on the banks of the river Ganges.[431] (Interestingly, there was considerable and ongoing political and public concern in Britain about the prevalence of infanticide in India, and especially the systematic killing of female babies in some parts of that country).[432] Even so, Victorian women who were accused of infanticide were usually treated with considerable leniency. Few were convicted. The 1803 Act, which repealed that of 1624, had incorporated a provision allowing juries acquitting defendants of murdering their newborn offspring to return a verdict of guilty to the lesser offence of concealing a birth, a crime which carried a maximum sentence of two years imprisonment. More than 60 years later, Byles J. ventured the opinion that nearly all cases in which a conviction for this offence was secured were actually instances of murder.[433]

Those women who *were* convicted during the 1800s of the full crime routinely received pardons. No woman was executed for killing her own baby (below the age of 12 months) after 1849. Like Defoe, over a century earlier, many observers attributed this to an overly sympathetic attitude on the part of judges and juries. Some barristers claimed that they seized "every favourable scrap of evidence" to acquit, even in cases where there was no real doubt as to guilt. Like Defoe, several Victorian observers also feared that women contemplating the crime were well aware of this in advance of committing their

[429]OBSP, Trial of Sarah Russell, 3rd July 1782.
[430]OBSP, Trial of Mary Tate, 30th June 1714.
[431]William L Langer, "Infanticide: a historical survey", *History of Childhood Quarterly*, vol.1, 1974, p.360.
[432]See for example Edward Moor, *Hindu Infanticide*, London, J. Johnson and Co., 1811, p.9.
[433]Katherine O'Donovan, "The Medicalisation of Infanticide", *Criminal Law Review*, 1984, p.261.

offences. There was particular concern that, despite the claimed prevalence of infanticide in the capital, a 'sympathetic' approach to the crime was especially common at the Old Bailey.[434] Such attitudes ultimately found a legislative outlet in the 1922 Infanticide Act, which made the maternal killing of "newly-born" infants manslaughter in certain circumstances. It was passed because it was practically impossible to secure convictions for murder in these cases (even though any death sentence passed was certain to be commuted).

## Conclusion

Patterns of infanticide in the Metropolitan area are broadly similar to wider English trends, albeit with a number of situational differences that are explained by a largely urban environment. Generally, however, no special paradigm is necessary to distinguish them from rural developments. By the late 1600s, a national transformation was underway in the levels of prosecution and conviction for the crime, and these continued to fall during the 1700s. (Indeed, there was a European wide change during this period in social and legal attitudes towards infanticide).[435] This process was reflected in the Metropolis, albeit that the fall in conviction rates was slower than in provincial society. This is, perhaps, a small indication that London, although seen as a corrupting location by contemporaries, and a dissolvent of traditional social mores by many modern scholars, preserved at least some older values during the 1700s. In London, as elsewhere, it seems that the decline in prosecution was not primarily a matter of incidence but rather the result of a marginalizing of the 1624 Act combined with a general reduction in willingness to return guilty verdicts for infanticide (irrespective of the statute). Although observers like Defoe had to assume, if only for the purposes of argument, that eighteenth century jurors were genuinely being taken in by the explanations being proffered by accused women, it seems much more likely that their 'not guilty' verdicts were indicative of a major change in legal and social attitudes.

Why this occurred must be a matter of conjecture. Nevertheless, there are several plausible explanations for such a change in outlook. Probably amongst the most significant, was a growth in notions of due process. This was reflected in a more clearly enunciated burden and standard of proof, the advent of

---

[434] Ann R Higginbotham, "'Sin of the Age"; Infanticide and Illegitimacy in Victorian London', *Victorian Studies*, vol. 32, no. 3, 1989, p. 319.

[435] For example, in Germany, during the eighteenth century, the imposition of the death penalty for infanticide became progressively rarer as punishment for the crime was increasingly confined to a term of imprisonment. See on this: Susanne Kord, "Women and Children, Women as Childkillers: Infanticide in Eighteenth-Century Germany", *Eighteenth-Century Studies* vol.26, no.3, 1993, pp.449-446, at p.451. Similarly, in France, during the 1700s, women were very rarely convicted of the offence, because courts insisted on strict standards of proof or were persuaded that the accused woman's emotional state rendered them legally insane. See on this Tracey Rizzo: "Between Dishonor and Death: infanticides in the *Causes celebres* of eighteenth-century France" *Women's History Review*, vol.13, no.1, 2004, at p.11

defence counsel, the expansion of evidential rules (hearsay was expressly excluded at Mercy Hornby's hearing in 1734) and the widespread use of expert evidence. Indeed, the crime appears to have made a major contribution to the development of forensic practice and criminal law in many of these areas. Thus, legal representation could lead to imaginative defences even in apparently hopeless cases. At the trial of Mary Mullen, in 1757, defence counsel argued that the defendant was innocent, although her baby's throat had been cut, because in the pain of a difficult childbirth an unassisted mother might accidentally slash its throat when she meant to cut an umbilical cord that was wrapped around the infant's neck.[436] It is apparent that infanticide ceased to be viewed as a 'crime apart' during the 1700s, in much the same way that witchcraft had after 1660. As a result, juries accepted that they would have to let numerous guilty women go free if they wished to avoid the risk of convicting the innocent.

However, the process appears to have gone further than this, as judges and juries acquitted women who, in their hearts, they must have believed to be guilty, *provided* that the evidence allowed the possibility of a charitable interpretation. Could anyone really have accepted Sarah Hunter's claim, in 1769, that she gave birth entirely unwittingly and: "...awaked in the morning and found there was a child...I can give no account how I did it"?[437] This change was not simply a reflection of judicial policy. In the following century, Keating J. observed, in a written memorandum to the 1866 Commission on Capital Punishment, that whatever judges might do to inform jurors about the substantive law and the evidence in an infanticide case, they would wholly disregard it and "eagerly adopt the wildest suggestions which the ingenuity of counsel can furnish." Juries would simply not convict for what was, theoretically, a capital offence.[438]

As a result, other explanations for the reduction in conviction levels, apart from the simple growth of legal propriety, must be sought. These might include a general decline in Puritanical forms of religion, especially amongst members of the 'political' nation and an apparent change in sexual mores during the era. This had a number of practical consequences, not least in a near tripling of illegitimacy during the eighteenth century. In turn, this *may* have engendered male guilt, a feeling that the escaped seducer was at least as responsible for what had occurred as the woman prosecuted. Many legal decision makers, drawn from the upper and middling social orders, would have indulged in extra-marital sexual dalliances. They may have agreed with Dr. William Hunter, in 1783, that in most cases it was the father of the child who was "really criminal." Frequently, the mother was simply weak and deluded by a man, who: "Having obtained gratification ... thinks no more of his promises."[439] Sympathy for the predicament of females who were the recipients of male sexual attentions,

---

[436]OBSP, Trial of Mary Mussen, 26th May 1757.
[437]OBSP, Trial of Sarah Hunter, 28th June 1769.
[438]O'Donovan, "The Medicalisation of Infanticide", p.261.
[439]Hunter, *On the Uncertainty of the Signs of Murder*, p.6.

whether prostitutes or single women, accompanied by a feeling of male responsibility for the absence of restraint that encouraged such illicit liaisons, seems to have influenced legal attitudes towards a number of eighteenth-century offences, and frequently led to a benign application of the criminal law.[440]

The decline may also have reflected a more open recognition that committing bastards to the care of the parish was often a belated death sentence in any event. As Jonas Hanway pointed out, infants who went on the parish would usually be given to a "poor, decrepid woman, or a nurse, in whose hands it would die soon." The sooner this happened, the smaller the expense that would be incurred by the parish; something of which even apparently 'worthy' parochial officers were well aware.[441] Thus, a satire from 1768 involved Churchwardens jocularly enquiring about the fates of nine illegitimate babies put out to nurse the previous week, and asking their custodian, 'Mother Careless', how many were still living. She immediately replies "only two."[442] It has been observed, albeit with slight exaggeration, that it was widely known and, effectively, tacitly accepted, that being committed to the workhouse or put out to parish nursing meant almost certain death for the infants concerned.[443]

Interestingly, this change in attitude also ran counter to several of the era's other trends. Thus, newborn babies appear to have been excepted from a growing intolerance, both legal and social, towards attacks on wives, children and servants that seems to have occurred from about 1750.[444] Additionally, the decline in popular willingness to convict proceeded even as the post-1690 'Reformation of Manners' campaign, addressing general immorality, was at its peak. Furthermore, it occurred as provision for looking after pregnant women who went 'on the parish' increased. Indeed, it has been argued that London's eighteenth-century parochial and hospital provision was "uniquely well designed" for women in this situation. There were several lying in hospitals and almost 70 parish workhouses, small and large.[445] It also seems that in many circumstances eighteenth-century women who had babies out of wedlock did not have to conform to a model of ashamed, and so 'respectable', illegitimacy to receive charitable relief (for example, from the Foundling Hospital), even if it was politic to do so; economic need, rather than personal shame, was usually the most important factor in allotting assistance, at least until the 1790s (when a

---

[440]Anthony Simpson, "The mouth of strange women is a deep pit': Male guilt and legal attitudes toward prostitution in Georgian London", *Journal of Criminal Justice and Popular Culture*, 1996, vol. 4(3) 50-79, p. 53.

[441]Hanway, *A Candid historical Account*, p.21.

[442]Sir D Downright, *The Bastard Child, or a Feast for the Church-wardens*, London, 1768, p.31.

[443]Linebaugh, *The London Hanged*, p.149.

[444]John M Beattie, "Violence and society in early-modern England", *Perspectives in Criminal Law, Essays in Honour of John Edwards*, A Doob and E L Greenspan (Eds.), Ontario, Aurora, Ontario, 1985, pp.50-51.

[445]Hitchcock, "Unlawfully begotten on her body", pp.74-81.

change becomes apparent).[446] This, combined with a huge reduction in the use of active punishment for bastard bearing, such as commitment to a house of correction, might have led the courts to feel that there was less excuse for such acts than in the previous century.

Whatever the reasons, the eighteenth century saw a revival of the medieval notion that infanticide was different to other homicides. Indeed, with hindsight, it is the period immediately after 1624 that must be seen as being legally 'unusual' from a historical perspective. The 'long' eighteenth century (1688 onwards) witnessed a return to what might be viewed as a 'traditional' approach towards infanticide, found in medieval, Victorian and modern England. This is not to suggest that people became blasé about the killing of newborn babies, merely that contemporary observers did not feel that it normally warranted execution. In this, they may have been demonstrating that certain factors inherent to the crime, such as the fact that it does not create a sense of social insecurity, that the infant is perceived as being less capable of suffering than an adult or older child, that the loss to its family is not as great and that frequently the motivation behind its commission is (or at least was) to hide shame, mean that many are predisposed not to view it as being quite the same as other forms of killing.[447]

---

[446]Evans, '"Unfortunate Objects', p.131.
[447]John C Smith, *Smith and Hogan: Criminal Law*, 8th edn., London, Butterworths, 1996, p.394.

1. 'Gin Lane', Hogarth (1751)
*As this print suggests, many women participated in the era's epidemic level of spirit consumption.*

*2. 'Harlot's Progress', Plate 4, Hogarth (1732)*
*A woman at work beating hemp in the London Bridewell; she is under the close supervision of the jailer and his wife.*

*3. 'Four Stages of Cruelty', Plate 3, Hogarth (1751)*
*The print portrays a traditional image of a violent man and a victimised and corrupted woman.*

PLATE C

*4. A portrait of the notorious murderer Sarah Malcolm while she was in Newgate Prison; Hogarth (1733)*

*5. Portrait of Captain Thomas Coram, Hogarth (1740)*
*The founder of the London Foundling Hospital, an institution that may have made a small contribution*
*to reducing the incidence of neo-natal infanticide perpetrated by unmarried women.*

*6. The London Foundling Hospital, Hogarth (1739)*
*An anticipation of the work of the hospital, which was established that year.*

*7. 'Industry and Idleness', Plate 7; Hogarth (1747)*
*A prostitute steals from her client; this was a habitual risk when having connection with street-walkers.*

*8. 'Harlot's Progress', Plate 3; Hogarth (1732)*
*The magistrate Sir John Gonson arrests a prostitute in a room off Drury Lane; such judicial activism*
*against street-walkers was usually fairly sporadic.*

*9. 'Harlot's Progress', Plate 5; Hogarth (1732).*
*The death of a prostitute. Street-walkers suffered high rates of mortality from disease and the hardships associated with their lives. However, many survived to return to normal proletarian life.*

# Chapter 5: Instrumental Crime

## Introduction

This chapter will consider the nature and incidence of female perpetrated instrumental crime in the Metropolitan area during the eighteenth century. In particular, it will consider why women resorted to such offences, how their crimes differed from those of men, and how they fared when prosecuted for them. Although many crimes are, potentially, 'instrumental', in that they are aimed at securing goods, services or money, consideration will be limited to its most common and traditional manifestations: theft (in its various forms), burglary, house-breaking, robbery and receiving stolen goods. It will not consider instances of female perpetrated coining and uttering (a relatively common crime amongst women) or fraud. As will be seen, conventional instrumental crimes made up the great majority of prosecuted offences, whether committed by men or women, but were especially common amongst the latter.

Researching such crimes is more complicated than investigating offences like murder and rape because many lesser instrumental crimes were prosecuted at forums other than the Old Bailey. Amongst the most important of these were the three inferior 'quarter' sessions held (usually eight times a year) for Middlesex, the City and Westminster at Hick's Hall, the Guildhall Justice Room etc. These courts would hear most indicted cases of petty theft (under a shilling in value) and some prosecutions for receiving stolen goods (technically often only a misdemeanour).[448] This greatly limits the statistical value of 'counting' the gender distribution of several of the minor offences against property that were also occasionally prosecuted at the higher forum (an average of ten cases of petty theft were indicted at the Bailey each year during the century). Additionally, and further complicating matters, there was a tendency after the mid-century to create summary only misdemeanours, tried without a jury by magistrates sitting at petty sessions, to ensure the conviction of those suspected of specific forms of theft, in situations where essential legal elements of the felony would otherwise be hard to establish. The penalties imposed after conviction for such offences were usually relatively light.[449] Prosecutions for such offences are unlikely to have been 'gender neutral'.

---

[448] Thomas Dogherty, *The Crown Circuit Companion*, vol.1, London, Printed for E and R Brooke, 1799, pp.36-39.
[449] See generally Bruce P. Smith "The Presumption of Innocence and the English Law of theft: 1750-1850" *Law and History Review*, 2005, vol. 23, no. 1, pp.133-173.

## The Incidence of Female Instrumental Crime

Although eighteenth-century women *generally* committed far fewer crimes than men (or at least were prosecuted much less frequently), Metropolitan women were notably *more* prone to offending, when compared to men, than their Victorian or modern counterparts or, for that matter, their rural contemporaries and forbears. Thus, at the Old Bailey, they made up over a quarter of all defendants tried in the 150-year period after 1675. Female involvement in crime was especially marked in the late seventeenth and early eighteenth centuries when, a detailed study of the gender of defendants tried at the Bailey suggests, women made up over a third of that court's caseload. At one point, they constituted more than 40 per cent of all Metropolitan indictments and, in the City of London (whose trials were kept separate from those for Middlesex), between 1690 and 1713, they made up a narrow majority of those indicted for property offences (51.2 per cent).[450] Although urban areas appear to be criminogenic, explaining higher rates of crime generally in such environments, this does not account for there being a much higher *proportion* of female offenders.[451]

Of course, explanations for the high level of Metropolitan female prosecution *other* than simple incidence can be advanced for this peak in the early 1700s. Given the dearth of detective and policing agencies, a considerable proportion of prosecutions were of felons who had been caught 'red handed', and it was usually easier to detain women than men. Furthermore, women, unlike men, could not be offered enlistment in lieu of prosecution if apprehended during wartime (a frequent occurrence for men in a century of conflict). The number of male criminals 'at large' in the city would also be reduced by military recruitment at such times, increasing the proportion of female offenders. Additionally, the extension of benefit of clergy to women on the same basis as men (in 1692) may have made people more willing to prosecute females. Nevertheless, and as this also suggests, the high number of female defendants is especially notable because there normally appears to have been a greater *reluctance* on the part of victims to indict women than there was for male offenders, in a system that allowed enormous private discretion as to the decision to prosecute. Anecdotal accounts suggest that women fared slightly better in making appeals to their intended victims' mercy when urging them not to prosecute at all. It also seems that some men were deterred by a fear of appearing ridiculous if they prosecuted females.[452] Even where they did take action, many preferred to proceed against women in circumstances where they could be confident that they would receive lenient punishments (and which would also entail less disruption for the victim); for example, by using local

---

[450]John Beattie, *Policing and Punishment in London, 1660-1750*, Oxford, OUP, 2001, p.65.

[451] Edward Glaeser and Bruce Sacerdote, "Why Is there More crime in Cities?", *Journal of Political Economy*, 1999, vol. 107, no. 6, pp.225-229, pp.225-226.

[452]Peter King, *Crime, Justice and Discretion in England: 1740-1820*, Oxford, OUP, 2000, p.200.

forums.[453] Significantly, only 17 per cent of the small number of petty thefts that were indicted as such at the Old Bailey involved female defendants.

Additionally, women who were minor thieves (especially if they were also prostitutes) were disproportionately likely to be diverted from the mainstream criminal justice system into the Bridewell (if from the City) or one of the Middlesex Houses of Correction (if from that county), where they would be dealt with for vagrancy or disorderly conduct, rather than being indicted for the substantive offences for which they had initially been arrested. The Bridewell Court met every two or three weeks and was presided over by the Governors of that prison (amongst them being several City Aldermen and the Lord Mayor). It would hear allegations against those committed to the institution and would then decide whether to discharge the prisoner concerned or to impose a term of forced work (normally beating hemp) and incarceration. Sometimes, especially in the early part of the century, this would be accompanied by a beating. Thus, in the 1720s, some shopkeepers complained that shoplifters were inadequately punished because, provided the circumstances were: "...not notorious, and the [stolen] goods secured, the criminals escape with a Bridewell whipping, and soon return to their trade."[454] In the years from 1703 to 1705, 70 per cent of those who appeared before the City Bridewell Court were female.[455] As a result, it seems that the high number of women prosecuted at the Old Bailey during the eighteenth century reflects (and very possibly understates) real levels of female offending. Furthermore, it is clear from statistical analysis that this was due to the relative 'over-representation' of women in property crimes rather than offences of violence, disorder or criminal damage.[456]

Female involvement in crime appears to have declined slowly after the 1720s, before increasing briefly in the 1770s, though not again matching its peak in the early part of the century. A close examination of the Sessions Papers suggests that the 1780s *may* have been a significant decade in the transition to a more 'modern' gender distribution in Metropolitan crime.[457] Even so, in 1789, women still made up almost a third of Newgate's criminal inmates (146 of 499) whether awaiting trial or post-conviction disposals such as execution or transportation.[458] However, the number of female defendants continued to decline, gradually but inexorably, in the years after 1800. This process may have

[453]Robert Shoemaker, *Prosecution and Punishment: Petty Crime and the law in London and rural Middlesex, c.1660-1725*, Cambridge, CUP, 1991, p.214.

[454]Anon, *The Great Grievance of Traders and Shopkeepers, by the Notorious Practise of Stealing their Goods out of their Shops and warehouses by persons commonly called shop-lifters* ND but c.1720, London, at p.1.

[455]Beattie, *Policing and Punishment*, pp.24-33, p.66 and pp.313-314.

[456]Malcolm Feeley and Deborah Little, "The Vanishing Female: The Decline of Women in the Criminal Process, 1687-1912", *Law and Society Review*, 1991, vol. 25, no. 4, pp.719-757, p.721 and p.736. On female violence see chapters two, three and six.

[457]Lynn Mackay, "Why they stole: women in the Old Bailey, 1779-1789", *Journal of Social History*, 1999, vol. 32, p.624.

[458]John Howard, *Account of the Present State of the Prisons, Houses of Correction, and Hospitals in London and Westminster*, London, 1789, pp.2-3.

been aided by the era's increasing preoccupation with, and prosecution of, juvenile delinquency in urban areas. This phenomenon was highly gendered, being primarily limited to males.[459] By the final decade of the nineteenth century, women made up only 10 per cent of defendants at the Old Bailey, a pattern that (largely) continued throughout the following century. By this point, crime had come to be perceived as an essentially masculine problem and female deviance was increasingly seen as a manifestation of sexual or biological pathology - 'mad not bad' – that might more properly be addressed by agencies other than the criminal law (such as inebriates' asylums).[460] This was an interpretation that the high number of female offenders in the early 1700s would have precluded.

Additionally, it can be noted that Metropolitan women in the 1700s were far more likely to offend than their rural counterparts and predecessors. Thus, in Essex, between 1740 and 1804, only 13 per cent of those indicted at Assizes and Quarter Sessions for property offences were female, a pattern that was broadly matched elsewhere on the Home Circuit.[461] Similar patterns are revealed for this period in counties such as Somerset, Berkshire and Gloucestershire, with the proportion of female indictments rarely going above 16 per cent (though Cornwall, where, as late as 1805-7, 25 per cent of indictments were of women, is something of an exception).[462]

The high level of female prosecution in the eighteenth-century Metropolis (especially during the era's initial decades) was also at variance to earlier, rural, patterns. For example, between 1591 and 1618, women made up less than 15 per cent of all those prosecuted on indictment in Hertfordshire, at *both* the county's Assizes and Quarter Sessions.[463] Similarly, in Yorkshire, Northamptonshire and Norfolk, during the first half of the fourteenth century, only one woman was accused of felony for every nine males, a figure that remains almost exactly the same when larceny is considered on its own.[464] It appears that female offending rates in London in the late seventeenth and early eighteenth centuries were also significantly (though less markedly) higher than amongst their immediate Metropolitan predecessors. Beattie's work suggests that about a third of indictments there between 1670 and 1689 involved women.

This urban bias towards female offending during the era also applied to London's extensions south of the river, such as Lambeth and the built-up parts of North Surrey, where women were markedly more prone to committing crimes than those found in adjacent but mainly rural counties such as Sussex and

---

[459]Peter King, "The rise of juvenile delinquency in England 1780-1840: changing patterns of perception and prosecution", *Past and Present*, 1998, vol. 160, 1998, pp.116-166, at p.130.

[460]Lucia Zedner, *Women, Crime and Custody in Victorian England*, Oxford, OUP, 1991, p.296.

[461]King, *Crime, Justice and Discretion in England*, pp.196-199.

[462]Peter King, *Crime and Law in England, 1750-1850*, Cambridge, CUP, 2006, pp.202-206.

[463]Anon, *The Caterpillars of this Nation Anatomised*, London, 1659, p.4.

[464]Barbara Hanawalt, "The Female Felon in Fourteenth-Century England", *Viator*, 1974, vol. 5, pp.253 –268, at p.254 and p.268.

even the agrarian parts of Surrey itself.[465] It also accords with some evidence from Newcastle, where, between 1718 and the end of the century, the incidence of theft amongst women was markedly higher than in the surrounding countryside; until 1783, over half the prosecutions for that crime conducted at the city's Quarter Sessions involved female defendants.[466] However, it should also be noted that the apparently heavier involvement of urban women in instrumental crime during the eighteenth century was, to some extent, a European wide phenomenon, not a purely English one. For example, at times, almost half of the defendants in Ghent and Amsterdam were female. Similarly, in the town of Leiden, women constituted between 41 per cent and 44 per cent of those prosecuted between 1678 and 1794. Although, like Metropolitan women, they were less likely to commit offences of violence, they heavily outnumbered men accused of receiving and fencing stolen goods (65 cases compared to 39) and were only marginally less represented in conventional theft.[467]

## Explanations for the High Incidence of Female Crime

A number of potential explanations for the high incidence of female deviance in the eighteenth-century Metropolis have been advanced, three of which deserve specific consideration.

### Opportunity to Offend

Cities often provide greater opportunities to offend than rural areas. However, this alone does not explain *proportionately* greater female involvement in crime. Nevertheless, differential opportunity theory would suggest that it might be accounted for by the increased chances that were available to women to commit property crimes, as a result of the unprecedented level of female waged employment found at this time in the London area. Conversely, changes in such employment *could* explain its subsequent decline. If, as is sometimes (and controversially) suggested, women were increasingly confined to the domestic sphere during the late eighteenth and early nineteenth centuries, while public work was progressively limited to men, their opportunities to offend would necessarily also have been greatly reduced.[468]

---

[465]John Beattie, "The Criminality of Women in Eighteenth Century England", *Journal of Social History*, 1974, vol.8/4, pp.80-116, at p.96. John Beattie, *Crime and the Courts in England 1660-1800*, Oxford, OUP, 1986, p.169.

[466]Gwenda Morgan and Peter Rushton, *Rogues, Thieves and the Rule of Law: The Problem of Law Enforcement in Northeast England*, London, University College London Press, 1998, p.100. However, Newcastle had a much higher number of married women as defendants in theft cases than did the London area.

[467]E. Kloek, "Criminality and Gender in Leiden's Confessieboken, 1678-1794", *Criminal Justice History*, vol. 11, 1990, p.8.

[468]For a discussion of this see generally Robert Shoemaker *Gender in English Society 1650-1850: The Emergence of Separate Spheres?*, London, Longman,1998.

*Loss of Male 'Control'*

By contrast, aspects of 'control theory' might suggest that rural women in this era, living in 'traditional' patriarchal societies, were normally subjected to strict social and paternal constraints. They were kept under close observation in their neighbourhoods, places where male authority figures, such as clerics and magistrates, were also more immediate. As a result, their smaller representation in offending when compared to men can, in part, be explained by contrasts in opportunity, training, socially expected behaviour and socialised habits of obedience.[469] As Jonas Hanway observed, women were normally less likely to be afflicted by severe guilt because from a: "...habit of obedience they live more submissively to the decrees of heaven; perhaps being less deeply engaged in views of avarice and ambition."[470]

However, these controls became attenuated in the Metropolis, where there were more single, working, women, many of whom had migrated from the country to what was a large, frenetic and socially mobile city. In this environment, they were often dependant on their own wits to survive and enjoyed greater freedom to offend as well as to enter legitimate activities.[471] It is *possible* that patriarchal authority over urban women was particularly (and temporarily) weakened during this period because of the transitional nature of the era's economy. In the move from the traditional modes of production that had been prevalent before the late seventeenth century, and the rise of industrial capitalism a hundred years later, women were of unprecedented economic importance, potentially weakening male control. Although highly speculative, such a rationale does at least avoid local explanations for what was, to some extent, a European wide urban phenomenon.[472] Nevertheless, one of the most important explanations for female instrumental crime was simple need.

*Need*

It has been suggested that most eighteenth-century urban women stole for similar reasons to men: as a means of survival in what was a harsh environment, or as a way of supplementing inadequate wages.[473] Almost three quarters of Metropolitan women worked for a living, and there was no objection to women taking employment; this is considerably more than was the case in the mid-nineteenth century. However, they were largely denied access to male trades, especially well remunerated positions such as those organized by gilds or livery

---

[469]Beattie, "The Criminality of Women", p.96.

[470]Jonas Hanway, *Advice from Farmer Trueman to his Daughter*, 2nd edn. pp.67-71.

[471]See on this Lucia Zedner, "Women, Crime, and Penal Responses: A Historical Account", Michael Tonry (Ed.), *Crime and Justice; A Review of Research*, 1991, vol. xx, at p.247

[472]For a discussion of possible explanations see Malcolm Feeley, "The decline of women in the criminal process; a comparative history", *Criminal Justice History*, 1994, vol. 15, pp.235-274, at pp.253-274.

[473]John Beattie, "Hard Pressed to Make Ends Meet': Women and Crime in Augustan London", *Women and History*, Valerie Firth (Ed.), Toronto, 1995, p.106.

companies.[474] When women engaged in paid work, it was often in relatively unskilled, insecure, seasonal and poorly paid occupations that were the subject of intense competition. Compounding such problems, there may have been a gender imbalance in the capital as a result of disproportionate levels of female migration.[475] It is even 'possible' that, in London, women's earnings showed no significant increase throughout the entire of the eighteenth century.[476] As a result, it has been observed that the "hardships of the age" bore especially severely on females.[477] This was particularly the case for single women, as female wages were often premised on their not being the sole breadwinner. Certainly, a quite disproportionate number of indicted women were unmarried.[478]

At the start of the eighteenth century, about 80 per cent of women prosecuted at the Old Bailey were either listed as spinsters or (in only five per cent of cases) widows.[479] Of course, it is possible (indeed likely) that women living alone, independent of fathers, husbands and masters, prompted alarm in a patriarchal society, encouraging increased prosecution levels, while the legal advantages of married women have already been noted. Nevertheless, their high indictment rate probably also reflects incidence; because life was especially difficult for single females, they were particularly likely to resort to crimes such as theft. Many appear to have led a hand-to-mouth existence, in which crime was merely one facet of lives that encompassed prostitution, begging and poorly remunerated 'legitimate' forms of employment, such as selling newspapers, fish and vegetables in the streets. Exacerbating their difficulties, many were not even native Londoners; 56 per cent of women indicted at the Bailey between 1791 and 1793 were migrants from other parts of England, the British Isles (especially Ireland) or even continental Europe. London born female criminals only predominated amongst the very young (most non-native women arrived in the Metropolis as adults).[480] This meant that many were beyond the reach of family assistance if they got into difficulties.

Need was regularly advanced at court as an explanation for crime. Although, legally, necessity was not a defence in English law, defendants frequently referred to poverty as something that had compelled them to offend, often speaking in quasi-psychological terms of a desperation that had overwhelmed their powers of self-restraint.[481] Of course, as it was also an excuse

---

[474] Peter Earle "The female labour market in London in the late seventeenth and early eighteenth centuries" *Economic History Review*, 1989, 2nd series, XLII, 3, pp.328-353, at p.342 and p.346.

[475] Beattie, *Policing and Punishment*, p.69.

[476] L.D. Schwarz, 1985, "The standard of living in the long run: London 1700-1860." *The Economic History Review*, vol.38, no.1, 1985, pp.24-41, at p.31

[477] Dorothy George, *London Life in the Eighteenth Century*, London, Penguin Books, 1965, p.174.

[478] Peter King, "Female offenders, work and life-cycle change in late-eighteenth-century London", *Continuity and Change* vol. 11, 1996, pp. 61-90, at p.68.

[479] Beattie, *Policing and Punishment*, p.71.

[480] Peter King, "Female offenders", pp. 72-74.

[481] Dana Rabin, "Searching for the Self in Eighteenth-Century English Criminal Trials, 1730-1800", *Eighteenth-Century Life*, 2003, vol. 27, no.1, pp.85-106, at p.93.

that was likely to garner sympathy (whether true or not), some caution is necessary before accepting its veracity. Even so, and, arguably, reflecting a popular acceptance of the special problems Metropolitan women faced, such claims often attracted leniency from both judges and jurors. Women who pleaded distress were almost twice as likely to be found 'not guilty', or to have their sentences reduced, as were men who advanced it as an excuse.[482] Thus, Margaret Ellis, accused of snatching a money box worth over £5 from a shop, did not deny the crime, but instead told the jury that she had a: "…very bad husband, who made her sell all her goods, and left her with two small children." Although convicted, her death sentence was conveniently respited for pregnancy.[483]

Similarly, in 1759, after Elizabeth Rosdell was convicted of stealing lace from Harden Elderton's shop in Bishopsgate-street, her prosecutor was generous, telling the court that he had made enquiries about her in the parish and discovered that she had lived honestly there in the past until "necessity has drove her to do this." Rosdell, like Ellis, did not seek to deny the allegation and, although convicted, was found guilty only to the formalised value of 10d. (i.e. non-capital petty theft).[484] By contrast, it has been argued that one reason that women in Buenos Aires were very rarely prosecuted for instrumental crimes such as theft (as opposed to interpersonal offences), during the second half of the eighteenth century, was that, in this Latin American society, they were not forced to be economically independent to anything like the same degree as men. They would usually rely on husbands and lovers for their subsistence.[485]

However, although their motivations may have been broadly similar to those of men, the need/crime link appears to have been subtler amongst Metropolitan females. Thus, in the economically straitened 1780s, the number of men prosecuted for theft increased greatly, but that of women did not. It is likely that the authorities were targeting men for prosecution, expecting an increase in male crime in a post-war environment. Nevertheless, women may also have been resorting to expedients to survive in 'hard times' that were less commonly used by men. For example, during the late eighteenth century women always made up between two-thirds and three-quarters of the inmates of the large workhouse of St. Martin in the Fields. Similarly, they constituted a clear majority of the clients of the charitable Mendicity Society.[486] When combined with the ready availability of prostitution (for many) and a female willingness to have recourse to begging, such expedients may explain why the number of women resorting to theft in difficult times increased much more modestly than that of men.

---

[482]MacKay, "Why they stole: women in the Old Bailey", p.627.

[483]OBSP, Trial of Margaret Ellis, 26th April 1704.

[484]OBSP, Trial of Elizabeth Rosdell, 24th Oct. 1759.

[485] Susan Socolow, "Women and Crime: Buenos Aires, 1757-1797" *Journal of Latin American Studies*, 1980, vol.12, no.1, pp.39-54, at p.42

[486]MacKay, "Why they stole: women in the Old Bailey", p.634.

## 'Passive' Participants in Crime?

Despite the high incidence of female offending, some gender stereotypes for the era still maintain that women were more likely to play a passive and dependent role in the execution of crimes, often relying on male assistance or leadership, and also stealing items of lesser value than men. Additionally, it is claimed that male instrumental crimes were more likely to be committed outdoors, to involve robbery and to require "alacrity, physical strength, boldness, bravura and speed." By contrast, it is suggested that women tended to work indoors and relied upon "quiet, intelligence, stealth and quickness."[487] In recent years, some scholars, such as Garthine Walker, have challenged the generality of these assumptions, suggesting that not only was women's criminality greater than is sometimes assumed, but also that most female thieves did not act as assistants to male criminals and did not steal less valuable goods than men.[488] Some, but not all, aspects of Walker's analysis are borne out by prosecutions in eighteenth-century London. However, some aspects of the 'traditional' stereotype are also supported.

On an individual basis, it is not difficult to find women who were prominent in the eighteenth-century Metropolitan underworld. Although they may have been 'untypical', their presence meant that there was no shortage of available role models for women minded to resort to crime. For example, Jack Sheppard, a notorious felon and Newgate escapee, appears to have been heavily influenced in his criminal career by various mistresses. It was claimed that Elizabeth Lyon ('Edgeworth Bess'), a "large masculine woman", had dominated the young and physically frail man, frequently beating him when in drink, and directing all his criminal enterprises. She was followed by the unflatteringly named 'Mrs Maggot', an aggressive woman who apparently despised Shepherd and: "…only made use of him to go and steal money." It was claimed that Maggot enjoyed most of the proceeds of his crimes.[489] Even Jonathan Wild, the master criminal behind much organised crime in the Metropolis in the first quarter of the century, appears to have been heavily influenced early in his career by Mary Milliner, a habitual criminal with a detailed knowledge of London's

---

[487]Peter Linebough, *The London Hanged: Crime and Civil Society in the Eighteenth Century*, London, Penguin, 1991, p.339.

[488]Garthine Walker, "Women, theft and the world of Stolen Goods", *Women, Crime and the Courts in Early Modern England*, J. Kermode et al (Eds.) London, UCL Press, 1994, pp. 81-105, at pp.81-99.

[489]Arthur Hayward (Ed.), *Lives of the Most Remarkable Criminals: Who have been Condemned and Executed for Murder, the Highway, Housebreaking, Street Robberies, Coining or other offences. Collected from Original Papers and Authentic Memoirs, and Published in 1735*, London, Routledge and Sons, 1927, pp.182-184. After Sheppard's execution in 1724, Elizabeth Lyon continued to be a formative influence on numerous other young men on the cusp of a life of crime, in one case "seducing a shopkeeper's son to go a thieving with her."

underworld, whom he met while incarcerated in the Compter prison. He subsequently married her.[490]

On a less personal basis, it seems that a propensity to form criminal associations, rather than acting alone, was no greater amongst women in the 1780s than with men: about 29 per cent of both male and female thieves acted with accomplices. Nor, it seems, and taken overall, did women take items of lesser value than male thieves. Thus, they were slightly less likely to take items valued at under 10s, and a little more prone to stealing things worth between 10s and £10. They were significantly less likely than men to steal objects worth more than this amount, but two-thirds of thieves, of both genders, stole goods worth (or at least valued) at less than 40s.[491] However, and at variance to Walker's study, women *did* manifest a greater propensity to act with males when taking accomplices, than did men to work with females; those accused of theft were more than twice as likely to have committed their crimes with men than vice versa. Admittedly, the number of such inter-gender partnerships was, at first sight, quite small, three per cent for men and just over seven per cent for women.[492] Nevertheless, the quantification of cases involving male/female collaboration must be approached with considerable caution, especially where the parties were married to each other or cohabited.

*Feme Covert and Instrumental Crime*

The doctrine of Coverture (discussed in detail in chapter two) meant that the law was reluctant to find that a married woman who stole with, and in the presence of, her husband - unless it was in an 'overtly' active role - was implicated in the crime, even as an accessory. The doctrine did not apply if a woman stole at her husband's command, but in his absence: "...much less is she excused if she commit a theft of her own voluntary act." Additionally, it did not apply to a few serious instrumental felonies, such as robbery.[493]

The criminal implications of *feme covert* were increasingly restricted by tighter interpretation during the 1700s, even for theft. Thus, in 1775, when a man and his wife were tried at Hick's Hall for stealing iron hoops from the water pipes running into the New River, both were convicted, and the woman received what was, arguably, the more draconian sentence (six months imprisonment while her husband was only sentenced to a month and a public flogging).[494] Nevertheless, women received a considerable measure of protection if involved in criminal ventures with their husbands; for example, in 1792, Ann Cropper was acquitted of burglary, despite being found with stolen goods on her person, although her husband was convicted and sentenced to death.

---

[490]Gerald Howson, *Thief-Taker General: The Rise and fall of Jonathan Wild*, Hutchinson, London, 1970, at p.18.

[491]MacKay, "Why they stole: women in the Old Bailey", at p.624.

[492]MacKay, "Why they stole: women in the Old Bailey", at p.636.

[493]Anon, *The Laws Respecting Women*, London, Printed for J. Johnson, 1777, p.70.

[494]*Middlesex Journal*, Feb. 18-21, 1775

On many occasions, the protection of *feme covert* seems to have extended to co-habitants who were not legally married. This indulgence towards women was particularly important as 'habitual' female criminals tended to have spouses or partners who were also felons. Thus, to take an extreme example, the notorious shoplifter Anne Harris, though only 20, had twice become a 'hempen widow' before her own execution in 1708.[495] As a result, the number of 'married' women who assisted their partners in criminal ventures, especially theft, is probably very significantly greater than the records suggest. Even where the presumption in *feme covert* did not, strictly speaking, apply, some women would still allege duress, perhaps hoping that the sympathy it engendered would result in jury nullification. Amongst them was Jane Heybourn who, when questioned by a magistrate in 1735, unavailingly claimed that she had a husband in the 'Scotch Guards' stationed at the Tower, who "often beat her to make her do such things." It should also be noted that where *feme covert* operated, it *reduced* the already high number of eighteenth century women being prosecuted, further suggesting that the 'headline' figures may, if anything, understate female criminal involvement.

Some other aspects of the traditional female criminal stereotype *are* clearly accurate. Women tended to steal, rather than rob, a crime that involved the use, or threat of, violence. Additionally, they were much less likely to be involved in crimes like burglary (a nocturnal crime committed between 9 pm and 6 am) and, albeit to a lesser extent, house-breaking (its diurnal counterpart). This may also have been due to the inherent risk of confrontation and violence involved in breaking into private premises. However, there were many exceptions to the general pattern and there were few areas of criminal activity in which women were completely absent.

## Female Burglary and Housebreaking

Between the start of 1700 and the end of 1799, only 62 women were convicted of burglary at the Old Bailey (in reality, perhaps a maximum of 70 to allow for missing sessions papers early in the century), an average of about one every 18 months. This compares to well over 1,200 men convicted of the offence during the same period, making the female level five per cent of that of men. This confirms the point made at the trial of Martha Harman, convicted of burglary in 1676, despite it being "a crime rarely attempted by that sex." Interestingly, of the 62 women, a high proportion committed their crimes alone or with other females. This might suggest that women who were unusual enough to commit such offences rarely looked for male assistance. Alternatively, it may be that this form of crime was considered so much a male provenance that women who were so singular as to engage in it could not find men willing to work with them. Typically, Jane Heybourn acted alone when she hid in the Three Cups tavern

---

[495] J L Rayner and G T Crook (Eds.) *The Complete Newgate Calendar*, vol.11, London, Privately printed for the Navarre Society, 1926, p.205.

near Bedford Row, waiting for the owner to go to bed. When he had done so, she emerged, in the small hours, broke open a cupboard and helped herself to a silver tankard and spoons.[496] Breaking into properties during daylight hours was, proportionately, more common amongst females. A total of 54 women were convicted of housebreaking during the century, about 20 per cent of the male total.

## Female Robbery

Relatively few women were indicted for street robbery, 76 being convicted at the Bailey during the century (perhaps 80 allowing for statistical gaps), making an average of less than one a year. However, this is still about 33 per cent of the male total (220 men), so that, although the use or threat of violence was (legally) an inherent part of the crime, robbery was much less gender specific than burglary. Of course, some of these women had worked with male associates. Thus, Margaret Greenaway and Ann Rush of Saint Bride's parish robbed George Thorn of his hat and cash in 1745, after luring him down a back alley. When he resisted their demands for money, and tried to detain them, they were joined by three men, armed with sticks and knives, who forced Thorn to surrender his valuables to the women.[497] However, as with female burglars (though less markedly so), the majority acted without male assistance. Where females did act without men, they sometimes victimised children (a crime strongly associated with women) or other women. For example, in 1735, Jane Leg robbed an infant in St. James's Park of her cap, coat and frock. (Leg was a habitual criminal who had been acquitted twice during the previous year at the same court).[498] Margaret Bowden was robbed of her gown and cash in Petticoat Lane by a group of three women who accosted her one evening and asked Bowden "to treat them."[499]

Nevertheless, a significant number of female robbers, acting without male assistance, robbed adult men. Mary Kitching ('Fat Moll') and Elizabeth Alexander were indicted for robbing seventeen-year-old James Jennings, in Whitechapel. They accosted Jennings when he stopped to urinate in the street one night, followed him and then bundled him into a building. There, they rifled his pockets for cash, before Jennings managed to summon help. He admitted that he "cried sadly, and was much frightened" by his experience.[500] Similarly, Eleanor Geary was found guilty of robbing a coachman named William Johnson of half a guinea. Johnson was going down an alley, early one evening, carrying a message, when he was hustled into a house by a pair of women who demanded drink from him. Alcohol was purchased, but, while there, Johnson claimed that

---

[496]OBSP, Trial of Jane Heybourn, 16th January 1735.
[497]OBSP, Trial of Margaret Greenaway and Ann Rush, 30th May 1745.
[498]OBSP, Trial of Jane Leg, 11th Sept. 1735.
[499]OBSP, Trial of Mary Forster and others, 7th July 1773.
[500]OBSP, Trial of Mary Kitching, 21st Oct. 1761.

Geary held him while the other woman picked his pocket. Johnson, too, found this a terrifying experience: "I was so much frightened, that a Child of ten Years old might have managed me."[501] Although, in some of these cases, their victims may have been intoxicated, it is clear that those females who were unusual enough to have recourse to robbery could be highly intimidating.

## Female Theft

Women were most commonly associated with straightforward offences of larceny. There were significant differences between what the sexes stole, how they carried out their thefts and the immediate circumstances in which they offended. Many of these were consistent over time. These gender distinctions in appropriation patterns resulted, in part, from the different opportunities to offend that males and females experienced in their everyday lives. Thus, female defendants were much more likely than male ones to know their prosecutors and, for that matter, other witnesses at their trials. In 1788, only a quarter of males, but over 55 per cent of females, fell into this category. Arguably, this was because the daily lives of women were more socially and geographically circumscribed than those of men. Although certainly not confined to domestic duties, many were responsible for household management (if not necessarily their own). Even allowing for trips to local taps, shops and taverns, their lives were spatially more constrained than those of working men, many of whom would travel considerable distances in the course of their employment, whether making deliveries or as jobbing labourers. As a result, women's opportunities for theft were more likely to occur within their own neighbourhoods and were also more likely to involve stealing from someone they knew.[502]

However, while such geographic constraints *partly* account for women's predilection to steal from acquaintances, it was also a result of their greater recourse to social 'borrowing networks'. These were informal arrangements between landlords and tenants, neighbours, friends and acquaintances, involving the loan of goods and money. They were an important expedient for many poorer women trying to make ends meet or deal with an immediate crisis. Nevertheless, such arrangements could go wrong in a number of ways, leading to the 'injured party' bringing theft charges. Thus, women might be late returning goods they had borrowed or have some other type of dispute with the lenders. Those accused usually admitted they had made use of the item and, occasionally, even a prosecutor would concede that a defendant had not meant to take the item on a permanent basis (this usually resulted in an acquittal). Frequently, problems arose because women pawned such goods, usually claiming that they had been in distress but had intended to redeem the item at a later date. Typically, in 1782, Ann Mitchell claimed that she had regularly

---

[501]OBSP, Trial of Eleanor Geary, 7th Dec. 1743.
[502]MacKay, "Why they stole: women in the Old Bailey", p.630.

pledged borrowed goods in the past and always returned them.[503] Another common scenario occurred when women who were legally in possession of others' goods, either in the course of their businesses (such as washerwomen) or as a result of taking furnished lodgings, pawned such items. Thus, in 1775, Elizabeth Beete accused Elizabeth Johnson at the Bow Street Court of pledging a looking-glass and tablecloth from her lodgings, and was bound over to prosecute her at the Old Bailey.[504]

There were also significant differences in *what* the genders stole. Perhaps counter-intuitively, men were more likely to steal foodstuffs, especially liquor, tea, coffee or sugar. This was because such commodities were often stolen from the wharves and warehouses where many males either worked or sought employment. Unsurprisingly, men were also more likely to take industrial or agricultural materials, such as roofing-lead (a uniquely male crime), horses and tools. These tended to come from places of work (even if the thief was not an employee), building sites, sheds or tavern stables. These were places in which females had less cause to be present.[505]

To consider an extreme example of this phenomenon, animal theft in the Metropolitan area (in this case, primarily rural and suburban Middlesex) was overwhelmingly a male preserve. Only 40 women were prosecuted for the crime between the start of 1700 and the end of 1799, and of these, about a dozen committed their alleged crimes with husbands or other male colleagues. Additionally, just over half of these cases involved the theft of poultry, whether hens, cocks, geese, turkeys or ducks; looking after such fowl was often a woman's job. Female theft of larger animals was rarer: seven pigs, four horses and a similar number of sheep, with the odd donkey or cow making up the remainder. Women were also particularly likely to be assisted by males in cases involving larger animals. Altogether, only five women were convicted of the full offence charged, and two of these stole poultry, though, in the most serious case, Sarah Todd stole a horse from a tavern in Gray's Inn lane. (Her socially injurious crime also attracted a death sentence).[506] Six other women were convicted of the lesser offence of (petty) theft to the value of 10d. All six of these cases involved either poultry or rabbits. In comparison, over 1,500 men were accused of animal theft. Over half were convicted of the full offence charged, and another 150 of theft to the value of 10d. Additionally, a very much higher proportion of these cases involved large animals, especially horses, which were often taken from outside taverns or at markets: less than ten per cent of male cases involved poultry. Thus, men were far more likely to commit animal theft, usually took beasts of much greater size and value than women, and were more likely to be convicted when prosecuted.

---

[503]MacKay, "Why they stole: women in the Old Bailey", p.631.
[504]*The Middlesex Journal*, Jan. 31st –Feb. 2nd 1775
[505]MacKay, "Why they stole: women in the Old Bailey", p.625.
[506]OBSP, Trial of Sarah Todd, 16th Jan. 1755.

By contrast, although both men and women were heavily concerned in stealing clothes and household goods, the number of females involved in this activity was proportionately greater than that of males (the objects of female theft tended to be gender related rather than gender specific, few being unique to women). Women were more likely to both need, and have an intimate knowledge of, the value of such items, given their family responsibilities and that clothes were the largest category of household expenditure. They could also easily be pawned or sold in the city's extensive second-hand garment market. Nevertheless, it seems that a significant number of women stole clothes for personal use, despite the risk of identification, either because they needed the garment or because they found it attractive in what was an increasingly fashion conscious age.[507] This pattern was not novel to London or the eighteenth century. It was even more marked in seventeenth-century Cheshire.[508] Women were also more likely to steal money, watches and jewellery, though this was, in large part, a result of the high incidence of prostitutes stealing from their clients.[509]

However, female criminal careers, like male ones, were usually relatively fluid. Mary ('Moll') Jones' life provides a fairly typical progression. She was born in Chancery Lane, and started her working life manufacturing scarves, but seems to have drifted into crime after marrying an extravagant apprentice. Initially, she worked as a pickpocket, but abandoned this form of crime after being arrested, convicted and clergied for the offence. She then became a shoplifter, experiencing success in this field for several years, until caught and hanged in 1691.[510] Nevertheless, as Jones' career also suggests, women were particularly associated with certain forms of theft. Foremost amongst these were shoplifting, pick-pocketing and stealing when employed as domestic servants.

## Shoplifting

The 'Shoplifting Act' of 1699 made the offence of "privately stealing" goods worth five or more shillings from retail premises a capital offence by removing it from benefit of clergy (though it had to be prosecuted under an appropriately worded indictment). Its enactment reflected concern at an apparent growth in such crime in the Metropolitan area, at the same time as London was witnessing a rapid expansion in its number of shops and a transformation in the nature of its retail industry. However, prosecutions under the 1699 Act appear to have been comparatively rare, at least when compared to the huge number of cases

---

[507]Beverley Lemire, "The Theft of Clothes and Popular Consumerism in Early Modern England", *Journal of Social History*, 1990, pp.255-276, at p.264

[508]Garthine Walker, *Crime, Gender and Social Order in Early Modern England*, Cambridge, CUP, 2003, p.163.

[509]MacKay, "Why they stole: women in the Old Bailey", p.625.

[510]Captain Charles Johnson, *A General and True History of the Lives and Actions of the most Famous Highwaymen, Murders, Street-Robbers etc.*, Birmingham, 1742, p.301.

that must have occurred throughout the Metropolis.[511] Instead, some form of summary justice might be imposed on the perpetrator (for example, a beating), or the victim might accept financial payment in lieu of prosecution (compounding). Thus, in 1719, Mary Sutton unavailingly attempted to buy off a shopkeeper's wife who had caught her red handed; she "desir'd her not to be in a passion, and put 3 Half Crowns in her hand, and bid her say she bought it and did not steal it."[512] Doubtless many others were more successful in such circumstances. Alternatively, the victim might allow a prosecution to be brought in the Bridewell court or, if they did choose to have recourse to prosecution by indictment, prefer one for petty theft (alleging that the value of the goods stolen was under a shilling) or for simple grand larceny (over a shilling but less than five shillings in worth or, if more than this sum, without alleging that the technical requirements of the 1699 Act were made out). As a result, in the 1720s it was claimed that a combination of compounding and a reluctance to go to the expense and trouble of prosecuting detained shoplifters meant that only one in ten who were apprehended were actually brought to court, while nine out of ten of those few who were convicted were clergied, whipped or, at most, transported.[513]

Even when prosecutions were brought under the 1699 Act, acquittals or convictions for lesser offences (petty or simple grand larceny) were frequently returned, many juries, like that in Sarah Thorne's case in 1703, merely finding an accused woman "guilty to the value of 4s. and 10d."[514] This latter sum was almost as much a 'ritual' one as 10d. was in those situations where juries wished to return a finding of petty theft; for example, in 1707, the shoplifter Mary Floyd had her 19 yards of muslin valued at that very small sum.[515] It became increasingly easy to return such lesser verdicts, as the century advanced, because the definition of shoplifting set out in the 1699 Act was interpreted progressively more strictly; this was largely, it seems, because the crime came to be seen as a less serious offence than had been the case in the early 1700s. For example, the statutory requirement that the theft be committed "privately" came to be defined as being committed completely "unseen." By the end of the century, if a shop assistant witnessed such a crime being committed, before apprehending its perpetrator, perhaps having been alerted by suspicious behaviour, an acquittal or a partial verdict of simple larceny would usually ensue. By then, convictions for the full offence normally occurred where there had been exacerbating factors, for example, if particularly valuable items had been taken or the thief had

---

[511]Tammy C. Whitlock, *Crime, Gender and Consumer Culture in Nineteenth-century England,* Ashgate Publishing, Aldershot, 2005, at p.130

[512]OBSP, 8th April 1719, Trial of Mary Sutton.

[513]Anon, *The Great Grievance,* at p.1

[514] OBSP, 13th Oct. 1703, Trial of Sarah Thorne.

[515]OBSP, Trial of Mary Floyd, 23rd April 1707.

struggled violently when detained.[516] This also encouraged victims to indict for simple grand larceny (rather than the graver offence) from the beginning of a prosecution.

Females were always heavily associated with shoplifting. During the century, 183 women and 202 men were convicted of the offence at the Old Bailey (and women had a lower conviction rate than men). Between 1780 and 1823, 56 per cent of all shoplifting prosecutions at the Old Bailey involved women. Other females were convicted at that forum, or one of London's inferior sessions, for taking goods worth more than five shillings from a shop but outside the terms of the 1699 Act, appropriating goods worth less than five shillings from retail premises (both of which were simple larceny) or takings goods of under a shilling in value (petty larceny), and it is probable that women were more likely to be prosecuted for stealing such lesser sums. Women were certainly dominant in some *types* of shoplifting, such as the theft of cloth. This is not surprising, as a high proportion of those who stole fabric were needle and clothing workers (commonly a female occupation), stealing the raw materials of their trade. Thus, of the women convicted of shoplifting at the Old Bailey between 1780 and 1823, 64 per cent had been found guilty of stealing unmade up textiles, such as gingham, muslin or lace. In these cases they were also often older than the typical offender (20 per cent of women convicted of shoplifting in the years between 1791 and 1823 were aged from 30 to 40, compared to only 11 per cent of men).[517]

Periodically, shoplifting would become especially prevalent, something that might prompt retailers to petition the government to take special initiatives to deal with the problem. This might be done via an increased use of accomplice evidence in such cases, offering enhanced rewards to those securing convictions and refusing post-conviction reprieves. This occurred in 1726, and one result was the conviction and execution of a large group of female shoplifters. Among them were Jane Holmes, Katherine Fitzpatrick and Mary Robinson, all of whom were hanged that year. (After the mid-century, almost all women convicted under the 1699 Shoplifting Act were pardoned, even if it was on condition of transportation).

A number of fairly standard techniques seem to have been employed by shoplifters. Thus, women would sometimes work in pairs, one distracting the shopkeeper, perhaps by haggling over ('cheapening') an item, while the other concealed goods about her person. Some, like Elizabeth Rosdell in 1759, would personally distract the shopkeeper while acting alone. She was convicted of stealing six yards of expensive black silk lace from a shop in Bishopsgate after asking to examine some of the cloth and then agreeing to purchase a small amount. While the owner was cutting this for her, she knocked another piece of

---

[516]Deirdre Palk, *Gender, Crime and Judicial Discretion: 1780-1830*, Boydell Press, Woodbridge, 2006, at, p.70.
[517]Palk, *Gender, Crime and Judicial Discretion*, at p.39 and pp57-59.

material off the counter and hid it. Unfortunately for her, the shopkeeper noticed what she was doing and detained her in the street. Rosdell was then taken into a backroom, searched and the stolen lace discovered under her stays.[518] As this incident suggests, the voluminous female clothes of the era could be pressed into service to conceal stolen items. Typically, after Mary Davis took a pair of leather shoes from a cobbler's shop she was able to secret them under her cloak.[519] In the 1720s, Mary Robinson and Jane Holmes developed a sophisticated technique to steal even larger amounts of cloth from drapers' shops, on one occasion taking 80 yards of Mantua silk. They secured two large hooks under their petticoats, on which they could hang a full roll of the material, while an associate distracted the shopkeepers. Robinson's exceptional age, she was 70 when executed in 1726, may also have reduced their suspicions.[520] The sums stolen could be extensive. According to a confederation of London shopkeepers, one early eighteenth-century female shoplifter admitted, shortly before execution, that during her thieving career she had stolen goods "to the value of twelve thousand pounds" from retail premises.[521]

## Pick-pocketing

Legally, pick-pocketing was a particular type of theft, one that involved "privately" (i.e. secretly) stealing from another's person goods worth more than a shilling. This was a capital offence as, unlike other forms of (simple grand) larceny at this value, it had been put beyond the ambit of benefit of clergy by an Elizabethan statute (Blackstone thought that this was due to the ease with which the offence could be committed and the difficulty of preventing it).[522] Picking pockets of goods below a shilling in value remained petty theft and thus, of course, not even theoretically capital. Additionally, openly 'snatching' goods worth more than 12d. from the person might not qualify, as it was not done secretly. As the century advanced, the technical requirements for an offence of pick-pocketing to be made out (like those of shoplifting), and especially the meaning of "privately", came to be interpreted increasingly strictly. By the final decades of the eighteenth century, an accretion of case law defined the offence as occurring only in those situations in which the theft occurred without any 'knowledge' (constructive or actual) on the part of the loser and (effectively) without the victim having been grossly careless in his conduct; for example, by being intoxicated or asleep with a prostitute when the theft occurred.[523] Of course, it was always open to prosecutors to indict for simple grand larceny (a clergyable offence), or for juries to convict of such a lesser offence. The small number of women found fully guilty over the course of the century (about 12

---

[518]OBSP, Trial of Elizabeth Rosdell, 24th Oct. 1759.
[519]OBSP, Trial of Mary Davis, 24th Oct. 1787.
[520]Hayward (Ed.), *Lives of the Most Remarkable Criminals*, pp.381-383.
[521]Anon, *The Great Grievance*, at p.1
[522]Blackstone, *Commentaries on the Laws of England*, 1769, vol. 4, at p.241.
[523]Palk, *Gender, Crime and Judicial Discretion*, at pp.69-70.

per cent of all female indictments for the crime) compared to those situations that resulted in a finding of guilty of a lesser offence (about 30 per cent), indicate that both were frequent occurrences.

Many, probably a majority, of pickpockets were female, especially in London, where it was noted as early as the 1650s that "as many women as men" were involved in the crime.[524] Court records show that this was still the case in the eighteenth century. Thus, between January 1700 and December 1799, at least 125 women were convicted of pick-pocketing at the Old Bailey alone. This was fractionally higher than the number of men (118) found guilty of the offence at the same forum during the period. The discrepancy is slightly higher still, when acquittals are considered as well. Between 1780 and 1808, 53 per cent of those accused of pick-pocketing at the Old Bailey were women.[525]

Some women achieved special notoriety for their success in this arena. In the 1730s, an Irishwoman named Mary Young was popularly known as 'Jenny Diver' because of her skill; she led a successful gang of predominantly female pick-pockets.[526] Although twice transported, under different names, she swiftly returned to London and crime, prior to her final arrest and execution at Tyburn in 1741.[527] Other 'professionals' had even longer careers. In 1728, when 'Moll' King and Sarah Fox were arrested for picking a gentleman's pocket in a theatre, it was noted that they had been pickpockets for over 30 years.[528] The same year, after Judith Holloway was capitally convicted of picking a woman's pocket of a silver snuffbox in Bishopsgate Street, it was observed that she had been a "noted pickpocket for above forty years."[529]

Part of the explanation for this heavy female involvement in pick-pocketing is probably physical; women (like children) were more likely to have small hands and a delicate 'touch'. Indeed, in the previous century, and despite her name, an absence of this quality had prompted Moll Cutpurse to move into receiving: "I had no great promising symptoms of a lucky mercurial in my fingers, for they had not been used to any slight and fine work."[530] However, there was another, more important, reason: the victims of female pickpockets tended to be men. Of the 125 convicted women, 107 had male victims and only 17 had female ones, although in six of these cases, the male owner (usually a husband) of the stolen items was also named on the indictment (the status of one victim is unclear from the report). In part, the disparity is readily explicable. More men were abroad in the streets and they were more likely to be carrying valuable objects, such as

---

[524] Anon, *The Caterpillars of this Nation Anatomised*, London, 1659, p.4.

[525] Palk, *Gender, Crime and Judicial Discretion*, at p.69.

[526] *The Gentleman's Magazine*, vol. 11, March 1741, p.162.

[527] Rev. Gordon, *The Life and Circumstantial Account of the extraordinary and Surprising Exploits, Travils, robberies and Escapes of the Famous Jenny Diver*, London, 1745, p.8.

[528] *The Weekly Journal*, 4th May 1728.

[529] *The Flying-Post*, 7th December 1728.

[530] Anon, *The Life and Death of Mrs Mary Frith, Commonly Called Mal Cutpurse*, London, Printed for W. Gilbertson, 1662, p.3.

time-pieces or significant amounts of cash, especially if they were from the upper social orders or engaged in business. As a typical example can be considered Mary Freeman's victim in 1734, a gentleman who lost 15 guineas, a silver snuffbox and two gold rings.[531] Male fashions in clothing may also have made men more vulnerable to theft. However, a great many cases of female perpetrated pick pocketing in which men were victims had, as their contextual background, the use of 'sexual attraction' to get close to their targets. Thus, women might flirt with men in streets and public houses before helping themselves to their goods and prostitutes might steal from their clients.

*Theft by Prostitutes*

Many prostitutes stole from men, before, during or after intercourse. Their high numbers in the Metropolitan area meant that they inevitably made up a major element in female instrumental crime. The ad hoc and temporary recourse to prostitution by many poorer Metropolitan women can make distinguishing professional 'whores' from drunk or flirtatious women difficult. Nevertheless, according to one estimate, nearly a fifth of the females tried at the Old Bailey during the eighteenth century had sexual transactions for money as the immediate background to their offences.[532]

Prostitutes were usually opportunistic thieves, taking advantage of men when the chance presented itself. Indeed, according to the magistrate John Fielding, given that necessity was usually the motive force behind both activities, it was natural that whores would "generally join the thief to the prostitute."[533] Mary Standford might be considered 'typical' of such women. From a respectable background in the country, she was sent to London to enter service. However, she lost most of her appointments due to her "forward behaviour" and, after being seduced by a footman, became a prostitute, working the area between Temple Bar and Ludgate Hill. She also graduated to picking her clients' pockets when the opportunity presented itself. In due course, she had a baby out of wedlock, increasing her need for money. Continuing with prostitution, she eventually attracted a client who alleged that she had picked his pocket of four guineas and a silk handkerchief. Although Standford claimed the money was a gift, she was arrested, tried and (unusually for a woman in this situation) convicted of the full offence.[534]

Many of the victims of such prostitutes were intoxicated. Thus, Ann Southerwood accosted Alexander Chance while he was coming across London

---

[531] *The Daily Journal,* 17th Sept. 1734

[532] Peter King, "Gender, Crime and justice in late eighteenth-and early nineteenth-century England", *Gender and Crime in Modern Europe,* M. Arnot et al (Eds.), London, University College London press, 1998, pp.44-74, at p.46 and pp.62-64.

[533] John Fielding, *A Plan for a Preservatory and Reformation for the benefit of Deserted Girls, and Penitent Prostitutes,* London, 1758, p.4.

[534] Hayward (Ed.), *Lives of the Most Remarkable Criminals,* pp.368-371.

a cameo for William Hogarth in his print 'Cruelty in Perfection' (1751). However, most maids who stole acted alone and on their own initiative. Inevitably, they would usually have a detailed knowledge of their masters' premises, allowing them to take secreted treasures and other valuables.

Female servants who were prosecuted for stealing from their employers tended to have been recently taken on, rather than old retainers. Some had been in service for only a matter of days, many for just a few weeks.[546] Typically, one night in 1711, Mary Stotter stole goods worth 11s. from her master of only a week and made off, being subsequently arrested with them still in her possession. (At trial, she was convicted, but found guilty only to the value of 10d.).[547] Similarly, in 1798, Susannah Taylor, aged 58, was indicted for stealing clothes, linen and silverware worth over £12 from her master of three weeks, a Stoke Newington sadler. She ransacked his house overnight and then immediately pledged the items with several local pawnbrokers (to lessen suspicion about the provenance of the large amount of goods she was disposing of) before disappearing. Even so, she was only convicted of stealing goods to the value of 39s. and sentenced to two years in the House of Correction.[548] In passing, it should be noted that the three types of item that Taylor appropriated featured especially prominently amongst those goods stolen by domestic servants, presumably, this was largely because of their ready marketability.

Of course, this does not *necessarily* mean that longer serving maids did not steal. They may have mastered techniques to avoid discovery or, more likely, come to informal arrangements with their masters after detection. These might involve working without pay until they had made good any loss, or simply being dismissed without a reference or back-pay by an employer whose familiarity with the individual made him (or her) too compassionate to go to the trouble and expense of pursuing a matter through the courts. Even newly employed women would attempt such stratagems. Thus, in 1718, Ann Smith, who had been in service for less than two weeks, stole 13 guineas, some petty cash and jewelry from her master. When he caught up with her in Covent Garden, after she had disposed of some of the items and the money, she unavailingly tried to negotiate, admitting the crime and proposing that: "…if her master would not prosecute her, she would go to service and pay him the rest of the money which she had embezzled."[549] The following year, the similarly situated Hannah Wyfield was more successful, only being prosecuted when she fell behind in her efforts to reimburse her erstwhile employer. Nevertheless, although recourse to such measures undoubtedly helps explain why longer serving servants were less likely to be processed through the criminal justice system, it is also plausible that, having developed some loyalty to their masters, they were inherently less likely

---

[546] Humfrey, "Female Servants and Women's Criminality", p.61.

[547] OBSP, Trial of Mary Stotter, 16th May 1711.

[548] OBSP, Trial of Susannah Taylor, 12th Sept. 1798.

[549] OBSP, Trial of Ann Smith, 27th Feb. 1718.

to steal. Additionally, and further bolstering the number of recently employed maids prosecuted, it is possible that a few women deliberately sought domestic employment with a view to the criminal opportunities it presented, and would merely wait until a chance to steal appeared.

Servants also posed a more insidious and subtle threat. As Defoe noted, at least if a maid was a: "...downright thief she strips you, at once, and you know your loss." More problematic were those who took favours from tradesmen in exchange for allocating custom or, even worse, pilfered from their employers. He was incensed that such petty theft was often tacitly ignored. Nevertheless, defining this type of embezzlement as 'stealing' presents difficult problems as to where the realm of time-sanctioned work-connected perquisites and allowances ended, and theft began. Many of these benefits were regarded by servants as part of their entitlements.[550] Even Defoe acknowledged that pilfering servants did not view taking tea, sugar and wine or similar commodities as theft and thought that if they did: "...not directly take your pewter from your shelf, or your linen from your drawers, they are very honest."[551]

As some of the cases already cited suggest, although the eighteenth century saw regularly published diatribes against dishonest servants, the Old Bailey juries that tried them seem to have been remarkably benign. They frequently indulged in 'pious perjury' to down-value stolen goods below the strategic levels at which offences ceased to be petty thefts (a shilling) or, alternatively, became unclergyable and thus capital felonies (40 shillings). Jurors seem to have felt that, depending on the case, transportation, branding and discharge, flogging or a short spell of imprisonment, rather than execution, met the gravity of most situations. Thus, of 95 trials between 1715 and 1721 in which female servants were prosecuted for stealing from their masters, only ten ultimately received the death penalty, the rest being given lesser penalties. (Furthermore, several of the condemned women very probably had their sentences commuted to 14 years transportation or some other disposal). Those female servants who were capitally convicted would often have done something to aggravate their offences: stolen quite exceptional amounts of money; refused to co-operate by providing information after arrest as to what they had done with the stolen items; adopted a defiant or insolent tone with the authorities and the court, or stolen immediately after being taken on (though frequently, even this did not prevent a benign outcome).[552]

Why middle ranking jurors, most of whom would have had a maid at the very least, should show such lenience is difficult to explain. It is possible that these crimes were viewed as an occupational hazard of employing servants. Perhaps more significantly, such thefts, usually committed stealthily by women,

---

[550]Bridget Hill, *Servants: English Domestics in the Eighteenth Century*, 1996, Oxford, Clarendon Press, pp.45-46.
[551]Moreton (Defoe), *Every-Body's Business*, pp.7-9.
[552]Humfrey, "Female Servants and Women's Criminality" pp.74-75.

involved no potential risk of violence, something that was always a matter of acute contemporary concern. Where this was not the case, the judicial process could be ruthless. When Grace Tripp was tried for murder after letting a robber named Peters, who was also her lover, into Lord Torrington's house, during which crime another servant had her throat slit, the authorities made an example of her. Although Peters was the actual killer, he was granted immunity from prosecution and allowed to turn Crown evidence against Tripp. She was convicted and executed, despite being a minor actor in the process (she had held a candle during the murder), only 19 years old and having been promised marriage by Peters in exchange for facilitating entry to her employer's house.[553]

The large-scale employment of females as servants had another, indirect, affect on female crime. Many women who came to London seeking domestic service did so without prearranged 'places' and with limited financial resources. Some failed to secure employment on arrival in the city and swiftly found themselves destitute and a long way from any possibility of family assistance. Others, who had initially been taken on, quickly lost their positions. In these circumstances, they might turn to prostitution and/or crime to support themselves. As a result, for women, the years around 20, when many arrived in the Metropolis, tended to produce a peak in offending.[554] In passing, it should also be noted that a significant number of former servants used the knowledge gained in the course of their employment to return to their masters' premises, after discharge, and steal, especially if their initial departure had been acrimonious. Additionally, the possibility that masters might occasionally make unfounded allegations of theft against their servants as part of a dispute over wages etc. cannot be precluded.

## Receivers

London provided easy access to receivers, both small-scale dealers, often operating from the cover of legitimate businesses such as pawnbrokers, second-hand garment sellers or tavern keepers, and those who dealt on a larger, even quasi commercial, scale. As far back as the medieval period this crime had been disproportionately associated with women. However, the eighteenth century saw an especially heavy female involvement. Some estimates suggest that the offence made up 5 per cent of all female indictments and that women made up well over 40 per cent of those convicted of receiving stolen property in the Metropolis. According to the Sessions Papers, almost 2,000 people were prosecuted at the Bailey for the crime during the century, and nearly half of them were women. Even this does not necessarily reflect the respective proportions prosecuted for the crime as, often being a misdemeanour, it was also indicted at the various inferior sessions held in the Metropolis, and women were usually more (rather than less) likely to be tried at these forums.

---

[553]Rayner and Crook, *The Complete Newgate Calendar*, vol. II, pp.213-214.
[554]King, "Female offenders", p.80.

In lower class households women would often be responsible for managing the family budget, whether this involved purchasing food, negotiating with tradesmen or pawning items when times were hard and redeeming them when money was available.[555] This also gave them an understanding of the value of household items, something that facilitated receiving. The women involved were often widows, possibly attracted to the crime as a way of supplementing meagre incomes or to ward off indigence. They would also have had many years to make valuable 'business' contacts and secure premises from which to operate. Thus, in 1731, Sarah Hewlet from St. Sepulchre's parish, allegedly a notorious "common Receiver of stolen Goods", was convicted of receiving four pounds of stolen bacon. She appears to have been a Fagin like criminal mastermind, arranging low level crimes from her gin shop. At her trial, it was claimed that she had enticed and encouraged young boys to steal, lodged them in her house and paid them small amounts of money, usually just a few pence or shillings, for quite valuable items, which she then made them spend in her premises on "Gin and Hot-pots." Despite being convicted, Hewlet was merely fined and sentenced to a short term in prison.[556]

Several female receivers specialised in clothes and fabric. For example, in 1765, Rachael Freeman was arrested after one of her regular suppliers, a woman caught shop-lifting in a linen-draper's, named her to the authorities and her premises were searched.[557] That many women worked in taverns and coffee-shops also furnished opportunities for small scale receiving from, and disposal to, customers. According to Patrick Colquhoun, writing at the end of the century, some larger scale female receivers also worked as brothel keepers. However, as the relatively small numbers of both male and female receivers who were found guilty (about a quarter of those women indicted for the crime at the Old Bailey) suggests, they were extremely difficult to convict, despite legislation in 1691 and further Acts reinforcing this statute in 1702 and 1706. Almost no women at all were convicted of the crime at the Bailey in the first six years of the century.

## Trial and Disposal

As some of the cases cited suggest, women accused of instrumental crimes (like those accused of most other offences) were more likely than their male counterparts to receive favourable outcomes from the era's criminal litigation process, whether in the form of outright acquittal, being convicted of lesser offences than those charged, milder punishments imposed after conviction, or reprieves from sentences of death. This was an aspect of the general lenience manifest towards female defendants examined in chapter two. It was not a new

---

[555] J M Golby and A W Purdue, *The Civilisation of the Crowd: Popular Culture in England 1750-1900*, Sutton Publishing, Stroud, 1999, p.141.
[556] OBSP, Trial of Sarah Hewlet, 28th April 1731.
[557] Lemire, "The Theft of Clothes and Popular Consumerism", p.267.

phenomenon. Even in the late seventeenth century, Metropolitan juries were far more likely to reduce a charge for an indicted woman than for a man. Thus, in burglary cases, it occurred in only 33 per cent of trials involving men, but fully 64 per cent for women.[558] This continued unabated in the following century. Although petty theft (under a shilling in value) was rarely prosecuted *per se* at the Bailey during the eighteenth century (due to its trivial nature), it was a very frequently returned 'lesser' verdict, largely as a result of juries committing 'pious perjury' by down valuing goods to this non-capital amount. A scrutiny of the Old Bailey Sessions Papers indicates that women were more than twice as likely as men to receive such a disposal. Additionally they were more likely to receive outright acquittals; in the late eighteenth and early nineteenth centuries (1780-1820), most male property offenders from the London area who were tried at the Bailey were convicted (c. 61 per cent), but only a minority of females were found guilty.[559]

If convicted, women were also treated more leniently than men. Thus, only eight per cent of female property offenders were sentenced to death during the two decades immediately before and after 1800, compared to 13 per cent of men. Even more significantly, in practice hardly any women (one individual or 0.15 per cent) were actually executed for such crimes (rather than being subsequently reprieved) during this period, whereas 89 men (2.85 per cent) were hanged. Even earlier in the century, female instrumental crime that actually resulted in executions had often occurred during short term 'panics', such as that over shoplifting in 1726, or involved specially aggravating factors. Thus, Anne Harris was executed after she had been clergied and burned in the face by the executioner (it was one of his talks) so often at the beginning of the century that there was "no more room left for the hangman to stigmatise her." Similarly, in 1749, Mary Dimer was hanged for participating in a violent robbery near Tower Hill, during which her accomplice viciously beat their victim, despite the latter's plea for clemency on her behalf. Women were also more likely to be fined and less likely to be subjected to a sentence of transportation than men.[560]

Of course, it is possible that they received more lenient treatment because they were not as 'hardened' as male criminals, perhaps committing less serious examples of the crimes with which they were charged, or having fewer previous convictions. Modern disparities in sentencing between male and female offenders, which are still generally favourable to women, are usually attributed to gender related contextual factors rather than gender bias. Women present fewer problematic (or aggravating) characteristics to the present-day justice system.[561] However, in the eighteenth century this does not appear to have been the case.

---

[558]Val Edwards, "German Princesses and Common Prostitutes: Women and Crime in Restoration London", *Holdsworth Law Review*, vol.6, 1981, pp.2-16, at pp.9-13.

[559]King, "Gender, crime and justice...", pp.44-74, at p.46 and pp.62-64.

[560]King, "The rise of juvenile delinquency in England", p.62.

[561]Barry Godfrey et al, "Explaining Gendered Sentencing Patterns for Violent Men and Women in the Late-Victorian and Edwardian Period", *British Journal of Criminology*, vol. 45, 2005, p.696-697.

The available evidence suggests that female defendants at the Old Bailey were no more likely than men to be neophytes to crime or to be markedly less hardened offenders.[562] Other explanations must be sought for their milder treatment.

It is probable that, because men were expected to be aggressive, male instrumental crime, of any sort, was perceived as more threatening than that committed by women, and so was more likely to be prosecuted to conviction and to receive severe punishment. Certainly, women were unlikely to be swept up in the draconian penal regimes that often accompanied the crime/prosecution surges that followed large-scale post-war demobilisations (such as that of the 1780s). Much female theft could also be seen as an inherent hazard of employing servants carelessly or voluntarily associating with prostitutes. It was not the work of anonymous strangers, emerging from the shadows to victimise members of the public who were otherwise powerless to protect themselves. Women may also have been treated more leniently because it was felt that their inherent natures meant they were easily led astray by others. Perhaps most importantly, and as previously noted, it may have been because a claim of need or pressure of circumstances was much more readily accepted as a legitimate motive behind their crimes. (Draconian sentences would also force any children of female convicts on to their parishes, something that was always acutely unpopular amongst well to do ratepayers).[563]

It should also be noted that, unlike the high incidence of female prosecution, the historical record suggests that there was nothing unusual or specific to the criminal justice system of the eighteenth-century Metropolis in this lenient treatment of female thieves. Women accused of property offences have frequently received more favourable outcomes than their male counterparts, something that was apparent even in the medieval period.[564]

## Conclusion

It is sometimes suggested that English society started to become truly 'modern' in the eighteenth century. However, when it comes to the commission of instrumental crime, modern Metropolitan women lag behind their forbears of the 1700s. The (historically) unusually high level of female offending during this era, when compared to that of men, was probably the result of a combination of circumstances rather than any one cause. Nevertheless, it is apparent that single Metropolitan women were much more likely to commit and be prosecuted for theft than their married counterparts. In part, this is a reflection of a differential in levels of law enforcement. The doctrine of *feme covert* and, even more importantly, the social attitudes that underpinned it, meant that married women and those acting with men were less likely to be indicted. However, to a larger

---

[562]King, "The rise of juvenile delinquency in England", p.62.
[563]King, "The rise of juvenile delinquency in England", pp.63-64.
[564]Hanawalt, "The Female Felon in Fourteenth-Century England", p.266.

extent, it seems to reflect incidence; single women were more likely to offend as a result of the economic precariousness and social isolation that often characterised their lives combined with their unprecedented degree of independence and lack of 'supervision' in the Metropolitan environment.

In these circumstances, crime could become an attractive option in a city (and its surroundings) where numerous opportunities for offending readily presented themselves, some of which women were ideally situated to exploit. Thus, the commoditisation of sex, and the relative informality with which it often occurred, at variance to 'normal' practice in most rural areas, provided the background for much crime. Similarly, the continuous demand for (and heavy turnover of) maids and the plethora of urban retail premises gave many women exposure to temptation in a large city that provided both the opportunity to readily dispose of stolen goods and also a real chance of escaping post-crime detection. For older women, accumulated trading and dealing skills, contacts and their understanding of the value of consumer goods, meant that they might experience financial success when involved in disposing of the proceeds of others' crimes, even if they came from instrumental offences in which females were not well represented (such as burglary). Perhaps compounding these problems, the Metropolitan area was also large enough for specifically female criminal groups to develop (such as Diver's gang), into which women could slip, finding in them the economic and, perhaps, emotional support that was so often lacking for strangers in the capital.

Even so, the high level of female prosecution for theft in the Metropolis during the eighteenth century, and the 'active' involvement of many of its perpetrators, does not appear to have eliminated (though it may have reduced) the traditional 'chivalry' shown by the courts and many (usually male) property owners towards women, something that was normally denied to able-bodied men. This is, perhaps, significant. It is sometimes argued that, in eighteenth-century England, offences against the person were viewed much less seriously than those against property. However, the indulgence shown towards many women might suggest that it was not instrumental crime *per se* that occasioned alarm, but rather the context in which it occurred. Unlike their male counterparts, female thieves were more likely to be seen as pathetic rather than menacing; when they were, their crimes were also seen as relatively minor, even where they involved quite significant sums of money or valuable goods and, as was often the case, considerable deliberation. By contrast, nocturnal burglaries, largely committed by males, always involved the possibility of very serious violence, as householders, roused from their slumbers, might confront desperate men, in disadvantageous circumstances. Finally, the early decades of the eighteenth century challenge behavioural stereotypes by indicating that, although women *may* be inherently less violent than men, in the right environment they are just as capable of criminal dishonesty. Nevertheless, the conjunction of circumstances necessary for this to occur appears to be highly unusual and historically very rare.

# Chapter 6: Rape

## Introduction

This chapter will examine legal and social attitudes towards rape in the Metropolitan area. In doing so, it will draw general conclusions about the nature of prosecuted rapes during the eighteenth century, while identifying those features of the crime that were more commonly found in what was often an urban or suburban, rather than rural, environment. Additionally, it will focus closely on the somewhat neglected area of forensic practice in rape cases. Understanding this is vital when drawing other interpretations from the legal record. Thus, some recent analysis of notorious rape trials from the era, such as the case of *Abraham v Thornton* in 1817, has been flawed by a failure to examine the case in the context of the criminal litigation process, and to understand the impact that this had on both the evidence adduced and the eventual verdict.[565]

In early modern England, rape was an infrequently prosecuted offence, normally making up about one per cent of indicted felonies. Thus, the Surrey Assizes averaged one prosecution a year between 1660 and 1800, and those for Sussex only one every four years.[566] Guilty verdicts were even rarer, though the majority of those convicted were also executed.[567] This made rape unusual. In public, it was universally acknowledged in both elite and popular debate to be the "greatest offense next to murder", in the words of the sixteenth century jurist Sir Anthony Fitzherbert. As an eighteenth-century complainant freely conceded (albeit not entirely accurately), it: "...was a crime for which a man must lose his life."[568] However, unlike murder, rape seems to have been an offence that only rarely got to court, and was difficult to prosecute successfully when it did. Even in the early 1800s, three times as many murder trials came before the English courts as those for rape. There were good reasons for this. Legally, the definition of rape was uncertain and, even more importantly, it was hard to substantiate with admissible evidence. Magistrates were reluctant to commit men accused of the crime for trial, grand juries often refused to indict them when they did, and, if indicted, petty juries were frequently unwilling to

[565]Roy Porter (1986) "Rape-Does it have a Historical Meaning?" in *Rape an Historical and Cultural Enquiry*, S Tomaselli and R Porter (Eds.) Oxford, p.227
[566]John M Beattie (1986) *Crime and the Courts in England: 1660-1800*, OUP, Oxford, p.126.
[567]Garthine Walker, "Rereading Rape and Sexual Violence in Early Modern England" in *Gender and History*, April 1998, vol. 10, p.1.
[568]OBSP, Trial of Richard Green, 10th May 1769.

convict them.[569] As a result, and even by modern standards, there was probably massive under-reporting of the crime.

## The Statistical Picture

A total of 45 people, both men and women (prosecuted as accessories) were convicted of rape between January 1700 and the end of 1799.[570] These convicts emerged from the trials of 281 people indicted for the crime (i.e. cases that were not thrown out prior to trial by the Grand Jury returning a bill of indictment 'ignoramus'). This produces a conviction rate of circa 16 per cent. The number of convictions per decade varied over the course of the 1700s, and, given the population increase over the course of the century, the per capita rate fluctuated even more. Thus, six men were found guilty in the final decade of the century; one man in the 1780s; seven in the 1770s; eight in the 1760s; two in the 1750s; four in the 1740s; eight in the 1730s and five in the 1720s. The eight men convicted in the 1730s came from a group of 34 put on trial; the eight in the 1760s from a group of 26, too small a difference on these very low numbers to carry any significance.

Broadly speaking, such results appear to be in alignment with most other findings for the era, though Anthony Simpson's work suggests that conviction rates varied more substantially when broken down into lustrums (the years between 1755 and 1759 produced no convictions, while in those between 1795 and 1799, 38 per cent of defendants were found guilty).[571] Nevertheless, taken overall, there was little variation in the proportion of defendants found guilty over the course of the century. Whatever measure is used, conviction rates were much lower than those for most other felonies, such as larceny and burglary. In the early 1800s, they stood at 17 per cent, compared to 63.1 per cent for all indictable crimes taken together.[572]

Professor Beattie has identified a tangible increase in the number of rape prosecutions brought in Surrey during the eighteenth century; though small, it clearly outstripped the county's population growth. Thus, in the years between 1660 and 1689 there were eight cases, while between 1780 and 1802 there were 13. He suggests that this indicates that women were more willing to bring attacks to court, perhaps because the courts themselves became less hostile to

---

[569]Cynthia B Herrup (1999) *A House in Gross Disorder: Sex, Law, and the Second Earl of Castlehaven*, OUP, New York, pp.122-123.

[570]The online OBSP search lists 53 individuals due to mistaken multiple reporting of some defendants. Gaps in the records might suggest c.50 as a plausible figure.

[571]Antony E Simpson, "Vulnerability and the Age of Female Consent: Legal Innovation and its Effect on Prosecutions for Rape in Eighteenth-Century London" in *Sexual Underworlds of the Enlightenment*, 1987, G S Rousseau and R Porter (Eds.), Manchester University Press, Manchester, pp.188-192.

[572]A D Harvey, *Sex in Georgian England: attitudes and prejudices from the 1720s to the 1820s*, Duckworth, London, 1994, p.77.

such actions.[573] However, such an increase was not matched north of the Thames. The number of prosecutions and convictions remained relatively constant despite a very major population growth in the Metropolis, which grew from just under 600,000 people at the start of the century to just over a million at its end. Thus, in the half century from January 1700 to December 1749, 130 people were tried for the crime, and 21 convictions resulted. In the following 50 years, there were 24 convictions from about 151 trials. This suggests, if anything, a major decline in the per capita rate for the area. Why this should occur, at variance to the pattern in Surrey, is difficult to determine, but it does suggest that a 'softening' in forensic practice that encouraged complainants to come forward was unlikely.

## Historical Background to the Crime

During the medieval period rape was often seen as a crime against (another man's) property, i.e. as a form of theft. Indeed, rape and abduction (often termed ravishment) were closely linked by the Statutes of Westminster as well as in the medieval mindset, and not properly distinguished until after 1500 (abduction remained a separate felony). Even a mid-Tudor definition could declare that rape occurred where a man: "...ravisheth or taketh a[nother] man's wife, wydowe or maide against her will."[574] It was thought that one of the most serious dangers faced by a rape victim, if single, was her loss of 'marketability'. As a result, rape was sometimes the precursor to marriage in medieval England, especially amongst the upper classes or where the victim's family had earlier opposed a relationship.[575]

However, a significant change in attitudes towards the crime seems to have occurred during the early modern era. By the mid-seventeenth century, legal definitions had altered, and medieval jurisprudential views substantially abandoned. Rape had become a 'sexual' crime in which it was the woman's innocence that was in issue.[576] By the eighteenth century, it was clearly the complainant who was the crime's victim. However, 'medieval' attitudes and practices lingered. Abduction continued a modest existence. Thus, in November 1690, a royal proclamation called for the arrest of Sir John Johnstone, who had kidnapped a 13 year old "virgin of great wealth", from Great Queen Street, with a view to ravishing and forcing her into marriage.[577] Similarly, in the 1700s,

---

[573]Beattie, *Crime and the Courts in England: 1660-1800*, pp. 126-131.
[574]Wilhelm Middleton, *The Boke For A Justyce of Peace*, London, 1545, f.Bii.
[575]For rape in England during the fourteenth century, see B Hanawalt, *Crime and conflict in English Communities, 1300-1348*, Harvard University Press, Cambridge/London, 1979, p.106.
[576]Manon Van de Heijden, "Women as victims of sexual and domestic violence in Seventeenth-Century Holland: Criminal cases of Rape, Incest and maltreatment in Rotterdam and Delft" in *Journal of Social History*, 2000, vol. 33, no. 33, p.623.
[577]15th Nov 1690, Printed by Charles Bull, London.

several Metropolitan rapists, such as John Sheridan, offered marriage to their victims in lieu of being prosecuted.[578]

## The Eighteenth-Century Legal Definition of Rape

Rape defendants were usually adult and adolescent males. Boys below the age of fourteen could not be guilty of rape as, for this crime, the law assumed they had an "imbecility of body as well as mind."[579] Although, of course, a woman could not be a principal to rape, she could, like a man, be an accessory.[580] Indeed, a woman could still be prosecuted as an accessory even if the principal was still at liberty, as occurred with Lucy Roberts in 1758. Under common law, an accessory was as criminally liable as the principal. As a result, women made up c. 5 per cent of rape defendants. Any female could be the victim of rape, although a man could not rape his wife (a situation that has only been fully abandoned in the common law world over the last 30 years).

Eighteenth century courts applied varying definitions to the essential elements of the crime. Consequently, at the start of the 1800s, an observer could note that during the previous century a: "…very considerable doubt ha[d] arisen as to what shall be considered sufficient evidence of the actual commission of this offence."[581] There was no dispute that rape involved having "unlawful and carnal knowledge of a woman, by force against her will."[582] However, there was considerable doubt as to whether 'carnal knowledge' required both penetration and the emission of 'seed' or simply penetration. The latter certainly had to be present, however shallow. Ejaculation without penetration was not rape.[583] But penetration without ejaculation posed greater problems. The authorities appeared to conflict on this issue; indeed, some jurists, such as Coke, expressed conflicting views within the body of their own work. Thus, after the Reverend Russen's trial in 1777, the 12 judges, sitting together in London, decided that any penetration, even if it did not break the hymen, was enough, without any need for a 'spermatic injection'. This appears to have been the dominant view at the time.

However, only a few years later, *Hill's Case* (1781), another special verdict, was considered by the assembled judges and, on this occasion, a majority concluded that penetration without emission was not rape. Nevertheless, it seems that emission would normally be assumed from penetration, especially where the man finished coitus of his own volition, *unless* the contrary appeared

[578]OBSP, Trial of John Sheridan, 13th April 1768.
[579]William Blackstone, *Commentaries on the Laws of England* Book IV, Clarendon Press, Oxford, 1769, p.212.
[580]OBSP, Trial of Hugh Leeson and Sarah Blandford, 27th Apr 1715.
[581]Edward Hyde, *A Treatise of the Pleas of the Crown*, vol. 1, printed by A. Strahan, London, 1803, p.436.
[582]William Hawkins, *A Treatise of the Pleas of the Crown*, Book 1, 2nd Edition, London, 1724, p.108.
[583]Sir Edward Coke, *The third part of the institutes of the laws of England*, printed for A Crooke, London, 1669, p.60.

clearly on the evidence.[584] At the Old Bailey, simple penetration often appears to have been sufficient. However, *in practice*, it seems that supporting this with evidence of ejaculation was highly desirable and something that the courts would expressly enquire into. Thus, in 1796, Ann Thacker was questioned by the court until she gave an affirmative response not only to the defendant having secreted something wet but also to the question: "Was he in your body at the time something warm came from him?"[585] Early in the nineteenth century, the need for emission was expressly abandoned by statute (9 Geo.4. c31 s16).[586]

## The Inchoate Offence

Assault with intent to rape (i.e. attempted rape) was an indictable misdemeanour. As such, it could be prosecuted either at the Old Bailey (the Metropolitan equivalent of the Assizes) or at the various quarter sessions held for Middlesex, the City and Westminster. Most such cases, both nationally and in the London area, appear to have gone to the inferior courts, and only 11 are recorded as having been heard at the Old Bailey between 1714 and the end of the century. By contrast, the City of London Sessions alone heard 77 cases of assault with intent to rape between 1740 and 1830.[587] Of the 11 Old Bailey cases, seven were brought in the 1720s and the last in 1742. There were usually special reasons explaining why these cases were heard at the higher forum. Sometimes, they were prosecuted there after a rape trial in the same court had produced a 'not guilty' verdict because the issue of penetration was not made out, despite the rest of the evidence being strong. Thus, in 1725, Samuel Street was convicted of the misdemeanour at the Old Bailey sessions immediately following those at which he had been acquitted of raping the same complainant.[588]

Very importantly, because it was a misdemeanour and not a felony, a jury considering a full rape indictment could not return a lesser verdict of guilty to the inchoate crime, whether because they genuinely felt the full offence had not been made out (for lack of penetration) or as 'pious perjury' aimed at ameliorating the death for felony rule, in the way that they could, for example, down value larceny to petty theft. Thus, in 1788, when a jury tried to return a verdict of guilty of attempted rape on a single substantive count, the presiding judge warned them that they must either convict or acquit the prisoner. Very reluctantly, they eventually returned a 'not guilty' verdict. However, and for the same reason, an acquittal on a rape indictment did not preclude a subsequent prosecution for assault with intent to rape, despite the doctrine of *autrefois acquit* being well established. Thus, the judge in the 1788 trial shared the jury's view of

---

[584]Hyde, *A Treatise of the Pleas of the Crown*, p.439.
[585]OBSP, Trial of Thomas Davenport, 17th Feb. 1796.
[586]J F Archbold, *A Summary of the Law Relative to Pleading and Evidence in Criminal Cases*, 3rd Edition, Pheney, London, 1828, p.287.
[587]Simpson, "Vulnerability and the Age of Female Consent…", p.189.
[588]OBSP, Trial of Samuel Street, 13th Oct. 1725.

the merits of the case, remanded the defendant in custody and awarded the victim's father five guineas from public funds to pursue a misdemeanour prosecution.[589] Similarly, in 1751, after a surgeon giving expert evidence at a rape trial observed that the little girl who was the alleged victim was too young for a man to be able to enter her, and stated that this view had been shared by all his fellow surgeons at the London Hospital, the defendant was acquitted: "…but another bill for a misdemeanour was preferred against him to be tried at Guildhall."[590]

Occasionally, a misdemeanour count for the lesser crime would be indicted at the same time as a rape count, so that jurors had a lesser offence on which to convict as an alternative. This occurred at the trial of Robert Lander in August 1725. However, it was very unusual, perhaps because it conveyed a lack of confidence in the more serious count, discouraging a conviction (as even the courts occasionally acknowledged) or because of legal differences between the two types of crime.[591] Obviously, a failure on the lesser count would make a subsequent prosecution for the more serious offence unsuccessful. Thus, in 1734, Betteridge May's prosecution of her alleged assailant appears to have failed largely because she had already tried to prefer an indictment for rape at Hick's Hall (the location of the Middlesex sessions), which had been thrown out by the Grand Jury there, and then unsuccessfully prosecuted him for assault with intent to rape.

The punishment for an attempt was much milder than for the completed offence; it could involve any combination of fine, flogging or a short sentence of imprisonment. Thus, in April 1730, George Rouson was tried at Hick's Hall for the 'rape' of a nine year old child (actually assault with intent to rape) and sentenced to be whipped twice from Islington turn-pike to the local Church, and then to be kept to hard labour at Clerkenwell Bridewell for a year.[592] In 1725, Samuel Street was fined and imprisoned for six months after being convicted of the same offence at the Old Bailey. However, even the misdemeanour was not a generic crime, covering a wide range of sexual assaults; its *mens rea*, an intent to rape, had to be made out. This made attempted rape slightly more difficult to prosecute successfully than some other misdemeanors. It only applied to attacks that fell just short of the capital crime. Prior to their decline into non-existence after the Civil War, many lesser, but (to modern eyes) still serious, sexual assaults had been dealt with by the Church courts. Arguably, the disappearance of these courts left a lacuna in the offence repertoire that was not to be filled until the creation of the crime of 'indecent assault on a female person' in 1861 (24 & 25 Vict., c.100, s.52). In the eighteenth century, sexual assaults committed without intent to rape would normally be prosecuted as simple assaults, as occurred

---

[589]OBSP, Trial of Joseph Fyson, 25th June 1788.
[590]OBSP, Trial of Christopher Larkin, 3rd July 1751.
[591]OBSP, Trial of James Purse, 10th May 1780.
[592]*Grub-street Journal*, 16th April 1730.

when the 'London Monster', whose penchant was slashing women's buttocks with a blade, was tried at the Bailey in 1790.[593]

Legally, the misdemeanour differed from the capital crime only in not requiring penetration. In practical terms, however, it was viewed much less seriously. As a result, it has been suggested that many misdemeanor prosecutions were brought when, in reality, the full (and capital) crime had been committed. It was easier to prove than the completed offence and the relatively mild penalty encouraged conviction. Additionally, as a misdemeanour, it could be compounded quite legally. Significantly, perhaps, Anne Bond's initial complaint against the infamous Colonel Charteris was only for the inchoate offence, and *may* have been sworn as a hoped for prelude to obtaining damages from Charteris in a civil action.[594] Professor Beattie suggests that the decision to 'down charge' rape to attempt was more common in urban, rather than rural, environments. Thus, the urban parishes of Surrey (such as Lambeth) witnessed a proportionately much greater number of prosecutions for the inchoate offence than for the full crime, whereas in the rural areas it was little higher. This may have been because of the potential support, encouragement and outrage available from family and friends in such areas when compared to the higher proportion of more isolated, single, women found in the city.[595]

## The Social Background to Rape

### Intimates and Strangers

Stranger rapes were comparatively rare, or at least rarely prosecuted. They included some assaults that were committed in the course of other serious crimes, such as burglary or robbery, and the occasional gang rape. Thus, in 1735, Margaret Maccullough was brutally attacked by seven men who had earlier assaulted another woman and "stopped her Mouth with Mud and Human Dung", before changing their target. A witness heard the leader of the gang, a blacksmith, exhort his colleagues to "Take a Colly-flower Stalk [erect penis?] and –[fuck?] the Bitch to death."[596] Such cases could involve up to 20 men. As today, stranger rape, if it came to court, was most likely to produce a conviction. It was also much less likely to result in a reprieve if there was a guilty finding.

However, the great majority of rapes were committed by intimates and acquaintances. Anna Clark's study of 45 rape cases tried at the Old Bailey

---

[593]Jan Bondeson, *The London Monster,* Free Association Books, London, 2000, pp.91-93.
[594]Antony E Simpson, "Popular Perceptions of Rape as a Capital Crime in 18th Century England: the Press and the Trial of Francis Charteris in the Old Bailey, February 1730" in *Law and History Review*, 2004, vol.22, no.1, p.32.
[595]Beattie, *Crime and the Courts in England: 1660-1800*, p.130.
[596]OBSP, Trial of John Whitney, 11th Sept. 1735.

between 1770 and 1799 suggests that only 27 per cent involved strangers.[597] Of course, much depends on the definition of 'stranger'; does it include those known only by sight etc? Sometimes, such attacks occurred incestuously, committed, for example, by fathers or step-fathers. Thus, a newspaper from 1726 could laconically note that the proprietor of a tavern in Hog lane had been committed to Newgate "for ravishing his own child, a girl of about 11 or 12 years of age."[598] The frequent practice of sharing beds amongst the poor facilitated such behaviour. More commonly, however, prosecuted rapes were committed by employers, fellow employees, lodgers or neighbours, with considerable variation in the degree of previous social intimacy.

*Social Status of Victims and Defendants*

Using a contemporary social classification (that of the magistrate Patrick Colquhoun) Clark concluded that in London, between 1770 and 1779, the most common social combination in rape cases involved lower class victims with lower class assailants (47 per cent of a 36 case sample in which the social class for both parties could be identified). However, in so far as there were social distinctions between prosecuted rapists and their victims, it seems that defendants tended to be a little more prosperous than complainants. Thus, lower class victims with 'middle class' attackers made up 22 per cent of the sample, while middle class victims with lower class assailants constituted only 17 per cent.[599] Although there were no upper class attackers (or victims) in Clark's study, Colonel Charteris was certainly not unique in being a 'gentleman' accused of attacking a working woman. Within 30 years of his hearing, Lord Baltimore was tried at the Surrey Assizes for raping a London based milliner, though in his case a controversial acquittal resulted.[600] However, where children were victims, their attackers might be lodgers or apprentices in their parents' houses and thus, marginally, their social inferiors.

In a relatively high proportion of rapes, particularly those involving post-pubescent females, the victims were servants. A few of these cases, especially where a servant's employers were the defendants and of high social status, became *causes celebres*. More commonly, however, servants would be victimized by members of the middling social orders. Such prosperous men still had natural advantages if their testimony was pitted against their inferiors. When it came to weighing evidence, it was assumed that men of "easy circumstances" were less likely to commit perjury.[601] There are obvious explanations for the apparently

---

[597] Anna K Clark, *Women's silence, men's violence: sexual assault in England, 1770-1845*, Pandora Press, London, 1987, p.138.

[598] *Weekly Journal, or The British Gazetteer*, 4th June 1726.

[599] Clark, *Women's silence, men's violence*, p.135.

[600] Wallace Shugg, "The baron and the milliner: Lord Baltimore's rape trial as a mirror of class tensions in mid-Georgian London", *Maryland Historical Magazine*, 1988, vol. 83, pp. 310-330.

[601] Humphrey Gilbert, *The Law of Evidence*, 2nd. Edition, Printed by Catherine Lintot, London, 1760, p.158.

high number of servant victims; 'routine activity theory' provides one. It predicts that crimes are likeliest to occur when three conditions are present: a motivated offender; a suitable target, be it property or a person, and the absence of a capable guardian.[602] Servants were obviously vulnerable; many were young and, especially in London, a long way from their family homes and thus potential guardians. Their immediate neighbours might not know or care about them. Additionally, they were highly dependant on their employers, making them easy targets for their masters, his male relatives or even fellow employees. In larger houses, female domestics would often work well away from the servants' quarters, and according to a known routine. This meant that men could anticipate when they would be isolated. Additionally, in some cases, they might be asked to perform quite intimate functions, such as putting their masters to bed, which provided further opportunities for the men concerned. Others would be expected to wait up late, for their employers, if they went out for the night.[603]

Indeed, there were regular instances of men, like Colonel Charteris, deliberately employing girls with the sole intention of seducing them, and some domestic employment agencies appear to have acted as procurers for this purpose. Other women were (unwittingly) recruited by brothels. Thus, in an experience that was resonant of passages in John Cleland's *Fanny Hill* (1747), Ann Cooley was taken on as a 'domestic servant' by Lucy Roberts, who appears to have been a madam serving a wealthy clientele. A week into her employment, Cooley was plied with drink and introduced to a 'gentleman' who, allegedly, forced himself on her before throwing her half a guinea and leaving. Roberts was acquitted, though the court sent Cooley to hospital to be cured of the venereal disease she had contracted and ordered that the house be indicted as one of ill repute.[604] Servants were also vulnerable to defence claims of malicious prosecution. Typically, when Bond warned Charteris that she intended to prosecute him for rape, he immediately alleged that she had stolen £20.

Not uncommonly, the rape of a servant would follow a series of incidents in which the attacker had forced physical contact on the woman. Thus, it was claimed that Thomas Coles had 'stroked' and 'cuddled up' to his eventual victim, a newly employed servant, as well as putting his hand up her petticoats and kissing her (despite her protestations) in the days preceding the full attack.[605] In 1763, Mary Heather claimed that during three months spent as a servant before she was raped, her master had made "frequent attempts on her chastity, generally two or three times in a week." On one occasion, he had even pulled off

[602]Jessica Warner and R Griller, "'My Pappa is out, and my Mamma is asleep." minors, their routine activities, and interpersonal violence in an early modern town, 1653-1781' in *Journal of Social History*, 2003, vol. 36, p.562.
[603]Bridget Hill, *Servants: English Domestics in the Eighteenth Century*, 1996, Clarendon Press, Oxford, pp.45-46.
[604]OBSP, Trial of Lucy Roberts, 13th Jan. 1758.
[605]OBSP, Trial of Thomas Cole, 9th Dec. 1789.

most of her clothes.[606] The brutal reality was that inequalities of class, position, age and gender (i.e. of power) meant that the dividing line between a master 'seducing' and 'raping' his female employee would often have been tenuous. To a young girl, perhaps up from the country and alone in the Metropolis, dependant on her position for shelter, food and income, the pressure to be 'accommodating' must have been considerable; significantly, Heather stayed in her position, despite her master's improper conduct. Even Colonel Charteris tried every ploy in his seduction repertoire before raping Anne Bond. This included offering her money, fine clothes, the chance to live in a house and promising to find her a husband in due course.[607] Maids from indigent backgrounds were in a similar position. When William Jackson was accused of rape at the Bow Street police office by a servant girl that had been apprenticed to him from his local asylum, the charges were dismissed, as the examination of his victim suggested that she had consented to his desires on previous occasions, though the "fact of his seducing her was clearly proved." Significantly, at the same examination, Jackson was successfully charged with cruelly horse whipping another asylum girl who had been apprenticed to him.[608]

Motivations for rape differed. Since the 1970s, several feminist writers, such as Susan Brownmiller, have stressed that rape is often an instrument of male domination over women, a political act, designed to punish or humiliate females rather than being motivated purely by sexual desire. This probably applied to some eighteenth century rapes, such as the previously cited case of Margaret MacCullough. However, during the 1700s, and the large number of Metropolitan prostitutes notwithstanding, opportunities for legitimate sexual intercourse were more restricted than in the modern era (abstinence was a common method of birth control even within marriage). This may have engendered widespread male sexual frustration and meant that a higher proportion of eighteenth-century rapes were motivated by simple lust than today.[609] This is certainly the 'feel' of the Sessions Papers.

## The Rape of Small Children

Many eighteenth-century rape victims, over a third, were children, as can be seen by analysing the trials of all 33 people indicted for the crime between the start of 1730 and the end of 1739. For over half of them (17), their victims were under 16. Ten of them allegedly attacked children under the age of 10, including a two year old, an infant of three years ten months and a six year old. Two of the girls were aged ten or eleven and at least five between twelve and fifteen. Many of those aged 16 or over were young adults or adolescents, some being described as

---

[606]OBSP, Trial of John Medows, 14th Sept. 1763.

[607]Anon, *The Tryal of Colonel Francis Charteris*, printed for Sylvanus Pergat, London, 1730, p.4.

[608]*The Times*, Oct 21st, 1791, at p.3.

[609]Edward Shorter, "On Writing the History of Rape", *Signs: Journal of Women in Culture and Society*, 1977, vol.3, no.2, at pp.471-482, at p.473.

'girls' and obviously still teenagers. This profile is in accordance with most other studies, and was something that contemporary observers were well aware of. Writing in 1699, one commentator deplored the 'fact' that rape had become increasingly commonplace and was committed: "…in the most scandalous manner too, upon the bodies of meer children."[610] Whether the level of such cases reflected incidence (as appears likely) or a willingness to prosecute, is not entirely clear, though the latter appears improbable. The age of defendants varied greatly, though apprentices, like the fifteen-year-old James Booty, tended to be young. Age was not given consistently in the Sessions Papers until the 1790s, and then only when defendants were convicted. The six rape convictions from that decade involved three men in their 20s, and one from each of the following decades, with the youngest man being 26, the oldest 52, and the average 36 years and four months, though the sample is too small to draw too many conclusions.

The very high percentage of young children found amongst rape victims probably reflects both their vulnerability and adult willingness to take advantage of it. In the early modern period, children had been exposed to most aspects of the grown-up world, often being treated as small adults, rather than being segregated from it. Unfortunately, this may have meant that there were fewer psychological inhibitions to cross-generational sexual relations. It is also possible that such attitudes were compounded by a contemporary 'defloration mania', itself perhaps motivated by anxiety at the endemic level of venereal disease.[611] There was a widespread popular belief that intercourse with a virgin could cure such afflictions. Nevertheless, this type of conduct, even if widespread, was certainly not socially approved. Evidence from contemporary newspapers indicates that women would often mob child molesters outside court, and communities might punish acquitted individuals informally.[612] The era was a transitional period in adult/child relations. Lawrence Stone has suggested that during the seventeenth and eighteenth centuries, parents became increasingly 'attached' to their children emotionally. This made them more willing to protect their offspring from the adult world, including sexual depredations, explaining the subsequent decline in child victimisation.[613] It should also be noted that there was nothing unique to eighteenth–century London, or indeed England, in

---

[610]Anon, *The Tryal and Condemnation of Mervin, Lord Audley Earl of Castlehaven*, London, 1699, Preface p.6.

[611]Simpson, "Vulnerability and the Age of Female Consent", p.187.

[612]J Gammon, "'A denial of innocence": female juvenile victims of rape and the English legal system in the eighteenth century' in *Childhood in question: children, parents and the state*, A J Fletcher and S Hussey (Eds.), Manchester University Press, Manchester, 1999, p. 91.

[613]Lawrence Stone, *The Family, Sex and Marriage in England, 1500-1800*, London, Weidenfeld and Nicholson, 1977, p.405

this. The same pattern of frequent sexual assaults on small children and minors was manifest in Ireland during the 1700s.[614]

Although a third of Metropolitan rape victims might be under the age of ten, the ancient law of rape had required that victims be at least that age if the offence was to be charged as a felony, rather than merely a misdemeanour. Following the problems occasioned by an Elizabethan rape prosecution, in which the victim was seven years old, a statute of 1576 (18 Eliz. C.7) made it felony, without benefit of clergy, to "unlawfully and carnally know any woman child under the age of ten years."[615] As a result, consent became irrelevant, such girls being considered "incapable of judgment and discretion."[616] This created an offence that in modern parlance would be termed 'statutory rape'. Its effect can be seen in numerous cases at the Old Bailey. Thus, and typically, William Macdonnel was indicted in 1741 for raping eight-year-old Elizabeth Hurst, an infant "within the age of 10 years...against the form of the statute."[617] The dividing line was crucial. In the case of Grace Pitts the presiding judge pointed out to the jury that although the child was only a few months over ten, it still took her beyond the reach of the statute which: "...makes her Consent not necessary; consequently he [the defendant] is indicted now in the same Manner as he would have been in a Fact committed on a Woman of mature Age." This meant that as well as proving intercourse with the alleged victim, the Crown had to show that it was done by force. Consent obtained from a girl of ten or eleven by deceit, though deplorable, was still, in some measure, agreement, and so did not constitute rape. The defendant was acquitted.

Nevertheless, although a ten year old could give sufficient agreement to preclude a rape charge, the age of consent in eighteenth century England was actually set at 12 years, the legal age for female marriage (it was 14 for men). However, the two-year period between 10 and 12 was little protected. Technically, it seems to have been a common law misdemeanour to have had consensual intercourse with a girl of such an age, but it was very rarely prosecuted, even in the inferior courts.[618] Early in the following century it was put on a statutory basis (9 Geo.4 c31 s17) and made an offence for which hard labour could be imposed. It is possible that the neglect shown towards this misdemeanour in the eighteenth century, which could have been a useful penal provision given that consent became irrelevant, reflected a combination of legal indifference and ignorance. The area was poorly covered by contemporary legal texts and many lawyers may even have been unaware of the crime.[619]

---

[614]James Kelly, "A Most Inhuman and Barbarous Piece of Villainy'; An Exploration of the Crime of Rape in Eighteenth-Century Ireland", *Eighteenth-Century Ireland*, 1995, vol.10, pp.78-107, at p.86.
[615]Mortimer Levine, "A More than Ordinary Case of 'Rape', 13 and 14 Elizabeth 1", *American Journal Of Legal History*, 1963, vol. 7, p.163.
[616]Blackstone, *Commentaries on the Laws of England*, Book IV, p.212.
[617]OBSP, Trial of William Macdonnel, 14th Oct. 1741.
[618]Hyde, *A Treatise of the Pleas of the Crown*, p.436.
[619]Simpson, "Vulnerability and the Age of Female Consent", p.187.

With small children, the exposure of rape was often accidental. Thus, finding the yellow and green stains produced by venereal disease discharges on linen might alert parents, as could the presence of dried semen on clothes. Typically, Elizabeth Robinson's mother found "something unusual in her linen" and called in a midwife to examine her daughter.[620] Similarly, the Reverend Benjamin Russen's rape of one of his pupils at the Bethnal Green Charity School, came to light when the girl's older sister was washing her linen and noticed "some yellow stuff as stiff as buckram."[621] In pre-menstrual girls, the presence of blood on linen was also a potential indicator, as might be signs of squirming or some other form of evident physical discomfort in the genital area.

## Problems in Prosecuting Rape

In the early modern era, criminal prosecutions were largely founded on charges brought and pursued by private individuals. This applied as much to rape as to other serious felonies. However, there were many factors discouraging complainants from such action, over and above the inherent distress involved. Prosecuting rape, like any other grave crime, was potentially expensive; court fees alone might cost well over a guinea. Calling a doctor to provide medical evidence would be significantly more. Nevertheless, most rape victims were poor.[622] Even worse, if the accused man was acquitted, he might have the financial resources and motivation to bring an action for malicious prosecution against the complainant. Occasionally, an unsuccessful complainant would be prosecuted for perjury. This undoubtedly discouraged many victims from initiating prosecutions, especially for the completed offence. Sometimes, however, they might get assistance from a well to do friend or colleague. Thus, Ann Bond was largely able to pursue her attacker because a previous employer, Mary Parsons, engaged an attorney on her behalf and accompanied Bond and the lawyer to Hicks' Hall to lodge a complaint against Colonel Charteris.[623] Lord Baltimore's victim also received help from a similar source.

Nevertheless, reporting the crime to a magistrate did not guarantee that the matter would go before a Grand Jury, let alone come to trial. Although the discretion of JPs and Aldermen (ex officio magistrates for the City of London) to dismiss allegations of rape was very limited in theory (as it was for all felonies), in practice, it seems, they weeded out many 'flimsy' rape cases at an early stage. Indeed, it has been suggested that in the City, less than 15 per cent of rape charges were committed for trial. This could be done by dismissing them outright, adjudicating them summarily as instances of common assault, or sending them to a Grand Jury as attempts. As a result, many rape victims lost

---

[620]OBSP, Trial of Daniel Bonnely, 13th July 1715.
[621]OBSP, Trial of Benjamin Russen, 15th Oct. 1777.
[622]Clark, "*Women's silence, men's violence*", pp. 21-45.
[623]Simpson, "Popular Perceptions of Rape", p.32.

control over how their crime was to be defined as soon as it reached a magistrate.[624] Thus, the records of the Guildhall Justice Room's minute books for the years between 1780 and 1796, suggest that of 17 allegations of rape or assault with intent to rape of women of over 12 years of age, only one went for trial at the Old Bailey (the defendant was acquitted), three other men were charged but not prosecuted, in four cases the magistrates dismissed the charges, and nine men were not even apprehended.[625] This seems to have occurred elsewhere in the Metropolitan area. Henry Justice, a Hackney JP, recorded in his notebook that he had received a belated claim of rape from Ursula Bridgman, a married woman. However, he concluded "yet on ye relation [it] did not appear to be a force" and did not commit for trial. (Interestingly, despite Norris being a very active magistrate, it is his only mention of the full offence in a period spanning more than eleven years).[626]

### The Evidence Adduced at Trial.

In opening a rape prosecution to an Old Bailey jury in 1789, the distinguished barrister William Garrow summed up the problems attendant on most rape cases, then as now. They were difficult for courts and juries to consider because by the very: "...nature of the offence, it is almost always attended with a secrecy which makes it necessary for Courts and Juries to find their way as they can, and to judge from the probability and improbability of the story told by the person who complains of the injury."[627] Mathew Hale's warning that, although rape was difficult to prove in a forensic environment, it was even "harder to be defended" by an innocent man, was regularly put to juries by both the judiciary and defence lawyers, as occurred at Alexander Lawson's trial at Hick's Hall for assault with intent to commit rape (he was acquitted).[628] Contemporary notions about evidence often put complainants at a disadvantage. Prosecutions suffered from the traditional reluctance of juries to convict on capital charges in cases where most of the evidence was victim generated. Finally, complainants were always female, defendants usually male. In the eighteenth century, women were usually felt to be more governed by their emotions and less 'rational' than men, yet the most important aspect of the Crown's case was usually the complainant's testimony.

### The Role of Complainant Reputation

Complainant credibility went to the heart of rape cases. Blackstone felt that it was an indication of the compassionate nature of English law that, unlike some

---

[624]Simpson, "Popular Perceptions of Rape", p.52.

[625]Clark, "*Women's silence, men's violence*", p.53.

[626]Ruth Paley (Ed.), *Justice in Eighteenth-Century Hackney: The Justicing Notebook of Henry Norris and the Hackney Petty Sessions Book*, London Record Society, London, 1991, pp.22-23.

[627]OBSP, Trial of Thomas Cole, 9th Dec. 1789.

[628]*The Times*, Sept.14th 1789, p.4.

Civil law jurisdictions, even a prostitute could be the victim of, and prosecute, a rape.[629] However, the experience of Elizabeth Galloway, a prostitute who accused the Scottish Lord John Drummond (an erstwhile client) of the crime in 1715, would suggest that there was not much truth in this, though she did get her case past three examining JPs and had Drummond committed to Newgate for five days before the matter was thrown out by the Middlesex Grand Jury at the Old Bailey. (That his Lordship was a notorious Roman Catholic might explain why the case progressed as far as it did).[630] In reality, as even Blackstone candidly noted, the reputation of the victim was vital in any prosecution for the crime. As late as 1790, Lord Kenyon, presiding over a rape trial at the Old Bailey, was prepared to enunciate this in the clearest terms. Although, as he pointed out to the jury, even a prostitute could be the victim of rape: "Generally speaking, it was expected that the person who complained of this offence should produce an untainted and an unsullied character." As the complainant could not do this, an acquittal ensued.[631]

Far more even than today, rape trials were as much an examination of the complainant as of the accused man. Chastity played a crucial role. Women of bad reputation had little prospect of success, and any suggestion that a complainant had been sexually active outside marriage would hugely undermine her case. Indeed, in early modern Europe generally, the sexual assault of virgins and continent married women was considered more serious than that of 'fornicators'.[632] Thus, a contemporary medical source advised on the tell tale signs that indicated that a: "…female hath accustomed herself to venereal habits, and of consequence is less to be believed upon a deposition for a rape."[633] Unsurprisingly, defendants would also regularly adduce bad character evidence to suggest that the complainant was a loose and immoral woman, something that might also account for her contracting venereal disease where this was part of the prosecution case. Typically, in 1731, one witness claimed that a rape complainant, Sarah Matts, was a: "…common vile Woman. The greatest Black-guard may lie with her for 6 d. … She always had the Character of a Whore and a Thief." Given that Matts had been convicted (and then whipped) for petty larceny at the same court, only eight months earlier, the ensuing acquittal is not surprising.[634] Less obviously, twelve-year-old Anne Barnard's prosecution of a soldier, in February 1754, appears to have failed because she came from a rough part of Westminster, full of "whores and wickedness", and had a witness come forward to say that she was a "very imprudent girl in playing with the boys."

---

[629]Blackstone, *Commentaries on the Laws of England*, Book iv, p.213.
[630]Anon, *The Case of the Lord John Drummond in Relation to a Rape*, Printed for J. Roberts, London, 1715, p.3.
[631]*The Times*, Nov 2nd, 1790, at p.3
[632]Heijden, "Women as victims of sexual and domestic violence in Seventeenth-Century Holland", p.623.
[633]S Farr (Ed.), *Elements of Medical Jurisprudence*, printed for T. Becket, London, 1788, p.45.
[634]OBSP, Trial of John Ellis, 8th Dec. 1731.

However, reputation was viewed as so important that many complainants were also allowed to call witnesses to say that they were 'modest', chaste and trustworthy women, likely to be telling the truth. This was at variance to the general common law practice of not allowing prosecutors to call what were, effectively, 'oath helpers' to boost their credibility. Thus, at the trial of Hugh Leeson in 1715, his victim, Mary May: "...call'd Witnesses to her Reputation, who gave her the Character of a very industrious, honest Woman; amongst whom was a Minister, who marry'd her to her Husband about 8 Years ago, had administer'd the Sacrament to her, and heard among her Neighbours that she liv'd a very honest, regular Life."[635] After the trial, Leeson went into print to deplore the worth of such complainant character evidence, claiming that May's church going was a charade and asserting that even the: "...most abandoned prostitute may have these things to plead in bar of publick censure."[636] A few years later, however, Anne Bond called three former employers to state that she was a "modest" young woman who would not tell lies.[637]

As with all felonies, a defendant could call witnesses to his good character, including sexual morality; this was often a vital part of the trial process and especially favourable to those with 'connections'. Thus, in 1757, Christian Streeter, a young country woman recently arrived in the Metropolis from Sussex, was allegedly lured to the home of Daniel Laskey and raped. At his trial, Laskey called almost a dozen witnesses to vouch for his character and to claim that he was not the sort of man to commit such a crime. Among them were an Earl, a Lord, four Knights and a City Alderman. An acquittal followed.[638] Of course, most defendants had to make do with much more mundane character witnesses, such as employers and business colleagues or even friends and casual acquaintances.

## The Competence of Child Witnesses

As a general rule, only those who were under oath could testify in eighteenth century courts, something that, for example, precluded the evidence of Quakers in even the most serious crimes. However, before the latter decades of the century, cases involving the rape of children under 12 years of age were occasionally accorded special treatment. In his *History of the Pleas of the Crown*, written in the previous century, Sir Matthew Hale had suggested that children who did not have the "sense and understanding" to appreciate the obligation imposed by an oath could still give evidence, in such cases, albeit unsworn. This was a privilege that was denied to child witnesses in most other types of case. Hale's justification for this indulgence was pragmatic: sexual crimes against

---

[635] OBSP, Trial of Hugh Leeson and Sarah Blandford, 27 Apr 1715.
[636] Hugh Leeson, *Capt. Leeson's Case: Being an Account of his Tryal, for Committing a Rape*, Printed for J. Roberts, London, 1715, p.11
[637] Anon, *The Tryal of Colonel Francis Charteris*, p.15.
[638] OBSP, Trial of Daniel Laskey, 20th April 1757.

children were usually committed in private so that it would often be impossible to convict the guilty without a relaxation of normal practice. However, he was also adamant that, if a child was unsworn, some sort of corroboration of their testimony was necessary.[639] This general analysis was still being accepted by Blackstone well into the following century, and there are occasional instances of such evidence being received at the Old Bailey. Thus, in December 1707, Elizabeth Berry, an infant, gave (presumably) unsworn testimony about her rape.[640] As late as 1769, John Gyles was acquitted after standing trial for the rape of eight year old Ann Wallis during which: "The child was examined, but not upon oath; [and] the account she gave was short of proving the fact."[641]

Nevertheless, such testimony was very rarely allowed at the Old Bailey during the eighteenth century, and seems to have been acutely unpopular with both jurors and judges. For example, at the trial of Daniel Bonnely, in 1715, the complainant said that the accused man threw her upon a bed and penetrated her: "...but she not understanding the meaning of an Oath, what she said was not taken as Evidence, and he was acquitted."[642] (Though why they first received her testimony is not clear). Normally, as with Mary Reynolds, a few months short of her tenth birthday, it was almost certain that the complainant "not being examined upon oath, he [the defendant] was acquitted."[643] Eventually, in 1779, reception of the testimony of unsworn children was expressly rejected by the judges meeting in London to consider the case of *Brasier*.[644] At this trial for the attempted rape of a five year old, the evidence of the victim had been received at the Reading Assizes. However, the 12 assembled Westminster judges (i.e. the country's highest judicial figures) subsequently decided that, although children of any age could give sworn evidence if they understood the religious sanction behind an oath and were capable of distinguishing good from evil, they could not testify except when so sworn. It was not until the late nineteenth century that the Criminal Law Amendment Act of 1885 (48 & 49 Vict., c. 69, s. 4) would again allow the receipt of unsworn testimony from children, though, as Hale had originally suggested, this statute required that it be corroborated by "other material evidence."

Mathew Hale proposed that the competence of children below the age of 12 should always be considered carefully, and, in the eighteenth century, many who were slightly above this limit, such as Catherine Glass, were also "interrogated concerning the Nature of an Oath" before being sworn.[645] Indeed,

---

[639]Mathew Hale, *History of the Pleas of the Crown*, Book 1, Printed by E and R Nut, London, 1736, pp.634-5.
[640]OBSP, Trial of William Kite, 10th Dec. 1707.
[641]OBSP, Trial of John Gyles, 5th April 1769.
[642]OBSP, Trial of Daniel Bonnely, 13th Jul 1715.
[643]OBSP, Trial of Thomas Crosby, 7th Dec. 1757.
[644]R v Brasier (1779) 1 Leach 199.
[645]OBSP, Trial of Ann Glass, 14th Jul 1742.

in 1789, Ann Barrett, although fully 14, was also questioned on the issue. The matter could be raised either by a presiding judge or by the defendant (the latter was especially likely where the accused man was legally represented). However, age was not the only determining criteria. In 1733, Mary Faucet, an 'intelligent' child who had received the rudiments of religious instruction, though only just over nine, satisfied the test and was able to give sworn testimony, albeit that the presiding judge took the opportunity to warn her not to take away a man's life by giving false evidence.[646] This last step appears to have been almost standard practice with sworn child rape complainants. However, there were limits for even the cleverest child. In 1788, when the court rather optimistically questioned the father of Kitty Sweetman, who was six years and eight months old, asking him whether she was a "quick or backward child of her age", her father had to concede that she was not competent to take an oath.[647]

Compounding these problems, the courts also became progressively stricter about receiving reported speech (hearsay), preventing the restriction being circumvented. In the late seventeenth century, near contemporaneous accounts from infants about their victimisation in rape cases, repeated by family members, had often been received at trial.[648] This changed quite early in the following century, although as late as 1727, Thomas Padget appears to have been convicted of rape almost entirely on the evidence of a five-year-old girl's father and nurse, neither of whom can have been present when the crime was committed.[649] By then, however, such an approach was highly unusual. More typical was a case from 1754, in which the victim was only six and thus unsworn. This produced the usual difficulty in establishing penetration; there being: "...no other evidence against the prisoner than hearsay from the child's mouth it was not judged sufficient."[650]

In the absence of a victim's testimony, securing a conviction became difficult. As the case above suggests, the issue of penetration, in particular, was extremely hard to prove. Such cases normally required special features, such as the defendant being caught in flagrente or, failing this, making admissions when questioned, before a guilty verdict would be returned. Thus, in 1722, James Booty, accused of raping a five year old, "confest it" when examined and was subsequently convicted. Similarly, in 1739, John Adamson was found guilty of raping Catherine Walgrave, although she was still two months shy of her fourth birthday, because he admitted the crime to the child's father. Adamson later complained that he had only made admissions because his master had promised to be merciful if he did so.[651] Nevertheless, despite such evidential problems, Simpson suggests that between 1730 and 1830, the conviction rate for the rape

---

[646] OBSP, Trial of John Cannon, 12th Sept. 1733.
[647] OBSP, Trial of Joseph Fyson, 25th June 1788.
[648] John Langbein, The Origins of Adversary Criminal Trial, OUP, Oxford, 2003, pp.239-240.
[649] OBSP, Trial of Thomas Padget, 22nd Feb. 1727.
[650] OBSP, Trial of William Kirk, 30th May 1754.
[651] OBSP, Trial of John Adamson, 17th Jan 1739.

of those under 10 was, at 18 per cent, fractionally higher than the general trend.[652] This was probably because attacks on children excited jury sympathy and precluded consent as a defence.

## Expert Medical Testimony

Medical evidence was highly valued by the courts in rape cases. Indeed, it was normally necessary if a conviction was to be obtained. At one trial in 1748, a surgeon who happened to be in the Old Bailey on other business was even asked to give an opinion in a rape case that was otherwise lacking in such expert testimony.[653] Occasionally, the court would adjourn briefly during a hearing, so that doctors could update their medical examination of complainants, especially children thought to be infected with venereal disease, in the privacy of the Mayor's parlour. As a result, rape was the third most common type of case in which medical evidence was called at the Old Bailey. Additionally, although prosecution medical experts outnumbered those called by defendants by a ratio of three to one, the disparity was significantly smaller than for other types of crime. Unsurprisingly, surgeons predominated as experts in rape cases, in one sample, they appear eighteen times, compared to only four for apothecaries, and one each for midwives and physicians.[654]

Some of the arrangements behind such examinations are revealed by the trial of William Kirk. James Moffatt, a surgeon, was summoned to Justice Cox's house, where he found the accused man being held and was told that he was suspected of raping a seven-year-old girl, who was also present. The JP, a woman and the surgeon then retired upstairs to carry out an intimate inspection of the complainant. When this was done, the two men decided to examine Kirk in a back room; he was found to have a very severe genital infection, with 'ruptures' so big that they could barely produce his penis for scrutiny. They also examined his underwear for signs of venereal disease discharges.[655] Obviously, it was often much harder for experts instructed by a defendant to examine a complainant, many being turned away. Thus, when Samuel Graff instructed a Dr. Dearing to examine his alleged victim, her mother refused to allow it, saying that they had "already employ'd an able surgeon, who was master of his business." Dearing was forced to challenge the complainant's expert witness at trial, without the benefit of seeing the girl.[656] Judges and jurors at the Bailey would often attempt to get medical experts to commit themselves firmly on the

---

[652]Simpson, "Vulnerability and the Age of Female Consent", p.187.
[653]OBSP, Trial of William Page, 15th Jan. 1748.
[654]Stephan Landsman, "One Hundred Years Of Rectitude: Medical Witnesses At The Old Bailey: 1717-1817", *Law and History Review*, 1998, vol. 16, pp.452-461. There was a tendency for prosecution medical evidence to be adduced at the end of the Crown's case. By contrast, defendants who called such evidence commonly opened their cases with it.
[655]OBSP, Trial of William Kirk, 30th May 1754.
[656]OBSP, Trial of Samuel Graff, 6th Dec. 1721.

essential elements of rape, particularly penetration. However, doctors tended to rely on indirect proofs, including the simultaneous presence of venereal disease in both the victim and defendant and generalized observations about the condition of the victim's genitalia. Many medical men preferred to give a "doubtful" rather than a "certain" opinion about whether intercourse had occurred.[657]

Medical testimony was especially valuable when small children were the victims, as evidence could be given of injuries and damage to the infants' genitalia that made consent appear less likely in those over ten, and penetration more probable in those below that age. Thus, in 1748, 13 year old Hepzibah Dover was examined by a mid-wife who declared at trial that the girl's "private parts appeared to be scratched, and in a most miserable pickle."[658] Doctors were usually more scientific in their analysis, describing the presence of classic indicia for rape. Thus, in 1752, Thomas Renton, a Scottish qualified surgeon, was summoned by the magistrate Henry Fielding to his Bow Street office to examine Catharine Poor, a child suspected of having been raped. He found the injuries indicative of great violence, with the: "…outward lips of her womb somewhat swelled, and the skin in several places torn. Upon opening the inward lips they were a good deal inflamed with a laceration and confusion on the left side of the inward lip."[659] As this suggests, damage to female genitalia, evidenced by the presence of blood, swelling and inflammation, was viewed as an indication of rape, especially if a child was involved. However, as today, as these symptoms could also: "…be induced by other means, or are not inconsistent with consent having been obtained, they can only be considered as corroborative."[660] Sadly, on several occasions during the century, the Sessions Papers record that surgeons refused to examine girls who were thought to have been rape victims when they realized that it was with a view to criminal proceedings. They were unwilling to risk being subpoenaed to give evidence at any ensuing trial at the Old Bailey.

*The Presence of Venereal Disease*

Something that quickly becomes apparent from any detailed study of rape cases during the 1700s is the astonishing number of victims (at least a third) who, apparently, became infected with the "foul disease", i.e. some form of venereal disease, as a result of their attack. Thus, among the 18 complainants in the five years from 1750 to 1753, the Sessions papers mention 11 instances of suspected infection with another being possible (well over half). Of course, a few alleged cases were probably misdiagnosed. Nevertheless, in the case of small children (where the incidence appears much higher than amongst adult victims) the

---

[657]Landsman, "One Hundred Years Of Rectitude", pp.452-461.
[658]OBSP, Trail of William Garner, 7th Sept. 1748.
[659]OBSP, Trial of Patrick White, 25th June 1752.
[660]Farr (Ed.), *Elements of Medical Jurisprudence*, p.43.

discovery of disease was one of the most common means by which the crime came to light. It was well known, even at the time, that the only way in which venereal disease could normally be contracted was by "lewd and filthy dalliance."[661]

In part, the level of sexually transmitted disease reflects its high incidence in the metropolitan area generally during the period. Syphilis ('pox') and gonorrhoea (or 'clap') reached endemic levels and claimed numerous prominent victims including the regularly infected James Boswell. Indeed, early editions of the Sessions Papers were replete with advertisements offering dubious cures for these afflictions, and even Native American remedies for the disease were discussed.[662] There was also a flourishing trade in cat-gut condoms, sold to prevent infection. Of course, it is possible that rape defendants were more sexually active and probable that they were more likely to have had recourse to prostitutes than the average person. Additionally, becoming infected may have driven several women into reporting attacks when they would otherwise have remained silent. However, in the case of adolescent and adult women it could also give rise to defences based on claims that the accused man was actually an innocent 'patsy', being blamed by a (possibly married) woman, trying to avoid opprobrium for catching a disease from a lover. Some defendants called doctors to establish that they themselves were 'clean' of the disease if the complainant proved to be infected.

## Defences

There were (and are) a limited number of defences to allegations of rape. Foremost amongst them were claims that the allegation was maliciously fabricated, either because no sexual intercourse had occurred at all, or because it had occurred, but with consent. Both of these situations appear regularly in the Sessions Papers. Additionally, several more technical defences were sometimes run, for example a denial that any penetration (an essential element of the crime) had occurred or, in the case of stranger rape, an allegation of mistaken identification.

### Compounding, Extortion and Malicious Prosecutions

Some rape prosecutions were clearly malicious, or at least unfounded. Their number is hard to establish, though it was probably quite small. False allegations might be made for a variety of reasons: extorting money, exacting revenge or hiding an embarrassing personal situation being foremost amongst them. Thus, one defendant claimed that a complainant had only alleged rape about what was a consensual sexual relationship because he had had her arrested for smuggling

---

[661]Dr D Turner, *Syphilis. A Practical Disseration on the Venereal Disease.* 2nd edition, London, 1724, p. 40 and p.14.
[662]Sept.1-3, 1757 *The London Chronicle or Universal Evening Post.*

in clothes to a Newgate inmate to facilitate an escape attempt.[663] On another occasion, an independent witness claimed that a complainant had admitted to him that she had made a malicious allegation as the only way in which she could be revenged on a fellow servant who had been the author of unpleasant gossip about her. False accusations could also be made to avoid shame. Thus, when a somewhat inebriated Elizabeth Stone was caught *in flagrente*, by neighbours who had been secretly observing her enjoying a 'threesome' with two local youths, she eventually claimed that it had been against her will. Her husband gave her the option of prosecuting for rape and "clear[ing] up her character" or being thrown out, as he was unwilling to be cuckolded by boys. At trial, the jury quickly indicated to the judge that they had heard enough, and acquitted.[664] Similarly, the youthful Henry Burt was acquitted after the 13-year-old complainant admitted that "she came to him about a month after [the alleged rape] and undrest her self, came into the Bed, and lay with him all night." The initial complaint seems to have been prompted by her father's fury at an apparently consensual liaison; the court accepted Burt's view that he "was eager and she not very unwilling."[665]

The courts were especially sensitive to the possibility of monetary blackmail motivating rape allegations. Indeed, even where the court was satisfied that a rape had actually occurred, an offer by the victim to settle the matter for a financial payment appears to have prejudiced the prospects of a subsequent criminal prosecution. Strictly speaking, offering financial compensation to avoid a rape prosecution was illegal, being the offence of 'compounding a felony', though, as assault with intent to rape was only a misdemeanor, it was quite legitimate to reach a monetary settlement for the lesser offence. In practice, paying off complainants appears to have been widespread for both crimes. This was reflected in the literature of the era. In Henry Fielding's 1730 comedy, *Rape upon Rape*, 'Squeezum' assumes a monetary payment will settle a rape allegation.[666] In reality, the Reverend Green's alleged victim, a servant employed in the house where he lodged, did not go directly for a magistrate after being raped, but asked the cleric the following morning what he thought of receiving a "lawyer's letter" with a view to prompting him to: "...do justice some way or other, or be brought to shame."[667] There has been an academic debate as to the extent to which an evinced willingness to negotiate the settlement of a rape allegation was a defence or prosecution 'strategy'. According to Simpson, a few highly publicised cases led to the emergence of the 'blackmail myth', a belief that

---

[663]Heijden, "Women as victims of sexual and domestic violence in Seventeenth-Century Holland", p.623.

[664]OBSP, Trial of Simon Frazier, Thomas Hodges and John Hasley, 11th Sept. 1771.

[665]OBSP, Trial of Henry Burt, 1st May 1717.

[666]Henry Fielding, *Rape upon Rape: or the Justice caught in his Own Trap*, Printed for J. Watts, London, 1730, p. 55.

[667]OBSP, 10th May 1769, Trial of Richard Green.

extortion was widespread.[668] By contrast, Edelstein suggests that this was rarely the case, compositions were simply easier than proceeding with the enormous difficulties of a rape prosecution.[669]

Occasionally, women may have fabricated allegations with a view to blackmail, just as men periodically made false allegations of attempted sodomy to obtain money from those who were afraid of the attendant publicity.[670] Thus, at the Trial of William Willis in 1715, for the rape of his maid, Phebe Shaw, it was claimed that the girl's mother had put her up to the action to get money after Phebe was dismissed from her employment for theft. However, several witnesses gave evidence that "made it look like a malicious Prosecution, upon which the Prisoner was acquitted."[671] Similarly, in 1718, Robert Shales, John Wood and Mary Wood were indicted at Hick's Hall (the Middlesex Sessions) for conspiring to fraudulently charge the Baron de Bothmar with raping Margaret Medull.[672] However, the judiciary were aware of such possibilities and, on occasion, would grant an acquitted rape defendant a copy of his indictment to facilitate a subsequent civil action against the complainant for malicious prosecution.

Most accommodations, if reached, probably occurred quite early in the process, before recognisances had been entered into by prosecution witnesses. These would be discharged when the witness appeared to testify at the trial on indictment. If they failed to appear they would usually lose whatever sum they were bound over in ('estreatment'), though the defendant would then be found 'not guilty'. Thus, in 1785, Mary Twigg (the complainant) and Martha Twigg (a witness) being: "…called on their recognizances, and not appearing, the prisoner was acquitted."[673] This probably meant that compounding became more expensive as a case progressed. Whatever its effect, there were only seven cases of rape complainants failing to appear against an indicted defendant between December 1714 and the end of the century. Thus, in 1765, Jane Lawson did not appear to prosecute her alleged attacker, her recognisance being escheated as a result, and the accused man acquitted.[674] Even more intriguingly, Elizabeth Jones, who accused three men of raping her, indicated to the examining Justice that she was satisfied that they should be bailed pending trial. Subsequently, the men appeared for their hearing and the "witness [was] called, but none

---

[668]Antony E Simpson, '"Blackmail myth" and the prosecution of rape and its attempt in 18th Century London: the creation of a legal tradition' in *Journal of Criminal Law and Criminology* 77, 1986, pp. 101-150.

[669]Laurie Edelstein, "An Accusation easily to be made?: Rape and Malcious prosecution in eighteenth century England", *American Journal of Legal History*, 1998, vol. 42, pp.351-390.

[670]For a discussion of this regular phenomenon see *The Post Boy*, 16-18 October 1707.

[671]OBSP, Trial of William Willis, 7th Dec. 1715.

[672]*Weekly Journal, or The British Gazetteer*, 20th Sept. 1718.

[673]OBSP, Trial of Robert Spencer, 14th Dec. 1785.

[674]OBSP, Trial of John Daniel, 18th Sept. 1765.

appearing, the prisoners were acquitted." It must be a matter of speculation as to what dealings may have lain behind these events.[675]

The sums involved varied considerably, depending on which offence was charged, the defendant's ability to pay, the extent of the injury etc. Sometimes it might be portrayed as a 'reimbursement' for time and trouble spent in pursuing the matter and seeking medical help. Thus, in 1735, Phillip Brown, an apprentice described as a 'boy', was indicted for assaulting his master's 11-year-old daughter with intent to rape her. He was acquitted, primarily, it seems, because his mother came to court to say that the child's father had offered to "make it up for three guineas, if he might be indemnified."[676] For the full offence, however, the amounts negotiated could be far more substantial. Thus, Colonel Charteris was rumoured to have offered £300 to Bond after proceedings were underway. This was an extreme case; more 'typically', in 1742, a defendant claimed that the rape allegation had been made to "extort some money," and asserted that the victim had intimated that she would not settle for less than £50.[677]

### Consent

As Burt's case indicates (and as today) a simple claim of consent to otherwise admitted intercourse was a frequently used defence. Although publicly deplored by clerics, eighteenth-century London witnessed a high level of 'fornication', that is sex outside the confines of marriage. This was found amongst all social classes and appears to have increased markedly from its incidence during the 1600s.[678] Amongst lower class women, in particular, sexual mores were more flexible than they were to be in the Victorian era, so that illegitimacy was not uncommon and cohabitation relatively frequent.[679] The prevalence of casual sexual encounters was undoubtedly a major factor behind the city's epidemic of venereal disease, and neither judges nor jurors were so naïve that they did not appreciate that such liaisons were commonplace (many, no doubt, also indulged in them). Thus, Robert Laskey was quick to point out at trial that he had encountered his alleged victim near Rosamond's pond in St. James's park, during the early afternoon, where it was notorious that people walked "with an intent to be picked up."

Defendants, while denying rape, might freely admit that they were 'saucy' or 'impudent' fellows, given to chance dalliances with women. Periodically, such behaviour could occasion difficulties, as John Motherill, an itinerant Metropolitan tailor, discovered in a notorious case from 1785. He met a woman in the street and swiftly made advances to her, and to which, he claimed, she was very receptive. He then persuaded her to accompany him to a local churchyard,

---

[675] OBSP, Trial of Henry Fawkener et al, 16th Jan 1747.

[676] OBSP, Trial of Phillip Brown, 11th Sept. 1735.

[677] OBSP, Trial of William Remue, 8th Dec. 1742.

[678] Tim Hitchcock, "'Unlawfully begotten on her body': Illegitimacy and the Parish Poor in St Luke's Chelsea", *Chronicling Poverty*, 1997, P King et al (Eds.), pp.70-87.

[679] Clark , "*Women's silence, men's violence*", p.27.

where she agreed to his proposal that they be as "familiar as man and wife." According to the defendant, he then: "****** *** [fucked her?] without the least resistance." Subsequently, however, the woman alleged rape. At trial, Motherill was acquitted without even giving evidence. Although he freely admitted that his 'unchaste' behaviour was deplorable, he also asked how many other young men (he was 25) would not have behaved in a similar fashion.[680]

Where consent was in issue, many of the problems that plague the courts today in 'date rape' cases, those involving an admitted degree of prior social intimacy between the parties, also troubled their eighteenth-century predecessors. Indeed, 'seduction', particularly of the 'innocent', was an eighteenth century preoccupation. Heavy-handed 'flirtation' and pressure, especially where there were inequalities of power, was normal, blurring the dividing line between consent and force, so that Jonathan Swift could talk of female agreement obtained "half by force and half by consent." Typically, Henry Williams, a witness in another man's rape trial, was adamant that he would never force a woman into intercourse: "...otherwise than by talking her over, and making her drink, as a Man must always do in such Cases; for you know a Woman must be coax'd a little, though she's never so willing."[681] Obviously, 'coaxing' might cover a range of behaviour.

## 'Unequivocal' Victims

Eighteenth century judges, lawyers and jurors were imbued with notions as to how 'genuine' rape victims were likely to behave. Of course, to modern observers, many of these attitudes demonstrate a complete ignorance of victim psychology and are heavily influenced by stereotypic beliefs about the nature of the crime and about women. Nevertheless, such notions were highly influential on the forensic process. In particular, male judges and jurors were reluctant to convict if women were not 'unequivocal victims', able to demonstrate that their conduct and character were beyond question.[682] Although the early modern belief that women were often innately more lustful than men seems to have waned swiftly during the era, there appears to have been a popular suspicion that some rape victims 'invited' their treatment. However, and unlike the modern era, to eighteenth century eyes it seems that this might involve even minor acts of female independence or eccentricity.

Perhaps indicative of such attitudes was the long-standing belief, still widely held by legal observers in the seventeenth century, and retained by many complainants in the following one, that rape could not produce pregnancy, so that any ensuing pregnancy was indicative of consent to intercourse. This belief

---

[680] John Motherill, *The Case of John Motherill. The Brighthelmstone Taylor Who was Tried at East Grinstead for A Rape*. London, 1786, pp.3-12.
[681] OBSP, Trial of John Ellis, 8th Dec. 1731.
[682] K Stevenson, "Unequivocal victims: the historical roots of the mystification of the female complainant in rape cases", *Feminist Legal Studies*, 2000, vol. 8, pp.343-344.

appears to have been based on a thirteenth-century legal tract. Although, in 1716, the jurist William Hawkins observed that the "philosophy of this notion may very well be doubted of," echoing earlier criticisms made by Mathew Hale, it still occasionally cropped up in the cross-examination of rape complainants at the Old Bailey until the 1750s, and was only definitively rejected by legal tracts towards the end of the century.[683] Even one contemporary medical observer felt that conception could only take place in rape situations if the victim's "lust was excited."[684]

In the 1760s, William Blackstone identified the factors that were conducive to a conviction for rape in eighteenth century England. He argued that if a complainant was of "good fame [reputation]; if she presently discovered [quickly revealed] the offence, and made search for the offender; if the party accused fled for it; these and the like are concurring circumstances, which give greater probability to her evidence."[685] Reputation has already been addressed. Very importantly, women were expected to make an outcry while being raped and then to complain about the crime, at the very first opportunity open to them, afterwards. These were being considered in an almost mechanistic fashion even by the late seventeenth century.[686] Indeed, examination on these topics was so *de rigeur* that, in several cases, the observer noting the trial for the publishers of the Sessions Papers could summarise the questions and answers as if they were near formalities.[687] A failure to cry out or complain could be fatal to a prosecution. Typically, Mathew Cave, an adolescent London apprentice accused of raping his employer's young daughter was acquitted, largely, it seems, because he returned from the field where the crime was allegedly committed to his master's premises, together with the girl, and worked there for a further month so that: "…it was not proved to the Satisfaction of the Court that it was a Rape; he coming Home with the Child: she making no Discovery of it, till she was forced to it; and his continuing to work in the Yard." His allegation of consent was accepted.[688]

## Recent Complaint

As the eminent American judge Oliver Wendell Holmes noted, the need to make a swift complaint was an: "…ancient requirement that a woman should make hue and cry as a preliminary to an appeal of rape."[689] This had survived the late medieval move to indictment as the main form of prosecution and was still considered an important, albeit not legally vital, prerequisite to a rape allegation in the eighteenth century. As a result, Blackstone felt that it was proper that the

---

[683] Elise Histed, "Medieval Rape: A conceivable Defence?" in *Cambridge Law Journal*, 2004, vol. 63(3), pp.743-769, at p.744 and pp. 765-769.

[684] Farr (Ed.), *Elements of Medical Jurisprudence*, p.43.

[685] Blackstone, *Commentaries on the Laws of England*, Book IV, p.213.

[686] See for example, OBSP, Trial of an anonymous 'Lusty Man', 6th Sept. 1677.

[687] OBSP, Trial of John Clark, 21st April 1762.

[688] OBSP, Trial of Matthew Cave, 14th Oct. 1747.

[689] In the case of *Commonwealth v Cleary* (1898) 172 Mass 175.

woman making the allegation: "...should immediately after, *dum recens fuerit maleficium*, go to the next town, and there make discovery to some credible persons of the injury she has suffered."[690] Interestingly, the same pre-requisites for an accusation of rape, if even more strictly interpreted, applied in contemporary Germany.[691] Whatever its legal origins, the courts were intensely suspicious of belated claims. Blackstone's assertion that jurors were reluctant to convict on stale complaints is amply borne out by the records. Late complaints, and the reasons behind them, would be vigorously questioned, and a failure to provide a very convincing explanation would usually lead to an acquittal. Thus, a 12 year old who slept on her attack for several days was asked why she didn't immediately tell her mother. Her admission that it was only when her mother asked how she came to lose two shillings, with which she had earlier been entrusted, that she told her, seems to have been fatal to the prosecution case.[692]

## Simultaneous Outcry

Linked to this doctrine was an intense suspicion of women who failed to make an "outcry" *during* the assault, especially when within earshot of potential witnesses. This was always considered a strong indication that no attack had occurred, and something about which the courts would also vigorously examine complainants.[693] One of the reasons that the Reverend Green may have been acquitted of raping a servant, was that he was able to call the landlord of a neighbouring tavern to say that his establishment, the: "...next house to where the girl lives is so contiguous, that if she had called out lustily, she must have been heard."[694] So fundamental was this that, in 1789, prosecuting counsel could assume that jurors would: "...naturally enquire whether she [the complainant] cried out." He felt it necessary to explain in advance that her failure to do so was because the attacker had made it physically impossible by smothering her.[695]

Many eighteenth century commentators were also firmly wedded to the view that, physically, rape was almost impossible if a fully-grown woman was absolutely determined to preserve her virtue. Thus, an observer from 1715 could claim that the: "...perpetration of it [rape] in Adult Persons is so very difficult, that it requires something of an implicit Belief to be credited."[696] Another contemporary medical source was equally convinced that: "...rape, by which is meant a compleat, full, and entire coition, which is made without any consent of the woman, seems to be impossible, unless some very extraordinary

---

[690]Blackstone, *Commentaries on the Laws of England*, Book IV, p. 211.
[691]Eva Lacour, "Faces of violence Revisited. A Typology of Violence in Early Modern Germany", *Journal of Social History*, vol.34, no.3, pp.649-667.
[692]OBSP, Trial of William Page, 15th Jan 1748.
[693]Blackstone, *Commentaries on the Laws of England*, Book IV, p.214.
[694]OBSP, Trial of Richard Green, 10th May 1769.
[695]OBSP, Trial of Thomas Cole, 9th Dec. 1789.
[696]Anon (1715) *The Case of the Ld. John Drummond in Relation to a Rape*, Printed for J. Roberts, London, p.3.

circumstances occurs, for a woman always possesses sufficient power, by drawing back her limbs, and by the force of her hands, to prevent the insertion of the penis."[697] Thus, at his trial, in 1715, Captain Leeson demanded to know how a "little man", like himself, only 5 feet 6 inches tall, could possibly have overpowered a large woman "without her concurrence", especially when her arms were free to resist.[698] Complainants would be closely questioned about the steps they had taken to resist, and there was a suspicion that any failure to struggle adequately was indicative of a lack of virtue.

## The Trial Process in Rape Cases

### The Use of Counsel at Trial

Throughout the era, counsel could actively assist prosecutors and, by the early eighteenth century, the Crown was increasingly willing to pay for counsel in Metropolitan rape cases. By contrast, at the start of the 1700s, the privilege of legal representation was not open to those facing felony counts as defendants, unless it was to argue a point of pure law. However, in the 1730s, English courts, beginning with the Old Bailey, abandoned their centuries-old rule forbidding defendants from being actively represented by counsel. By the 1750s, if the defendant was well to do, both prosecution and defence might be legally represented in rape cases. The full impact of such representation on the typical rape trial is hard to assess. However, as with other hearings, it usually meant that the complainant's evidence was explored more thoroughly. Thus, in 1793, Sarah Tipple was expertly cross-examined by experienced defence counsel, a barrister named Knollys, when she swore that her master had raped her. Knollys probed inconsistencies in her story and focussed in great detail on the mechanics of the alleged rape, asking her exactly how the accused man had restrained her while the offence was carried out, while pointing out that the slender defendant was "not two or three ton weight." An acquittal ensued.[699] Similarly, in 1787, a Mr. Davidson was prosecuted at the Westminster Quarter Sessions for the attempted rape of his charwoman. Fortunately for him, he was wealthy enough to afford expert legal counsel in the form of William Garrow. The celebrated barrister's cross-examination of the complainant was so devastating that it "clearly appeared to the Court and Jury, that the whole of the charge was a fabrication." As a result, the accused man was immediately acquitted, without having to call any evidence in his own defence.[700]

---

[697]Farr (Ed.), "Elements of Medical Jurisprudence ", p.42.
[698]Leeson, Capt. Leeson's Case, p.12.
[699]OBSP, Trial of John Curtis, 20th Feb. 1793.
[700]The Times, Oct. 19, 1787, p.3.

*Examination of Rape Complainants*

Then as now the forensic examination of rape complainants was both intimate and often highly distressing for the woman concerned. However, given the technical requirements for the crime, and the traditional English emphasis on publicly given oral evidence, there was no alternative for complainants to answering humiliating questions in open court, even in an era that prized modesty. As prosecuting counsel at the trial of John Hunter warned the jury, the evidence that must be put in front of them so that they could reach a verdict, though obscene, had to be heard in public: "...from the Mouth of the Witnesses." Perhaps unsurprisingly, some women, like twelve year old Martha Flanders, found giving evidence about the physical minutiae of their attacks extremely hard and it was with: "...great Difficulty that the Court could get her to speak particularly of the Affair."[701] Customary expressions, such as the defendant's penis being his 'yard', and any emitted semen his 'nastiness', might be employed, *provided* that the essential facts were revealed. However, complainants like Elizabeth Midwinter, who tried to resort to excessive euphemism to avoid intimate accounts were repeatedly enjoined to go into detail and advised that: "In prosecutions of this kind it is absolutely necessary to be very full, particular, and explicit."[702] Nevertheless, there was a tendency for forensic language to become slightly less 'earthy' and more clinical as the century advanced, something that may have been encouraged by court clerks and which also probably reflected a shift in cultural mores. Thus, 'cock' increasingly became 'private parts'.[703]

## Penal Disposal

Although rape was a capital offence until 1841, convicted rapists, like other felons, could obtain a royal pardon that would save them from having their sentences carried out. Execution rates varied by decade. Everyone convicted of rape between 1795 and 1804 (five men) went to the gallows. However, only one of the five men convicted between 1770 and 1774 was executed.[704] Much would depend on the inherent gravity of their crimes. In 1798, Dennis Nugent, a 48 year old Irishman convicted of raping an eight year old in circumstances that were too disgusting for the (increasingly sensitive) Sessions papers to report "did not entertain the least prospect of a pardon." He publicly acknowledged the justice of his sentence at the gallows.[705] Nevertheless, even early in the century, a number of convicted rapists avoided their sentences. Near the start of the period, William Pheasant, convicted of raping Deborah Wise, an infant of less than ten years of age, at her Dancing School, initially bribing her silence with

---

[701]OBSP, Trial of Matthew Cave, 14th Oct. 1747.

[702]OBSP, Trial of James Purse, 10th May 1780.

[703]Gammon, "'A denial of innocence'", p.89.

[704]Simpson, "Vulnerability and the Age of Female Consent", p.187.

[705]Anon, *The Last Dying Speeches and Confessions, Confessions and Adventures of the Three Unfortunate Malefactors, Executed this morning before the Debtors Door, Newgate*, London, 1798, pp.3-4.

pennies and fruit: "… obtained His Majesty's most Gracious Pardon, which is now under the Seals."[706] Later, they had almost an even chance of being reprieved.[707] Influential contacts were important in the pardoning process. Captain Leeson claimed that, after his conviction, one of the trial jurors intimated that he had been unwilling to return a guilty verdict, but gave in to the wishes of the majority because he knew Leeson the "such interest at court, that he would not die of it." The juryman proved right.[708]

## Conclusion

Any historico-legal approach towards rape will tend to resonate with the concerns of modern observers.[709] Many of the issues raised by the eighteenth century experience are still very topical today. Indeed, much of the modern law of rape was forged or developed during this period. Some of its more arcane aspects, such as the admissibility of a recent complaint as an exception to the general rule against previous consistent cases, still survive in several common law jurisdictions. Many others, like the mandatory warning to juries about the desirability of complainant corroboration (which emerged from the era's suspicion of complainants) or the marital exemption, have only been abolished in recent decades. Arguably, given the legal attitudes towards the crime that lingered into the twentieth century, it is unsurprising that women 200 years earlier had a mountain to climb in bringing successful prosecutions. As a result, it is also quite understandable that many women sought alternative solutions to their wrongs (such as compounding or civil litigation), or simply ignored them altogether. Those who did seek to pursue matters through the Metropolitan courts, and their numbers seem to have fallen proportionately rather than increased during the century (perhaps because evidential rules became tighter), would often fall at one of the numerous fences that had to be cleared before trial: examining magistrates; Grand Juries etc. Even if they got a 'day in court', the odds were stacked against them. However, the reasons for their lack of forensic success are, perhaps, slightly less obvious than might at first appear.

It is usually suggested that ingrained social, and especially, patriarchal attitudes towards rape meant that complainants were readily disbelieved. Certainly, the records of the Old Bailey lend credence to this view. Although the eighteenth century was committed to a 'black letter' definition of rape that was similar to that of the modern era, its investigative and forensic process was very different. The era was largely devoid of any understanding of rape trauma syndrome and (ostensibly) possessed an image of how 'genuine' victims were supposed to behave that bore little relationship to reality. A failure to resist adequately, cry out to the requisite degree during an attack or any tardiness in

---

[706]OBSP, Trial of William Pheasant, 13th January 1699 and *The Flying Post*, 24-26 January 1699.

[707]Simpson, "Popular Perceptions of Rape", p.53.

[708]Leeson, *Capt. Leeson's Case*, p.4.

[709]Stevenson, "Unequivocal victims", p.346.

reporting the incident were often assumed to be the hallmarks of fabrication. In the modern era, these have been termed 'Rape myths', stereotypical beliefs about the nature of the crime that put women at a disadvantage, and which also mean that observers are unlikely to define a rape as such, even though it meets the legal criteria for the offence.

However, simple disbelief does not *fully* explain the low level of successful rape prosecutions. Here, the willingness of a trial jury to convict Robert Lander of attempted rape while acquitting him of the complete offence, when he was (very unusually) indicted for both, is suggestive. No issue was taken during the trial over penetration, the evidence of which was quite unequivocal, the victim stating that the defendant's member was "in me about a quarter of an hour." It was obviously a situation in which the complainant was either lying altogether or in which the defendant (a man of previous good character) was guilty of rape. Nevertheless, the jury availed themselves of the chance to convict of the lesser offence. There must be a strong suspicion that they thought him guilty but not deserving of death, and would have acquitted altogether in the absence of an attempt being charged.[710] Many acquittal verdicts in similar cases, in which there was no alternative count available, were probably returned by juries that actually believed a defendant to be 'guilty' but were not prepared to see him hanged. Significantly, attempted rapes tried at the City of London Quarter Sessions in the eighteenth century produced a conviction rate of 47 per cent, well over twice that of the completed offence.[711]

Unlike murder, and *pace* Sir Anthony Fitzherbert, it seems that whatever lip service was paid to the gravity of rape in public, such views were highly qualified and contextualised in private. Eighteenth-century rape investigations and trials involved a moral as well as legal judgment on the victim. If her status or conduct appeared to be at all 'flawed' a verdict was likely to go against her. Any number of factors could be fatal to prosecution success: an absence of justification for being beyond the reach of male protectors, previous social connection with the attacker, the consumption of alcohol, a dubious personal history or a willingness to consider financial settlement. However, it seems that these issues went not just to complainant credibility, as is sometimes suggested, but to the very gravity with which the offence itself was considered. The rape of 'blemished' women did not raise public anxiety, especially amongst the middling orders found on juries, and was not considered to be anything like as serious as contemporary notions of the 'ideal-typical' rape, one in which a woman of spotless virtue was overwhelmed, through no fault of her own, despite struggling to her utmost. Even if blemished complainants were believed - as they often must have been – jurors seem to have been willing to acquit. This was even more likely if they thought that the victim had actively 'encouraged' her victimisation, while

---

[710]OBSP, Trial of Robert Lander, 27th Aug. 1725.

[711]Simpson, "Vulnerability and the Age of Female Consent", p.189. Similarly, five of the 11 attempt trials at the Bailey produced guilty verdicts (four of these occurring in the 1720s).

anything that could be remotely redefined as 'seduction', however heavy handed, would produce an acquittal.

However, this does not necessarily mean that rape was a 'tool' used to terrorise women into subjection. Eighteenth-century England took, by modern standards, a remarkably 'robust' attitude towards the body (as opposed to property) and preserved most of the early modern era's high tolerance for non-lethal physical violence. Thus, only the gravest assaults were classified as felonies rather than misdemeanours. It is, perhaps, not surprising that such attitudes also readily extended to sexual violence. Indeed, a Middlesex cleric, who suggested that members of his community were succouring those who had carried out the sadistic rape and murder of a local woman, contrasted their apparent reluctance to expose those responsible with the enthusiasm with which they would "run the whole country over in the pursuit of a petty thief."[712] Rape could be the subject of callous jokes in jest books aimed (from their price) at the upper and middle classes.[713] It was also not unique in witnessing a degree of de facto tolerance for what was publicly a deprecated crime. Consensual sodomy was a capital offence, and, ostensibly, considered so grave a "crime [as] not to be named among Christians."[714] However, although vehemently deplored, and despite rare but well publicized executions, numerous eighteenth century Metropolitan homosexuals, arrested in circumstances where the evidence appeared very strong, were discharged without further action being taken, charged with the inchoate offence, or acquitted altogether. Additionally, several of those convicted were subsequently pardoned, rather than executed. As D'Archenholz noted, in practice, it was "very uncommon to see a person convicted and punished for this crime."[715] Judges and jurors would never openly defend the practice, but were, it seems, reluctant to see homosexuals hanged.[716]

Ultimately, it is necessary to distinguish social values that are descriptive from those that are normative. The eighteenth century saw a marked divergence between the popular (male) interpretation of rape and its strict legal definition. This facilitated great prosecutorial discretion. In many cases, it was probably thought unreasonable to hang a man, possessed of the strong sexual imperative attributed to him by the era, for doing what came 'naturally'. However, in exceptional cases, and for whatever reason, the strict letter of the law could be invoked. By contrast, the past 200 years, as well as putting children sexually 'off-limits', has seen a progressive narrowing in the divergence between legal and

---

[712]Anon, *A Sermon Preach'd at Isleworth in the County of Middlesex, On Sunday, Feb 10, 1722, Occasioned by the Rape and murder committed on the Body of Anne Bristow, January 22, on Smalbury-Green in that Parish,* Printed for J. Roberts, London, 1723, pp.11-12.

[713]Simon Dickie, "Hilarity and Pitilessness in the Mid-Eighteenth Century: English Jestbook Humor", *Eighteenth-Century Studies,* 2003, vol.37, no.1, pp.1-22, at pp.3-4.

[714]Anon (Ed.), *The Tryal and Condemnation of Mervin, Lord Audley Earl of Castlehaven,* p.12.

[715]Johann Wilhelm D'Archenholz, *A Picture of England,* Dublin, 1791, p.197

[716]Netta Murray Goldsmith, *The Worst of Crimes: Homosexuality and the Law in Eighteenth Century London,* Ashgate, Aldershot, 1988, pp.34-36.

popular definitions of rape. This process has been influenced by such diverse factors as the rise of feminism and an increasingly professional forensic hearing, though the ongoing debate over 'date rape' suggests that it is not yet complete. In a symbiotic development, changes in the legal process have not merely reflected changes in social attitudes, but have also helped inform and shape those attitudes.

# Chapter 7: Domestic Violence

## Introduction

This chapter will consider the position of Metropolitan women as both the victims and authors of domestic violence, taken in its widest sense, during the eighteenth century. Thus, while it will focus on 'wife-beating', it will also briefly consider situations in which women 'battered' their husbands or were the perpetrators of violence towards domestic servants and children. Whatever the immediate background to domestic violence, it should be remembered that the eighteenth century witnessed a relatively high tolerance for non-lethal violence, of all types, that was not planned or exercised in the course of committing crimes such as burglary and robbery. For much of the era, assaults of all but the most serious kind were viewed as quasi-civil matters, an attitude that only gradually disappeared during the early 1800s.[717] Low level violence, in particular, appears to have been a more common form of social 'interaction' than is the case today, albeit already in decline by comparison with previous centuries. Specifically domestic violence must be seen against this backdrop. It was often an accepted, if sometimes regretted, facet of everyday life, in a society where recourse to blows was not considered to be beyond the pale by many ordinary people.

Some aspects of domestic violence, such as the 'reasonable' physical chastisement of apprentices by their masters and children by their parents, guardians or schoolteachers, were expressly and unquestionably sanctioned by the law and so were not properly viewed as 'violence' at all. Others, such as the corporal punishment of wives, adult servants and undergraduates, existed in an increasingly murky legal twilight. Considering these phenomena for the eighteenth century as a whole is particularly difficult as, during its course, there were significant changes in both legal and social attitudes towards domestic violence and especially as to where the dividing line between legitimate chastisement and illegal violence should be drawn. The years after 1750, in particular, saw a reduced general tolerance for such conduct.[718] Indeed, to an extent, the era is illustrative of the processes by which some forms of violence become stigmatised while others are tacitly ignored. Nevertheless, even where domestic abuse was, technically, illegal, it is also clear that jurisprudential theory

---

[717] Anon, *Taking Stock: What do we know about interpersonal violence?*, ESRC Violence Research Programme, London, 2002, at p.9.

[718] John M Beattie, "Violence and society in early-modern England", in *Perspectives in Criminal Law, Essays in Honour of John Edwards*, A Doob and E L Greenspan (Eds.), Ontario, Aurora, Ontario, 1985, pp.50-51.

and practical reality (and the social attitudes that underlay such realities) often co-existed uneasily.

## Wife-beating

It is trite (because obvious) to say that domestic inequality shaped gender relations in the home during this period. Violence could be the clearest form of coercion in male/female relationships. In many respects, and as already noted, eighteenth-century England was a highly patriarchal society. In theory, religious tradition, aspects of scripture (even if selectively cited), ancient custom and the law, taken together, vested considerable powers in a husband whose sense of personal honour often extended to upholding his 'authority' in domestic as well as public life. Illustrative of this, parents whose adult daughters fled back to them to escape abusive spouses could find themselves being the subject of a writ of habeas corpus in the Court of King's Bench, aimed at securing the forcible return of their child. As Lord Mansfield pointed out, a husband had a "right to the custody of his wife," though that court would be reluctant to order a return if the husband's cruelty was deemed to have been 'excessive'.[719]

Wife beating existed in a social environment in which a woman's obedience to her spouse was, in theory, axiomatic. Unsurprisingly, this also produced a culture that was rich in exoneration for such behaviour. Indicative of this, many men, accused of physically mistreating their wives, would react not by denying that the violence had occurred, but by seeking to justify it; for example, by stressing their spouse's disobedience or personal failings, whether it was in her choice of friends, financial extravagance, refusal to perform household duties or even to provide sexual services.[720] Such a reaction was particularly common in the early years of the century. In an extreme case, when Matthias Brinsden was convicted of murdering his wife with a knife in 1722, he not only appeared devoid of grief, but also stressed his deceased spouse's manifold faults and: "...insisted on trifling allegations; said his wife lov'd Brandy and Geneva, disobey'd his commands, and would not be easy to live as he liv'd."[721] Women who did take legal action against their husbands often tacitly accepted the legitimacy of such 'deserved' chastisement by stressing that they themselves had been beaten *despite* according to the ideal model of a dutiful wife.

However, these attitudes declined markedly as the century advanced, especially amongst the middling and upper social orders. This was manifest in a number of ways. For example, there was an increased tendency for men appearing in the Church courts to flatly deny, rather than seek to justify, having

---

[719]Elizabeth Foyster, *Marital Violence: An English Family History, 1660-1857*, Cambridge, CUP, 2005, p.176.

[720]Margaret Hunt, "Wife Beating, Domesticity and Women's Independence in Eighteenth-Century London", *Gender & History*, Spring 1992, vol. 4, no. 1, pp.10-33, at p.18.

[721]Rev. Thomas Purney, *The Ordinary of Newgate's Account of the Behaviour, Confession and Last Dying Speech of Matthias Brinsden, who was executed at Tyburn, for the murther of his wife Hannah Brinsden* London, 1722, at p.3

used violence towards their wives. In 1721, Jacob Bor had been quite open about his use of 'moderate correction' against his spouse, after she 'provoked' him with her drunkenness and use of foul language. A century later, defendants in that forum were much less likely to be so ingenuous.[722] A similar trend can be detected in the civil courts. The explanation for such a change has been attributed to a variety of factors, from a widespread and ongoing 'gentling' of manners in society (one that had started over a century earlier), via the rise of a culture of 'politeness' (especially common in bourgeois society), to a change in marriage from being a patriarchal to an increasingly companionate and affectionate institution. Doubtless, all of these played some part in the process.

## The Right to 'Correct' a Wife

The theoretical underpinnings of a husband's legal right to physically 'correct' his wife had always been fairly slender. The earliest published mention of the subject appears to have been a passing remark in Sir Antony Fitzherbert's *The New Natura Brevium* of 1516. Sir Antony had observed that a woman could not bind her husband over to keep the peace if the violence she had suffered at his hands was merely that which was attendant on the lawful "governance and chastisement" of a wife. This was picked up by both William Lambarde and Michael Dalton and repeated in their own magistrates' handbooks, which were published over the following two centuries. It was reiterated by Mathew Bacon in his *New Abridgement of the Law* of 1736 and by Richard Burn in his much reissued *Justice of the Peace* of 1755.[723] As a result, in the 1760s, the jurist William Blackstone, although obviously uneasy about the practice, still felt unable to condemn the legality of spousal correction altogether, despite observing that since the reign of Charles II, society having become 'politer,' the justifications for its use had been increasingly doubted.[724] As late as 1807, a lawyers' primer declared that a husband could quite legally keep his wife: "...by force within the bounds of duty, and may beat her, but not in a violent or cruel manner." Violent, in this context, appears to have meant excessively or in illegitimate circumstances. Arguably, the legality of physical chastisement of a spouse (as well as her forcible confinement), in any form, however mild, was only expressly and quite unequivocally rejected in *R v Jackson* in 1891.[725]

Despite this, the legal right to chastise had been questioned for at least a century before 1700. In Calvin's Geneva, all spouse beating had been made a crime, something that influenced much Puritan opinion in England, which was strongly hostile to the practice. In 1609, William Heale, an Oxford divine, was adamant that it was unlawful for men to beat their wives. His book was reissued (without attribution), and in an expanded form, in 1682. Heale based his views

---

[722]Foyster, *Marital Violence*, p.121.
[723]Maeve Doggett, *Marriage, Wife-Beating and the Law in Victorian England*, London, Weidenfeld and Nicolson, 1992, pp.8-10
[724]William Blackstone, *Commentaries on the Laws of England*, Oxford, 1765, vol. I at p.433.
[725]Foyster, *Marital Violence*, p.40.

on a variety of religious, jurisprudential and ethical grounds. Thus, he felt that beating was something that a man would do to a slave, should slavery be institutionalised, not a spouse. Additionally, if a husband could lawfully beat his wife, she would be "legally bounde to indure his beating." In reality, even in the early 1600s, a wife could (sometimes) leave her husband because of his violent behaviour and he could still be forced to support her financially.

Heale was well aware (though dismissive) of the numerous contemporary suggestions that this only applied if the beating was 'excessive' and that otherwise the "law authorizeth a man to beat his wife but slightlie, and not in such sorte as may cause her departure...[in reality, he felt] how little so ever it bee they are not bound to take it." He also alluded to other attempts to reconcile practice with theory. Thus, he appreciated that some early seventeenth-century observers were already sanctioning the legality of wife-beating while stressing that it was not the 'done' thing, that is: "...in the strictnesse of law, for a husband to beate his wife is lawful, but it is inconvenient in the decencie of manners."[726] This seems to have been the (regretful) view of William Gough, in 1631, who complained that wives did not: "...have so good remedy by the helpe of law against cruell husbands, as servants may have against cruell masters." Nevertheless, Gough felt that it was morally wrong for husbands to beat their wives in any circumstances except for self-defence.[727]

Heale's views were extreme (and legally wrong) for the early 1600s. Indeed, they were published in response to other works that expressly upheld such a right and were, in turn, challenged by writers in the decades after 1609. Although a man's legal right to 'moderately' chastise his spouse may have been questioned, it was very rarely denied outright during the 1600s, though there was universal agreement that it should be 'reasonable', that is commensurate with the behaviour to be corrected, and not inflicted with a: "... sword or a bar of iron, nor any other weapon or instrument to kill them."[728] Even in the post-Restoration decades of the seventeenth century, husbands appearing in ecclesiastical court 'divorce' cases, where cruelty was alleged, would often stress that any beatings that they had administered had been restrained and controlled, rather than denying them altogether. Thus, one pointed out that the smack that he had given to his wife's mouth had been administered with "the back of his hand" and not resulted in any issue of blood. Another claimed merely to have given his spouse a "little light tap upon her head" which, he felt, would not have hurt a baby. Others stressed that their blows had been to the body and not resulted in bruising. Most of them also claimed to have administered correction with a cool head and with clear justification, rather than in anger.[729]

---

[726]William Heale, *An Apologie for Women*, Oxford, 1609, pp.45-49.
[727]William Gough, *Domesticall Duties*, London, 1634, at p.397
[728]C. Robbins (Ed.), *The Diary of John Milward Esq., September 1666 to May 1668*, Cambridge, CUP, 1938, pp.167-168.
[729] Elizabeth Foyster, "Male Honour, Social Control and Wife Beating in Late Stuart England" in *Transactions of the Royal Historical Society*, 6th Series, vol. 6, 1996, pp.215-224, at p.223

Judicial and legal attitudes became stricter during the following century. In its officially sanctioned manifestations, domestic violence of all types had to be kept within progressively narrower limits if it was to be considered 'legal'. Thus, if a master went 'too far' in administering physical chastisement, his apprentice could petition the JPs to release him from his articles or, in more serious cases, invoke the criminal law. Similarly, although, in the right circumstances, controlled male physical violence might be commended, if it was directed towards those identified as 'vulnerable', such as women, it was likely to be condemned. Additionally, when it came to spouses, the law was clear that 'correction' was supposed to be a response to a specific (and serious) fault or mistake on the part of a wife; it was not to be a general outlet for a husband's anger or a response to a trivial matter of household economy.[730] A reflection of this concern was that 'divorce' petitions in the Church courts during the 1700s would often stress that the domestic violence alleged was committed in a 'fury', 'passion' or 'rage'.[731] Indeed, witnesses appearing on the part of abused wives would frequently claim that their husbands became 'mad men' when beating their spouses.[732] Presumably, this would negate any suggestion that it was legitimate and considered 'correction'.

By 1750, overt recognition of the *legal* right of a man to beat his wife, to any degree, was often half-hearted. The widespread indignation in 1782 at the supposed late eighteenth-century 'rule of thumb' for Assizes, about the maximum thickness of a rod that could legitimately be used on a wife is indicative of a change in attitudes.[733] Although, in reality, Sir Francis Buller, the notoriously stern judge to whom this pronouncement was attributed, does not appear to have made it, unless in a social context, a popular belief that he had given such a judgment led to him being publicly ridiculed and the subject of a vicious satirical cartoon by James Gillray, caricaturing him as 'Judge Thumb'.[734] By the early part of the following century, magisterial attitudes in the London area make it clear that the practice was legally frowned upon, even in its more modest manifestations. In 1824, the Lord Mayor, presiding over the hearings at the Mansion House, claimed to be appalled at the constant attacks that were made on wives, and which came before him on so regular a basis that he was "daily reprobating the practice."[735]

This ongoing uncertainty about the state of the law allowed individual judges and magistrates during the eighteenth century considerable latitude to

---

[730]Susan Dwyer Amussen, "Being Stirred to Much Unquietness: Violence and Domestic Violence in Early Modern England", *Journal of Women's History*, Summer 1994, vol.6, no.2, pp.70-89, at p.82.

[731]Joanne Bailey, *Unquiet Lives: Marriage and Marriage Breakdown in England, 1660-1800*, CUP, Cambridge, 2003, at p.11.

[732]Foyster, "Male Honour, Social Control and Wife Beating", p.221.

[733]Amussen, "Being Stirred to Much Unquietness", pp.70-75.

[734]Henry Ansgar Kelly, "Rule of Thumb and the Folklaw of the Husband's Stick", *Journal of Legal Education*, 1994, vol. 44 (3), pp.341-365.

[735]*The Times*, Oct.7, 1824, at p.3.

impose their own personal marital ideology on the cases that came before them. As early as 1674, in *Lord Leigh's Case*, this flexibility had permitted the eminent judge and Lord Chief Justice, Mathew Hale, to deny that lawful chastisement extended to beating, and to conclude that it was limited to "admonition and confinement to the house, in case of her [a wife's] extravagance." Despite his reputation, his views were not generally followed on this matter in the immediately ensuing years, but would become more widespread in the next century.[736]

There was nothing unique to England in this process of gradual decline in the perceived legitimacy of wife-beating. In Norway, it was freely acknowledged that a husband could legally chastise his wife until the seventeenth century. In that country, there was the same distinction between legitimate correction and illegal violence as was found in England, the degree, motive and manner of its administration also being the determining factors. However, between the late 1600s and the early 1800s this was increasingly questioned and doubted, until being formally abolished in 1842.[737] A similar transformation, over the same period, occurred in Scotland. In the 1690s, Church court records north of the border contain numerous instances of wife beating in which the perpetrator was merely mildly reprimanded, while his spouse received equal blame for provoking such behaviour. Nevertheless, by 1846, a Scottish legal expert could note that even though, in the past, physical chastisement was allowed, and the doctrine was still claimed by some to be the law, it was highly unlikely that the Scottish courts would sanction it in practice.[738]

## Social Attitudes to Wife-beating

Whatever the legal position, by the early 1700s, wife beating was also condemned by much educated opinion as brutish and unmanly. It was at variance to an expanding culture of civility.[739] Early in the century, men such as Richard Steele and Joseph Addison used the pages of journals like the *Tatler* and *Spectator* to deplore the physical mistreatment of wives, calling for men to moderate their anger towards their spouses and to avoid what they euphemistically termed 'unkindness' and 'tyranny' in marriage. It has even been suggested that the rise of such attitudes may have done women a disservice, by driving abusive behaviour underground, and preventing it being properly discussed in public, though such an analysis has also been strongly challenged.[740] Most contemporary observers stressed that even if they found their spouses to

---

[736]Doggett, *Marriage, Wife-Beating and the Law in Victorian England*, pp.8-11.

[737]F.L. Naeshagen, "Private Law Enforcement in Norwegian History: The Husband's Right to Chastise His Wife", *Scandinavian Journal of History*, 2002, vol. 27(1), pp.19-29, at p. 27.

[738]Leah Leneman, "'A tyrant and tormentor': violence against wives in eighteenth-and early nineteenth-century Scotland", *Continuity and Change*, 1997, vol. 12.1, pp.31-54, at p.50.

[739]Elizabeth Foyster "Creating a Veil of Silence? Politeness and Marital violence in the English Household", *Transactions of the Royal Historical Society*, 2002, vol. 12, pp.395-415, at pp.396-398.

[740]Hunt, "Wife Beating, Domesticity and Women's Independence..", p.10.

be irritating and unreasonable, good husbands would bear with their faults. A wise man would: "…rather manage his wife, than [have recourse to] downright force and violence."[741]

Newspapers also reported incidents of wife-beating with growing distaste.[742] It was often identified as demeaning and dishonourable. Of course, it continued to exist in the upper and middling social orders, throughout the century, but it was increasingly 'discreet'. It was comparatively rare for it to extend beyond occasional blows, particularly to the body (rather than the face), as many gentlemen and prosperous tradesmen were afraid of the public disgrace they would incur if their spouse was seen with obvious wounds. The change in attitudes also led to greater attempts at concealing physically abusive relationships. It seems that wealthier women who received injuries such as black eyes, increasingly used cosmetics to hide their bruises.

Ironically, this change in attitudes towards violence also risked encouraging ostensibly 'legal' but abusive behaviour in other forms. For example, some wealthy men during the era resorted to committing their wives to private mad houses, not because they had genuine psychiatric problems, but because they found the women irritating or uncongenial and because the 'right' of a husband to confine his spouse was legally more uncertain than that of beating her (even Mathew Hale had accepted it), allowing some men to test their authority to its limits. The number of such establishments had grown swiftly in the eighteenth century, and there was no attempt to regulate them by statute until 1774. Prior to this date, there was no need for husbands to prove that their wives were mad to incarcerate them, though, if the women concerned were able to communicate with the outside world, they might be 'rescued' by family or friends, or have a writ of habeus corpus issued on their behalf in the Court of King's Bench. Thus, in 1766, Hannah Mackenzie escaped from Peter Day's Madhouse in Paddington by throwing money and a message to a gardener working in neighbouring premises.[743] Such allegations could also form part of divorce petitions; in 1711, Elizabeth Spinke complained to the Consistory Court that she had been committed to such an establishment in Stoke Newington for six weeks, against her will. When Catherine Bickerton sought to divorce her husband Theophilus, *a mensa et thoro*, at Doctors Commons in 1795, it was noted that, as well as beating her without provocation, he had frequently "threatened to send her to a private mad-house."[744]

Amongst 'ordinary' men, the situation was somewhat different, and the reality of everyday domestic violence often continued to be grim. Although some sections of the working class appear to have been affected by the wider

---

[741] Anon, *The Art of Governing a Wife*, London, J. Robinson, 1747, at p.20.
[742] Elizabeth Foyster, "At the limits of liberty: married women and confinement in eighteenth-century England", *Continuity and Change*, 2002, vol.17, pp.39-62, p.40.
[743] Foyster, "At the limits of liberty", pp.45-46.
[744] *The Times*, Jan. 12th 1795, at p.4

change in attitudes, as Blackstone realistically noted, in this respect the: "…lower rank of people, who were always fond of the old common law, still claim and exert their ancient privilege [to beat their wives]."[745] Poorer families frequently had definitions of acceptable intimate violence that differed from those held by the middling and upper orders. Daniel Defoe was not wholly exaggerating when he observed that "every vagabond thinks that he may cripple his wife at pleasure." Thus, it was considered quite normal when a woman developed a serious drink problem for her husband to attempt to "beat her out of this wicked course."[746] Indeed, at a proletarian level, attitudes towards inter-gender violence generally, whether domestic or not, were quite frequently not 'chivalrous' during the 1700s, and some of the female victims of such attacks do not appear to have expected special protection because of their sex. For example, in 1722, James Butler assaulted Elizabeth Pember outside her house in West Smithfield while he was intoxicated. He struck her in the face, knocking out one of her teeth, and putting her thumb out of joint when she held up her hand to ward off the blow. Nevertheless, his victim intervened on his behalf and, at her urging, his fine and custodial sentence were reduced.[747]

Throughout the eighteenth century, violence within marriage was not invariably viewed as deviant behaviour (even if not considered ideal) by the mass of people. It could still be a feature of a 'normal' and fully viable relationship.[748] Indeed, even late in the following century, the jurist Fitzjames Stephen could remark that "instances of brutality" towards women seldom reached the newspapers because they were so common. According to the Victorian feminist and polemical writer, Matilda Blake, women were so little protected by the law during the 1800s that men could "beat, torture and violently assault them" almost at will.[749] Although this was a major exaggeration, it rested on a kernel of truth, something that was far more apparent in the 1700s, when the sustained Victorian campaign against domestic violence (manifest in statutes such as the Matrimonial Causes Act of 1853) still lay far in the future. It was not until the nineteenth century that male violence, especially when it was directed against women, and even if it was practised by the working class, was to become a subject of acute concern amongst the political nation (this being an especially

---

[745]Blackstone, *Commentaries on the Laws of England,* vol I, at p.433.

[746]Anon, *The Last Speech and Confession of Sarah Elestone at the place of execution who was burned for killing her husband April 24 1678 with her deportment in prison since her condemnation,* printed for T.D. 1678, at pp.1-2.

[747]OBSP, Trial of James Butler, 28th Feb. 1722.

[748]Foyster, *Marital Violence,* p.4.

[749]Susan Edwards, "'Kicked, Beaten, Jumped On until They Are Crushed', All under Man's Wing and Protection: The Victorian Dilemma with Domestic Violence" in *Criminal Conversations, Victorian Crimes, Social Panic, and Moral Outrage* Judith Rowbotham and Kim Stevenson (Eds.), Ohio State University Press, Columbus, 2005, at pp.247-250.

late manifestation of what has been termed the post-medieval 'civilising offensive').[750]

## Informal Remedies for Wife-beating

In many situations, involvement by close relatives and intimate friends was more effective at limiting spousal violence than formal recourse to the law. In rural communities, it was difficult to produce the social isolation from family and neighbours that accompanies much modern domestic abuse. The relatively public nature of daily life amongst the poor during the eighteenth century facilitated the monitoring of family life, including domestic violence, by outsiders.[751] This obviously also went on in the London area throughout the 1700s. Nevertheless, in the Metropolitan environment, such intervention was less likely to occur or to be effective. At first sight, this might appear strange. Urban life amongst the poor was often devoid of privacy, as many couples and families crammed into over-crowded apartments in multi-residency houses. Against this, however, London was also characterised by the transience of many of its domestic arrangements and by the fact that a large number of its inhabitants, especially women, were migrants from the provinces. This meant that they would often be far from parents and siblings generally, and fathers and brothers in particular, people whose blood ties (and physical strength) meant they were inherently more likely to intervene effectively in cases of domestic violence. Additionally, and again in part due to migration, the common practice of living under a parental roof when first married, a time when patterns of marital behaviour are being established, was rarer in the Metropolis than in rural areas.

Of course, even in the absence of family and friends, strangers might intervene to prevent excessive abuse. For example, in Robert Hallam's case, neighbours had sometimes become involved when he had attacked his wife on earlier occasions (although his male apprentice, despite being roused by the noise of the final and fatal assault on the woman, and her cries of "murder", had returned to bed rather than become involved).[752] Nevertheless, this was not devoid of risk. Thus, in 1803, when a lodger began his "usual exercise of beating his wife," his landlord, alarmed by her cries of "murder" (a customary response to violence) intervened by gently commenting on the "impropriety of his behaviour." Despite the restrained nature of his involvement, the landlord was viciously attacked and struck with a poker by the husband.[753] For many, turning a blind eye was easier and certainly safer. Even local peace officers, especially watchmen, might be very reluctant to intervene where they were familiar with the husbands concerned in the abuse, if only for social reasons. This sometimes

---

[750] Martin Wiener, *Men of Blood: Violence, Manliness, and Criminal Justice in Victorian England*, New York, CUP, 2004, at pp.9-12.

[751] Amussen, "'Being Stirred to Much Unquietness:'", p.82.

[752] OBSP, Trial of Robert Hallam, 14th Jan. 1732.

[753] *The Times*, Jan. 10th 1803, p.3.

occurred despite severe beatings being administered almost under their noses.[754] Outside intervention could also be counter-productive for the women concerned, resulting in them receiving even worse treatment from their spouses, as can be seen in the case of the wife-killer John Wilkinson. Wilkinson was a Moorfields shoemaker who, having been left a widower, swiftly married a woman with a small inheritance, even though she "bordered upon idiotism." He quickly started to beat and abuse her. However, his neighbours: "...reproaches to Williamson for his barbarity used always to end in further ill-usage of the poor woman."[755]

In these circumstances, a perhaps surprising degree of isolation could be achieved, in even the most built up areas. As was noted with astonishment after the prolonged abuse to which the infamous Elizabeth Brownrigg's servant girls had been subjected was publicly revealed: "Who could have believed, that two wretches of the age of 15 or sixteen years, could, in such a Metropolis as London, and such a neighbourhood as Fetter-lane, continue to suffer as Mitchell and Clifford suffered, for two years, without discovery or escape."[756] In this case, the crime only came to light because a journeyman baker, whose master lived next door to the family, and who had at first been unwilling to "declare what he suspected", kept the house under close scrutiny. A fear of being sanctioned for bad-naming an apparently reputable local family appears to have led to his initial reluctance to act.[757] Similarly, Wilkinson's wife was beaten, ill treated and starved to death in the matrimonial home, although within walking distance of her legal guardian, and despite the presence of a female lodger in the same house. Again, it was acknowledged by contemporary observers that the husband's cruelty was: "...the more astonishing, considering her friends were so near."[758] The reduced effectiveness of informal intervention, combined with the generally liberating effect of the Metropolitan environment on women, *may* explain an apparently greater willingness on the part of the city's married females to have recourse to secular officials when suffering spousal abuse than was manifest by their rural counterparts.

## Formal Legal Action

Formal legal action could be taken in a variety of forums, using several different mechanisms. However, unless the consequences were particularly grave, for example, a death or very serious injury ensued, it was rare for prosecutions on indictment (i.e. before a jury) to be brought as a result of domestic violence, even though, and contrary to the normal situation, a wife could testify against

---

[754]See for example 'Law Report' in *The Times*, Dec. 19th, 1806, p.3

[755]Anon, *God's Revenge Against Murder!*, London, 1810, at p.33

[756]*The Gentleman's Magazine*, vol.37, 1767, at p.437.

[757]Anon, *An Appeal for Humanity in an Account of the Life and Cruel Actions of Elizabeth Brownrigg*, London, 1767, at p.10.

[758]Anon, *God's Revenge Against Murder!*, London, 1810, at p.35

her husband "in case of violent injuries to her person."[759] This reluctance to indict husbands had always been present, in all parts of the country, whether rural or urban. For example, in the years between 1620 and 1680, of the 579 assaults indicted at the Essex Quarter Sessions, none involved wife beating, despite there being evidence of numerous informal complaints about the practice.[760] Although prosecution by indictment was slightly more common in the Metropolitan area during the following century, it remained rare. Thus, nearly all of the cases of domestic violence that reached the Old Bailey had involved a killing, and were indicted as murder, a tiny number (fewer than 10) of very serious assaults apart. Amongst the latter were cases such as that of William Lee, who, in 1763, took a razor to his wife's neck.

## Domestic Homicide

As the cases at the Old Bailey indicate, the most acute forms of domestic violence could result in homicide. This accounted for a significant proportion of female murder victims, and most of those killed were wives or partners. Indeed, some contemporary observers feared that although Englishmen were not prone to jealousy, in the way of many 'continentals', they still had a marked and singular predilection for killing their spouses.[761] In the first two decades of the eighteenth century, of the 16 men indicted at the Old Bailey for murdering a female (some sessions papers for this period are missing), four had killed their wives and two their daughters. At least one other man had killed his lover. These years may have been slightly unusual (proportions for subsequent decades often being somewhat lower), nevertheless, even during the remainder of the century, a high percentage of males who were tried for killing women were accused of murdering their partners or (less commonly) daughters.

Sometimes, in these cases, it is apparent that the final, lethal, assault was merely the culmination of a long period of domestic abuse. For example, in a notorious murder case from 1732, in which Robert Hallam killed his pregnant wife by throwing her out of a first floor window, the defenestration had been preceded by a history of extreme domestic violence. His victim bore the marks of numerous previous attacks and neighbours noted that she had been beaten like an ox on earlier occasions. As a result, when they heard her cries, they normally merely observed to each other that: "Hallam's a beating his wife, according to custom." Although denying her murder (he claimed she committed suicide), even Hallam conceded at the Tyburn gallows that he had regularly thrashed her.[762]

In other cases, the killing seems to have been an exceptional event in an otherwise fairly 'normal' domestic life and not necessarily indicative of an

---

[759] J. Chitty, *A Practical Treatise on the Criminal Law*, vol.1, London, 1816, p.595.

[760] James Sharpe, "Domestic Homicide in Early Modern England," *Historical Journal*, 1981, vol. 24, p.31.

[761] Hayward (Ed), *Lives of the Most Remarkable Criminals*, pp.217-219

[762] OBSP, Trial of Robert Hallam, 14th Jan. 1732, *Gentleman's Magazine*, vol.2, 1732, p.627.

'abusive' relationship. Thus, in 1719, Isaac Smith stabbed his wife to death after an argument over who was to go for drink, during which he had apparently called her "Bitch and Toad and such like names." When he realized what he had done, he immediately observed that he had: "…kill'd the best of Wives, and must be hang'd for it." He was duly convicted and sentenced to death.[763] Occasionally, even women might acknowledge that their conduct had gone beyond accepted norms in provoking their spouses to such behaviour. Isaac Ingram was merely convicted of manslaughter, after being indicted for murdering his wife by throwing a poker at her. He appears to have received this favourable verdict largely because, in the month during which she 'lingered' prior to expiring from her wound, she "freely forgave her husband", stated that he had thrown the implement "at random" and asked that he not be prosecuted. Additionally, she counselled "all women to forbear provoking language" towards their spouses, and admitted that her husband had been annoyed with her because she had refused his entreaties to come down to breakfast.[764]

Even so, such verdicts should not be taken to suggest that wife-killing was viewed lightly by the authorities. In 1722, when Matthias Brinsden was awaiting execution for the murder of his wife Hannah, the Newgate Ordinary went out of his way to stress the enormity of his crime, preaching a sermon to the assembled prisoners on the evils of uxoricide and man's natural indebtedness to woman.[765] Almost 70 years later, when William Cooper was acquitted of murdering his wife, who had died some weeks after he had beaten her, and where the evidence suggested that she might have died from a bilious complaint rather than the effects of her beating, Chief Baron Hotham took the opportunity to admonish the defendant from the Bench: "…my conscience tells me that your conduct has been by no means such as entitles you to stand well in the esteem of any man in this Court." [766] It also appears that the eighteenth century witnessed a major transformation in attitudes towards lethal domestic violence, and, in particular, an increasing degree of popular concern about wife-killers. In the 1600s, the incidence of popular broadsides and chapbooks suggests that female husband killers were a major social pre-occupation. By the early 1800s, however, the focus was overwhelmingly on male spouse killers.[767] Additionally, it must always be remembered that, although detailed evidence for such cases is much more readily available than that for lower level manifestations of domestic violence, they were not remotely 'typical' of the phenomenon. Domestic violence was usually part of an ongoing relationship, not the means by which one came to an end.

---

[763] OBSP, Trial of Isaac Smith, 25th Feb. 1719.

[764] OBSP, Isaac Ingram, 28th Feb. 1722.

[765] Purney, *Last Dying Speech of Matthias Brinsden*, p.3

[766] *The Times*, Oct 30, 1790, p.4

[767] Martin J. Wiener, "Alice Arden to Bill Sikes: Changing Nightmares of Intimate Violence in England, 1558-1869", *Journal of British Studies* (2001) vol.40, pp.184-212, at p.187

## Prosecution at Quarter Sessions

Of course, if indicted, domestic assaults occasioning serious but not lethal, or necessarily life threatening, injuries, such as broken limbs, would normally be determined at the three Quarter Sessions found in the Metropolis.[768] However, even in these forums, the number of women prosecuting assaults committed by their husbands appears to have been relatively modest. Bringing a prosecution on indictment to deal with abusive spouses was usually very much a last resort. It is a mistake to view the gradual repudiation by the courts of the legal right of a man to chastise his wife as necessarily indicative of how the justice system would respond to marital violence in practice. Chastisement could be formally condemned as illegal and wrong while being tacitly condoned, or at least ignored.[769] Although culturally diverse understandings of violence were, in theory, subject to a single legal analysis when presented in the courtroom, the courts and policing agencies were extremely reluctant to become involved in domestic matters or to risk undermining a man's authority in his own home, except in the most blatant cases.

For less serious examples of wife-beating, legal theory and practice often co-existed uneasily, occasionally coming into conflict when a wife insisted on applying the strict letter of the law to her domestic circumstances. This was frequently in the face of strong discouragement from the relevant authorities. Thus, in 1803, Joseph Brandon was indicted at the Middlesex Quarter Sessions (held at Hick's Hall) by his wife for a series of assaults committed during domestic arguments over money. She had required a modest degree of medical attention for her injuries (severe bruising etc.) and had, she claimed, also suffered considerable emotional trauma as a result. At an earlier hearing, the parties (who were Jewish) had unavailingly been urged by both counsel and the court to go home and settle the matter in an "amicable way." At trial, the City's Common Serjeant, presiding over the hearing, openly regretted that they had not done this, something that should occur, he felt, in "all cases of dispute between man and wife." He also reminded the jury that the only evidence against the husband was that of his wife, and asked them: "...what the situation of all married men must be, if they were liable to be dragged before courts of justice in order to gratify the vindictive spleen with which their wives might be actuated." Nevertheless, the case was allowed to proceed, and despite the judge's apparent encouragement to acquit, the defendant was duly convicted of assault. However, he was then sentenced to a very modest 40s fine, despite being a reasonably prosperous man, and was bound over to keep the peace in future.[770]

---

[768]Bailey, *Unquiet Lives*, p.114.
[769]Reva B. Siegel, "'The Rule of Love': Wife Beating as Prerogative and Privacy", *Yale Law Journal*, 1996, vol. 106, pp.2117-2207, at pp.2130-2132.
[770]*The Times*, Sept. 14th, 1803, p.4

**Summary Solutions**

Relatively informal and personal intervention by JPs, or low-level prosecution in local forums, remained the preferred treatment for those who assaulted their spouses or lovers, if formal action was taken by victims. In some (probably many) cases, a JP might not take any formal proceedings at all against a violent husband, but instead sought to deal with the matter on a purely personal basis, perhaps admonishing and warning him, so that it was "made up" between the parties. This traditional part of the magisterial role was especially common in the provinces, but undoubtedly occurred in the Metropolis as well. However, there, the pressure of judicial work and the relatively modest social status of some Middlesex magistrates (especially that of the 'trading justices' who took office for the attendant fees), something that reduced their personal authority, combined with a lack of intimate involvement between JPs and populace in what was a much less static society, probably reduced both its incidence and effectiveness. Unfortunately, by their nature, instances of informal settlement were usually totally unrecorded, making their frequency difficult to estimate.

**Binding Over of Abusive Spouses**

Summary courts were heavily involved in dealing with assaults of all types (not just domestic ones), which made up a majority of the offences heard by such forums, especially in urban areas. Thus, in Hackney, during the 1730s, almost three times as many assaults as property offences came before the magistrates for disposal.[771] When it came to domestic violence, magistrates' binding over and recognisance procedures were particularly important. It had always been accepted by JPs that if a man did more than "chaste his wife with discretion", that is, if his correction became "outrageous," she could petition for him to be bound over.[772] This process occurred on a fairly regular basis throughout the Metropolitan area. Typically, it was adopted in January 1740, when Rebecca Child claimed that she went "in danger of her life" as a result of her husband's frequent beatings and threats.[773]

Despite this, the use of recognisances to deal with domestic violence (or any other type of crime) has often been neglected by modern historians. Under the procedure, an accused person promised to appear at the following Quarter Sessions, and sometimes (especially early in the century) to be of good behaviour or to keep the peace in the interim. The defendant would also have to provide sureties (often two) to guarantee his (or her) appearance. In 64 per cent of cases in eighteenth-century Middlesex, one of these would be the defendant on his own account. However, others could stand surety on behalf of (and with) the

---

[771]Peter King, "The Summary Courts and Social Relations in Eighteenth-Century England" *Past & Present*, no. 183, 2004, pp.125-173, at p.137

[772]William Fleetwood, *The Office of a Justice of Peace, Together with Instructions, How and in What Manner Statutes shall be Expounded*. London, printed by Ralph Wood for W Lee, 1657, p.31.

[773]Ruth Paley, *Justice in Eighteenth-Century Hackney: The Justicing Notebook of Henry Norris and the Hackney Petty Sessions Book*, London, London Record Society, 1991, at p.56.

principal. Usually, the sum would be £20 or more. The defendant was *normally* only inconvenienced by the process, unless they were unable to find the necessary sureties, when they might be committed to a Bridewell or House of Correction. (It was for this reason that a City clergyman observed that the only prostitutes who were effectively punished by use of the recognisance procedure were the "meaner sort," who were devoid of "any friend to appear for security").[774] At the sessions immediately after the issuing of the recognisance, the defendant would usually appear, pay a small fee to the Quarter Sessions clerk (typically 2s 4d.) and the document would be marked *ven & exon*, signifying that they 'came and were exonerated'. They were then free to leave court, poorer only by time, a few shillings, inconvenience and (perhaps) embarrassing publicity. However, a failure to appear would result in their sureties having their recognisances estreated and forfeit to the Crown. In practice, this very rarely happended, as the Sessions' Clerks were extremely efficient in 'chasing' sureties and allowing them the opportunity to 'respite' the estreatment for the sum of 14s. 8d.[775]

A study of the Westminster Quarter Sessions between 1680 and 1720 reveals that women could effectively prosecute even a relatively minor incident of domestic violence using this procedure, and were, in many respects, advantaged when compared to servants and apprentices in doing so (the latter often had to establish a contractual violation as well as violence). Between 1685 and 1720 the Westminster justices alone bound over 154 men for 'assault' at the instigation of their wives. Another 16 men were bound over for 'beating' their spouses, two for 'threatening' violence and four to "keep the peace" towards their wives. Of course, this must be kept in perspective. Even at the start of this period, Westminster had a population of 60,000 (soon to grow), and the 176 recognisances amount to an average of only five a year. Nevertheless, it is clear that the procedure was well known.

Because recognisances were not bound by a set legal formula, the language used by JPs when describing the various incidents was relatively unfettered and often highly descriptive. Some assaults were clearly fairly extreme. In these situations, the wording in the recognisance might use phrases such as "barbarous" or "inhuman" and would also sometimes stipulate specific attacks that were deemed to be beyond any acceptable notion of spousal correction; for example, that the complainant had had "three teeth [knocked] out of her head." Another woman had almost had her eye put out, yet another had had a knife broken against her stays, accompanied by threats to "murder" her. However, and significantly, in half the cases considered, the spousal violence appears to have been less extreme, the magistrate simply stating that there had been an

---

[774]Anon ('A clergyman of the City of London'), *Friendly Advice to the Fair Sex*, London, printed for G. Kearsly, 1758, at p.vi
[775]Norma Landau, "Appearance at the Quarter Sessions of Eighteenth-Century Middlesex", *London Journal* vol. 23 (2), 1998, pp.30-51, at pp.34-35.

'assault' or 'beating', perhaps with some resultant bruising. It would seem that some recognisances were even issued for purely threatening words (technically still an assault). Thus, it is apparent that the procedure was not limited to cases in which extreme violence had been shown towards abused spouses, but instead had a relatively modest threshold for judicial involvement.[776]

This phenomenon was certainly not confined to Westminster. The rest of Middlesex and the City produced similar results. Thus, Thomasin Wheeler from Hackney appears to have had a violent and indolent spouse, John, who beat her and also neglected his family (they had two children). However, Thomasin did not supinely accept his behaviour. She regularly involved the local JPs in dealing with her husband during the 1730s, frequently cropping up both in court records and the Justicing Notebook of the local magistrate, Henry Norris. Thus, in February 1731, she complained to the JP that John had beaten and abused her when she was sick, refused the family maintenance and even threatened to kill her. She was duly issued with a warrant for his arrest. In June the following year she came forward again with similar allegations and, on this occasion, John was actually committed to the New Prison because he could not provide sureties to ensure his appearance at the next Quarter Sessions to answer for the assault. However, in a pattern that was to recur, Thomasin doubtless feeling that she had taught him a sufficient lesson, John was discharged from prison within two weeks at the "desire of his wife in her hope of his amendment." This abusive, but judicially supervised, relationship continued over the next two years, with Thomasin periodically bringing similar claims against her husband then making up with him (sometimes he also deserted her).[777] Upper class and Aristocratic women might also use the binding over procedure when dealing with spousal violence, though, in their cases, it might be ordered by the Court of King's Bench, which heard three or four such cases a year. Amongst them was that of Lord Vane, who was bound over to keep the peace towards his wife in 1744, despite arguing that "by the common law he had power to govern, rule and chastise her reasonably." In 1758, the notorious Lord Ferrers had to find sureties of £10,000 in a similar situation.[778]

As the Wheeler case also suggests, allegations of assault made to JPs by wives were frequently accompanied by complaints about a husband's unwillingness to provide for his spouse and children. Indeed, for some women, it was the lack of financial support that appears to have rankled, rather than the occasional blow. Thus, in 1733, Hannah Preston's grievance against her spouse was his: "…beating her last Wednesday and especially for neglecting to make any provision for his family." The couple had three small children.[779] Of course,

---

[776]Jennine Hurl-Eamon, "Domestic Violence Prosecuted: Women Binding Over Their Husbands for Assault at Westminster Quarter Sessions, 1685-1720", *Journal of Family History*, 2001, vol. 26, no. 4, pp.435-454, at p.417 and p.439

[777]Paley, *Justice in Eighteenth-Century Hackney*, pp.26-27.

[778]Doggett, *Marriage, Wife-Beating and the Law in Victorian England*, p.11.

[779]Paley, *Justice in Eighteenth-Century Hackney*, p.21

there were also inherent dangers in involving the law in this manner. Vincent Davis appears to have been infuriated when, late one night, he returned home drunk and abused his wife: "...upon which she got a warrant for him and sent him to New Prison." After this, he could "never endure her", and his viciousness increased: "...often beating and abusing her, until the neighbours cried out in shame." He eventually stabbed her to death, for which he was duly executed.[780]

## The Church Courts

Other legal forums also became involved in dealing with wife-beating. By 1700, the Church Courts had largely ceased to be active in punishing such behaviour, as they had done (albeit with very modest sanctions) in previous centuries. However, they still had jurisdiction over legal separations, and could order them for domestic violence. Throughout all of Catholic, and most of Protestant, Europe, including England, divorce in the modern sense was not normally possible. Occasionally, an annulment might be granted that allowed remarriage; for example, where the original marriage was within prohibited degrees of kinship. However, in these situations the parties' original nuptials were not perceived to have been valid, rather than being put aside. In England, an Act of Parliament was necessary to produce a divorce that would allow remarriage. Nevertheless, a formal separation *a mensa et thoro* (from bed and board), that did not allow remarriage, but which dissolved many of the legal consequences of marriage (such as coverture), could be granted by the ecclesiastical Consistory Court (or Court of Arches). This was usually done for adultery. For example, in 1809, Jesse Gregson was granted a divorce *a mensa et thoro* against his wife Grace by that forum, on the ground of the latter's adultery with their coachman.[781] (If a woman wished to divorce her husband for the same reason, the court would normally look for aggravating features, such as the transmission of venereal disease by her spouse).[782]

Nevertheless, such 'divorces' could also be granted on the grounds of extreme "cruelty" manifest by serious domestic violence.[783] In these situations, maintenance could also be ordered against the husband. Thus, in 1711, when Elizabeth Spinke petitioned the Consistory Court for a divorce from her physician husband, John, she alleged that he beat her, cut her arms with a knife and threatened to murder her. She called neighbours to support these allegations. In response, he claimed that she was an unchaste and profligate social climber. However, her allegations were accepted by the court, and the 'divorce' ordered, with John being required to pay her £28 a year (in four

---

[780]Hayward (Ed), *Lives of the Most Remarkable Criminals*, pp.217-219.
[781]*The Times*, Jan, 27, 1809, p.3
[782]Douglas Hay and N. Rogers, *Eighteenth-Century English Society*, Oxford, OUP, 1987, at p.42
[783]Blackstone, *Commentaries on the Laws of England*, Oxford, Clarendon Press, vol.1, at p.440. Interestingly, such grounds were the same in eighteenth century Germany.

quarterly instalments of £7). This modest amount would allow her to live (probably with relatives) without falling into complete destitution.

Such requests appear to have been more readily granted as the century advanced. Prior to c.1750, it was normal for those petitioning the Church Courts to claim that they feared for their lives. This does not seem to have been absolutely essential (though still very common) after the mid-century, suggesting a slightly more liberal approach on the part of the courts.[784] Typically, though, such a claim was made in 1789, when a Mrs. Evans asked for divorce in Doctors Commons. Her husband, Thomas, had apparently treated her extremely harshly, so that she had given birth two months prematurely. Later, while she was lying in bed, he: "…assaulted her with his knees, and violently drove her head against the bed posts, so that she was found in the morning bloody and much bruised." On another occasion, he had "without any provocation … and with great violence pulled her down." Being, she claimed, in fear of her life, she eventually moved in with a relative, though she noticed a man lurking in the street outside the house, who, she believed, was acting for some malign purpose at the behest of her husband. (She also attempted to get her spouse bound over to keep the peace by the local magistrates, and unsuccessfully tried to negotiate a separation agreement with him).[785]

The cost of obtaining a judicially sanctioned separation was around £20 and could sometimes be even higher. This was almost a year's wages for some poorer members of the Metropolitan working-class, and several months' worth for many others, so that, in practice, it was an option that was only open to the rich and middling social orders. Because of this, it seems that as the century advanced, 'summary divorce' was introduced on a *de facto* basis. This appears to have been a (summary) court approved, and supervised, separation on terms. Essentially, it was a poor man's divorce *a mensa et thoro*, one which saved recourse to the "tedious and expensive forms of an application to Doctors Commons."[786] Thus, in 1761, Thomas Rottam, who had beaten his wife and then abandoned her agreed with the City justices that he should give her 3s 6d. a week. In 1775, Ann Hands secured 7s.[787] Similarly, in 1809, an Irish carpenter named McMillan and his wife Rachael, who made allegations of violence (on the part of the wife) and extravagance, dissolute living and adultery (on the part of the husband) against each other, agreed a separation with weekly maintenance and a division of the household furniture, under the supervision of a magistrate sitting at the Guildhall.[788] The procedure may have replaced a variety of other, rather archaic, mechanisms by which poorer married couples separated, such as

---

[784]Bailey, *Unquiet Lives*, p.116.

[785]*The Times*, May 18, 1789., p.3

[786]*The Times*, July 31, 1810, p.3. Doctors Commons provided the Metropolitan base for the ecclesiastical and Admiralty lawyers.

[787] Randolph Trumbach, *Sex and the Gender Revolution: Heterosexuality and the Third Gender in Enlightenment London*, vol.1, Chicago: University of Chicago Press, 1998, at p.360.

[788]*The Times*, August 30, 1809, p.3.

the 'wife sale', in which a woman was sold to another man, often her lover, for a nominal sum in front of witnesses. For example, in 1795, a woman lodged a complaint with the Westminster Magistrates against a man who had assaulted her. When he argued in his defence that he was her husband, and that she was co-habiting with another man, provoking him to such action, she produced a bill of sale evidencing that she had been 'sold' for a guinea to one James Clark in front of witnesses who had also signed the document.[789]

## Female Perpetrated Domestic Violence

### Husband Battering

In the modern era, domestic violence has been a major subject for feminist analysis. Much of the literature has suggested that it is a unitary phenomenon, rooted in a patriarchal social order in which women are always the victims of male violence. However, in recent decades, this has been qualified by research that has revealed a (perhaps) surprising amount of female perpetrated domestic violence, in which either men or lesbian co-habitees are the victims of attacks by their partners. The same research suggests that a considerable number of men who are violent to their partners are in relationships where such violence is readily reciprocated, rather than passively endured.[790] Some (albeit a very small minority) have even argued that many instances of wife-beating are precipitated by initial domestic assaults committed by the females who are themselves subsequently victimised.[791] Whatever the position, it is apparent that not all violence within intimate relationships is the same. In some, "mutual battery" occurs between individuals vying for dominance in the relationship, in others, both parties use physical force in the context of an argument. In many cases, of course, a dominant partner (usually male) uses violence along with emotional and psychological abuse to maintain control over the other; this is the 'classic' background to wife-beating. Although the exact extent and motivation of female instigated domestic violence is a matter of fierce controversy in the modern era, it is clearly not insignificant, even if much more rare than that committed by men.

This raises obvious questions as to the extent to which women in historical times might also have been the perpetrators of domestic violence. As has already been noted, the reality of eighteenth-century domestic life in the Metropolis could be radically different to the patriarchal ideal. Some women had always subverted the approved gender order and dominated or abused their husbands. This had been a subject of male concern for centuries prior to 1700, and various forms of informal sanction evolved to deal with men who were perceived as

---

[789]Hay and Rogers, *Eighteenth-Century English Society*, at p.53.
[790]Malcolm J. George, "Riding the Donkey Backwards: Men as the Unacceptable Victims of Marital Violence", *The Journal of Men's Studies*, 1994, vol.3, no.2, pp.137-159, at pp.137-141.
[791]Russell and Emerson Dobash, "Women's violence to Men in Intimate Relationships", *British Journal of Criminology*, 2004, vol. 44, at pp.324-325,

having been humiliated by their wives and so 'let down' their sex. These included the charivari rituals or Skimmington rides of the early modern era, which lingered into the eighteenth century, and that involved the infliction of public shame on the men targeted. In Skimmington (or Stang) riding the beaten husband would be publicly portrayed riding back to front, holding a horse or donkey's tale; occasionally, he would even be forced to ride in person on the animal. This would be conducted to the sound of discordant music, produced by rattling pots and pans, and played by his neighbours.[792] Instances of this occurred regularly in Tudor and Jacobean London and probably lingered into the early 1700s.

Other evidence from the eighteenth century, such as the large number of contemporary prints satirising husband-beating wives, also rebut any suggestion that all women in this period were timid and passive towards their spouses. Even when they were on the receiving end of male violence, many women were not at all reluctant to respond. Thus, when one Southwark woman took to heavy drinking, selling household goods to fund her alcoholism, it prompted her felt maker husband to "chastise her with blows." However, she was not slow to reply in kind, and the ensuing battles were so furious that their neighbours were regularly forced to "part them at all hours of the night." This situation persisted for several years, until the wife fatally stabbed her spouse.[793]

Of course, such female violence was inherently less likely to be reported or recorded if it did not result in death. For the years between 1685 and 1720 only three recognizances for assault, in which a husband accused his wife, can be found among the 7, 234 issued at the Westminster Quarter Sessions. One of these accused a woman of "cruelly beating" her spouse to the endangerment of his life, another of "assaulting and beating" him. (In the third case, the wife had been assisted by another male).[794] However, for a man, being the victim of spousal abuse was humiliating. It was likely to result in popular ridicule and contempt. Judicial 'robustness' in dismissing domestic violence allegations was also especially marked if a man was the victim. For example, when, in 1775, Ann Connolly was brought before the magistrate sitting at the Guildhall, accused of "violently assaulting" her husband, she was discharged after: "It appeared on the constable's oath that the surgeon had declared him to be out of danger." [795] As a result, it is likely that these three cases were the tip of a much larger iceberg of husband-battering, though its true extent is almost impossible to estimate.

---

[792]There is a very good portrayal of a Skimmington Ride, from c.1600, on a frieze in the hall of Montacute House.

[793]Anon, *The Last Speech and Confession of Sarah Elestone*, pp.1-2. For domestic murders perpetrated by women see chapter three.

[794]Jennine Hurl-Eamon, *Gender and Petty Violence in London, 1680-1720*, Columbus, Ohio State University Press, 2005, at p. 66

[795] Minute Book of the Guildhall Justice Room 28th Nov. to 15th Jan., 1775/76, LMA CLA 00501, entry for 13th Dec.

*Children*

It was accepted without question that parents could legally use violence against their children, and women (often mothers) were frequently the perpetrators of such behaviour, especially where smaller infants and girls were involved. The courts were highly reluctant to become involved in such cases, unless the chastisement was quite extreme, sometimes even waiting for a death to ensue before acting, and several female perpetrated murders occurred in this context (dealt with in chapter three). Homicides were, of course, 'untypical.' Much more common would be instances of women going beyond the bounds of legitimate physical chastisement of their children, or those for whom they had custody, and inflicting serious but non-lethal injuries. Although these limits were set quite generously, so that only the most serious cases were likely to result in legal action, there was a gradual, albeit very slow, decline in tolerance for child abuse, as there was for most other forms of domestic violence, during the course of the century.

*Domestic Servants*

Husbands and children were not the only recipients of such female instigated abuse. Women could assault or beat domestic servants and this, too, occasionally resulted in deaths.[796] Such attacks often occurred in a 'disciplinary' context, although the physical chastisement of adult (non-apprentice) servants for these purposes was of (increasingly) doubtful legality. In the seventeenth century, Samuel Pepys had alluded quite regularly in his diary to servants being beaten. This became very much rarer during the 1700s, so that it has been observed, with only slight exaggeration, that the whipping of domestic staff and workers was: "…certainly socially impossible in England by the eighteenth century (except for apprentices and very young servants, perhaps, and seafarers)."[797] As this comment suggests, apprentices were clearly, and quite legally, subject to 'reasonable' physical correction by their masters (though not their wives). For other domestics, much would depend on the age and gender of the individual being 'corrected'. Physical punishment of younger and female servants was much more likely to be condoned (provided it was kept within moderate limits) than that of older and male domestic staff. Female perpetrated physical chastisement was most common where female domestics were involved, as this was traditionally seen as being within a mistress's sphere, it was normally a "great reproach for a man to beat a maid-servant" (and vice versa).[798]

Cases such as that of Sarah Metyard or Elizabeth Brownrigg, in which a maid died from her mistress's beatings, became notorious in the Metropolitan area (and are dealt with in chapter three). However, low-level physical abuse was

---

[796]Malcolm J. George, "Skimmington Revisited", *The Journal of Men's Studies*, vol.10, no.2, pp.111-127.

[797]Gwenda Morgan and Peter Rushton, "Visible Bodies: Power, Subordination and Identity in the Eighteenth-Century Atlantic World", *Journal of Social History*, 2005, vol.39, no.1, pp.39-64.

[798]Gough, *Domesticall Duties*, p.671.

far more common. Thus, Lady Francis Pennoyer appears to have regularly beaten her female employees in Herefordshire during the mid-century, apparently taking an unhealthy pleasure from the process. Typically, in 1760, she overheard one of her maids speaking 'impertinently' (though "truthfully") in the housekeepers' room and decided to put her in her place. Being, she claimed, reluctant to dismiss her out of hand, because the maid came from a poor home, she gave her a choice, "either to be well whipped, or to leave the house instantly." The young woman accepted a beating, and the following morning was made to kneel down and ask forgiveness. She was told to prepare herself and Lady Francis noted that she then "whipped her well" during which the maid cried out freely.[799] It is likely that such scenarios were repeated, in similar circumstances, quite widely in houses that employed servants. Of course, in this case the maid had 'consented' to being beaten. However, this was not invariably the case, particularly where younger domestics were involved.

Nevertheless, as the century advanced, the constraints on disciplining even youthful female maids appear to have become steadily stricter, especially after c.1750. Thus, in a notorious case from 1788, George and Sarah Metcalf were accused of assaulting their maid. They had thrashed her for breaking a plate and misplacing a stool. To receive her beating, Metcalf had been laid across a chair, a table and her master's knee, and had been gagged and bound to prevent her from crying out. She had then been beaten with a rod that had been pickled in brine, as a result of which she was covered in bruises and the blood "ran down from her side to her stockings." Sarah had taken a very active part in the proceedings, wielding the rod at least as much as her husband. The punishment they administered was considered extreme and quite excessive by most contemporary observers, *The Times* noting that it was characterised by "inhumanity and cruelty." Even so, and despite the gravity of the maid's wounds, defence counsel for the Metcalfs, when addressing the Middlesex sessions jury at Hick's Hall, still felt able to emphasize that the "instrument of correction" employed (the rod) was actually the "most proper thing in the world" to use in a beating. Although it might draw blood, it was unlikely to inflict permanent injury. He also stressed that the alleged assault was not to be considered in the same way as one between two men, because "by the law of this country, a master might with propriety moderately correct and chastise his servant." The key questions for the jury, he suggested, were whether the rod was an appropriate instrument to administer chastisement, and whether the girl had received more than a moderate degree of correction. This was an old-fashioned view of the law by 1788, and one that found little favour with the Bench. The Chairman firmly directed the trial jury that "no authority which a master has over his servant could justify such a beating." He also pointed out that it had been far more severe than any court imposed whipping. Additionally, he stressed that masters and servants were essentially equal in respect to their bodily

[799]William Andrews, *Bygone Punishments*, London, William Andrews & Co., 1899, at pp.225-226

integrity. Both defendants were convicted, though the penalties imposed were fairly moderate. George was fined £20 and his wife was imprisoned for 14 days. This was, presumably, to ensure that she, rather than her husband's purse, was also punished, but may reflect additional disquiet at a woman becoming so actively involved in such violence.[800]

## Conclusion

Throughout the eighteenth century numerous Metropolitan women suffered from domestic violence at the hands of their partners and spouses. This was officially sanctioned to only the most modest degree, but was often tacitly accepted in practice, in even fairly extreme forms, by both the relevant authorities and the wider society. However, any form of spousal violence that had the potential to be lethal was legally and socially totally unacceptable, and was liable to severe punishment, even in the early 1700s. Additionally, as the century advanced, the courts appear to have become stricter in their attitudes towards wife-beating, reflecting a gradual change in social mores.

Most women who suffered domestic abuse accepted it as part of the allotted order of things; others 'fought back' but did not seek outside intervention. Where they did seek an external remedy, it was usually via informal solutions involving family, friends and neighbours, or, if they had recourse to the criminal justice system, via low level magisterial intervention. Their better educated and more affluent sisters were also able to use the Church courts to some effect. Although women were much more likely to be the victims of domestic violence, rather than its perpetrators, this was not invariably the case. Husband battering and the (excessive) beating of servants and children by women were regular phenomena within the Metropolis, even if rarely reported. It seems that a considerable number of urban women were not remotely fastidious about the use of violence in a domestic context. Although the level of such cases is impossible to quantify precisely, those involving husbands are, like so many other features of eighteenth-century urban life, indicative of a significant difference between social theory and practical reality in inter-gender and domestic relationships during this period.

---

[800] *The Times*, Oct. 21, 1788, at p.3.

# Chapter 8: Prostitution

## Introduction

Traditionally, prostitution has been the single form of 'deviance' most closely associated with women. This chapter will consider the origins, incidence and nature of female prostitution in the Metropolitan area, with a particular focus on prostitutes' experiences with law enforcement agencies and the wider criminal justice system. Prostitution was seen as a major Metropolitan problem throughout the eighteenth century, if only because of the huge amount of women who went 'on the town'. The occasional and part-time nature of the trade for many of them makes assessing their numbers accurately very difficult. Some figures were ludicrously exaggerated. In 1728, it was claimed that as many as 62,500 prostitutes worked in and about London, though very little reliance can be placed on so precise a figure, especially as it would make them almost 8 per cent of the total population.[801] The following year, another observer merely declared that the city "abounded" with streetwalkers.[802] Later in the century, during the 1780s, the visiting German Johann D'Archenholtz concluded that there were 50,000 full-time prostitutes in the Metropolis "without reckoning kept mistresses" (though he appears to have derived this figure largely from Patrick Colquhoun's work).[803] Other foreigners produced similar assessments, at almost the same time; another German, Frederick Augustus Wenderborn, placed it at 40,000 women.[804] More realistically, in the 1750s, Saunders Welch though that there was a hard-core of over 3,000 full-time 'professional prostitutes', with others more peripherally involved. Whatever the figure, it was clearly substantial.

Not only were prostitutes a highly visible presence on many of London's streets, but they were also linked to forms of crime other than 'victimless' offences against morality. The risks of associating with them included being robbed by their 'bullies' (essentially pimps) and even, in exceptional cases, being physically attacked or murdered.[805] Prostitutes themselves regularly stole from their clients. Indeed, to many observers, the terms prostitute and thief were almost synonymous. Thus, a newspaper could refer to Cheapside being infested during the late evening by "herds of prostitutes of the lower or pickpocket

---

[801]James Dalton, *A Genuine Narrative of all the Street Robberies Committed since October last*, London, 1728, p.41.

[802]Anon, *Hell upon Earth: or the Town in an Uproar*, London, J. Roberts, 1729, p.B1 and p.12.

[803]Johann Wilhelm D'Archenholz, *A Picture of England*, Dublin, 1791, p.188.

[804]Frederick Augustus Wenderborn, *A View of England Towards the Close of the 18th Century*, vol.1, London, 1791, p.288.

[805]Saunders Welch, *A Proposal to render effectual a Plan to remove the nuisance of Common Prostitutes from the streets of this Metropolis*, London, 1758, p.8.

class."[806] Even worse, they did not necessarily confine their attentions to the men who resorted to them of their own volition, often being connected to crimes committed against ordinary members of the public, even if they had not tried to form sexual liaisons with the women concerned. Thus, in 1787, it was reported that three prostitutes had accosted a gentleman at Charing Cross and: "...by gathering round him contrived to pick his pocket of three guineas."[807] Additionally, it was feared that liaisons with prostitutes encouraged employed men, whether clerks, tradesmen or apprentices, to commit crimes against their masters to support their sexual indulgences or at the behest of the women concerned.[808] Thus, when Elizabeth Elye was accused of keeping a brothel, it was noted that one of her clients was a mercer's apprentice, who "used to bring his masters goods to the prisoner, and give them to her."[809] In the early eighteenth century, London Grand Juries regularly warned of the corrupting influence of 'lewd women' on otherwise honest young men, a theme that was also frequently touched on by the Newgate Ordinary in his *Account.*[810]

Prostitutes could also be the root cause of major outbreaks of disorder. It was the involvement of prostitutes and their bullies in robbing sailor clients that precipitated the Penlez riots of 1749, after one of their victims summoned his shipmates to exact revenge.[811] Perhaps even more importantly, they were closely associated with routine low-level disturbances, such as the use of profanities and the commission of acts of 'lewdness' in public. Thus, in the rougher parts of urban Middlesex, it was noted that prostitutes would sit out in the streets during the day, swearing, playing cards and drinking gin. If respectable people passed by, "especially decent women", they would often be greeted with a torrent of obscenities.[812] Typically, in 1803, a prostitute was brought before the Alderman sitting at the Guildhall, charged with having obstructed a gentleman and his wife in Aldersgate Street, using such indecent language in the process as "must shock and terrify any modest woman."[813] Indeed, it was a decreased tolerance for the rowdiness associated with street prostitution, as much as its inherent sexual immorality, in a society that increasingly stressed the middle class values of restraint and sobriety, that appears to have been the motive force behind many purity campaigns towards the end of the century.

## Social Background of Metropolitan Prostitutes

For much of the century, there was particular concern about "well brought up" women, from relatively genteel circumstances, who fell into prostitution via a

---

[806]*The Times,* July 10, 1788 p.3
[807]*The Times* Oct. 27, 1787, p.3
[808]Anon, *A Letter to the Right Reverend the Lord Bishop of London,* London, 1808, p.12.
[809]OBSP, Trial of Elizabeth Elye, 31st May 1693.
[810]John Beattie, *Policing and Punishment in London, 1660-1750,* Oxford, OUP, 2001, p.93.
[811]Welch, *A Proposal to render effectual a Plan..,* p.8.
[812]*The Times,* Sept. 6, 1787, p.2.
[813]*The Times,* Feb. 2, 1803, p.3.

seduction and subsequent abandonment that left them destitute and without reputation.[814] It was feared that the women involved, perhaps deflowered with the help of alcohol and drugs, and unable to continue living with their parents, would turn to the cause of their downfall for succour. Such men would then pay for the woman's flight to London, where he would publicly display her: "…for a single season; at the end of which he contrives to lodge her in a brothel, and abandons her for ever." In due course, the woman would acquire venereal disease and would no longer be of any use to the mistress of the 'stew' concerned, who would throw her out onto the streets.[815]

A published letter (even if apocryphal), supposedly sent by a prostitute incarcerated in Newgate while awaiting execution for stealing a watch, reveals the typical 'life cycle' that, it was feared, such women went through. The author was from comfortable, if reduced, provincial circumstances but had been 'debauched' by a Baronet after her arrival in London and subsequently sent to an upmarket bawdy house. There, the madam had taken most of her income while she contracted numerous venereal infections. In due course, her physical appearance deteriorated, so that she was eventually ejected from the house and forced to continue whoring on the streets as the only alternative to starving.[816] Another contemporary 'factional' account described the experiences of a poor clergyman's daughter of considerable beauty, who was orphaned at fifteen. She entered service in a grand but irreligious house that gradually wore down her own moral beliefs. In due course, she was seduced by the son of the house, made pregnant and abandoned before being enticed by fraud into a brothel where she was beaten into prostituting herself. After this establishment closed down, she, too, ended up working the streets.[817]

However, although making good copy, such women were not typical of Metropolitan prostitutes. As even some contemporary observers noted, most were the children of: "…miserable and vicious parents, whose daily apprehensions of absolute destitution, of rags to cover their nakedness, or bread to allay the painful cravings of hunger, have led them early to initiate their offspring in the mysteries of vice that they may exchange the horrors of impending starvation for the less dreaded miseries of prostitution."[818] Of 25 women arrested one night in May 1758, and then examined in detail by the magistrate John Fielding, the vast majority had been born into pauperism, and

---

[814]M Ludovicus, *A Particular but Melancholy Account of the Great Hardship, Difficulties, and miseries that Those Unhappy and much to be pitied Creatures, the Common Women of the Town, Are plung'd into at this Juncture*, London, 1752, p.7.

[815]Anon, *Thoughts on Means of Alleviating the Miseries attendant upon Common Prostitution*, London, Printed for T. Cadell, 1799, pp.15-19.

[816]Daniel Defoe, *Some Considerations upon Street-Walkers with A proposal for lowering the present number of them*, London, printed for A. Moore, 1726, pp.16-18.

[817]Anon, *Penitents in the Magdalen House*, vol.1, London, printed for John Rivington, 1760, pp.20-100.

[818]Anon, *Thoughts on Means of Alleviating the Miseries …*, p.26.

many had been orphaned or abandoned by their parents.[819] Many observers were well aware of the reality of such women's life choices, one even accepting that although their activity was not lawful: "…where it is carry'd on from Principle of extreme Necessity, I believe it very much qualifies the guilt."[820]

For such women, being a prostitute was usually not an identity, merely an expedient, a facet of their ordinary lives, prompted by need and a lack of ready alternatives. As a result, it was often a seasonal or part-time occupation, frequently interspersed with other forms of unskilled and poorly remunerated work, such as domestic service, dress-making, street vending and mendicancy. Indeed, for a considerable number of female beggars, a willingness to give their bodies, as well as their thanks, for alms donated by male passers-by seems to have been a part of their reduced status.[821] In some cases, poor married women were forced into prostitution by their husbands; among them was a Frenchman charged with beating his spouse in a "most inhuman manner" because she was not bringing home enough money from her street walking.[822]

Occasional prostitution seems to have been especially common amongst the female domestic servants who poured into London from "all corners of the universe" but subsequently lost their positions.[823] Echoing comments made by Daniel Defoe a decade earlier, Father Poussin was convinced that a large proportion of maids from the provinces would have recourse to street-walking if they were between situations, often moving directly "from bawdy house to service."[824] As a result, a few observers, such as Bernard De Mandeville, could even argue that men who employed prostitutes were actually doing a laudable act, furnishing them with the: "…means of subsistence, in the only, or at least most, innocent way that she is capable of procuring it."[825]

More commonly, they would lament the dearth of other economic opportunities available to such women, something that pushed them into the 'profession'. Towards the end of the century, some even claimed that women were being driven into prostitution because men were taking many of the few legitimate employments that were traditionally open to them, such as shop-work, millinery and perfumery. As they were excluded from numerous other types of position by their sex, this made their financial position even more precarious.[826] Such an analysis was also taken up by several of the female writers of the age.

---

[819]Tony Henderson, *Disorderly Women in Eighteenth-Century London: Prostitution and Control in the Metropolis, 1730-1830,* London, Longmans, 1999, p.14. Henderson's excellent book provides the fullest account of London's prostitution problem at his time.

[820]Ludovicus, *A Particular but Melancholy Account …,* p.27

[821]Tim Hitchcock, *Down and Out in Eighteenth-Century London,* London, Hambledon & London, 2004, pp.93-95.

[822]*The Times,* 1798 July 16th, p.3

[823]Anon, *Satan's Harvest Home,* London, 1749, p.3.

[824]Father Poussin, *Pretty Doings in a Protestant Nation,* London, 1734, p.5.

[825]Bernard De Mandeville, *A Modest Defence of Public Stews,* Glasgow, printed by Henry Mordaunt, 1730, p.24.

[826]*The Times,* Nov. 10 1785, p.3.

Thus, Priscilla Wakefield and Mary Radcliffe both stressed that prostitution was a result of the gendered division of labour, male usurpation of female employments and the impact of female dependency on men.[827] Perhaps reflecting the transient and temporary nature of much street-walking, although the term 'prostitute' first makes an isolated appearance in the Old Bailey Sessions Papers in 1685, it was not used regularly until the 1760s. Synonyms, such as 'whoring', despite encompassing prostitution, were not limited to those who provided sex on a commercial basis. Women who committed 'fornication' might also be the recipients of such a label. Prostitutes, by contrast, were specifically confined to what in the modern era are sometimes termed 'sex workers'.

Of course, for a few eighteenth-century women, prostitution was a true 'profession', followed with a degree of deliberation. Amongst them were some of those recorded in *Harris's List of Covent Garden Ladies*, a guide to Metropolitan prostitutes, their addresses and appearances, sales of which reached 8,000 a year at the start of the 1790s.[828] Nevertheless, such women were always in a minority, and the 'elite' high-earning members of their profession were even rarer. It was widely thought that the latter were the cast off mistresses of wealthy gentlemen; they were socially accomplished and could affect genteel airs and graces.[829] However, for most of the women concerned, prostitution was a poorly remunerated and corrupting mode of life. As D'Archenholz stressed, when talking of London's artistically talented high class prostitutes: "I now speak only of a few, for it is very uncommon, not to say impossible, to find such precious qualities among those vile prostitutes, whose kind of life stifles in their breasts every seed of virtue, if any indeed ever existed therein."[830] Many could scarcely earn a living, walking around Drury Lane and Fleet Street for hours on end before becoming so desperate for business that they accepted a customer who had haggled them down to a few pence.[831]

Most prostitutes, almost 60 per cent, came from the English provinces or remoter parts of the British Isles, such as Ireland. However, this was about the same proportion as for adult female Londoners generally (or, for that matter, female Old Bailey defendants). Many were very young. The magistrate Sir John Fielding claimed that during "search nights" in the 1750s, when local constables would arrest up to 40 women at a time, more than half of those detained would be under the age of 18, and many were as young as 12.[832] Some 35 years later, D'Archenholz was appalled to see girls of eight or nine offering themselves

---

[827]Vivien Jones, "Placing Jemima: women writers of the 1790s and the eighteenth century prostitution narrative", *Women's Writing*, vol.4, no.2, 1997, pp.201-220, at pp.206-207.
[828]D'Archenholz, *A Picture of England*, p.197.
[829]Richard King, *The Frauds of London Detected*, London, 1770, p.95.
[830]D'Archenholz, *A Picture of England*, p.193
[831]Anon, *The Whores and Bawd's Answer to the Fifteen Comforts of Whoring*, London, 1706, p.6.
[832]John Fielding, *A Plan for a Preservation and Reformatory for the Benefit of Deserted Girls and Penitent Prostitutes*, London, 1758, p.6.

(though they were well below the era's 12 year age of consent) and, even worse, finding customers.[833] Nevertheless, although a highly visible focus of public concern, these girls were not typical of most Metropolitan prostitutes, who were usually in their late teens or early twenties, while some were very much older.[834] According to D'Archenholz, women in their 50s and 60s would often emerge late at night, to press their faded charms on inebriated men leaving public houses, offering them cheap and immediate sex in the public streets.

Although prostitutes might begin their careers in their teens, it was widely believed that their lifestyle meant that they would "soon hasten to an untimely end, and finish their early days generally in extreme distress, in poverty and disease."[835] In 1785, *The Times* suggested that 5,000 streetwalkers a year died in the Metropolitan area alone. Frequently, their deaths would be occasioned by an untreated medical condition such as venereal disease, which was endemic amongst prostitutes (and those who had regular recourse to them).[836] 'Cures', which often involved using mercury, were expensive and largely ineffectual; indeed, contemporary medicine could not even distinguish between gonorrhoea and syphilis, while the use of sheep-gut condoms were the only prophylactics available against infection. Many women would compound their problems with alcoholism. One prostitute observed that towards the end of her career almost all her earnings were spent on purchasing spirits and that: "Drunkenness, which was at first a relief, now became an incurable disease."[837] Robert Bembridge was acquitted of murder (but convicted of manslaughter) after stabbing a prostitute to death with his sword, when a pair of surgeons gave evidence that the wound she had received would not have been mortal but for the fact that there was an inflammation in the dead woman's lungs: "...occasion'd by her hard drinking, and the cold place she lay in."[838] In the 1770s, *Harris's List* recorded that several of the women detailed in its pages were alcoholics, with remarks such as: "Brandy is what she has the strongest passion for."[839] Not untypically, a prostitute committed to Tothill Fields Bridewell in 1729, was so drunk when arrested that it was necessary to carry her there in a wheel-barrow.[840]

Simple despair claimed a number of other women, among them being Sarah Knight, who plied for trade in the alleys around Union Street in Westminster. One night in 1774, and somewhat the worse for drink, she was arrested and detained in a cell at the local Watchhouse. While there, she hanged herself from a doorpost with the white silk ribbon she used to attract custom.[841] Nevertheless,

---

[833]D'Archenholz, *A Picture of England*, p.193.

[834]Henderson, *Disorderly Women in Eighteenth-Century London*, pp.20-21.

[835]Wenderborn, *A View of England Towards the Close of the 18th Century*, p.291.

[836]Poussin, *Pretty Doings in a Protestant Nation*, p.41.

[837]Defoe, *Some Considerations upon Street-Walkers ...*, pp.16-18.

[838]OBSP, Trial of Robert Bembridge, 6th December 1721.

[839]Anon, *Harris's List of Covent Garden Ladies*, London, Printed for H. Ranger, 1773, p.D4.

[840]*Weekly Journal, or the British Gazetteer*, 16th November 1728.

[841]Hitchcock, *Down and Out in Eighteenth-Century London*, p.90.

despite such cases, an early death was not invariably the streetwalker's fate. For many, prostitution appears to have been merely a temporary interlude in their lives, from which they retired to marry or return to a more mundane form of low waged employment, such as street-vending.

Prostitutes could be found throughout the London area. In the words of Father Poussin, a long-term resident of Drury Lane, they were as numerous between Whitechapel and Charing Cross "as mackerel after thunder in hot seasons."[842] However, they tended to concentrate in locations at or near the centre of the Metropolis, where potential clients were plentiful, and particularly favoured places where police control was relatively weak. This meant that there was a significant continuity in some prostitution 'hotspots' during the century, such as the area in and around Covent Garden. Others waxed and waned during an era of rapid urban growth and change. In particular, the number of prostitutes working within the 'square mile' of the City appears to have fallen, in both absolute and proportionate numbers, as the area's population declined in relation to that of other locations. At various times, Fleet Street, the Strand, Charing Cross, Hyde Park, Marylebone, Leadenhall Street, Whitechapel and Petticoat Lane were all considered as centres of Metropolitan prostitution.[843] The areas around theatres, such as Drury Lane, were always hotspots for streetwalkers, and some women actively sought their clients inside such buildings. There were complaints in 1786 that they were availing themselves of half-price tickets, which permitted them to enter for the latter part of a play, to ply for trade, so that the boxes were often "crowded with prostitutes."[844]

## Work

Many contemporary observers were concerned that streetwalkers were often controlled by 'bullies', violent men who robbed the women of much of their earnings and were widely viewed as "cowardly, monsters."[845] According to one commentator, such pimps often doubled as thief-takers or bailiffs in their spare time, employments that required the use or threat of violence. The same individual felt that their characters were a "compound of every vice" and that they treated their women in a barbarous fashion, taking the bulk of their earnings while allowing them only pocket-money in exchange.[846] John Furnace, a notorious bully, was typical of the public perception of such men; he was convicted at the Westminster Sessions of stabbing a Drury Lane Watchman in the side during the small hours of the night, after being asked to make less noise.[847]

---

[842]Poussin, *Pretty Doings in a Protestant Nation*, p.2.
[843]Henderson, *Disorderly Women in Eighteenth-Century London*, p.52.
[844]*The Times*, Aug. 17, 1786, at p.1.
[845]Anon, *Thoughts on Means of Alleviating the Miseries…*, p.21
[846]Ludovicus, *A Particular but Melancholy Account…*, pp.14-15.
[847]*The Times*, April 18th, 1803.

There was also widespread concern about the numerous brothels that could, allegedly, be found in the London area, typically with 14 or 15 young women in each.[848] As with prostitutes, the relative informality of some of these establishments makes calculating their numbers difficult. Many low-grade taverns effectively doubled as ad hoc brothels; men could buy drink and meet women in the front room, negotiate terms, and then rent a back room to take them for sexual liaisons.[849] It was thought that formal brothels were frequently presided over by an aged and highly corrupting 'bawd', who lodged and clothed the women at extortionate rates.[850] Such women were widely believed to be former prostitutes who, having reached their 40s, were no longer capable of attracting customers; instead, they lured young girls into the trade.[851] In a notorious *cause celebre* from 1753, the willingness of the London 'mob' to accept Elizabeth Canning's bizarre explanation for her four-week absence from her employer is indicative of popular attitudes towards both madams and the recruitment of prostitutes. Canning claimed that she had been abducted in the City and driven to Enfield, where she was imprisoned in the attic of a brothel by one 'Mother Wells', in an attempt to force her into prostitution. Sir Crisp Gascoyne, the Lord Mayor, who sided with Wells and her gipsy attendant in doubting the whole story, and who ensured a pardon for the two women after they were convicted at the Old Bailey, was publicly vilified, and had his coach attacked in the street (Canning was eventually found guilty of perjury and transported, despite having the support of the magistrate Henry Fielding).[852]

And, of course, bullies, bawds and brothels all existed in numbers. Edward Hartey experienced all three in 1726, when he was 'picked up', while in an intoxicated condition, by Mary Blewit. She took him back to a house run by a bawd named Alice Gale. Once there, he was robbed by Blewit and, when he confronted her, was attacked by her bullies who: "...beat me, and kick'd me down stairs, and broke my nose, and then turn'd me out of doors." Once outside, they chased him about the streets, so that he would forget where the house was.[853] However, and contrary to many popular perceptions, it seems that most Metropolitan prostitutes operated independently of brothels, madams and bullies. As a result, much of their sexual activity took place in quiet and secluded public areas, such as darkened allies, or in cheap lodging houses, tavern rooms, bagnios or the woman's own accommodation. Famously, James Boswell even

---

[848]Anon, *A Letter to the Right Reverend the Lord Bishop of London*, London, 1808, p.14.

[849]Julie Peakman, *Lascivious Bodies: A Sexual History of the Eighteenth Century*, Atlantic Books, London, 2005, at p.11.

[850]D'Archenholz, *A Picture of England*, p.189.

[851]Anon, *The London-Bawd with Her Character and Life*, 3rd edn., London, Printed for John Gwillim, 1705, p.A2.

[852]Bevis Hillier, "The Mysterious Case of Elizabeth Canning" *History Today*, vol.53, issue 3, 2003, at pp.47-53. A huge number of theories have been advanced about this notorious case, including the suggestion that Canning had given birth to an illegitimate child during her absence.

[853]OBSP, Trial of Mary Blewit, 11th July 1726.

had a sexual encounter with a streetwalker while on Westminster Bridge. More typically, John Cooper, a constable, told the Bridewell court that one of the women he detained had taken a man to a private house where she "offered to lye with him and told him she would show him the Postures."[854] De Mandeville identified the use of such ad hoc expedients as part of the prostitution problem, and suggested that the trade would be 'healthier' if it was both legalised and regulated. He proposed that women be driven off the streets into specially appointed brothels, situated in designated areas of every town and city, within which groups of 20 prostitutes would be supervised by a matron and given access to physicians and infirmaries. In such an environment, he thought, the women would also become more 'civilised' and less prone to being disorderly or dishonest.[855] His views, though not typical, were certainly not unique, being reiterated, *inter alia*, by an anonymous observer in 1756, who went so far as to suggest Cupers Gardens as an appropriate Metropolitan venue for such houses. However, in a debate that continues to this day, others argued that licensing prostitution would officially sanction such activity. Additionally, it was feared that indulging sexually "irregular appetites" was likely to increase, rather than satisfy, them.[856]

Although, in some places, streetwalkers could readily be found throughout the day, in many others it was a predominantly nocturnal activity, and the women involved would "sally out towards the dusk, arraigned in their most gaudy colours."[857] As this comment suggests, prostitutes from all but the very lowest level of vagrant women would usually work in their 'finery', clothes signifying their availability and also adding to their allure, though these could be as simple and basic as a clean white silk ribbon. Workhouses would sometimes insist that prostitute inmates worked in these garments so that they lost their 'shine,' so reducing the chance of their returning to the trade. Prostitutes might approach potential clients with verbal suggestions and, depending on the environment, physical contact. Thus, when Charlotte Clarke successfully sought to attract a young man's attention, as he went about his business on Ludgate Hill, it was noted that he was: "... accosted in the usual manner by the lady, who took him under the arm, and brought him into a court."[858] However, prostitutes could solicit more aggressively, sometimes surrounding pedestrians in groups and overwhelming them with "caresses and entreaties."[859]

Some observers suggested that those who employed prostitutes were usually the "wild, the thoughtless, and the intoxicated."[860] However, in reality, many Metropolitan men, of widely differing backgrounds, seem to have had

---

[854]Beattie, *Policing and Punishment in London*, pp.245-246.
[855]De Mandeville, *A Modest Defence of Public Stews*, pp.30-31.
[856]Anon, *The Evils of Adultery and Prostitution*, London, 1792, p.11.
[857]D'Archenholz, *A Picture of England*, p.193.
[858]*The Times*, Aug.12, 1806, p.3.
[859]D'Archenholz, *A Picture of England*, p.193.
[860]Anon, *The Evils of Adultery and Prostitution*, pp.64-65.

recourse to them. Most of the women involved appear to have offered conventional intercourse on a 'one to one' basis. Heterosexual sodomy appears to have been frowned upon, and normally cost the client significantly more. Of the at least 600 men arrested for being with a prostitute in the City, Westminster and Middlesex, only 31 cases involved two women or (very rarely) two men with a single woman.[861]

Although prostitutes frequently worked in pairs or small clusters for mutual protection, and might even refer to themselves collectively as the 'sisterhood', they were also in fierce competition with each other. As a result, they might have their own areas, which they would defend against other streetwalkers, often violently. Sometimes 'new' women would have to pay a financial levy to be allowed to work, one woman noting that after she attempted to find a "fare" in the Fleet Street area: "I was drove from street to street by women of my own profession, who swore I should not come in their beats until I had paid my footing." In the process, they snatched her cap and handkerchief, 'finery' that she had made from an old apron to draw clients.[862] In another case, from 1787, an intruding woman was attacked and "violently beaten," having her head cut wide open in the process.[863] Local street-walkers might also use their financial links with neighbourhood watchmen to invoke the law when attempting to drive suspected 'interlopers' from their areas, having the women concerned arrested as prostitutes in the process.[864]

## Contemporary Attitudes Towards Prostitution

Throughout the century, two conflicting attitudes, whether express or implied, dominated the debate on prostitution. Most observers recognised that it was the source of many ills. Such men stressed the association of streetwalkers with crime, epidemic levels of venereal disease, disorder, immorality and the erosion of family life.[865] Even Bernard De Mandeville conceded that prostitution occasioned serious problems such as bastardy and its attendant risk of infanticide. However, many observers, including De Mandeville, felt that the fundamental problem was that the male sexual urge was innate; it was not an acquired habit, nor was it 'learnt' behaviour. As a result, its indulgence was an inevitable facet of human society.[866] Indeed, some medical commentators even

---

[861]Randolph Trumbach, *Sex and the Gender Revolution: Heterosexuality and the Third Gender in Enlightenment London*, vol.1, Chicago: University of Chicago Press, 1998, at p.156.

[862]George Stevens, *The Adventures of a Speculist, or, a Journey Through London*, London, vol. 1, 1788, p.211.

[863]*The Times*, Sept. 6, 1787, p.2.

[864]Anon, *The Midnight-Ramble Or, the Adventures of Two Noble Females*, London, Printed for B. Dickinson, 1754, at pp.10-11.

[865]Antony E. Simpson, "'The Mouth Of Strange Women Is A Deep Pit': Male Guilt And Legal Attitudes Toward Prostitution In Georgian London", *Journal of Criminal Justice and Popular Culture*, 1996, 4(3), pp. 50-79, at p.50.

[866]De Mandeville, *A Modest Defence of Public Stews*, pp.23-24.

questioned the physical desirability of sexual abstinence amongst men. Others argued that prostitutes, by alleviating male sexual tensions, safeguarded 'respectable' women from male attentions (an attitude that dated back to St. Augustine). Additionally, De Mandeville was certainly not alone in his belief that there was little worthwhile distinction between 'public' and 'private' whoring. The former constituted what was officially viewed as prostitution, i.e. contractual arrangements in which sex was overtly sold for cash; the latter, the seduction of young girls and married women. De Mandeville thought that the social consequences of this type of behaviour were often more serious than the effects of formal prostitution.[867] By contrast, other observers, such as Charles Horne, rejected any notion that prostitution resulted from: "…an inevitable necessity, produced by the most powerful, and (at the same time) universal law of nature." Horne noted that hunger was as innate to human beings as lust, but pointed out that it did not have to be satisfied by theft.[868]

**Contemporary Attitudes Towards Prostitutes**
Proletarian attitudes towards individual prostitutes (rather than their trade) were complex. Perhaps unsurprisingly, given their social provenance, such women often attracted popular sympathy and support, and heavy-handed attempts by the authorities to deal with them could excite acute hostility amongst poorer Londoners. Thus, one Sunday night in 1730, three youths were arrested after rescuing four detained prostitutes from the hands of a constable. They were part of a group of men, armed with sticks, who had come: to their assistance and who: "… beat the watch and Constables to such a degree that they were obliged to release them."[869] Similarly, the arrest of 'lewd' women by activist constables appears to have excited the ire of groups of off-duty soldiers on several occasions.[870]

However, although the vast majority of women who had recourse to prostitution were from the working class, this did not mean that lower class Londoners were invariably sympathetic towards them. Metropolitan brothels and stews had traditionally been a particular target for mobs of apprentices and their associates during Easter and May Day celebrations. Thus, a huge riot had developed when a group of youths gathered in Moorfields in 1668 to pull down local bawdy houses.[871] Such incidents continued into the following century, so that in 1705 it could still be observed that London's bawds were terrified by the approach of Shrove-Tuesday (a major apprentices' holiday): "…for she's more

---

[867]De Mandeville, *A Modest Defence of Public Stews*, p.26.
[868]Charles Horne, *Serious Thoughts on the Miseries of Seduction and Prostitution*, London, 1783, p.2.
[869]*Grub-street Journal*, 30 April, 1730.
[870]*Post Man*, 14-16 May, 1702.
[871]Anon, *The Tryals of such Persons (Peter Messenger, Richard Beasley… as under the Notion of London-Apprentices were tumultuously assembled in Moorfields* London, Robert Pawlet, 1668, pp.1-5.

afraid of the mob, than a debtor of a Serjeant."[872] Those who were involved in organising prostitution, such as the notorious bawd 'Mother Needham', stoned to death while being pilloried, could expect little sympathy from ordinary people, whatever their social backgrounds.

Similarly, there was never a uniform attitude towards prostitutes amongst 'respectable' Londoners. Sexual honour remained an important commodity for most women, both in their private and public lives. Many brought actions for defamation in the consistory court to protect it. These usually involved allegations that the defendant had called them 'whores' in public. However, this was often necessary to provide the plaintiff with *locus standi* in that forum. The great majority (83 per cent) of such women were married and, frequently, were disputing more general allegations of sexual incontinence, such as adultery. Even so, it is apparent that an allegation of prostitution, even if made in anger, could not lightly be ignored by well to do women, including those from the 'tradesman' class.[873]

Nevertheless, this did not preclude sympathy even amongst the respectable for prostitutes. At the start of the century, what might be termed the 'traditional' view of streetwalkers was widespread, though never entirely dominant. This suggested that such "strumpets" were the depraved and calculating corrupters of men who either entered the profession to satisfy their own unnatural lusts or through inherent "idleness" and for whom a savage penal response, involving flogging and transportation, was necessary.[874] After the mid-century, this attitude was supplemented by a growing tendency to see them as victims of circumstance, whether extreme poverty, child molestation, neglectful parents or an early seduction. Campaigners increasingly argued that, too often in the past, prostitutes had been judged excessively harshly and viewed with: "… detestation as infamous, when they ought to have been regarded with compassion as unhappy." It was also felt that such women were too easily considered to be irreclaimably vicious.[875] These views were shared by innovative magistrates, such as John Fielding and Saunders Welch, several reformist politicians and (unsurprisingly) most members of the new charities that sought to rescue fallen women.[876] Thus, Fielding stressed that many girls drawn into prostitution were not innately wicked, but rather vulnerable to predatory individuals because they were young, unprotected and female.[877]

---

[872]Anon, *The London-Bawd with Her Character and Life*, 3rd edn., London, Printed for John Gwillim, 1705, p.A4.

[873]Robert Shoemaker, *The London Mob*, London, Hambledon & London, 2004, pp.53-54.

[874]Daniel Defoe, *Some Considerations*, pp.1-20.

[875]Anon, *An Address to the Benevolent Public … on behalf of the London Female Penitent*, London, 1807, pp.3-4.

[876]Faramerz Dabhoiwala, "The pattern of sexual immorality in seventeenth-and eighteenth-century London", *Londinopolis: Essays in the Cultural and Social History of Early Modern London*, P. Griffiths et al (Eds.), Manchester, Manchester University Press, 2000, pp.86-106, at p.95.

[877]Fielding, *A Plan for a Preservation*, p.6.

The growth in such attitudes eventually bore fruit in the establishment of Jonas Hanway's Magdalen House in 1758. Between that year and the start of 1802, it took in 3,477 women, of whom only 476 were discharged as 'incorrigible', although many others seem to have lapsed back into prostitution after apparently successful work placements.[878] In 1789, this establishment was joined by the Lock asylum, which took twenty penitent prostitutes at a time, after they had been 'cured' of venereal disease at the specialist Lock Hospital (which treated many infected street-walkers) that had been established in 1746.[879]

## 'Double Standards' and Prostitution

Throughout early modern Europe, women were usually treated more strictly than men when formal action was taken over sexual 'crimes'. Females were disproportionately prosecuted for adultery, fornication, prostitution and producing illegitimate children. Men could be (and were) charged with these offences, but the authorities appear to have taken a more lenient attitude towards them.[880] This was largely the result of a system of endemic double standards when it came to sexual matters. Such attitudes were, to a considerable extent, mirrored in eighteenth-century London. (Though it should, perhaps, be noted that over 85 per cent of those convicted of bigamy at the Old Bailey during the 1700s were men). Thus, a prostitute might be the subject of public opprobrium, but the man who initially seduced her would often: "...obtain no other appellation by such villainy than that of man of gallantry."[881]

This lack of even-handedness was also reflected in Metropolitan policing. When constables such as John Welburne (a Farringdon officer) arrested prostitutes and their clients, the men would normally be released without more than a caution. By contrast, the women would often be committed to a house of correction or Bridewell.[882] As a typical example of this sexual double standard, can be considered a case from 1752, in which Deborah Knockley, a streetwalker, was caught with John Stamford in an "indecent posture" by a patrolling watchman, and produced with him the following day at the Guildhall Justice Room. Stamford was discharged "on promising not to offend again." Knockley, however, was committed to the Spitalfields Workhouse.[883] This remained the normal response to such couples throughout the century. Thus, after the City

---

[878]Anon, *An Address to the Benevolent Public ...* p.11

[879] Randolph Trumbach, *Sex and the Gender Revolution: Heterosexuality and the Third Gender in Enlightenment London*, vol.1, Chicago: University of Chicago Press, 1998, at p.188.

[880]Manon Van der Heijden, "Women as victims of sexual and domestic violence in 17th Century Holland: Criminal Cases of Rape, Incest and Maltreatment in Rotterdam and Delft", *Journal of Social History*, 2000, vol.33, no.3, p.623.

[881]Anon, *Penitents in the Magdalen House*, vol. 1, p.xv.

[882]OBSP, Trial of James Newbold, 12th Oct. 1743.

[883] Minute Book of the Guildhall Justice Room 25th May to 19th June, 1752, LMA CLA 00501, entry for 19th June.

Marshal raided what appears to have been a Jewish brothel in Hounsditch in 1775, the 14 occupants (seven women and seven men) found playing cribbage, were produced in front of the Lord Mayor. The women were committed to the Bridewell, while their clients were dismissed "on their promising not to offend again."[884] As a result, the Guildhall Justice Room documents only 22 cases between 1752 and 1796 of men being arrested in the City as patrons or associates of streetwalkers, only three of whom were subsequently prosecuted to conviction.

Nevertheless, by the latter decades of the seventeenth century, such an unequal approach towards sexual indiscretions was being questioned, albeit only tentatively. In particular, a significant number of middle-class men were beginning to argue that fornication was as distasteful in males as it was in females, and to be concerned about their reputation for sexual continence.[885] As one observer noted in 1696, men who used streetwalkers would be "very ill pleas'd" if their own wives had recourse to prostitutes, or their mothers and daughters were accused of being whores.[886] This change in attitudes gradually (and very slowly) increased over the course of the ensuing century, extending to the 'honest' poor. It may have been reinforced after the mid-century by a growth in 'new' ideals of romantic love and the increased value that was placed on domestic family life.[887]

It is also not quite true to say that the purchase of sex by male heterosexuals was invariably unpoliced during the 1700s. Some men were bound over by recognisance, and a handful more severely punished. Thus, when William Fuller was committed to the London Bridewell in the early 1700s, he shared his cell with a 77-year-old man, who had been sent to the institution for sleeping with two prostitutes simultaneously, and a boy of 13 who had been detained after paying half-a-crown for sex with a streetwalker.[888] Similarly, in 1730, an Irishman who had been surprised late one night in an "indecent manner" with a prostitute, in Drury-lane, was carried before the magistrate, Sir John Gonson and, along with the woman concerned, committed to Tothill-fields Bridewell (though the public manner of his conduct helps explain this disposal).[889]

There were also times in the early century when prostitutes' clients were on the receiving end of campaigns conducted by the members of the Society for the

---

884*The Middlesex Journal*, Jan. 19-21, 1775.

885Bernard Capp, "The Double Standard Revisited: Plebeian Women and Male Sexual Reputation in Early Modern England", *Past and Present*, no.162, 1999, pp.70-100, at p.98

886Anon, *The Night Walker: or Evening Rambles in Search after Lewd Women*, London, Printed for James Orme, 1696, p.A1.

887Randolph Trumbach, *Sex and the Gender Revolution: Heterosexuality and the Third Gender in Enlightenment London*, vol.1, Chicago: University of Chicago Press, 1998, at p.184.

888William Fuller, *Mr William Fuller's Trip to Bridewell: With a True Account of his Babarous Usage in the Pillory*, London, 1703, pp.9-14.

889*Grub-street Journal*, 3 September 1730

Reformation of Manners, which arrested several hundred men for being in the company of "lewd" women. An examination of the 31 sessions held between October 1700 and October 1709 in Westminster reveals that at least 234 recognisances were issued to men for lewd behaviour and/or their presence in a brothel. Although this makes up a very small proportion of the 11,893 prosecutions initiated by the societies in London during this period, the majority of which involved prostitutes, it is significant that they occurred at all. Perhaps even more surprisingly, many of the men concerned were not poor, but came from the prosperous middling social orders.[890]

**The Law on Prostitution**

There were regular complaints throughout the century that prostitutes were becoming more open in their behaviour, not even bothering to retire to a secluded place to conduct their nefarious activities, because the laws against them were useless: "...either from some defect in them, or a wilful neglect or partiality in their execution."[891] As this comment suggests, both the substantive law and its implementation were considered problematic and need to be examined.

It has been argued that eighteenth-century prostitutes were not generally treated harshly by the courts, and even suggested that real repression for such women only started in the 1830s.[892] To the extent that this is true, one probable explanation is that the legal position of prostitution was confused and uncertain throughout the 1700s. It was not expressly forbidden by any statute (such as the Vagrancy Acts) or at common law, and so could normally only be prosecuted if associated with some other offence against property, public order or decency. Indeed, it was not until the advent of the 1824 Vagrancy Act that soliciting was, in *some* circumstances, made an offence *per se*. The statute of 1752 against bawdy houses did not deal with street prostitution, though it may, occasionally, have been used (illegally) to address the problem.[893] Indeed, the laws used to regulate streetwalkers did not distinguish between prostitution and other forms of publicly lewd behaviour, although several contemporary observers felt that such a division was desirable. As a result, many eighteenth-century prostitutes were dealt with under a Jacobean statute of 1604, which authorised commitment to a house of correction after summary conviction by a magistrate, of anyone who was found to be "idle and disorderly." As there was little scope for higher judicial interpretation and supervision of this Act, it came to be construed quite broadly by JPs. Many, like Sir John Fielding, suggested that constables were

---

[890]Jennine Hurl-Eamon, "Policing male heterosexuality: the reformation of manners societies' campaign against the brothels in Westminster, 1690-1720", *Journal of Social History*, vol. 37, no.4, 2004, pp.1017-1035.

[891]Anon ('by a clergyman of the City of London'), *Friendly Advice to the Fair Sex*, London, Printed for G. Kearsly, 1758, at p.v.

[892]Simpson, 'The Mouth Of Strange Women Is A Deep Pit", p.61.

[893]Simpson, "The Mouth Of Strange Women Is A Deep Pit", p.56.

entitled to arrest 'Night-walkers' solely on the basis that they were prostitutes, and such arrests were often listed in the petty sessions under charges of "being a common prostitute." It was a swift, effective and cheap procedure, unlike most other forms of prosecution.

In practice, many poor women who were found wandering the streets late at night, were unable to explain how they made a living or why they were abroad at that hour, and so suspected of prostitution, were incarcerated under its provisions. This would normally entail a short period of imprisonment in a House of Correction or the Bridewell, compulsory labour (usually picking oakum or beating hemp) and, early in the century, the possibility of being flogged with a scourge made of holly fronds.[894] The inmates of such establishments always included large numbers of prostitutes.[895] This provision continued in force throughout the eighteenth century, so that an observer, writing in 1789, could still note that magistrates had enormous powers to deal with suspicious street people: "...even without any known crime actually committed." Generally, they could be detained and produced before the Justices if they could not maintain themselves, were not lawfully employed and refused work. The same commentator stressed that this power should be used against the 'army' of abandoned prostitutes who infested the areas around playhouses, who could be: "...deemed idle and disorderly persons, and be sent to the House of Correction to hard labour."[896]

As a result, prostitutes found at night in those parts of the city that were more strictly policed than others might be arrested by the constables, detained in a watch-house overnight, produced the following morning before the magistrates and sentenced to a month or so in custody.[897] Typically, one night in 1730, seven young women who were found walking the streets around Drury lane, and who could "give no satisfactory account of their manner of living", were arrested and committed by magistrates to hard labour in the Tothill-fields Bridewell.[898] Such a policy continued throughout the 1700s and into the following century, so that as late as January 1816, it was noted that fifteen of "those wretched females whom the Lord Mayor has determined to expel from the streets" had been arrested, convicted, and sentenced to a month in Bridewell. The Hatton Garden magistrates took similar action later the same year.[899]

The power was open to abuse, and many 'respectable' women found themselves on the receiving end of such policing. In 1705, Mrs. Elizabeth King prosecuted Thomas Bayly, a constable, at the Westminster Quarter Sessions, for

---

[894]Robert Shoemaker, *Prosecution and Punishment: Petty Crime and the Law in London and Rural Middlesex, c. 1660-1725*, Cambridge, CUP, 1991, pp.169-171. Anon, *Reports from Select Committees, Respecting The Arts-Masters and Apprentices of Bridewell Hospital*, London, 1799, p.8.

[895]Fuller, *Mr William Fuller's Trip to Bridewell*, pp.10-14

[896]*The Times*, Oct.14, 1789, p.3.

[897]Anon, *Thoughts on Means of Alleviating the Miseries ...*, pp.20-21

[898]*Grub-street Journal*, 3rd September 1730.

[899]Simpson, "The Mouth Of Strange Women Is A Deep Pit", pp.50-79, at p.62.

"using her in an indecent manner." He had arrested her as a common nightwalker, when he found her out after dark, and then asked to "put his hands up her coats."[900] There could be more serious consequences. In 1742, the High Constable of Westminster, while making a general search of the area: " ... did not scruple to commit to the Roundhouse any Person they found in the Streets, tho' not offering the least Disturbance." He sent 28 women to St. Martin's Roundhouse, many of whom were not even soliciting, but simply going about their lawful business or returning home from work. Tragedy struck when the prison's notorious keeper, William Bird, crammed them into the "Hole", a six-foot-square cell, which had its window locked shut. Despite their cries of 'murder', he left them unattended, so that four women were suffocated. The coroner's jury returned a verdict of wilful murder against Bird and he was committed to Newgate to await trial.[901] He subsequently received a 'special' verdict from a jury at the Old Bailey, unable to apply the criminal law to the special facts of the case.

However, and perhaps partly because of such cases, it appears that Sir John Fielding's attitude towards this area of the law was not typical of all magistrates, especially those in the City (rather than urban Middlesex). On many occasions, the square mile's Aldermen cautioned watchmen against arresting women who had merely solicited in a restrained manner, or discharged prostitutes who had been detained when standing quietly in the streets, even if in groups of women.[902] As a result, the numbers who were formally prosecuted at City of London petty sessions appear to have fluctuated wildly; from over 300 in 1786, and perhaps twice as many again in 1779 (the records are not complete) to almost none in the years 1790 and 1791.[903] In both the 1720s and the 1780s (probably throughout the century), it also seems that between 40 and 45 percent of arrested Metropolitan prostitutes were simply discharged by the magistrates with a verbal warning. [904]

**The Law on Brothels**
In the early decades of the eighteenth century, the term 'bawdy house' was not confined to formal brothels but also encompassed unlicensed establishments that provided alcohol and casual accommodation for streetwalkers; indeed, it seems to have extended to any premises where men and women met for the purposes of sexual immorality, whether tavern or lodging house.[905] Thus, in 1728, when Sir John Gonson charged the Westminster Grand Jury to present all

---

[900]Jennine Hurl-Eamon, "The Westminster Impostors: Impersonating Law Enforcement in Early Eighteenth-Century London", *Eighteenth-Century Studies*, vol.38, no.3, 2005, pp.461-483, at p.464
[901]*The Gentleman's Magazine*, 1742, vol. 12, p.386.
[902]Simpson, "The Mouth Of Strange Women Is A Deep Pit", p.57.
[903]Simpson, "The Mouth Of Strange Women Is A Deep Pit", p.69.
[904]Randolph Trumbach, *Sex and the Gender Revolution: Heterosexuality and the Third Gender in Enlightenment London*, vol.1, Chicago: University of Chicago Press, 1998, at pp.113-114.
[905]Dabhoiwala, "The pattern of sexual immorality", p.87.

bawdy and disorderly houses in the city, he urged that under such: "...denomination[s] you ought to reckon those many shops, where such numbers of the lower sort of people get drunk with Geneva."[906] All bawdy houses were deemed to be public nuisances per se, and, as such, their operators could be prosecuted and fined.[907] However, if Peter Wood's establishment is anything to go by, many brothels hid behind complicated financial arrangements, with different individuals owning the freehold of the premises, renting the property and paying the various taxes on it.[908] Additionally, their operators often used aliases and false home addresses. This made indicting them very difficult.

Brothels were specifically outlawed in 1752 by the 'Disorderly Houses Act' (25 Geo. 2, c.36). Nevertheless, securing convictions under the new provision appears to have been almost as difficult as it was at common law. The Act required that parishes fund the prosecution of any brothel found within their boundaries, provided that two residents 'paying scot and lot' attested to its existence. (If the prosecution was successful the parish was supposed to reward them with £10 apiece).[909] However, in practice, parishioners were often reluctant to come forward as witnesses. According to Sir John Fielding, this was partly for fear of being labelled as informers by their neighbours. Doubtless, both local officers and residents were also concerned about making powerful neighbourhood enemies.[910] Even if a matter came for trial, securing a conviction under the statute could be problematic. Thus, in January 1791, Hannah Davenport was prosecuted at the Clerkenwell Sessions House for keeping a bawdy house in Glanville Street. Her local constable, a Mr. Crane, who lived in the same street, gave evidence that whenever he passed her door he saw her, along with other women, "decoying and enticing" men of all backgrounds and ages (some as young as 12) into her house. Whenever a constable approached, the defendant would run inside and laugh at them through the window. Neighbours were also called to complain about the noise emanating from the property and the obscene language openly used by the accused woman. A coach-maker even testified that he had been a regular client of the defendant in the past, freely informing the court of "his own infamy." Despite this apparently damning evidence, Davenport was merely convicted of the (lesser) charge of keeping a disorderly house and imprisoned for three months.[911]

Sometimes, as a result of these difficulties, parish authorities would have recourse to measures that were of doubtful legality to force such houses out of

[906]Anon, *The Charge of Sir John Gonson, Kt. to the Grand Jury of the City and Liberty of Westminster*, Westminster, London, 2nd. Edn., 1728, p.23.
[907]William Blackstone, *Commentaries on the Laws of England*, vol. 4, Oxford, Clarendon Press, 1765-1769, p.168.
[908]OBSP, Trial of John Wilson et al, 6th Sept. 1749.
[909]Anon, *The Complete Parish Officer*, 1772, London, p.38.
    ˙mpson, "The Mouth Of Strange Women Is A Deep Pit", p.61.
    ˙e *Times,* Jan. 12th 1791, p.4.

existence; for example, by setting constables or watchmen on permanent duty outside them, with a lantern and candles, so that anyone entering could be publicly identified and, hopefully, humiliated.[912] Occasionally, such measures would go even further. Thus, in Shire Lane, in St. Dunstan's parish, there were several brothels whose presence was a longstanding irritant to the local churchwardens. The magistrates had not been able to suppress them, and even neighbourhood constables and watchmen were thought to be amongst their customers. Eventually, the parish authorities positioned watchmen permanently outside them with lanterns and instructions to escort any patrons of the houses along the lane, while asking them loudly how they had been "pleased" in their visit. It was hoped that this would make their clients the subjects of "public shame." However, a glazier, called into one of the brothels to repair a broken window, objected to such treatment and smashed the watchmen's lanterns as he left the premises. This was treated as an assault on a civil officer in the execution of his duty, and the glazier was arrested and taken to the Bow Street Court. There, however, the Bench swiftly dismissed the charge brought by the watchmen, asked the church-wardens why they did not indict the houses as nuisances in the proper manner, and demanded to know the legal basis for placing lantern men outside their doors to "insult the passenger on the King's highway." The glazier also threatened to prosecute the parish officers involved, and their supervising constables were bound over to be of future good behaviour.[913]

So secure did the proprietors of such establishments feel that, in 1790, a notorious brothel madam, 'Mother Hassel', sued her establishment's former occupants for the board, lodging and clothing that she had furnished to them at extortionate rates, for the purposes of prostitution. Unfortunately for her, the court concluded that, as the house and its business were illegal (because immoral), any contracts entered into within it were also unenforceable. Several similar cases were decided in much the same way at about the same time.[914] These were important legal decisions, as it was widely thought that the debts that the women in such establishments accrued, with the consequent threat of imprisonment for failure to pay them off, often forced them to submit to their bawd's "hellish designs."[915]

## The Policing Agencies Dealing with Prostitution

Despite widespread criticism as to the state of the substantive law, many observers felt that it was policing, not the law, that lay behind the Metropolis's problems with prostitutes. As one noted: "We want no new laws to prevent

---

[912] *The Times*, Aug. 14th 1788, p.2.
[913] *The Times*, Nov. 28, 1789, p.3.
[914] *The Times*, July 3, 1790, p.3.
[915] Jonas Hanway, *A Plan for Establishing a Charity-House, or Charity Houses for the Reception of Repenting Prostitutes, To be Called the Magdalene Charity*, London, 1758, at p.xxix.

these evils; we only want those we have to be enforced."[916] Nearly all Metropolitan agencies and officers became involved in controlling prostitutes. Foremost amongst them were parish beadles, constables, and their subordinate watchmen. Beadles held permanent full-time salaried positions within the parish. It was one of their responsibilities to help control the presence of prostitutes on public streets, though this could also make them acutely unpopular.[917] Typically, in May 1701, beadles assisted constables and JPs to detain almost 40 "lewd" women at the traditional fair held near Hyde Park, and sent them to the Westminster Bridewell in Tutle-fields.[918] Constables carried out similar operations; for example, in 1744, John Welburne, a Farringdon officer, noted that he had periodically raided a 'disorderly' house frequented by prostitutes in Love's Court in the same parish. He recalled that, when he went his rounds there, over the summer months: "I have called in between two and three in the Morning, and I never went in, but I found a Company of Women, and sometimes Men with them; and have taken them up sometimes, and carried them to the Watch-house, and they have been committed to the Workhouse." It appears that he usually took the watchman who was permanently assigned to duty in Love's Court with him when he did so.[919] City Marshalmen and, later in the century, the 'patroles' attached to various police offices also frequently became involved in dealing with Metropolitan streetwalkers.

### De Facto Tolerance for Prostitutes

Throughout the century, the authorities, whether JPs or parish officers, showed considerable de facto toleration for prostitution. As a result, many were able to pursue their activities quite openly. Thus, in 1786, it was noted that "dozens of infant prostitutes" paraded in front of Somerset House each night. Even worse, these girls appeared to be supervised by much older "harridans" who provided them with alluring clothes in which to entice prospective customers, receiving a share of the proceeds of any ensuing sexual transaction in exchange. However, despite such overt behaviour, no formal legal action was taken against them.[920] Constables and beadles usually adopted a laissez–faire attitude towards the prostitutes who were working their local streets, intervening selectively, on a case-by-case basis, and often only when a woman's behaviour occasioned severe local complaint, was associated with disorderly conduct or some other form of crime, or threatened to become locally disruptive.

Amongst their subordinates, in the Watch, such attitudes were even more pronounced, and the turning of a blind-eye to soliciting was frequently endemic, except when under acute pressure from their superiors.[921] Even where they did

---

[916]*The Times*, Oct.14, 1789, p.3.
[917]OBSP, Trial of Edmund Long, Henry Townley and Charles Savage, 17th Oct 1744.
[918]*English Post*, 12-14 May 1701.
[919]OBSP, Trial of James Newbold, 12th Oct. 1743.
   *Times*, 10th May, 1786, p.2.
   n, *A Letter to the Right Reverend the Lord Bishop of London*, London, 1808, p.34.

intervene, the most common response by watchmen appears to have been to disperse groups of streetwalkers, and to order them to 'move on', even if this entailed inflicting the women on another parish.[922] Typically, John Sylvester, a Fleet Street watchman, seeing an inebriated local barber being lured away by a notorious prostitute, threatened her with arrest, warned the barber about the risk, and called the woman a "saucy brimstone toad", but ultimately let her go off with the man when he made it clear that she was "a girl for his fancy."[923]

Such an approach lasted well into the following century. For example, in 1825, a Mr. Price was accosted by a prostitute, while walking along Cornhill, who took hold of his arm and, when rebuffed, followed him uttering "horrible" obscenities. However, when he asked a watchman to arrest her, the officer was unwilling to do more than "order her to go about her business."[924] There were, of course, de facto limits to what was acceptable street behaviour by prostitutes. Although soliciting might be tolerated, if it became too aggressive, involved excessive amounts of publicly voiced obscenities or impinged too heavily on other pedestrians, the Watch was likely to intervene. Such limits were flexible, and subject to variation over time, as what was deemed unacceptable conduct also changed.[925]

Accommodating attitudes were not confined to parish officers; there were regular complaints about the reluctance of many Metropolitan JPs to engage with the problem. Some observers expressed outrage at the: "Magistrates, who, with the law on their side ... [nevertheless] allow such swarms of prostitutes nightly to infest the streets."[926] Others pointed out that the 'shoals' of prostitutes crowding the streets of the Metropolis thronged around the very doors of the City's courts, without being punished, sometimes even conducting assignations in the entrance porch to the Mansion House itself, where criminal justice was administered.[927] In 1790, it was claimed that Covent Garden, Bow Street, Hart Street and Drury Lane, along with every small court, lane and alley around them, "swarmed" with brothels, despite local magistrates being inundated with complaints from members of the public.[928] This phenomenon invites explanation, and a number of reasons for such tolerance can be identified.

## Corruption

One explanation was simple bribery. Extortion from prostitutes by watchmen, beadles and even constables was a long-standing problem. Daniel Defoe had feared it was endemic in the 1720s.[929] It only rarely resulted in punishment.

---

[922]Henderson, *Disorderly Women in Eighteenth-Century London*, p.153.
[923]OBSP, Trial of Mary Blewit, 11th July 1726.
[924]*The Times*, August 9th 1825, p.3.
[925]Henderson, *Disorderly Women in Eighteenth-Century London*, pp.119-120.
[926]Anon, *The Evils of Adultery and Prostitution*, pp.64-65.
[927]Anon, *A Letter to the Right Reverend the Lord Bishop of London*, p.34.
[928]*The Times*, July 3, 1790, p.3.
[929]Daniel Defoe, *Parochial Tyranny*, London, 1727, at p.20

Watchmen inevitably became familiar with street-women, whose pitches could be almost as fixed as their own beats. Presents of gin or tobacco might be tendered or, more commonly, cash and free sexual relations, in exchange for tolerance. Some women even referred to the bribes they paid as 'gin money'. As a result, it was feared that: "A large share of the miserable earnings of vice [i.e. prostitution] is extorted in the streets by watchmen."[930] A failure to pay might lead to arrest, detention in the Watch-house overnight and being produced before a JP the following morning.[931]

Several observers alleged that this amounted to an informal "Impost on Whoring", and that those prostitutes who were unfortunate enough to be arrested normally came from the poorest stratum of the profession, being women who could not afford to carry the necessary half a crown to bribe local officers.[932] Those who were possessed of that sum were as "sure of protection, as a cheating director, and may sin on without danger." By contrast, the "poor needy wag-tail" was likely to be committed to Bridewell if caught.[933] This view was shared by a City clergyman, who observed that only the "meaner sort" of prostitutes were punished, those with "no money to corrupt."[934] This phenomenon continued to the end of the century and beyond. Beadles were particularly associated with extortion from the very prostitutes they were tasked with arresting, again, allegedly, acting against only the most wretched women.[935]

Additionally, general fraternisation, purely for social purposes, was widespread, if only because a watchman's life was often a lonely one and the local women were likely to become familiar faces. Thus, in a 'liberty' situated within Middlesex, but very close to the City of London, it was noted that the prostitutes had "their beats and stands as regular and uniform as the watchmen."[936] They would tell their sad stories to the officers while: "…treating them with Geneva and Tobacco for the Liberty of walking about their respective beats."[937] As a result, the minute books of parish vestries and wardmote courts contain numerous complaints about watchmen associating with prostitutes while on duty, such as that made against a supernumerary officer for "harbouring loose women in and about his Box." Even if they did not go this far, it was common for them to ignore prostitutes, and act in the manner of one McDonald, another supernumerary watchman, who, it was alleged, allowed: "…

---

[930]Andrew Moreton (Daniel Defoe), *Thoughts on Means of Alleviating the Miseries attendant upon Common Prostitution*, London, 1799, p.1.

[931]Samuel Leigh, *Leigh's New Picture of London*, London, printed by W. Clowes, 1819, p.98

[932]*The Times*, 13 June 1828, p.3

[933]Poussin, *Pretty Doings in a Protestant Nation*, p.3.

[934]Anon ('by a clergyman of the City of London'), *Friendly Advice to the Fair Sex*, London, printed for G. Kearsly, 1758, p.vi.

[935]Anon, *The Midnight Rambler or, New nocturnal Spy*, London, printed for J. Cooke, 1770, pp.107-108

*Times*, Sept. 6th 1787, p.2.

ı, *Low-Life or one Half of the World …*3rd. edn., London, 1764, pp.4-5.

Disorderly Women to be cursing and swearing in the street and making a riot and he in his box and took no notice of them."[938]

Worse still, even some JPs, especially those who could be numbered amongst Westminster's notorious 'Trading Justices', were also ambiguous about prostitution, for mercenary reasons. It was feared that several took bribes to overlook the operation of bawdy houses.[939] The magistrate William Blackborow was accused of threatening action against constables who 'took up' prostitutes living in the lucrative tenements that he owned. Similarly, it was alleged that Charles Whinyates blatantly used his office to extort complementary service from both prostitutes and brothels.[940] It was also claimed that many bawds ensured that they were on good terms with their local Justice's clerk, by allowing him free sexual favours in their brothels, knowing that he would act as an intermediary with the magistrate if it ever became necessary to make "her peace with the Justice of Quorum."[941]

## Physical and Legal Dangers in Excessive Activism

Another deterrent to the aggressive policing of prostitutes was its inherent risks, both physical and legal. Constables who made an excessive number of arrests might occasion public hostility. For an extreme example of this, can be considered the case of John Dent, who was murdered while on duty in 1709. Dent was a highly interventionist constable, and a member of the Society for the Reformation of Manners, who had distinguished himself, over several years, in prosecuting numerous disorderly houses and prostitutes.[942] His death occurred after he attempted to assist a colleague who was trying to detain known streetwalkers in the Covent Garden area. A serious disturbance ensued, during which Dent was fatally stabbed by one of a group of soldiers seeking to prevent the arrest.[943]

There were also some legal dangers associated with excessive activism when policing streetwalkers. An arrested but acquitted prostitute could sue the officer who detained her for false imprisonment, a longstanding right that was explicitly restated as late as 1803 in *Tooley's Case*. As a result, women detained in Westminster were usually convicted by the sessions courts as a matter of form, whether they were guilty or not. However, a considerable number of them were then discharged without any further punishment, if the evidence was thought to

---

[938]Henderson, *Disorderly-women in Eighteenth-Century London*, pp.110-111.

[939]Norma Landau, *The Justice of the Peace 1679-1760*, Berkeley, University of California Press, 1984, p.185.

[940]Norma Landau, "The Trading Justice's Trade", *Law, Crime and English Society: 1660-1830*, Cambridge, CUP, 2002, pp.47-50.

[941]Anon, *The London-Bawd with Her Character and Life*, 3rd edn., London, Printed for John Gwillim, 1705, p.A4.

[942]*Post Boy*, 19-22 March 1709.

[943]Thomas Bray, *The Tryals of Jeremy Tooley, William Arch, and John Clausson, Three Private Soldiers for the Murder of Mr.John Dent, Constable...* London, Printed for J. Wilford, 1732, p.4.

be weak.[944] Individual prostitutes with means (a small minority) could also enforce their theoretical civil rights. As a result, D'Archenholz noted that well to do prostitutes were seldom bothered by the magistrates; if a JP attempted to: "…trouble them in their apartments, they might turn him out of doors; for, as they pay the same taxes as the other parishioners, they are consequently entitled to the same privileges."[945]

Such legal risks were exacerbated because hostility towards the anti-prostitution reformers extended to some senior members of the judiciary, as can be seen in the proceedings resulting from the killing of constable Dent. At the ensuing murder trial, Lord Chief Justice Holt was deeply concerned about the legal basis for arresting the prostitute whose detention had precipitated the officer's murder, as she had not been engaged in any illicit activity when held. At Holt's suggestion, the jury returned a special verdict.[946] In due course, the 12 judges, sitting together at Serjeants' Inn, decided by a narrow majority that the defendants should be acquitted of murder and only convicted of manslaughter.[947] The revived reformation of manners movement eventually came to grief in the 1760s, after an adverse legal verdict from Judge Charles Pratt. Happy to have an opportunity to show his "dislike towards these reformers," Pratt refused to set aside as excessive an award of £300 damages made against several reforming constables accused of assaulting and falsely imprisoning the female keeper of an alleged brothel, the Rummer Tavern. This, when accompanied by the action's considerable legal costs, dealt a fatal blow to the society's funds, so that it collapsed in 1765. This was especially galling as the woman genuinely was a brothel keeper, and the society belatedly secured the conviction of the plaintiff's principal witness at the earlier trial.[948]

Frequently, the wisest policy for constables confronted by prostitution was to 'see no evil, hear no evil' unless it was very overt. This often resulted in officers swearing in their returns that their parishes were free from such forms of deviance, when this was transparently not the case. This attitude prompted the sarcastic observations of a 'reformed robber', in the 1750s, who noted that he must be mistaken in imagining there were any brothels in Covent-Garden: "…as the Constables, who have the utmost detestation of perjury, so clearly demonstrate by their oaths, and as it is highly incredible to argue, that the most active Justice in England would let any such houses remain under his very nose."[949] One of the long-term objects of reformers was to install men as parish officers who would not be susceptible to being pressured into applying local standards of order at the expense of the prescribed justice of the state.

---

[944]Simpson, "The Mouth Of Strange Women Is A Deep Pit", p.60.

[945]D'Archenholz, *A Picture of England*, p.189.

[946]Bray, *The Tryals of Jeremy Tooley, William Arch, and John Clausson*, pp.8 and 26.

[947]*Post Boy*, 29 November-1 December 1709.

[949]·)anna Innes, *William Payne of Bell Yard, Carpenter c.1718-1782: The Life and times of a London ·ving constable*, unpublished paper (in original version), privately circulated by the author.

·on, *A congratulatory Epistle From a Reformed Robber*, London, 1758, p.15.

Even if they were arrested, it was not uncommon for prostitutes to be quietly released without charge in the early hours of the following morning, having cooled their heals in a watch-house cell overnight, rather than being produced before a JP (though, in theory, this was illegal). This sometimes occurred upon the constable of the night: "...reflecting too that he may not be able to bring any sufficient charge against her."[950] Those who did proceed would often regret it, discovering that detaining street-women was more trouble than it was worth, being accompanied by much "expense, fatigue and loss of time."[951] The JPs, of course, only sat outside the normal hours of service of the Watchmen, who would have to attend court to give evidence when they might otherwise be sleeping.

## Anti-Prostitution Campaigns

This 'steady state' of relative inaction would periodically give way to pressure from private individuals, crusading organisations, activist magistrates or influential journals to 'do something' about prostitution. Thus, in 1787, several 'respectable' householders from the Strand petitioned the sitting magistrates at the Bow Street Police Office to take action over the area's large number of prostitutes. In response, they directed that 'privy' search warrants be regularly issued to the area's High Constable: "...'till the same shall be entirely removed."[952] Throughout the eighteenth century, some Metropolitan magistrates, parish vestries and Grand Juries attempted to pressurise their constables into acting more vigorously against streetwalkers. As a result, there would be periodic, intense, but usually short-lived, campaigns against prostitutes. These would include attempts to 'take up' women in large numbers, although such activity may not always have been aimed at moral reform. Until stipendiary magistrates were introduced in 1792, cynics claimed that Westminster magistrates (many of them 'trading justices') organized large-scale sweeps for prostitutes with the express purpose of extorting bail-money from them.[953]

Typically, in 1701, several JPs, accompanied by a very large number of constables and beadles, went to the May Fair held near Hyde Park and committed "near 40 lewd women to Bridewel in Tutle-fields."[954] Almost a century later, a 'search-night' held on a Monday evening in November 1785, in the area around St. Martin's Lane, produced numerous arrests, the women being detained by both watchmen and Bow Street Runners and then taken back to the St. Martin's parish Watch-house with "brutal authority." After being crammed into a cell there overnight, they were examined by magistrates the following day, some being committed to the Bridewell.[955] On another Monday night, some four

---

[950]Anon, *Thoughts on Means of Alleviating the Miseries,* pp.20-21.
[951]Anon, *Low-Life or one Half of the World* ...3rd. edn., p.12.
[952]*The Times,* Oct. 27, 1787, p.3.
[953]Simpson, "The Mouth Of Strange Women Is A Deep Pit", p.59.
[954]*English Post,* 12-14 May 1701.
[955]*The Times,* Nov. 10 1785 p.3.

years later, 50 such women were detained in and about the Strand, before being produced in front of Sir Sampson-Wright, the Bow Street magistrate, the following day. Again, a few were committed as disorderly women, while the remainder were simply discharged.[956]

On rare occasions, individual parish officers might launch crusades against prostitutes, whether out of personal conviction or a desire to secure rewards. When they did so, it was comparatively easy for them to detain large numbers of women very quickly. Thus, in the summer of 1694, John Cooper, a barber surgeon and constable from the Broad Street Ward of the City, along with his attendant Watchmen, committed at least 18 women to the Bridewell as 'nightwalkers'. Several others were produced before the Lord Mayor's court. Cooper appears to have been influenced by the rewards offered by the Society for the Reformation of Manners.[957] Similarly, the career of William Payne, a highly active constable and former member of the (refounded) Society for the Reformation of Manners, is indicative in this respect. A magistrate's notebook covering a period of five weeks in the autumn of 1777 shows that of 251 people brought before the sitting aldermen for summary trial or referral in that period, at least 105 had been arrested by Payne, a high proportion of whom were prostitutes. He usually worked in Fleet Street, where such women could readily be found on most evenings. However, and significantly, it appears that Payne was almost unique amongst local parish officers in such activism during these months.[958]

As the careers of both these constables suggest, the most important of the campaigning organisations were the associated Societies for the Reformation of Manners. The first of these was established in 1690 in Tower Hamlets. By 1701, there were nearly 20 similar associations in London and others followed over the next decade. However, and partly for generational reasons, they petered out in the 1740s, making it necessary to refound them in 1757. Nevertheless, they declined rapidly again after the mid-1760s. Although largely self-administering, the various societies operated within a loose confederation. Their members deplored Christians who limited their moral activity to personal spiritual observance and exhortation. Instead, they sought to reform the world by using the secular courts to suppress public manifestations of immorality, such as prostitution.[959] As private citizens, they might seek out offenders and either deliver them into the hands of local constables or secure information which could be passed on to neighbourhood JPs. The societies would sometimes also fund any ensuing prosecutions. Alternatively, members of the societies could themselves become highly interventionist local constables and take action

---

[956]*The Times,* Dec. 16 1789 p.4.
[957]Beattie, *Policing and Punishment in London 1660-1750,* pp.245-246.
[958]Innes, *William Payne of Bell Yard.*
[959]M.G. Smith, "Pastoral Discipline and the Church Courts: the Hexham Court 1680-1730", *Borthwick Papers,* York, 1982, no. 62, pp.9-10.

directly against miscreants. Thus, in the early 1760s, some London members actively petitioned to be sworn in as 'extra' constables so that, instead of being given jurisdiction over a single parish, they had authority to act anywhere in the City of London. The Court of Aldermen annually approved the appointment of several members of the society as constables on this basis.[960]

From their beginnings, the societies targeted prostitutes, and some members acquired a degree of expertise in their local street-walkers. Thus, City magistrates' minute books from late 1761 and early 1762, suggest that William Payne was actively assisting other reforming constables to deal with prostitutes and people found in brothels. By 1762, he was an acknowledged expert on the street-walkers of the Fleet Street area; if he recognised a woman as an 'old offender', rather than a neophyte to the trade, it would usually be enough to ensure that she was not released with a reprimand (as was common with new prostitutes) but instead sent to the Bridewell.[961]

However, much of the political nation, and many ordinary people, felt that their members were interfering busybodies who exercised their powers in an 'insolent' manner.[962] De Mandeville's defence of public stews was specifically aimed at the societies; he felt that their: "…endeavours to suppress lewdness, have only served to promote it."[963] They were also heavily criticised in the popular press. Additionally, the fragmentation of policing meant that pursuing a coherent strategy towards street-walkers within the entire Metropolitan area was almost impossible; there was always an acute temptation to 'off load' the problem onto neighbouring jurisdictions. Thus, it was noted in 1785 that a simultaneous campaign of "vigorous measures" against prostitutes in both the City and Westminster meant that each was attempting to push them into the other's area; the City's constables were even expressly ordered to drive the women past Temple Bar. As a result it was feared that: "…these wretched women must seek an asylum in the arms of old father Thames."[964] Nevertheless, even at a parochial level within Middlesex and the cities of London and Westminster, co-operation was difficult to establish, as wards and parishes sought to 'move on' women to their neighbours.

## Conclusion

Prostitution was a significant part of the economy of eighteenth-century London. It provided an essential safety net for many marginalised women and contributed financially towards a host of other businesses, such as the lower rungs of the rental market and the retail trade in alcohol. It existed largely because of the constant (male) demand for sexual services in and about the

---

[960]Innes, *William Payne of Bell Yard.*
[961]Innes *William Payne of Bell Yard*
[962]*The Gentleman's Magazine*, 1731, vol. 1, p.61.
[963]De Mandeville, *A Modest Defence of Public Stews*, p.v.
[964]*The Times*, Nov. 7th, 1785, p.3.

Metropolitan area and a chronic lack of economic opportunities and other forms of support for women. As a result, most thoughtful observers were realistic about any prospects of 'solving' the problem, accepting that at best it could only be ameliorated, and the number of women involved in the 'trade' reduced.[965] Throughout the century, the Metropolitan law enforcement agencies also appear to have tacitly accepted this analysis; their 'default' mode of operation being one of containment, placing limits on where, when and how streetwalkers could operate, rather than attempting to proscribe such conduct altogether. Although their relative inactivity was, in part, the result of endemic corruption amongst parish officers accompanied by the legal problems associated with prostitution, it also reflected a widespread acknowledgement that many women were forced into prostitution by factors that were beyond their control and, perhaps, a growing measure of official sympathy for their bleak predicament.

Nevertheless, prostitution was also closely linked to many other, much more serious, forms of criminal activity and disorder, as well as to other types of social problem within the Metropolis, such as epidemic levels of venereal disease. Because of this, law enforcement agencies would, periodically, be pressured into more intense, albeit localised and often short-lived, campaigns against prostitutes, especially those at the bottom end of the trade. These were usually relatively ineffectual, at least in the long term.

For most of the women involved, prostitution was a grim, unhealthy and sometimes dangerous existence, one in which intense competition usually made the rewards relatively modest; however, it was also normally just a facet of their existences rather than an identity, something from which they eventually escaped back to normal proletarian life. Many 'ordinary' female Londoners from the lower social orders had had some experience of going 'on the town,' at some point in their lives, even if it was not something that they later boasted about.

---

[965]Anon, *An Address to the Benevolent Public ...*, pp.3-4.

# BIBLIOGRAPHY

Amussen, Susan Dwyer (1994) "Being Stirred to Much Unquietness: Violence and Domestic Violence in Early Modern England", *Journal of Women's History*, vol. 6, no. 2, pp.70-89.

Andrew, Donna and McGowen, Randall (2001) *The Perreaus & Mrs. Rudd: Forgery and Betrayal in Eighteenth-Century London*, London: University of California Press.

Andrews, William (1899) *Bygone Punishments*, London: William Andrews & Co.

Anon, (1632) *The Laws Resolutions of Womens Rights: or, the Lawes Provision for Women*, London: John More.

Anon, (1662) *The Life and Death of Mrs Mary Frith, Commonly Called Mal Cutpurse*, London: Printed for W. Gilbertson.

Anon, (1677) *Horrid News From St. Martin's, or, Unheard-of Murder and Poison: Being a true relation how a girl not full sixteen years of age, murdered her own mother at one time and a servant-maid at another with Ratsbane*, London: printed for D.M.

Anon, (1678) *The Last Speech and Confession of Sarah Elestone at the place of execution who was burned for killing her husband April 24 1678 with her deportment in prison since her condemnation*, London: printed for T.D.

Anon ('A Citizen in London'), (1751) *The Vices of the cities of London and Westminster trac'd from their original …*, Dublin: G. Faulkner.

Anon ('By a clergyman of the City of London'), (1758) *Friendly Advice to the Fair Sex*, London: Printed for G. Kearsly.

Anon ('By a Lady of Quality'), (1721) *Women Triumphant or the Excellency of the Female Sex*, London.

Anon ('By Sophie, a person of quality'), (1739) *Women not Inferior to Men*, London: printed for John Hawkins.

Anon, (1659) *The Caterpillars of this Nation Anatomised*, London.

Anon, (1662) *The Life and Death of Mrs Mary Frith, Commonly Called Mal Cutpurse*, London: Printed for W. Gilbertson.

Anon, (1668) *The Tryals of such Persons (Peter Messenger, Richard Beasley… as under the Notion of London-Apprentices were tumultuously assembled in Moorfields*, London: Robert Pawlet.

Anon, (1678) *The Last Speech and Confession of Sarah Elestone at the place of execution who was burned for killing her husband April 24 1678 with her deportment in prison since her condemnation*, London: printed for T.D.

Anon, (1683) *An Assistance to Justices of the Peace, for the Easier Performance of their Duty*, London: Joseph Keble.

Anon, (1688) *A Hellish Murder Committed by a French Midwife, on the Body of her husband*, London.

Anon, (1696) *The Night Walker: or Evening Rambles in Search after Lewd Women*, London: Printed for James Orme.

Anon, (1699) *Concealed Murther Revealed*, London: Printed for William Aldredge.

Anon, (1699) *The Tryal and Condemnation of Mervin, Lord Audley Earl of Castlehaven*, London.

Anon, (1705) *The London-Bawd with Her Character and Life*, 3rd edn., London: Printed for John Gwillim.

Anon, (1706) *The Whores and Bawd's Answer to the Fifteen Comforts of Whoring*, London.

Anon, (1706) *Serious admonitions to youth, in a short account of the life, trial, condemnation and execution of Mrs Mary Channing who, for poisoning her husband, was burnt at Dorchester in the county of Dorset on Thursday, March the 21st 1706*, London: printed for Ben Bragg.

Anon, (1715) *The Case of the Ld. John Drummond in Relation to a Rape*, London: Printed for J. Roberts.

Anon, (ND but c.1720) *The Great Grievance of Traders and Shopkeepers, by the Notorious Practise of Stealing their Goods out of their Shops and warehouses by persons commonly called shop-lifters*, London,

Anon, (1723) *A Sermon Preach'd at Isleworth in the County of Middlesex, On Sunday, Feb 10, 1722, Occasioned by the Rape and murder committed on the Body of Anne Bristow, January 22, on Smalbury-Green in that Parish,* London: Printed for J. Roberts.

Anon, (1725) *A View of London and Westminster: or, the Town Spy, etc. By a German Gentleman,* London.

Anon, (1728) *The Charge of Sir John Gonson, Kt. to the Grand Jury of the City and Liberty of Westminster,* 2nd edn., London,

Anon, (1729) *Hell upon Earth: or the Town in an Uproar,* London: J. Roberts.

Anon, (1730) *The Tryal of Colonel Francis Charteris,* London: printed for Sylvanus Pergat.

Anon, (1732) *A Treatise of Feme Coverts or the Lady's Law,* London: Printed for R. Nott.

Anon, (female author) (1735) "The Hardships of the English Laws in Relation to Wives", in *Women in the Eighteenth Century,* V. Jones (Ed.), London.

Anon, (1738) *Baron and Feme: A treatise of Law and Equity Concerning Husbands and Wives,* 3rd edn., London: R. Nott.

Anon, (1740) *A Dialogue Between A Married Lady and a Maid,* London.

Anon, (1747) *The Art of Governing a Wife,* London: J. Robinson.

Anon, (1749) *Satan's Harvest Home,* London.

Anon, (1754) *The Midnight-Ramble Or, the Adventures of Two Noble Females,* London: Printed for B. Dickinson.

Anon, (1758) ('A clergyman of the City of London'), *Friendly Advice to the Fair Sex,* London: printed for G. Kearsly.

Anon, (1758) *A Congratulatory Epistle From a Reformed Robber,* London.

Anon, (1760) *Penitents in the Magdalen House,* vol.1, London: printed for John Rivington.

Anon, (1764) *Low-Life or one Half of the World …,* 3rd edn., London.

Anon, (1767) *An Appeal for Humanity in an Account of the Life and Cruel Actions of Elizabeth Brownrigg*, London.

Anon, (1770) *The Midnight Rambler or, New nocturnal Spy*, London: printed for J. Cooke.

Anon, (1772) *The Complete Parish Officer*, London.

Anon, (1773) *Harris's List of Covent Garden Ladies*, London: Printed for H. Ranger.

Anon, (1777) *The Laws Respecting Women*, London: Printed for J. Johnson.

Anon, (1792) *The Evils of Adultery and Prostitution*, London.

Anon, (1798) *The Last Dying Speeches and Confessions, Confessions and Adventures of the Three Unfortunate Malefactors, Executed this morning before the Debtors Door, Newgate*, London.

Anon, (1799) *Reports from Select Committees, Respecting The Arts-Masters and Apprentices of Bridewell Hospital*, London.

Anon, (1799) *Thoughts on Means of Alleviating the Miseries attendant upon Common Prostitution*, London: Printed for T. Cadell.

Anon, (1800) *Thoughts on the Frequency of Divorce in Modern Times*, London.

Anon, (1803) "The Criminal laws as they relate to capital offences" in *Journals of the House of Commons*, London, vol.33.

Anon, (1807) *An Address to the Benevolent Public … on behalf of the London Female Penitent*, London.

Anon, (1808) *A Letter to the Right Reverend the Lord Bishop of London …* , London.

Anon, (1810) *God's Revenge Against Murder!*, London.

Anon, (2002) *Taking Stock: What do we know about interpersonal violence?*, The ESRC Violence Research Programme, London.

Anon, (1699) *The Tryal and Condemnation of Mervin, Lord Audley Earl of Castlehaven*.

Archbold, J. F. (1828) *A Summary of the Law Relative to Pleading and Evidence in Criminal Cases*, 3rd edn., London: Pheney.

Babbington, Anthony (1999) *A House in Bow Street,* 2nd edn., Chichester: Barry Rose.

Babington, Zachary (1677) *Advise to Grand Jurors in Cases of Blood,* London: Printed for John Amery.

Bacon, Francis (1906) "On Judicature," *The Essays,* London: Everyman edn. J M Dent.

Bacon, Sir Francis (1641) *Cases of Treason,* London: printed by the Assignes of John More.

Bailey, Joanne (2002) "Favoured or oppressed? Married women, property and 'coverture' in England, 1660-1800" in *Continuity and Change,* vol. 17 (3), pp.351-372.

Bailey, Joanne (2003) *Unquiet Lives: Marriage and Marriage Breakdown in England, 1660-1800,* Cambridge: CUP.

Baker, John (1998) "The Three Languages of the Common Law" in *McGill Law Journal,* vol. 43, pp.5-24.

Baker, John H (1973) "Criminal Justice at Newgate 1616-1627" in *The Irish Jurist,* vol. 8, pp.307-322.

Baldwin, R. (1776) *Considerations on some laws relating to the office of Coroner,* Newcastle: printed for T. Saint.

Beattie, John (1974) "The Criminality of Women in Eighteenth Century England", *Journal of Social History,* vol.8/4, pp.80-116.

Beattie, John (1985) "Violence and Society in Early-Modern England," *Perspectives in Criminal law. Essays in Honour of John Edwards,* A. Doob et al (eds.), Ontario: Aurora.

Beattie, John (1986) *Crime and the Courts in England 1660-1800,* Oxford: OUP.

Beattie, John (1995) "Hard Pressed to Make Ends Meet': Women and Crime in Augustan London" in *Women and History,* Valerie Firth (Ed.), Toronto, p.106.

Beattie, John (2001) *Policing and Punishment in London, 1660-1750,* Oxford: OUP.

Bellamy, John G. (1998) *The Criminal Trial in Later Medieval England: Felony Before the Courts From Edward I to the Sixteenth Century*, Toronto: University of Toronto Press.

Bingham, Peregrine (1816) *The Law of Infancy and Coverture*, London: Butterworth & Son.

Blackstone, William (1765-9) *Commentaries on the Laws of England*, Oxford: Clarendon Press, vols 1-4.

Bohun, Edmund (1693) *The Justice of Peace: His Calling and Qualifications*, London.

Bond, D.F. (1965) *The Spectator*, vol. 1, Oxford: Oxford Clarendon Press.

Bondeson, Jan (2000) *The London Monster*, London: Free Association Books.

Bosworth, Mary (2001) "The Past as a Foreign Country? Some Methodological Implications of doing Historical Criminology" in *British Journal of Criminology*, vol. 41, no. 3, pp.431-442.

Bray, Thomas (1732) *The Tryals of Jeremy Tooley, William Arch, and John Clausson, Three Private Soldiers for the Murder of Mr. John Dent, Constable...* London: Printed for J. Wilford.

Burman, Michele et al (2001) "Researching girls and violence: facing the dilemmas of fieldwork" in *British Journal of Criminology*, vol. 41, pp.443-459.

Campbell, Ruth (1984) "Sentence of Death by Burning for Women" in *Journal of Legal History*, vol. 5, pp.44-48.

Capp, Bernard (1996) "Separate Domains? Women and Authority in Early Modern England" in *The Experience of Authority in Early Modern England*, P. Griffiths et al (eds.), Basingstoke: MacMillan, pp.117-145.

Capp, Bernard (1999) "The Double Standard Revisited: Plebeian Women and Male Sexual Reputation in Early Modern England" in *Past and Present*, no.162, pp.70-100

Chitty, J. (1816) *A Practical Treatise on the Criminal Law*, vol.1, London.

Clark, Anna K. (1987) *Women's silence, men's violence: sexual assault in England, 1770-1845*, London: Pandora Press.

Coke, Sir Edward (1644) *Institutes of the Lawes of England, Part Three, Concerning High Treason, and other Pleas of the Crown and Criminal causes*, London: W. Lee.

Colquhoun, Patrick (1796) *A Treatise on the Police of the Metropolis*, London: Printed by H. Fry.

Conley, Carolyn (1995) "No pedestals: women and violence in late nineteenth-century Ireland" in *Journal of Social History*, vol. 28, no. 4, pp.801-818.

Cornett, Judy M. (1997) "Hoodwink'd by custom: The exclusion of women from juries in Eighteenth-Century English Law and Literature" in *William and Mary Journal of Women and the Law*, vol. 4, pp.18-28.

Cotton, J. (2003) 'Homicide' in *Crime in England and Wales 2001/2002: Supplementary Volume*, C. Flood-Page and J. Taylor (eds.), pp.1-23, London: Home Office.

D'Archenholz, Johann Wilhelm (1791) *A Picture of England*, Dublin.

Dabhoiwala, Faramerz (2000) "The pattern of sexual immorality in seventeenth- and eighteenth-century London" in *Londinopolis: Essays in the Cultural and Social History of Early Modern London*, P. Griffiths et al (eds.), pp.86-106, Manchester: Manchester University Press,

Dabhoiwala, Faramerz (2006) "Summary Justice in Early Modern London" in *English Historical Review*, vol. cxxi, no. 492, at pp.796-822.

Dalton, James (1728) *A Genuine Narrative of all the Street Robberies Committed since October last*, London.

De Mandeville, Bernard (1724) *A Modest Defence of Publick Stews*, London: printed for A. Moore.

Defoe, Daniel (1726) *Some Considerations upon Street-Walkers with A proposal for lowering the present number of them*, London: printed for A. Moore.

Defoe, Daniel (1727) *Parochial Tyranny*, London.

Defoe, Daniel (1731) *The Generous Projector*, London: Printed for A. Dodd.

Devereaux, Simon (2005) "The Abolition of the Burning of Women in England Reconsidered" in *Crime, History & Societies*, vol. 9, no. 2, pp.73-98.

Dickie, Simon (2003) "Hilarity and Pitilessness in the Mid-Eighteenth Century: English Jestbook Humor" in *Eighteenth-Century Studies*, vol.37, no.1, pp.1-22.

Dickinson, J.P. and Sharpe, James A (2000) "Infanticide in early modern England: the Court of Great Sessions at Chester, 1650-1800" in *Infanticide: Historical Perspectives on Child Murder and Concealment, 1550-2000*, M. Jackson (Ed.), Aldershot: Ashgate.

Dobash, Russell and Dobash, Emerson (2004) "Women's violence to Men in Intimate Relationships" in *British Journal of Criminology*, vol. 44, pp.324-325.

Doggett, Maeve (1992) *Marriage, Wife-Beating and the Law in Victorian England* London: Weidenfeld and Nicolson.

Dogherty, Thomas (1799) *The Crown Circuit Companion*, vol.1, London: Printed for E and R Brooke.

Dolan, Frances (1994) *Dangerous Familiars: Representations of Domestic Crime in England, 1550-1700*, Ithaca and London: Cornell University Press.

Downright, Sir D. (1768) *The Bastard Child, or a Feast for the Church-wardens*, London.

Earle, Peter (1989) "The female labour market in London in the late seventeenth and early eighteenth centuries" in *Economic History Review*, 2nd series, vol. XLII, 3, pp.328-353.

Edelstein, Laurie (1998) "An Accusation easily to be made?: Rape and Malicious prosecution in eighteenth century England" in *American Journal of Legal History*, vol. 42, pp.351-390.

Edwards, Susan (2005) "'Kicked, Beaten, Jumped On until They Are Crushed', All under Man's Wing and Protection: The Victorian Dilemma with Domestic Violence" in *Criminal Conversations, Victorian Crimes, Social Panic, and Moral Outrage*, Judith Rowbotham and Kim Stevenson (eds.), Columbus: Ohio State University Press.

Edwards, Val (1981) "German Princesses and Common Prostitutes: Women and Crime in Restoration London" in *Holdsworth Law Review*, vol. 6, pp.2-16.

Eisner, Manuel (2001) "Modernization, Self-control and Lethal violence" in *British Journal of Criminology*, vol. 41, pp.618-638.

Elias, Norbert (1982) *The Civilising Process*, vols. 1 and 2, Oxford: Blackwells.

Emsley, Clive (2007) *Hard Men: The English and Violence Since 1750*, London, Hambledon and London.

Evans, Tanya (2005) "'Unfortunate Objects': London's Unmarried Mothers in the Eighteenth Century" in *Gender & History*, vol.17, no.1, pp.127-153.

Farr, Samuel (1788) *Elements of Medical Jurisprudence*, London: printed for T. Becket, London.

Feeley, Malcolm and Little, Deborah (1991) "The Vanishing Female: The Decline of Women in the Criminal Process, 1687-1912" in *Law and Society Review*, vol. 25, no. 4, pp.719-757.

Feeley, Malcolm (1994) "The decline of women in the criminal process; a comparative history" in *Criminal Justice History*, vol. 15, pp.235-274.

Fielding, Henry (1730) *Rape upon Rape: or the Justice caught in his Own Trap*, London: Printed for J. Watts.

Fielding, John (1758) *A Plan for a Preservatory and Reformation for the benefit of Deserted Girls, and Penitent Prostitutes*, London.

Fleetwood, William (1657) *The Office of a Justice of Peace, Together with Instructions, How and in What Manner Statutes shall be Expounded.* London: printed by Ralph Wood for W Lee.

Forbes, Thomas R. (1977) "Inquests into London and Middlesex Homicides, 1673-1782" in *Yale Journal of Biology and Medicine*, vol. 50, pp.207-220.

Forbes, Thomas R. (1982/3) "Deadly Parents: Child Homicide in Eighteenth- and Nineteenth-Century England" in *Journal of the History of Medicine and Allied Sciences*, vol. 41, pp.175-199.

Foyster, Elizabeth (1996) "Male Honour, Social Control and Wife Beating in Late Stuart England2 in *Transactions of the Royal Historical Society*, 6th Series, vol. 6, pp.215-224.

Foyster, Elizabeth (1999) *Manhood in Early Modern England: Honour, Sex and Marriage*, London and New York: Longman.

Foyster, Elizabeth (2002) "At the limits of liberty: married women and confinement in eighteenth-century England" in *Continuity and Change,* vol.17, pp.39-62.

Foyster, Elizabeth (2002) "Creating a Veil of Silence? Politeness and Marital violence in the English Household", in *Transactions of the Royal Historical Society*, vol. 12. pp.395-415.

Foyster, Elizabeth (2005) *Marital Violence: An English Family History, 1660-1857*, Cambridge: CUP.

Frost, Ginger (2004) "'She is but a Woman': Kitty Byron and the English Edwardian Criminal Justice System" in *Gender & History*, vol. 16, no. 3, pp.538-560.

Fuller, William (1703) *Mr William Fuller's Trip to Bridewell: With a True Account of his Babarous Usage in the Pillory*, London.

Gammon, J. (1999) ""A denial of innocence": female juvenile victims of rape and the English legal system in the eighteenth century" in *Childhood in question: children, parents and the state*, A J Fletcher and S Hussey (eds.), Manchester: Manchester University Press.

Garland, David (1990) *Punishment and Modern Society: A Study in Social Theory*, Oxford: Clarendon.

Gatrell, V.A.C. (1996) *The Hanging Tree: Execution and the English People 1770-1868*, Oxford: OUP.

George, Dorothy (1965) *London Life in the Eighteenth Century*, London: Penguin Books.

George, Malcolm J. (1994) "Riding the Donkey Backwards: Men as the Unacceptable Victims of Marital Violence" in *The Journal of Men's Studies*, vol.3, No.2, pp.137-159.

George, Malcolm J. (2002) "Skimmington Revisited" in *The Journal of Men's Studies*, vol.10, No.2, pp.111-127.

Gilbert, Humphrey (1760) *The Law of Evidence*, 2nd edn., London: Printed by Catherine Lintot.

Giles, William (1771) *A Treatise on Marriage*, London.

Gisborne, Thomas (1797) *An Enquiry into the Duties of the Female Sex*, London.

Glaeser, Edward and Sacerdote, Bruce (1999) "Why Is There More Crime in Cities?" in *Journal of Political Economy*, vol. 107, no. 6, pp.225-229.

Godfrey, Barry and Lawrence, Paul (2005) *Crime and Justice: 1750-1950*, Collompton: Willan Publishing.

Godfrey, Barry et al (2005) "Explaining Gendered Sentencing Patterns for Violent Men and Women in the Late-Victorian and Edwardian Period" in *British Journal of Criminology*, vol. 45, 2005, pp.696-697.

Golby, J.M. and Purdue, A.W. (1999) *The Civilisation of the Crowd: Popular Culture in England 1750-1900*, Stroud: Sutton Publishing.

Goldberg, Jeremy (1995) "Girls growing up in later medieval England" in *History Today*, vol. 45, pp.25-32.

Goldsmith, Netta Murray (1988) *The Worst of Crimes: Homosexuality and the Law in Eighteenth Century London*, Ashgate: Aldershot.

Gordon, Reverend (1745) *The Life and Circumstantial Account of the extraordinary and Surprising Exploits, Travils, robberies and Escapes of the Famous Jenny Diver*, London.

Gough, William (1634) *Domesticall Duties*, London.

Gowing, Laura (1997) "Secret Birth and Infanticide in Seventeenth-Century England" in *Past and Present*, vol.156, at pp.157-187.

Gowing, Laura (2001) "The Freedom of the Streets: Women and Social Space, 1560-1640" in *Londinopolis*, P. Griffiths et al (eds.), Manchester: Manchester University Press.

Hale, Mathew (1736) *History of the Pleas of the Crown*, Book 1, London: Printed by E & R Nut.

Hall, John (1708) *Memoirs of the Right Villainous John Hall*, London.

Halliday, Stephen (2006) *Newgate: London's Prototype of Hell*, Stroud: Sutton Publishing.

Hanawalt, Barbara (1974) "The Female Felon in Fourteenth-Century England" in *Viator*, vol. 5, pp.253 –268.

Hanawalt, Barbara (1979) *Crime and conflict in English Communities, 1300-1348*, Cambridge/London: Harvard University Press.

Hanway, Jonas (1758) *A Plan for establishing a Charity-House of Charity Houses for the reception of repenting prostitutes*, London.

Hanway, Jonas (1759) *A Candid historical Account of the Hospital for the Reception of exposed and Deserted Young Children*, London.

Hanway, Jonas (1789) *Advice from Farmer Trueman to his Daughter*, 2nd edn.,. Edinburgh.

Harvey, A. D. (1994) *Sex in Georgian England: attitudes and prejudices from the 1720s to the 1820s*, London: Duckworth.

Hawkins, William (1724) *A Treatise of the Pleas of the Crown*, Book 1, 2nd Edition, London.

Hay, Douglas and Rogers, Nicholas (1987) *Eighteenth-century English Society*, Oxford: OUP.

Hayward, Arthur (Ed.) (1927) *Lives of the Most Remarkable Criminals: Who have been Condemned and Executed for Murder, the Highway, Housebreaking, Street Robberies, Coining or other offences. Collected from Original Papers and Authentic Memoirs, 1735*. London: Routledge & Sons.

Heale, William (1609) *An Apologie for Women*, Oxford.

Henderson, Tony (1999) *Disorderly Women in Eighteenth-Century London: Prostitution and Control in the Metropolis, 1730-1830*, London: Longmans.

Herrup, Cynthia B. (1999) *A House in Gross Disorder: Sex, Law, and the Second Earl of Castlehaven*, New York: OUP.

Heywood, Eliza (1743) *A Present for a Servant-Maid*, London.

Higginbotham, Ann R. (1989) '"Sin of the Age"; Infanticide and Illegitimacy in Victorian London" in *Victorian Studies*, vol. 32, no. 3, p.319.

Hill, Bridget (1996) *Servants: English Domestics in the Eighteenth Century*, Oxford: Clarendon Press.

Hillier, Bevis (2003) "The Mysterious Case of Elizabeth Canning" in *History Today*, vol. 53, issue 3, pp.47-53.

Hindle, Steve (2003) "Crime and Popular Protest" at pp.130-147 in B Coward (Ed.) *A Companion to Stuart Britain*, Oxford: Blackwells.

Histed, Elise (2004) "Medieval Rape: A conceivable Defence?" in *Cambridge Law Journal*, vol. 63(3), pp.743-769.

Hitchcock, Tim (1997) "Unlawfully begotten on her body': Illegitimacy and the Parish Poor in St Luke's Chelsea" in *Chronicling Poverty*, P King et al (eds.), pp.70-87.

Hitchcock, Tim (2004) *Down and Out in Eighteenth-Century London*, London: Hambledon & London.

Hitchcock, Tim (2005) "Begging on the Streets of Eighteenth-Century London" in *Journal of British Studies*, vol.44.3, pp.478-498.

Hoffer, Peter C and Hull, N E H (1981) *Murdering Mothers: Infanticide in England and New England 1558-1803,* New York: New York University Press.

Horne, Charles (1783) *Serious Thoughts on the Miseries of Seduction and Prostitution*, London.

Howard, John (1789) *Account of the Present State of the Prisons, Houses of Correction, and Hospitals in London and Westminster,* London.

Howel, James (1657) *Londinopolis*, London.

Howson, Gerald (1970) *Thief-Taker General: The Rise and fall of Jonathan Wild*, London: Hutchinson.

Humfrey, Paula (1998) "Female Servants and Women's Criminality in Early Eighteenth-Century London" in *Criminal Justice in the Old World and the New*, G.T.Smith et al (eds.), Toronto: University of Toronto.

Hunt, Margaret (1992) "Wife Beating, Domesticity and Women's Independence in Eighteenth-Century London2, *Gender & History*, vol. 4, no. 1, pp.10-33.

Hunter, William (1812) *On the Uncertainty of the Signs of Murder in the Case of Bastard Children*, London: printed for J Callow (first published 1783).

Hurl-Eamon, Jennine (2001) "Domestic Violence Prosecuted: Women Binding Over Their Husbands for Assault at Westminster Quarter Sessions, 1685-1720" in *Journal of Family History*, vol. 26, no. 4, pp.435-454.

Hurl-Eamon, Jennine (2004) "Policing male heterosexuality: the reformation of manners societies' campaign against the brothels in Westminster, 1690-1720" in *Journal of Social History*, vol. 37, no. 4, pp.1017-1035.

Hurl-Eamon, Jennine (2005) "The Westminster Impostors: Impersonating Law Enforcement in Early Eighteenth-Century London" in *Eighteenth-Century Studies*, vol. 38, no. 3, pp.461-483.

Hurl-Eamon, Jennine (2005) *Gender and Petty Violence in London, 1680-1720*, Columbus: Ohio State University Press.

Hyde, Edward (1803) *A Treatise of the Pleas of the Crown*, vol. 1, London: printed by A. Strahan, London.

Innes, Joanna (ND) *William Payne of Bell Yard, Carpenter c.1718-1782: The Life and times of a London informing constable*, unpublished paper (in original version), privately circulated by the author.

Jackson, Mark (1994) "Suspicious infant deaths: the statute of 1624 and medical evidence at coroners' inquests" in *Legal Medicine in History*, M Clark and C Crawford (eds.), Cambridge: CUP.

Jackson, Mark (1996) *New-born child murder: women, illegitimacy and the courts in eighteenth-century England*, Manchester: Manchester University Press.

Johnson, Captain Charles (1742) *A General and True History of the Lives and Actions of the most Famous Highwaymen, Murders, Street-Robbers etc.*, Birmingham.

Jones, Vivien (1997) "Placing Jemima: women writers of the 1790s and the eighteenth century prostitution narrative" in *Women's Writing*, vol. 4, no. 2, pp.201-220.

Kasperson, Maria (2000) *Infanticide in Eighteenth Century Stockholm*, Paper delivered to The British Criminology Conference.

Kelly, Henry Ansgar (1994) "Rule of Thumb and the Folklaw of the Husband's Stick" in *Journal of Legal Education*, vol. 44 (3), pp.341-365.

Kelly, James (1995) "'A Most Inhuman and Barbarous Piece of Villainy'; An Exploration of the Crime of Rape in Eighteenth-Century Ireland" in *Eighteenth-Century Ireland*, vol. 10, pp.78-107.

King, Peter (1996) "Female offenders, work and life-cycle change in late-eighteenth-century London" in *Continuity and Change*, vol. 11, pp.61-90.

King, Peter (1998) "The rise of juvenile delinquency in England 1780-1840: changing patterns of perception and prosecution" in *Past and Present*, vol. 160, pp.116-166.

King, Peter (1999) "Gender, crime and justice in late eighteenth-and early nineteenth-century England" in *Gender and Crime in Modern Europe*, M. Arnot et al (eds.), London: University College London Press, pp.44-74.

King, Peter (2000) *Crime, Justice and Discretion in England: 1740-1820*, Oxford: OUP.

King, Peter (2004) "The Summary Courts and Social Relations in Eighteenth-Century England" in *Past & Present*, no. 183, pp.125-173.

King, Peter (2006) *Crime and Law in England, 1750-1850,* CUP: Cambridge.

King, Richard (1770) *The Frauds of London Detected*, London.

Kloek, E. (1990) "Criminality and Gender in Leiden's Confessieboken, 1678-1794" in *Criminal Justice History*, vol. 11, p.8.

Kord, Susanne (1993) "Women and Children, Women as Childkillers: Infanticide in Eighteenth-Century Germany" in *Eighteenth-Century Studies,* vol. 26, no. 3, pp.449-466.

Lacour, Eva (2001) "Faces of violence Revisited. A Typology of Violence in Early Modern Germany" in *Journal of Social History,* vol. 34, no. 3, pp.649-667.

Landau, Norma (1984) *The Justice of the Peace 1679-1760*, Berkeley: University of California Press.

Landau, Norma (1998) "Appearance at the Quarter Sessions of Eighteenth-Century Middlesex" in *London Journal*, vol. 23, pp.30-51.

Landau, Norma (2002) "The Trading Justice's Trade" in *Law, Crime and English Society: 1660-1830,* Cambridge: CUP, at pp.47-65.

Landsman, Stephen (1998) "One hundred years of rectitude: medical witnesses at the Old Bailey 1717-1817" in *Law and History Review*, vol.16, pp. 445-494

Langbein, John (1978) "The Criminal Trial Before the Lawyers" in *The University of Chicago Law Review*, vol. 45, pp.263-316.

Langbein, John (2003) *The Origins of Adversary Criminal Trial*, Oxford: OUP.

Langer, William L (1974) "Infanticide: a historical survey" in *History of Childhood Quarterly*, vol. 1, pp.353-365.

Leeson, H. (1715) *Capt. Leeson's Case: Being an Account of his Tryal, for Committing a Rape*, London: Printed for J. Roberts.

Leigh, Samuel (1819) *Leigh's New Picture of London*, London: Printed by W. Clowes.

Lemire, Beverley (1990) "The Theft of Clothes and Popular Consumerism in Early Modern England" in *Journal of Social History*, vol. 24, pp.255-276.

Leneman, Leah (1997) "'A tyrant and tormentor': violence against wives in eighteenth-and early nineteenth-century Scotland" in *Continuity and Change*, vol. 12.1, pp.31-54.

Levine, Mortimer (1963) "A More than Ordinary Case of 'Rape', 13 and 14 Elizabeth 1" in *American Journal Of Legal History*, vol. 7, no. 2, pp.159-164

Linebough, Peter (1991) *The London Hanged: Crime and Civil Society in the Eighteenth Century*, Harmondsworth: Penguin.

Lorrain, Rev. Paul (1701) *The Ordinary of Newgate his Account of the Behaviour Confessions, and Dying Speeches of the Condemned Criminals that were Executed at Tyburn on Wednesday Jan. 28th 1701*, London.

Lorrain, Rev. Paul (1703) *The Ordinary of Newgate his Account of the Behaviour, Confessions, and Dying words…21th of July 1703*, London.

Lorrain, Rev. Paul (1705) *The Ordinary of Newgate his Account of the Behaviour, Confessions, and Dying words…4th May 1705*, London.

Lorrain, Rev. Paul (1708) *The whole life and conversation, Birth, Education and Parentage of Deborah Churchill…*, London: Printed for J. Dutton.

Ludovicus, M. (1752) *A Particular but Melancholy Account of the Great Hardship, Difficulties, and miseries that Those Unhappy and much to be pitied Creatures, the Common Women of the Town, Are plung'd into at this Juncture*, London.

Macfarlane, Alan (1980) "Illegitimacy and illegitimates in English history", in *Bastardy and its Comparative History*, P Laslett, K Oosterveen and R Smith (eds.), London: Arnold & Co, 1992, p.71.

Mackay, Lynn (1999) "Why they stole: women in the Old Bailey, 1779-1789" in *Journal of Social History*, vol. 32, pp.623-639.

Malcolm, Sarah (1732) *A True Copy of the Paper Delivered the Night before her Execution by Sarah Malcolm*, London.

Malcomson, R.W. (1977) "Infanticide in the eighteenth century" in *Crime in England 1550-1800*, J.S. Cockburn (Ed.), London: Methuen.

McKenzie, Andrea (2005) "This Death Some Strong and Stout Hearted Man Doth Choose": The Practice of Peine Forte et Dure in Seventeenth- and Eighteenth-Century England" in *Law and History Review*, vol.23, no.2, pp.279-314.

Melling, Elizabeth (Ed.) (1969) *Crime and Punishment, Kentish Sources VI*, Maidstone: Kent County Council.

Mercer, E.D. and Goodacre, K. (1965) *Guide to the Middlesex sessions Records, 1549-1884,* London: Greater London Record Office.

Middleton, Wilhelm (1545) *The Boke For A Justyce of Peace*, London.

Misson, Henri (1719) *Memoirs and Observations in his Travels over England* (J. Ozell, Trans), London.

Monkkonen, Eric (Ed.) (1991) "Bound for America: A Profile of British Convicts Transported to the Colonies, 1718-1775" in *Crime and Justice in American History*, vol.1.

Moor, Edward (1811) *Hindu Infanticide,* London: J. Johnson and Co.

Moreton, Andrew (Daniel Defoe) (1725) *Every-Body's Business is No-Body's Business*, London.

Moreton, Andrew (Daniel Defoe) (1799) *Thoughts on Means of Alleviating the Miseries attendant upon Common Prostitution*, London.

Morgan, Gwenda and Rushton, Peter (1998) *Rogues, Thieves and the Rule of Law: The Problem of Law Enforcement in Northeast England,* London: University College London Press.

Morgan, Gwenda and Rushton, Peter (2005) "Visible Bodies: Power, Subordination and Identity in the Eighteenth-Century Atlantic World" in *Journal of Social History*, vol.39, no.1, pp.39-64.

Moritz, Karl (1886) *Travels in England in 1782*, London: Cassell and Company.

Morris, N. and Rothman, D. J. (eds.) (1995) *The Oxford History of the Prison*, Oxford: OUP.

Motherill, John (1786) *The Case of John Motherill. The Brighthelmstone Taylor Who was Tried at East Grinstead for A Rape*, London.

Naeshagen, F L (2002) "Private Law Enforcement in Norwegian History: The Husband's Right to Chastise His Wife", *Scandinavian Journal of History*, vol. 27(1), pp.19-29.

Norton, Rictor (2001) *Early Eighteenth-Century Newspaper Reports: A Sourcebook*, http://www.infopt.demon.co.uk/grub/grub.htm

O'Donovan, Katherine (1984) "The Medicalisation of Infanticide" in *Criminal Law Review*, p.261.

Paley, Ruth (Ed.) (1991) *Justice in Eighteenth-Century Hackney: The Justicing Notebook of Henry Norris and the Hackney Petty Sessions Book*, London: London Record Society.

Palk, Deirdre (2004) "'Fit Objects for Mercy': gender, the Bank of England and currency criminals" in *Women's Writing*, vol. 11, no. 2, pp.237-258.

Palk, Deidre (2006) *Gender, Crime and Judicial Discretion: 1780-1830*, Woodbridge: Boydell Press.

Parker, George (1781) *A View of Society and Manners in High and Low Life*, London.

Peakman, Julie (2005) *Lascivious Bodies: A Sexual History of the Eighteenth Century*, London: Atlantic Books.

Pearson, Patricia (1998) *When She Was Bad: How Women Get Away with Murder*, London: Virago Press.

Pike, Luke Owen (1876) *A History of Crime in England*, vol. 2, London: Smith Elder & Co.

Porter, Roy (1986) "Rape-Does it have a Historical Meaning?2 in *Rape an Historical and Cultural Enquiry*, S Tomaselli and R Porter (eds.) Oxford, at p.227.

Porter, Roy (1991) *English Society in the 18th Century*, London: Penguin.

Poussin, Father (1734) *Pretty Doings in a Protestant Nation*, London.

Purney, Rev. Thomas (1722) *The Ordinary of Newgate's Account of the Behaviour, Confession and Last Dying Speech of Matthias Brinsden, who was executed at Tyburn, for the murther of his wife Hannah Brinsden*, London.

Quarrell, W.H. and More, Margaret (Trans and eds.) (1934) *London in 1710 From the Travels of Zacharias Conrad Von Uffenbach*, London: Faber & Faber Ltd.

Rabin, Dana (2003) "Searching for the Self in Eighteenth-Century English Criminal Trials, 1730-1800" in *Eighteenth-Century Life*, vol. 27, no.1, pp.85-106.

Rabin, Dana (2005) "Drunkenness and Responsibility for Crime in the Eighteenth Century" in *Journal of British Studies,* vol.. 44.3, pp.457-477.

Rayner, J. L. and Crook, G. T. (eds.) (1926) *The Complete Newgate Calendar*, London: Privately printed for the Navarre Society, vols 1- 4.

Reynolds, Elaine (2002) "Sir John Fielding, Sir Charles Whitworth, and the Westminster Night Watch Act, 1770-1775" in *Criminal Justice History*, vol.16, pp.1-29.

Rizzo, Tracey (2004) "Between Dishonor and Death: infanticides in the *Causes celebres* of eighteenth-century France" in *Women's History Review*, vol.13, no.1, pp.5-21.

Robbins, Caroline (Ed.) (1938) *The Diary of John Milward Esq., September 1666 to May 1668*, Cambridge: CUP.

Rogers, Nicholas (1989) "Carnal Knowledge: Illegitimacy in Eighteenth-Century Westminster" in *Journal of Social History*, vol. xxiii, part 2, pp. 355-375.

Roughead, William (Ed.) (1914) *The Trial of Mary Blandy*, Edinburgh and London: William Hodge & Coy.

Ruff, Julius (2001) *Violence in Early Modern Europe 1500-1800*, Cambridge, CUP.

Schwarz, L.D. (1985), "The standard of living in the long run: London 1700-1860" in *The Economic History Review*, vol.38, no.1, pp.24-41.

Severn, Charles (1831) *First Lines of the Practice of midwifery: to which are added remarks on the forensic evidence requisite in cases of foeticide and infanticide,* London: published by S Highly.

Shapiro, Barbara (1986) "To a Moral Certainty: Theories of Knowledge and Anglo-American Juries 1600-1850" in *Hastings Law Journal*, vol. 38, pp.153-194.

Sharpe, James (1981) "Domestic Homicide in Early Modern England" in *Historical Journal*, vol.24, pp.29-48.

Sharpe, James (1994) "Women Witchcraft and the Legal Process" in Jenny Kermode and Garthine Walker, *Women, crime and the courts in early modern England*. London: UCL Press.

Shoemaker, Robert (1991) *Prosecution and Punishment: Petty Crime and the Law in London and Rural Middlesex, c. 1660-1725,* Cambridge: CUP.

Shoemaker, Robert (1998) *Gender in English Society 1650-1850: The Emergence of Separate Spheres?* London: Longman.

Shoemaker, Robert (2001) "Male Honour and the decline of public violence in eighteenth-century London" in *Social History*, vol.26, no.2, pp.190-208.

Shoemaker, Robert (2004) *The London Mob: Violence and Disorder in Eighteenth-Century England,* London: Hambledon and London.

Shorter, Edward (1977) "On Writing the History of Rape" in *Signs: Journal of Women in Culture and Society*, vol.3, no.2, pp.471-482.

Shugg, Wallace (1988) "The baron and the milliner: Lord Baltimore's rape trial as a mirror of class tensions in mid-Georgian London" in *Maryland Historical Magazine,* vol. 83, pp.310-330.

Siegel, Reva B. (1996) "'The Rule of Love': Wife Beating as Prerogative and Privacy" in *Yale Law Journal*, vol. 106, pp.2117-2207.

Simpson, Antony E. (1986) "'Blackmail myth" and the prosecution of rape and its attempt in 18th Century London: the creation of a legal tradition' in *Journal of Criminal Law and Criminology*, vol. 77, pp. 101-150.

Simpson, Antony E. (1987) "Vulnerability and the Age of Female Consent: Legal Innovation and its Effect on Prosecutions for Rape in Eighteenth-Century London" in *Sexual Underworlds of the Enlightenment*, G S Rousseau and R Porter (eds.), Manchester: Manchester University Press, pp.188-192.

Simpson, Antony E. (1996) "'The mouth of strange women is a deep pit': Male guilt and legal attitudes toward prostitution in Georgian London" in *Journal of Criminal Justice and Popular Culture*, vol. 4(3), pp.50-79.

Simpson, Antony E. (2004) "Popular Perceptions of Rape as a Capital Crime in 18th Century England: the Press and the Trial of Francis Charteris in the Old Bailey, February 1730" in *Law and History Review*, vol. 22, no. 1, pp.27-70.

Smith, Alexander (1719) *A Compleat history of the lives and robberies of the most notorious highwaymen ... for above an hundred years past,* vol. 2, London: Briscoe.

Smith, Bruce P (2005) "The Presumption of Innocence and the English Law of theft: 1750-1850" in *Law and History Review*, vol. 23, no. 1, pp.133-173.

Smith, John (1996) *Smith and Hogan: Criminal Law*, 8th edn., London: Butterworths.

Smith, M.G. (1982) "Pastoral Discipline and the Church Courts: the Hexham Court 1680-1730", York: *Borthwick Papers*, No. 62.

Smith, Rev. Samuel (1692) *The Ordinary of Newgate his Account of the Behaviour Confessions, and Dying Speeches of the Condemned Criminals that were Executed at Tyburn on 2nd. March 1692*, London

Smith, Thomas (1977) *Nakahara: Family Farming and Population in a Japanese Village, 1717-1830,* California: Stanford University Press.

Socolow, Susan (1980) "Women and Crime: Buenos Aires, 1757-1797" in *Journal of Latin American Studies*, vol. 12, no. 1, pp.39-54.

Soothill, K. et al (1991) *Homicide in Britain: A Comparative Study of Rates in Scotland and England and Wales*, Edinburgh: Scottish Executive Central Research Unit.

Spierenburg, Peter (1997) "How Violent were women? Court Cases in Amsterdam, 1650-1810" in *Crime, History & Societies*, vol.1, no. 1, pp.9-28.

Steffensmeier, Darrel and Allan, Emilie, (1996) "Gender and Crime: Toward a Gendered Theory of Female Offending" in *Annual Review of Sociology*, vol.22, pp.459-487.

Stevens, George (1788) *The Adventures of a Speculist, or, a Journey Through London,* vol.1, London.

Stevenson, K. (2000) "Unequivocal victims: the historical roots of the mystification of the female complainant in rape cases" in *Feminist Legal Studies*, vol. 8, pp.343-344.

Stone, Lawrence (1977) *The Family, Sex and Marriage in England, 1500-1800*, London: Weidenfeld and Nicholson.

Stone, Laurence (1985) "Debate: The History of Violence in England, A Rejoinder" in *Past & Present*, vol. 108, pp.214-216.

Swift, Jonathan (1901) *Journal to Stella*, London: Methuen & Co.

Taylor, Rev. John (1752) *The Ordinary of Newgate's Account...of the Sixteen Malefactors who were executed at Tyburn on Monday the 23rd of March, 1752*. London.

Trumbach, Randolph (1998) *Sex and the Gender Revolution: Heterosexuality and the Third Gender in Enlightenment London*, vol.1, Chicago: University of Chicago Press.

Turner, Dr D (1724) *Syphilis. A Practical Dissertation on the Venereal Disease.* 2nd edn., London.

Ulbricht, Otto (1988) "Infanticide in eighteenth-century Germany" in *The German Underworld*, Evans R.J. (Ed.), Routledge, p.111.

Van der Heijden, Manon (2000) "Women as victims of sexual and domestic violence in 17th Century Holland: Criminal Cases of Rape, Incest and Maltreatment in Rotterdam and Delft" in *Journal of Social History*, vol. 33, no. 3, p.623.

Van Muyden, Madame (Trans and Ed.) (1902) *A foreign View of England in the reigns of George I and George II*, London: John Murray.

Walker, Garthine (1994) "Women, theft and the world of Stolen Goods" in *Women, Crime and the Courts in Early Modern England*, J. Kermode et al (eds.) London: UCL Press, pp. 81-105.

Walker, Garthine (1998) "Rereading Rape and Sexual Violence in Early Modern England" in *Gender and History*, vol. 10, p.1.

Walker, Garthine (2003) *Crime, Gender and Social Order in Early Modern England*, Cambridge: CUP.

Warner, Jessica and Ivis, Frank (2000) "Gin and Gender in Early Eighteenth-century London" in *Eighteenth-Century Life*, vol. 24, pp.85-105.

Warner, Jessica (2003) "'My Pappa is out, and my Mamma is asleep': Minors, their routine activities, and interpersonal violence in an early modern town, 1653-1781" in *Journal of Social History*, vol. 36, issue 3, pp.561-584.

Warner, Jessica (2003) *Craze: Gin and Debauchery in an Age of Reason*, London: Profile Books.

Welch, Saunders (1758) *A Proposal to render effectual a Plan to remove the nuisance of Common Prostitutes from the streets of this Metropolis*, London.

Wenderborn, Frederick Augustus (1791) *A View of England Towards the Close of the 18th Century*, Dublin: printed for P. Wogan, vol.1.

Whitlock, Tammy C. (2005) *Crime, Gender and Consumer Culture in Nineteenth-century England*, Ashgate Publishing: Aldershot.

Wiener, Martin J (1999) "Judges v Jurors: Courtroom Tensions in Murder Trials and the Law of Criminal Responsibility in Nineteenth-Century England" in *Law and History Review*, vol. 17, no. 3, pp.467-506.

Wiener, Martin J (2001) 'Alice Arden to Bill Sikes: Changing Nightmares of Intimate Violence in England, 1558-1869' in *Journal of British Studies*, vol. 40, pp.184-212.

Wiener, Martin J (2004) *Men of Blood: Violence, Manliness, and Criminal Justice in Victorian England*, New York: CUP.

Wilkes, Rev. Wettenhall (1751) *A Letter of Genteel and Moral Advice to a Young Lady*, London.

William, R (Ed.) (1914), *The Trial of Mary Blandy*, Edinburgh and London, William Hodge & Coy.

Wrightson, Keith (1975) "Infanticide in earlier Seventeenth-Century England" in *Local Population Studies*, vol. 15, pp.10-21.

Wrigley, E.A. (1967) "A simple model of London's Importance in Changing English Society and Economy 1650-1750" in *Past and Present*, no.37.

Zedner, Lucia (1991) "Women, Crime, and Penal Responses: A Historical Account", in Michael Tonry (Ed.), *Crime and Justice; A Review of Research*, Chicago: University of Chicago Press.

Zedner, Lucia (1991) *Women, Crime and Custody in Victorian England*, Oxford: OUP.

Zunshine, Lisa (2005) *Illegitimacy in Eighteenth-Century England*, Columbus: Ohio State University Press.

## Contemporary Journals and Newspapers Cited

*Applebee's Original Weekly Journal*
*The British Journal*
*Daily Gazetteer*
*The Daily Journal*
*English Post*
*The Flying Post*
*The Gentleman's Magazine*
*Grub-street Journal*
*The London Chronicle or Universal Evening Post*
*The London Journal*
*London Post*
*The Middlesex Journal*
*Mist's Weekly Journal*
*The Post-Boy*
*The Spectator*
*The Tatler*
*The Times*
*Weekly Journal, or The British Gazetteer*

# INDEX